DEPREDATION and DECEIT

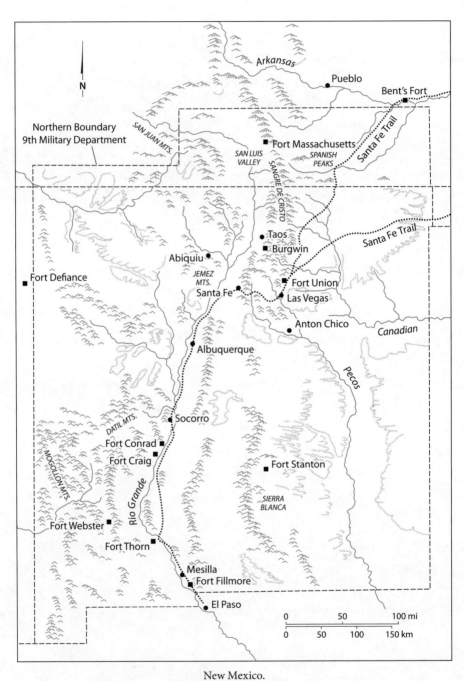

N

Arkansas

Pueblo

Bent's Fort

Northern Boundary
9th Military Department

SAN JUAN MTS.

Fort Massachusetts

SAN LUIS
VALLEY

SPANISH
PEAKS

Santa Fe Trail

SANGRE DE CRISTO

Taos

Burgwin

Santa Fe Trail

Abiquiu

JEMEZ
MTS.

Fort Defiance

Fort Union

Santa Fe

Las Vegas

Anton Chico

Canadian

Albuquerque

Pecos

Socorro

DATIL MTS.

Fort Conrad

Fort Craig

Fort Stanton

MOGOLLON MTS.

SIERRA
BLANCA

Rio Grande

Fort Webster

Fort Thorn

Mesilla

Fort Fillmore

El Paso

0		50		100 mi
0	50	100	150 km	

New Mexico.

Map by Bill Nelson. Copyright © 2017 by the University of Oklahoma Press.

DEPREDATION and DECEIT

*The Making of the
Jicarilla and Ute Wars
in New Mexico*

Gregory F. Michno

UNIVERSITY OF OKLAHOMA PRESS : NORMAN

Library of Congress Cataloging-in-Publication Data

Name: Michno, Gregory, 1948– author.
Title: Depredation and deceit : the making of the Jicarilla and Ute wars in New Mexico /
    Gregory F. Michno.
Description: Norman : University of Oklahoma Press, 2017. | Includes bibliographical
    references and index.
Identifiers: LCCN 2017001118 | ISBN 978-0-8061-5769-6 (hardcover : alk. paper)
Subjects: LCSH: Jicarilla Indians—Wars. | Indians of North America—Claims against—
    New Mexico—History—19th century. | Jicarilla Indians—New Mexico—History—19th
    century. | Ute Indians—New Mexico—History—19th century. | Ute Indians—Wars.
Classification: LCC E99.J5 M53 2017 | DDC 973.6/6—dc23
LC record available at https://lccn.loc.gov/2017001118

1 2 3 4 5 6 7 8 9 10

To Robert W. Larson
for his inspiration and faith in me

Contents

Illustrations

Maps

DEPREDATION and DECEIT

Introduction

The picturesque Sangre de Cristo Mountains are part of the Rocky Mountains and stretch nearly 250 miles from southern Colorado into northern New Mexico. The name is Spanish for "Blood of Christ" and according to legend may refer to the blood-red tints that the mountains take on during some sunrises and sunsets. More than blood, however, the mountains can be notorious for the heavy fall and winter fogs that snake through the valleys and climb the peaks, obscuring the landscape from view. Pathways become deceptive and seemingly well-trodden roads become unreliable. Likewise, the title's reference to "Depredation and Deceit" has several layers: despoliation, ruin, duplicity, fraud, and perhaps even the fog of war. Depredations and deceit certainly preceded the so-called Jicarilla and Ute Wars from 1849 to 1855. For those conflicts were completely unnecessary. They were caused, in major part, by American and Mexican greed and were bolstered by a depredation claims indemnification system that almost guaranteed war between the Indians and the whites—the salient objective that the system was established to prevent.

Enacting a law destined to guarantee war was certainly not the intent of Congress, but it involved a higher "law of unintended consequences" or the droll assessment that "no good deed shall go unpunished." How colonists could get along with the Indians was a question plaguing them from the early seventeenth century. Americans wanted land, and they viewed the newly discovered territories as uninhabited, regardless of the presence of the "uncivilized" Native peoples that currently occupied it. By the time the colonies became independent many treaties had failed, but both sides realized that some means of amity had to be reached to prevent endless war. The new United States made the Treaty of Hopewell with the Cherokees in 1785, which included stipulations that Indians who committed crimes against American citizens would be punished according to U.S. laws, while citizens who committed crimes against Indians would likewise be punished. One article rather sinisterly stated that "punishment of the innocent under the idea of retaliation, is unjust, and shall not be practiced on either side, except" during war, in which case the innocents apparently were fair game.[1]

To stifle potential conflict, the United States tried to regulate all trade and intercourse with the tribes, limiting who could trade among the Indians and what items were allowed—whiskey and guns being almost universally banned. An Ordinance for the Regulation of Indian Affairs was passed in 1786, and the famous Northwest Ordinance was passed in 1787. Among its tenets were the lines: "The utmost good faith shall always be observed towards the Indians, their lands and property shall never be taken from them without their consent; and in their property rights and liberty, they never shall be invaded or disturbed," followed by the kicker: "unless in just and lawful wars authorized by Congress."[2]

There always seemed to be contradictory intentions: try to curb white acquisitiveness but defend it. Three years after the Treaty of Hopewell, Americans were stealing Cherokee lands. Secretary of war Henry Knox was angered by the "avaricious desire of obtaining fertile lands possessed by the said Indians" of the whites, "who have so flagitiously stained the American name." The next year, Knox had the same problem with whites and the Wabash Indians in the Northwest Territory. He knew that the Indians had a right to the land and that it could not be taken from them without their consent or "in case of a just war." Irrespective of the wishes of the frontier whites, who "have the strongest prejudices against the Indians," to dispossess them of their land "would be a gross violation of the fundamental laws of nature." But if the Indians "persist in their depredations, the United States may with propriety inflict such punishment as they shall think proper."[3]

In 1789 the War Department was established, with Indian affairs under its jurisdiction. In 1790 and 1793 two Trade and Intercourse Acts were passed, both providing for the punishment of non-Indians who committed crimes against Indians residing in Indian country. In 1795, in his Seventh Annual Message, President George Washington reiterated the ongoing concern that whites "alienating" Indian lands were "the main cause of discontent and war" and that only by assuring justice to the Indians could the United States prevent the "frequent destruction of innocent women and children, who are chiefly the victims of retaliation." Washington believed that provisions were needed for "inflicting adequate penalties upon all those who" violated Indian rights and thus endangered the peace of the country.[4]

It seemed that the founding fathers and their generation understood that the main Indian problem came from white people and that the two groups had to work together to achieve peace. But it was still the Age of Enlightenment, and the founders' progeny had not yet disassembled that edifice into the coming phase of melancholy Romanticism and virulent racism. Yet it was necessary to prevent whites and Indians from killing each other over real or imagined theft, insult, or injury. A third intercourse act, the strongest yet, was approved on May 19, 1796, with the full title "An Act to Regulate Trade and Intercourse with the Indian Tribes and to Preserve Peace on the Frontiers." Some old treaty stipulations were rewritten. The issue of white encroachment was addressed in section 4. If any citizen went into Indian country and committed robbery, trespass, or other crime against any friendly Indian, "such offender shall forfeit a sum not exceeding one hundred dollars, and be imprisoned not exceeding twelve months." The offender must also pay the Indian "a sum equal to twice the just value of the property." If the offender was financially unable to make the payment, the money "shall be paid out of the treasury of the United States," provided that the Indians or the nation to which they belonged have not "sought private revenge, or attempted to obtain satisfaction by any force or violence."[5]

It was hoped that this would address the problem of white violations, but the settlers also complained about Indian intrusion. Northwest Territory governor Arthur St. Clair had been warning about increasing discontent among the frontier settlers over alleged Indian violence and infringement, and the alienation of these people was a very real concern. If Congress and the president wanted to maintain control of their fledgling country, they would have to do something to assuage the settlers' worries and give them some tangible benefit.[6]

Section 14 of the 1796 act gave the whites a gift: if any Indians entered an American state or territory and stole property or committed murder, violence, or outrage on any citizen, the citizen could apply to the superintendent, provide proofs of the crime, and make application to the guilty tribe for compensation. If the tribe did not make amends, "the United States guarantee to the party injured, an eventual indemnification," provided that the injured whites did not try to obtain private satisfaction or revenge. In addition, it was declared that the president could deduct a sum equal to the amount of property stolen or destroyed "by any such Indian, out of the annual stipend, which the United States are bound to pay to the tribe, to which such Indian shall belong."[7]

At first glance these articles might be seen as a just means to compensate both whites and Indians for injuries by the other party as well as a way to keep them from going to war. Unfortunately, deducting annuity money from a tribe because of one guilty individual was pure punishment of the innocent, just what some government officials had previously seen as abhorrent. And perhaps the biggest issue of all could be the problem of filing fraudulent claims. The act was debated in Congress; but strangely enough, the problem of fraud was never seen as a potentially nullifying issue.

What Congress seemed most concerned about was settlers who squatted on Indian land. The act's section 5 stated that any citizen who surveyed or settled on Indian land granted by treaty would also be subject to a fine of one thousand dollars and one year in prison. The military could remove the violator, whose land would be forfeited. Congress debated this for days in April 1796. Those who wanted to strike out the clause argued that Indians never really owned the land they occupied; the land was given to them by former treaties. Besides, the frontier lands were promised to veterans of the Revolutionary War. If the government reneged on its promise, it would only aggravate its citizens. James Madison argued that if Indians really had unqualified title to their land they could sell it to any foreign nation, and the United States could not allow that. In addition, he argued that forfeiting private real estate for any reason besides treason "was against the spirit of the Constitution." Albert Gallatin, with suspect logic, said that there was no proof that Indian depredations were "in general occasioned by previous injuries done to them." He believed that young Indian warriors went to war because it was in their nature and said that the government could not remove squatters from Indian land because it could not prevent them from moving there in the first place. The gist of their case was that the Indians only lived where they did by consent of the government and that it would not be good to anger the frontier people.[8]

On the other side, congressmen argued that the notion that the Indians did not own their land was contrary to natural justice, common sense, and fair play and that confiscating the land would cause more discontent among the Indians than it would among the settlers. After all, this was an act to preserve peace on the frontier. The idea that Indians had no right to the land they lived on, as Representative James Hillhouse said, "had caused great alarm among them, and was, in his opinion, one cause of the Indian wars." The wars did not harm the offenders but fell on "innocent frontier inhabitants." Theodore Sedgwick said that the prevailing idea that "civilized men could improve the land better, that they had thence a right to take from the natives," was no more than "a principle of plunder" that should never find support within the halls of Congress. In the end, thirty-six opted to strike out section 5, but forty-seven voted to retain it.

With the addition of section 5, section 14 might have been a pacifier to the frontier people. It is surprising, after all the debate over the other articles, that this one engendered so little comment. Only Connecticut representative Zephaniah Swift had an objection "to the clause which enacts that the losses sustained by the white people from the Indians on the frontier, shall be made good by the Government." He said that frontier settlers knew that their location placed them in jeopardy and was concerned that by guaranteeing to compensate for their losses, "*a door would be opened to fraud* [emphasis added], as it would be impossible to ascertain with precision the amount of any damage done by the Indians." Swift had foreseen the upcoming problem exactly. Representative Thomas Blount said that frontier settlers often turned their cattle loose to graze on Indian land. When they went to bring them in, "disputes would sometimes happen, which occasioned serious mischiefs." With those concerns, section 14 was altered. Swift was thereby satisfied that "the losses sustained by the frontier inhabitants could be deducted by the sum which government had stipulated to pay the Indians" and now had "no objection to the measure."

One might wonder how in the world fraud would be prevented by making the indemnification dollars come out of treaty funds instead of some other government funds. The person submitting a claim for losses did not care where the payment came from. In truth, claimants who were aware of the funding situation might even be more inclined to exaggerate a claim if they knew that the funds would be deducted from money due to their Indian adversaries. The congressmen must have known that such a clause would not lessen fraud one bit. They were probably satisfied that by this measure they had put a cap on fraud claims, limiting the possible payout to the amount held in the Indian annuity funds. In effect they had also denied sovereign immunity to the Indian nations, holding them liable for the acts of individuals. The whole would be punished for a guilty few. Washington's wish to provide justice for the Indians was severely compromised.[9]

The basic tenets of the 1796 act remained intact over the years. In 1802 another Trade and Intercourse Act was passed, but section 14 was almost the same, except that the time to wait for an Indian nation to respond to a claim was reduced from eighteen months to twelve. In 1834 a new Trade and Intercourse Act provided some significant changes, and this time the issue of depredations was encompassed mainly in section 17. Claims would no longer be paid for all Indians guilty of depredating, but only for those "belonging to any tribe in amity with the United States." In other words, indemnification would not be sought from those tribes at war with the United States, only from those at peace. The standard rationalization was that peaceful tribes would not likely be depredating; if they were, then they must be at war. This game was constantly played over the years by agents seeking to save government money.[10]

The claims were to be sent to the commissioner of Indian Affairs, a new office created in 1832. Claims now had time limits, having to be filed within three years of the alleged incident. The cap on funds was removed. If the Indian nation had no available annuity funds to repay a claim, "then the amount of the claim shall be paid from the treasury of the United States," which in effect removed the check on fraud, at least as it was conceived in minds of the framers of the 1796 Act. Non-Indians could now file a claim if any Indian molested them while they were "lawfully within" Indian country. This addition was certainly framed in response to the growing westward movement. Thousands of citizens needed protection as they took the trails west, believing it their "manifest destiny" to invade Indian country and spread their way of life from coast to coast. In addition, section 19 provided a significant change from the 1796 Act. Whereas the military before that had been able to arrest an offender found in the United States or its territories, now the military was given leave to go into Indian country to arrest any Indians accused of committing a crime.[11]

These clauses were to be responsible for uncounted mischiefs to come. Whites were free to file fraudulent claims and soldiers were free to march out to confront Indians and accuse them of depredations, not knowing whether the parties they accosted were guilty or innocent. War was almost inevitable.

The framers of the 1796 and 1834 acts seemed oblivious to the possibility that the depredation claim system they constructed to keep the peace would be a Pandora's box, resulting in thousands of fraudulent claims. In fact, the members of Congress likely could not have found a better way to do it if they had conspired to plan it that way. The law was not a conspiracy, but when the common people are shown an easy road to material gain without the threat of punishment, the outcome might have been predictable.

I have used Indian depredation claims extensively in previous publications and generally gave the white claimants the benefit of the doubt. The more I researched, however, the more I came to wonder if a significant number of them were exaggerating their losses or even filing claims for totally fabricated incidents.

What I have found in studying the claims of depredations in New Mexico in the years following the American invasion in 1846 led me to hypothesize that perhaps the "wars" against the depredating Indians, with my focus on the Jicarillas and Utes, were bogus, stirred up for little other reason than greed. Newly arriving Americans and the Nuevomexicano inhabitants, now "freed" from Mexican control and enjoying the fruits of U.S. citizenship, had found a sly new way if not to get rich then at least to enhance their economic situation. Making false depredation accusations unfortunately led to war, but what of it? As a result, U.S. entrepreneurs could acquire more Indian land and increase their wealth.

The Trade and Intercourse Act(s) taken in total, by opening up a wide pathway to defraud the Indians, probably caused some of the Indian wars of the nineteenth century. Anglo-Americans as well as Nuevomexicanos (and even the indigenous Indians) had their own self-interest at heart. Land was a basis for wealth, and nearly everyone sought to exploit it to a lesser or greater extent. Land was for farming, hunting, mining, stock-grazing, speculating, or a hundred other uses. To get more of it for yourself, another party had to be driven out. It was a zero-sum game. Falsely accusing Indians of robbery or murder and making claims for nonexistent losses was a comparatively simple way to get government money. And there was no penalty for making a false claim. In addition, the army would have to respond. Soldiers would search out the Indians assumed to be guilty and demand restitution and/or surrender of the guilty party. The waylaid Indians were usually innocent, or they would not have been so easily caught. They would resist, the inevitable shots would be fired, and a once friendly band would now be enemies, perpetuating a cycle of violence. The complaining citizens could even maintain that the army was not protecting them sufficiently and insist that militia volunteers were needed to punish the Indians. More Indian land and property could be confiscated. The army was often caught in the middle. Its duty, per the Trade and Intercourse Acts, was constabulary: it was there to keep the peace, protect both Indians and whites, or fight, as circumstances dictated. But the pre–Civil War army in the West seemed to savor its role as peacekeeper more than we might imagine. The records are replete with army officers questioning civilian allegations of Indian theft and murder. In numerous instances officers plainly stated that the Anglos and Nuevomexicanos were mendacious, to say the least. Many of their investigations into dire claims of robberies found the allegations to be bogus. The record shows this to be true on the New Mexico frontier in the 1840s and 1850s.

In addition, we find the puzzling phenomenon of an increased army presence resulting in more depredation claim filings as well as an increase in fighting.

When given the volatile mix of false accusations, public greed, and fabricated fear, the army, against its own volition, could become a destabilizing force on the frontier. These factors combined to cause much of the Jicarilla-Ute conflict, but New Mexico was not unique. The Trade and Intercourse Acts, far from ensuring a peaceful frontier, were manipulated by Americans who cared less for the spirit of the acts than for their own self-interest, who through their greed and dishonesty may have precipitated the very wars that they claimed to abhor.

1

The American Regime

The Jicarilla Apache Chief Lobo Blanco (White Wolf) stood on a high ridge at Point of Rocks, New Mexico, where the Santa Fe Trail approached the hills after many miles of traversing the rolling plains. It was a good vantage point. Lobo Blanco was hoping that some unsuspecting white men might come along, for his heart still ached for revenge. Two months before, in mid-August 1849, a small band of his people had set up camp about one-half mile from the small town of Las Vegas, on the high plains east of the Sangre de Cristo Mountains. They had only wanted to trade peacefully or they would not have brought the women and children so close to the town and the nearby soldier post.

Capt. Henry B. Judd, 3rd Artillery, was in command at the post. For months he and the military had been receiving reports from civilians that the Jicarillas had been raiding the settlements. On August 16, 1849, Judd wrote that "this band was undoubtedly in the many murders and robberies committed during the past year . . . especially at the town of Moro, and quite recently at the rancho of Mr. Waters [Samuel B. Watrous] near Barclay's Fort." Judd questioned some of the local "persons of respectability," who somehow recognized the warriors as the guilty ones. Judd's suspicions were confirmed by their efforts to get ammunition, plus the presence of more Indians who "were attempting a similar traffic" at the settlement of Las Valles about fifteen miles downriver from Las Vegas. Although the Jicarillas had camped with their families very close to town, Judd was sure that their attempt to procure powder and lead was "an evident design of committing depredations should a chance be presented."[1]

Judd forbade the local merchants to trade. He went out to talk with the Indians, but "from the contradictions, falsehoods and duplicity pervading their own statements I felt convinced that their object was anything but pacific," he reported. "I therefore determined to seize the party." He placed in command a twenty-five-year-old second lieutenant named Ambrose E. Burnside, long before he became famous for his signature muttonchop "sideburns" and infamous for leading the Union Army of the Potomac in a disastrous Civil War encounter at the 1862 Battle of Fredericksburg. Judd sent the local judge, Herman Grolman, to talk to the Jicarillas to learn their intentions and stall for time while Burnside prepared.

The wary Indians were not about to let the soldiers come so close. As the horsemen advanced menacingly, the Jicarillas sent a flight of arrows at them and fled. Burnside charged after them. Judd called the affair "a hand-to-hand conflict—the sabre being the only weapon used to advantage by our people." Burnside was slightly wounded below the ear, Lance Sergeant Ambrose was severely wounded by an arrow, and Private Meador received a bad contusion below the eye from the butt of a lance. The Indians received the worst of it, however. Judd said that only eight or ten warriors escaped. Three bodies were brought in, but "many of the dead remain in the ravines where they were sabred." The chase went for nine miles. They caught thirteen Indian ponies, but the prize was six women and children taken prisoner. The Jicarillas' Chief Chacón later insisted that the band was peaceful and only seeking to trade when the soldiers attacked them for no reason. Most ominous for the whites, one of the captured was Lobo Blanco's daughter.

Late in the day of October 24, 1849, Lobo Blanco spied two carriages approaching his lookout on Point of Rocks. He may have smiled, surprised yet pleased that the whites would be so foolish as to ride the trail in such small numbers without an escort.

The carriages belonged to James M. White, whose livelihood was advertised in the *Santa Fe Republican* newspaper, under the heading "J. M. White & Brother, Cheap Merchants, And Wholesale and Retail Dealers in Military Goods, Clothing and cloths, Dry Goods of all kinds, fashions and varieties, of the very latest stripe." The ad noted that the proprietors "are determined not to be undersold by anyone."[2]

White was returning to Santa Fe after purchasing stock in Kansas and Missouri for his stores in Santa Fe and El Paso. In spite of the danger, White brought along his wife, Ann, and his young daughter, Virginia. His employees, servants, and traveling partners manned thirteen goods-laden wagons. Despite the possible danger, White joined one of the wagon trains of Francis X. Aubrey, perhaps the most famous of all the merchants on the Santa Fe Trail, legendary for his fast mule trains and quick turnarounds. The train left Kansas City, Missouri, about September 15 but did not make good time. An early snowstorm hit the Oklahoma Panhandle and trapped the travelers for a while, while twenty of Aubrey's mules froze to death. When the weather let up, White continued with the train until impatience got the best of him. He left his wagons with Aubrey and pulled ahead in two carriages with his family and five other men.[3]

James White decided to rest for the evening, probably just beyond Palo Blanco Creek and east of Point of Rocks.[4] Lobo first rode up to the camp and asked for presents, but White refused to give any and demanded that the Indians leave. They rode away but returned once more to demand gifts. After being denied again, Lobo returned, this time with the rest of his band, and swept down on the little camp. They first shot down a mulatto servant, Ben Bushman, then a Mexican, who fell dead into the campfire. The others tried to run but did not get far. The Indians killed James White, Aubrey employee William Callaway, and two Germans, including a Mr. Lawberger. Just as Lieutenant Burnside had taken captives from Lobo's family, Lobo took Ann Dunn White, her daughter Virginia, and a black female servant prisoner. Not content with this coup, Lobo laid out the bodies of the men in line on the roadside next to the carriages, using them as bait, while his men concealed themselves behind a nearby hill. Shortly afterward a small party of Nuevomexicano buffalo hunters came by and investigated. As they examined the bodies and peered into the carriages, the Jicarillas struck again, killing some and wounding a Mexican boy while the others ran away. Lobo's warriors then plundered and destroyed the carriages, took their prisoners, and left the area.[5]

The next night another small party, including American merchant Charles Spencer, Alexander Barclay, George Simpson, and Isaac Adamson, passed by the massacre site. In the pale moonlight they saw carriage parts broken in pieces and bodies scattered on the ground. White's body was lanced several times, and wolves had eaten the lower half. A little rocking chair, probably Virginia's, was the only remaining undamaged object. The eerie scene spooked them. As Indian agent James S. Calhoun imaginatively explained it, "the hot breath of the Indians might be near enough to be scented." They hurried on to Las Vegas, hardly stopping to rest on a 78-hour ride. On the way they talked to a small party of Pueblo Indians, who claimed that they had just been in camp with a band of

Apaches where they saw a white woman, a child, and a black woman. Francis Aubrey passed the massacre site next and hurried on.[6]

Spencer later met with Calhoun and relayed the story. Calhoun quickly wrote to commissioner of Indian Affairs William Medill, asking that the army be spurred to act immediately to punish the Indians, protect the citizens, and rescue the prisoners. Calhoun wanted to send some Nuevomexicano traders to the Indians to try to purchase the captives; he regretted that he was "entirely destitute of the means" to do so yet still offered one thousand dollars to the person who "succeeds in bringing in to me Mrs. White and her daughter" (apparently forgetting about the black servant). Calhoun added that "if the money promised was the last cent I could command on earth, and I without the slightest hope of its reimbursement," he would gladly pay it nevertheless. Ominously, however, he also echoed the prevailing frontier impression that a white woman captured by the Indians would suffer a "fate worse than death," stating that "if the two captives are not to be liberated, it is to be hoped they are dead."

When James White and his party camped that evening near Point of Rocks they rode right into a burning powder keg. Americans and New Mexicans had made accusations that the Indians had been murdering and marauding and demanded army protection. The soldiers combed the Sangre de Cristo and surrounding plains, seeking to arrest and punish the guilty and recover stolen property. Sometimes they found the guilty parties, but sometimes they attacked the innocent. Many times the Indians had no idea why soldiers were trying to arrest or kill them and responded in kind. Chastisement and retribution were becoming near-weekly occurrences. The deaths of the White party were partially the result of a desire for vengeance but also the result of poorly thought out laws with Pollyanna-like expectations that contained the seeds of calamitous consequences.

Broken Promises

The Mexican War was picking up steam in the summer of 1846 when Gen. Stephen Watts Kearny arrived with his American "Army of the West" at Bent's Fort on the Arkansas River on July 31. Before crossing the river into Mexican territory, he issued a proclamation directing the people of New Mexico to remain at peace, accept their new leaders, and rest assured that "they will not be molested by the American army, but on the contrary, they will be respected and protected in all their rights, both civil and religious." The next day Kearny wrote a letter to New Mexican governor Manuel Armijo, stating that he was coming "as a friend" to take possession of the country. He requested Armijo "to submit to fate," behave, and not fight back. If so, Kearny would keep the peace and respect and protect everyone.[7]

Advancing on Santa Fe, Kearny stopped on August 17 at the small Mexican town of Las Vegas, which lay astride Gallinas Creek east of the mountains and only one long day's march from the capital. Kearny climbed atop an adobe roof along the town square and addressed the people, restating much of the same message and adding: "From the Mexican government you have never received protection. The Apaches and Navajos come down from the mountains and carry off your sheep, and even your women, whenever they please. My government will correct all this."[8]

Governor Armijo's heart was not in fighting, and Kearny's army reached Santa Fe unopposed on the evening of August 18. The next day in the city plaza he again addressed the people, telling them: "We come as friends, to better your condition and make you part of the republic of the United States." He promised no one would murder them, steal their property, molest their women, or change their religion. "You are no longer Mexican subjects; you are now become American citizens, subject only to the laws of the United States," he said. "I am your governor—henceforth look to me for protection."[9]

One month later Kearny had gone to "conquer" California. Near the Gila River he stopped and talked to Apache leader Mangas Coloradas. The two men professed friendship. Both were at war with the Mexicans and must have looked upon each other as potential allies. Kearny had made friends with the same Indians that he had promised the New Mexicans he would fight.[10]

The protection promise was repeated: at the conquest in 1846, in the 1848 Treaty of Guadalupe Hidalgo that ended the Mexican War, and in many other informal declarations. The Gadsden Treaty of 1853 reflected the realization that America could never live up to those pledges and "abrogated" them. But is a promise broken when it was never meant to be kept? It seemed that Congress enacted virtuous-sounding laws that looked fair and righteous on paper but were worthless in action and that a fair deal and equal treatment for Indians and Nuevomexicanos was never their intent. A major object of the Trade and Intercourse Acts was the contradictory desire to protect Indians as well as the whites who constantly intruded into Indian lands. A damage claim system was enacted that made it easy to defraud without punishment and harmed one of the parties that it was allegedly set up to protect. These acts, including those in 1802, 1822, 1832, and 1834, also had provisions to protect the Indians by prohibiting the sale of liquor.[11] Congress had an intimation of the physical and moral damage that could be done to a people with little inherited resistance to alcohol, let alone the outrageous swindling that would result from its use. But what was a fine of a few hundred dollars compared to the enormous profits that could be made? The government, naive and ineffective as it might be, tried to regulate the predatory behavior of its citizens but very often failed.

Congress may have had good intentions, but it could never hope to overcome the numbers and determination of the lawbreakers. Hence regulatory efforts were often seen as ineffective and even hypocritical. One of the army's constabulary duties was to prevent illegal liquor sales to the Indians, but it never had enough personnel to do so. Americans built distilleries in New Mexico shortly after Mexico achieved independence from Spain. American traders, licensed and unlicensed, brought whiskey to Indian Country with their first opportunity, while violations were routinely ignored in courts. Alexander Barclay, who worked as superintendent of stores and bookkeeper at Bent's Fort from 1838 to 1842, said that their business was in "trafficking with the tribes" and that for years the "fur trade [was] soaked in illicit alcohol." The traders were surprised that the army did not police them more. The Indian agents were reluctant to ask for help because the military would do little—they had too few resources themselves, and many did not see any harm in the practice.[12]

By 1853 agent Thomas Fitzpatrick said that the Trade and Intercourse Acts were "nothing more than a dead letter." The many white people constantly passing through Indian Country "pay no regard to such restrictions, traffic without license, furnish liquor to the Indians, and render all efforts to regulate intercourse a mere farce."[13]

When American scofflaws broke the rules, the army was too undermanned to stop them. It was astonishingly simple to subvert the alcohol bans of the Trade and Intercourse Acts that prohibited behavior that took advantage of the Indians. It was even easier to manipulate the depredation claim sections of those acts that *facilitated* taking advantage of the Indians. The red light did not work—it still led to the moral and physical degradation of entire tribes. The green light was worse—it led to death of innocents, war, stolen land, and the near-extermination of entire tribes. The acts failed because many Americans too often let greed supplant morality.

Merchant Conquest

The American army had arrived, making many promises, but most of the soldiers did not stay long to keep them. Kearny had brought a large force: about 1,600 men, including about 300 soldiers of the 1st Dragoons, 860 men of the 1st

Missouri Volunteers under Col. Alexander Doniphan, about 250 men of the Missouri Artillery Battalion under Maj. Meriwether L. Clark, and almost 200 other civilians and teamsters, along with 460 horses, 3,700 draft mules, and 15,000 cattle and oxen.[14]

These were not the first Americans in New Mexico. Traders and merchants had beat the army by decades. From the late 1700s on, scores of people had attempted trading with the New Mexicans but were usually dissuaded by strict Spanish prohibitions. U.S. Army expeditions such as Zebulon Pike's in 1806 were stopped cold, and Pike was arrested. French trader Jacques Clamorgan successfully sold goods in Santa Fe in 1807. In 1812 traders led by Robert McKnight and James Baird reached Taos but were arrested and their goods confiscated. Auguste Choteau had his wares impounded in 1817. William Becknell is generally called the father of the Santa Fe trade. He successfully opened a regular trade in 1821, no doubt helped by the Mexican Revolution, which removed an obstructionist Spain from the picture. Over the succeeding years the Santa Fe trade was in full swing, with numerous caravans traveling between Missouri and New Mexico, making profits for those bold enough to risk their money and lives. Josiah Gregg, one of the most famous merchants, began his regular caravans in 1831. Francis X. Aubrey made his first trip to Santa Fe one month before Kearny marched.[15]

By 1846, to the chagrin of the Mexican government, it appeared that the Spanish concern about wanton penetration of their territory by Americans was for real. Suddenly, along with the American merchant caravans came U.S. soldiers. It was fitting that Kearny's point man was the merchant James W. Magoffin, who had been engaged in the Santa Fe and Chihuahua trade since the late 1820s. He had married a relative of Governor Manuel Armijo and was selected to carry Kearny's letter to Armijo expressing his desire for a peaceful entry into New Mexico. Magoffin used Kearny's protection to bring along thirty of his goods-laden wagons. Also getting a prompt start in May 1846, seemingly unconcerned that there was a war going on, were trains under Josiah Gregg, George Doan, James Webb, W. S. McKnight, Norris Coburn, Jesse B. Turley, Francis Aubrey, Ben Pruett, George Peacock, and Sam Ralston, Albert Speyer, and Manuel Harmony. One man in an eastbound train counted 541 wagons heading west.[16]

It was an invasion of Americans bearing gifts. New Mexico would more easily be persuaded to accept its American master not by bullets but by consumer goods. If they did not already realize it, the locals and the Americans rolling in from the east would soon recognize that the army theoretically not only offered protection for their businesses and farms but would be a lucrative market in itself. Robert W. Frazer, who studied the situation extensively, concluded that between 1846 and the coming of the Civil War in 1861, "the army was the single most significant factor in the economic development of the Southwest."[17]

The New Mexicans, with little other choice, eyed the lures of protection and prosperity and took the bait. An onrush of American entrepreneurs could expand the economy and provide much-needed goods, services, and jobs. If the army built forts and roads and increased the number of soldiers, that would provide a market for New Mexican goods as well as inhibit Indian raids.

The Ugly American

The conquest may have been bloodless, but the Nuevomexicanos were not all pleased with the soldiers, particularly the volunteers' bad attitudes. George Ruxton, a former British officer traveling in the region, wrote: "Over all New Mexico . . . the most bitter feeling and most determined hostility existed against the Americans, who [were] not very anxious to conciliate the [Mexican] people, but by their bullying and overbearing demeanor toward them, have in a greater measure been the cause of this hatred." Col. Sterling Price had just arrived with 1,200 men of the 2nd Missouri Volunteers and 500 men of the Mormon Battalion. A citizen wrote to the *Niles' Register* that the soldiers were "a degenerate military mob, violators of law and order, heaping daily injury and insult upon the people." He criticized Price's inability to control his men, which "has produced among the New Mexicans the strongest feelings of distrust and hatred and a desire to rebel exists among the inhabitants."[18]

Kearny had offered army protection, but New Mexico suddenly lost its defenders when he marched to California and Colonel Doniphan rode off to conquer Chihuahua. When Kearny learned that Navajos had stolen stock from the small village of Polvadera, he addressed the townspeople on October 5, allowing the inhabitants of the Rio Abajo district "to form War Parties, to march into the Country of their enemies . . . to make reprisals and obtain redress for the many insults received by them." But he cautioned that they should not injure the elderly, women, or children. Kearny had given the citizens permission to attack Indians and recover stolen property, just what the Trade and Intercourse Acts wanted to prevent. Kearny delayed Doniphan's march to Mexico and ordered him to punish the Navajos and see to it that they would make no more trouble.[19]

Doniphan made a hurried campaign against the Navajos and forced them to sign a peace treaty of little substance and duration. Meanwhile dozens of merchants with hundreds of wagons waited at Valverde on the Rio Grande, hoping that Doniphan would return to the real task of getting them safely to the Mexican marketplaces. In their haste to make money, the traders were outpacing the army. Merchants nearly spearheading an invasion of a foreign country gave a new twist to the old term "camp followers." While they waited, George Ruxton again had an opportunity to note with disdain the Missouri Volunteers' lack of discipline, slovenliness, and insubordination.[20]

After Doniphan finally connected with the merchants on December 12, they hauled away to old Mexico. Doniphan never communicated the details of the treaty to New Mexican governor Charles Bent. Bent, another merchant and trader, had long been in the business of trading, buying, and selling to the New Mexicans and the Indians, with his brother William and partner Ceran St. Vrain. General Kearny appointed Charles Bent as governor of the territory, Donaciano Vigil as secretary, Richard Dallam as marshal, Francis P. Blair Jr. as district attorney, Charles Blumner treasurer, and Joab Houghton, Antonio José Otero, and Charles Beaubien as judges of superior court. All would be involved to a greater or lesser extent in the upcoming events. For Bent, it would be a lesser role. On December 26 he wrote to secretary of state James Buchanan about the treaty: "I am not able to state the terms, upon which it has been concluded, but so far as I have been able to learn, I have but little ground to hope that it will be permanent."[21]

About three weeks later Bent would be dead, killed in a revolt by the dissatisfied, angry Pueblo Indians and New Mexicans that Kearny had pacified in his bloodless conquest. One of the reasons for the rebellion was that American troops could not behave themselves. In Taos and especially in Santa Fe, Colonel Price's 2nd Missourians were often drunk and fought with themselves as well as the townsfolk, and the local women did not feel safe among them. Nuevomexicanos felt the sting of the conquerors' arrogant attitudes, plus the humiliation of surrendering without a fight, and the embarrassment and disgrace festered. There were rumors of a revolt, but Bent was not inclined to believe them. He had been living in the area for two decades, had a Mexican wife and children, and considered himself almost one of the locals.

Bent's reading of the local temper was dead wrong, because on January 19, 1847, New Mexicans and Indians from the nearby Taos Pueblo struck. Bent was killed, scalped, and decapitated. Several others were killed in Taos and at Simeon Turley's Mill north of town, where Turley had been distilling "Taos Lightning" for years. Down at Mora on the east slope of the Sangre de Cristo, mobs attacked and killed eight more Americans. Capt. I. R. Hendley and about eighty men battled the rebels in Mora, killing fifteen and capturing fifteen, but Hendley was shot and killed.

Colonel Price reacted quickly, marching north with companies of the 2nd Missouri and a company of mounted New Mexico volunteers under Ceran St. Vrain. Price fought and defeated the rebels at Canada, one day's march north of Santa Fe. On February 2 they fought the rebels at Taos Pueblo. Price killed about 150 of them, while losing 7 killed and 45 wounded. Some of the rebel leaders and followers were caught and hanged.[22]

Discontent slowly cooled after the executions. The Americans, however, never could get the fear of rebellion out of their minds. For years they saw conspirators and assassins waiting in the dark alleys or in the woods, and many of their actions would be predicated on the belief that an insurrection was always about to consume them. The Nuevomexicanos and Pueblo Indians came to realize that insurrection was not the solution: although the Americans with their obnoxious sense of cultural and racial superiority may have loathed them, they had not come to kill them—they were there mainly to make money. Once the locals caught on to the tricks, they also realized that a profit could be made.

New Mexico's Indians

Americans knew that the continent was full of "wild" Indians. They had been part of their westering experience from the early 1600s on, and the first trappers, traders, and explorers had supplied enough tales of wonders, romance, violence, and terror to fire every imagination. The American army, merchants, and immigrants entering New Mexico during the Mexican War were certain they would find a "savage" waiting behind every rock and tree. Strangely enough, for the great majority of newcomers, the hordes of the steppes and mountains failed to materialize.

Given the geographical position of the New Mexican settlements, one might imagine an island of "civilization" amid an ocean of Indians. The settlements generally followed along both banks of the Rio Grande, which flowed south roughly down the middle of the New Mexico Territory, and east and west of the river from a few miles to a score or two. If New Mexico was bisected with a north-south and an east-west line, the Jicarilla Apaches would generally be found in the northeast quadrant, the Mescaleros in the southeast, the Chihenne and Bedonkohe Chiricahuas in the southwest, and the Navajos in the northwest. To the south were Nednhi Apaches, and to the north were the Utes. Roaming in and out of the entire eastern half of the territory were the Comanches and Kiowas, and in the northeast were also the Arapahos and Cheyennes. New Mexico did not consist of an easily demarcated, advancing "frontier line" of settlement as posited by historian Frederick Jackson Turner. The standard Turnerian progression of settlement from east to west contrarily began in New Mexico from south to north then west to east. New Mexican settlements were set smack dab in the middle of the surrounding Indians. The Americans moving in were very conscious of that and would not cease their constant cries for military protection.

The Jicarillas were directly on the Americans' approach route along the Santa Fe Trail. Their name came from the Spanish, meaning "little basket makers." They got along reasonably well with the Spanish, especially as the warlike Comanches to the east drove the Jicarillas into the mountains around Taos, where in 1719 they asked for protection and even vowed to accept Christianity. When Comanches devastated a Jicarilla settlement on the Canadian River four years later, Jicarillas sought protection among the Picuris, Pecos, and Galisteo Pueblos. Eventually two branches developed. Those living mainly in the Sangre de Cristo were influenced by the Spanish and Pueblos; tended to have more permanent villages; farmed; made baskets, beadwork, and clay pots; were generally composed of the more elderly as well as young children; and became known as Olleros (mountain-valley people). Those living on the plains east of the mountains hunted buffalo; had fewer permanent dwellings; were more composed of young men and women; and were called the Llaneros (plains or grassland people).

In 1850 there were six principal Ollero village sites west of the Rio Grande: west of San Juan Pueblo, south of Ojo Caliente, in the canyons of El Rito, along the Chama River north and east of Abiquiu, and northwest of Abiquiu near Coyote. At these semipermanent sites they grew corn, beans, squash, and pumpkins. The Olleros migrated north toward the San Luis Valley in southern Colorado in the spring and back south in the fall. The Jicarillas and the Mexicans more or less peacefully coexisted.[23]

The Llaneros mainly resided in present Mora, San Miguel, and Colfax Counties, in the mountains and on the plains. A main agricultural center was along the Cimarron River, where they gathered nuts, wild fruit, seed-bearing grasses, greens, tubers, and herbs. Bands lived near Mora, Ocate, the Vermejo River, the Ponil River, Red River, and Ute Park. They also hunted elk and mountain sheep for part of the year, while following the migrating bison herds in eastern New Mexico, which moved south through the area in the fall and north in the spring. A number of Llanero village sites have been archaeologically excavated: an antelope hunting site east of Albuquerque near the present town of Moriarty;

sweathouses and hogans south of Las Vegas at Tecolote; a regular campsite at Ima, east of Santa Rosa atop the Llano Estacado on a major trail leading to the Bosque Redondo; a small village site east of Tucumcari near present San Jon; the Ritter Crossing site on the Canadian River near Logan; several sites along Ute Creek on trails from Mora to the buffalo hunting areas; several sites along Rabbit Ear Creek and Rabbit Ear Mountain northwest of Clayton; and a major campsite at Trinchera Pass, northwest of Folsom. Tucumcari Butte, Rabbit Ear Mountain, and Sierra Grande southeast of Capulin were sacred places on which "the Jicarillas laid their hands before going to hunt."[24]

The hunt was important, but farming was becoming more culturally and economically acceptable. In 1822 the Jicarillas petitioned the governor in Santa Fe for a grant of irrigable land at Cieneguilla (present-day Pilar), which would place them adjacent to some Hispanic families. Officials did not like the idea. One of them wrote: "That the Jicarilla nation has always been at peace with us cannot be denied and has rendered us some service, when as auxiliary forces they have joined us in campaign against our enemies, but . . . they acted from necessity, in consequence of being a persecuted tribe, timid, despicable and limited in force on account of their small numbers of warriors." The government did not want them around, noting "the just repugnance the people have, to having at this place such malicious and perverse Indians." The Spanish once needed the Jicarillas because of the Comanche threat. With that threat fading, they were an unwanted nuisance.[25]

That attitude persisted. General Kearny appointed Charles Bent governor, and one of his duties was overseeing Indian affairs. Bent's first report told Kearny that there were only about one hundred Jicarilla lodges in the territory. He described the Jicarillas as indolent and cowardly roamers. He claimed that most lived by theft, with the exception of a handful who bartered a small amount of pottery, which was more an annoyance than a benefit.[26] The picture that Bent painted was not of a people but of a few buzzing flies to be brushed away without a second thought.

The Jicarillas were a matrilocal society, meaning that families were established in the proximity of the bride's extended family. Each local group was independent and autonomous and had a civil leader who governed by persuasion. War leaders were only necessary during times of strife, again leading only by force of skill and personality. The Llaneros' leader in the early 1850s was Lobo Blanco; when he was slain, José Largo took his place. Other war leaders were San Pablo ("Red Coat"), Juan Julián, and José Antonio. The Ollero leaders were Francisco

Chacón, Huero Mundo, and Vicenti. Introduction of the horse and the need to hunt led to raiding activities, which always led to retaliation by the victimized party. Most raiding parties consisted of ten men or fewer, and they generally went out during the full moon. Whereas the Plains tribes would count coup, the Jicarillas did not see war as a game. They preferred to kill their enemies, but individual warriors did not take scalps. That practice was very limited and only performed on occasion by a party leader who already had made the necessary preparations with the medicine man. If they were defeated, no scalps could be taken. Southern Athapascan Apaches had more dread of the dead and ghosts than did the Plains tribes.[27]

The tribal halves mixed frequently, especially at annual fall gatherings, where they could feast and show their physical stamina in relay races. This ceremonial race derived from a Jicarilla origin story of a contest between the sun and the moon, and it was believed that the Jicarillas would starve if they stopped holding the race. The Olleros represented the sun and the animals and the Llaneros represented the moon and the plants, a model duality of the food resources of hunter-gatherers. If the Olleros won, animals would be in abundance the coming year; if the Llaneros won, plant foods would be in ample supply. Although the Jicarillas were increasingly turning toward farming, hunting was the foundation of the economy. But both depended on abundant land and continuous movement.[28]

The Jicarillas were being squeezed out of their own territory. It got worse when the Mexican government handed out large land grants to Mexicans and Americans. Spain had started the process, giving millions of acres to heads of Spanish families who would act as *empresarios* (entrepreneurs) to develop marginal lands and be a buffer between the settlements and the Indians. In New Mexico between 1821 and 1846, the government handed out at least sixteen grants of Jicarilla lands, all without permission. They included the Sangre de Cristo grant of about 280,000 acres, the Baca-Montoya grant of about 709,000 acres, the Anton Chico grant of about 585,000 acres, San Cristoval of 81,000 acres, Arroyo Hondo of 19,000 acres, Agua Negra of 17,000 acres, the Antonio Ortiz grant of about 164,000 acres, and the Mora–Las Vegas–Tecolote grant of about 1.3 million acres. The largest grant of all was given to Charles Beaubien and Guadalupe Miranda in 1841, involving more than 1.6 million acres in prime Jicarilla land in northern New Mexico and southern Colorado. Lucien B. Maxwell, who was married to one of Beaubien's daughters, purchased the grant in 1847. Like most of the other grantees, Maxwell allowed the Jicarillas to stay, mainly because trying to evict them would likely cause a war. The Mexican Colonization Law of 1828 stated that full title could not be given to the grantees until the Indians chose to abandon the land of their own volition, which would seldom be the case without coercion.[29]

Jicarilla life encompassed a territory that was to become the focal point of thousands of arriving Americans, soldiers, merchants, traders, emigrants, wagons, and animals. The space was limited, and the ecosystem was fragile. The Jicarillas had tried to coexist with the Spanish and Mexicans and had done an admirable job of it, but they were being pinched out of their sacred lands. They had helped the previous occupants when they could, but officials described them as despicable and timid, with warriors of little worth. Despite some thievery, the Jicarillas had never been at war with Spain or Mexico. But then came the Americans, who never could play well with others.

Outlaws and Indians

The arriving Americans may have feared the Indians, but the Jicarillas rarely troubled them at first. Navajos raided along the Rio Grande and to the west, and occasionally the Mescaleros and Chiricahuas would do the same in the southeast and southwest. The Utes sometimes stole stock, but they and the Jicarillas were not a serious threat to the newcomer Americans.

Some of the earliest word of marauding was received from east of the mountains in the spring of 1847. Uncertain if the raiders were Indians or the Mexican army, Colonel Price sent soldiers to investigate. Maj. Benjamin B. Edmonson of the 2nd Missouri took Companies B and F and a detachment of militia volunteers to San Miguel, about twenty miles southwest of Las Vegas. The locals told him that Cheyennes and Apaches were raiding in the area and had gone to the junction of the Mora River and Red River (Canadian) to join a band of 300 to 400 Mexicans, led by an outlaw named Manuel Cortés, who was involved in the uprising at Mora the previous January.[30]

Edmonson arrived at Las Vegas on May 20, but Indians and/or Mexicans had surprised a grazing party under Capt. Benjamin F. Robinson about forty-five miles to the northeast at Wagon Mound, killing one soldier, wounding two, and driving off or killing more than two hundred horses. Edmonson called in his other grazing party near the Ocate River and was able to get enough horses to mount the rangers and his remaining men (about eighty) and hurry to Robinson's camp.

Arriving there on the evening of May 24, Edmonson found that twelve government wagons had been attacked the previous day at Santa Clara Springs near

Wagon Mound. The "Indians" could not get at the wagons directly, so they drove the oxen off and killed seventy of them. Edmonson left thirty men for protection and picked up the raiders' trail heading east toward the Canadian. On May 26 they were "descending into the canon with great difficulty through the rocks, leading our horses and following the meanderings of the Indian trail" when they spotted three Indians watching them. When the sentinels rushed for their horses, Edmonson's men fired, killing one man and one horse. The other two escaped.[31]

Edmonson continued, reaching the Canadian in its 500-foot deep canyon, likely somewhere south of Carrizo Creek and north of Mora River. They struggled across the river, where the trail continued east up another defile. There the two men who had escaped were now charging toward them. Edmonson had fallen for the old trick of chasing after a few decoys while the main body waited to pounce. "The hills around us were, by this time, literally covered with Indians and Mexicans," Edmonson said, "who . . . opened fire upon us from every point occupied by them." The bottom of the canyon was extremely narrow, and the cliffs "so nearly perpendicular as to render a charge impossible."

For the rest of the day Edmonson moved his men to and fro, crossing the Canadian and recrossing, seeking shelter in the rocks. One spot appeared defensible, but it was "too far from the river to command access to water." He tried to figure how to extricate himself. Moving up one canyon they ran into "a large party of Mexicans rapidly descending the hill." The officers rallied twenty men and kept the Mexicans in check until the main body moved in to secure the ground. Some soldiers dismounted behind rocks while a detachment rushed to the river for water. The fight "continued without intermission about four hours, the enemy alternately advancing and retreating as new recruits arrived."

As the sun set, ammunition was low. Edmonson knew that he had to get out. "[A]s the enemy occupied the passes, I determined to reach the open ground at the top of the canyon before dark, which was effected in good order, except in fording the river, when the enemy, anticipating our movement, were concealed in considerable numbers, opened a hot fire—wounding two of our men and killing several horses." It was dark when they reached the top. They marched west until they found water and camped for the night. Edmonson said he had seventy-seven men and estimated his enemy to have had "from four to six hundred." He had one man killed and three wounded, a very slight loss for all they had endured. The enemy, he said, lost forty-one killed, but he could not ascertain their wounded, for "they were removed off the field as fast as they fell." Had Edmonson really decimated the enemy ranks as he had claimed, it would have been one of the greatest army victories over the Indians in the West. Edmonson maintained that he wanted to return to the canyon the next day and finish the job; but with little ammunition, they "were reluctantly compelled to suspend operations until a further supply could be obtained." Very likely his men were simply glad to get out of there alive.

They did resupply and after a few days returned to the canyon to retrieve the body of the dead soldier. The enemy was gone, Edmonson wrote, "not taking time to scalp or strip our man lost in the action, as is their custom." They followed the trail to a campsite where it appeared that stolen property had been divided up. Edmonson's horses, "fatigued and tender-footed," dictated that he return to his camp at Wagon Mound. He reported to Colonel Price that since May 26 "there has been no further depredations committed in, or marauding parties infesting, this portion of the territory."

Edmonson, in his close call, discovered why no east-west trails crossed the Canadian in that area: for about one hundred miles from near Springer in the north to near Conchas in the south, the river has cut a rough canyon, from five hundred to eight hundred feet deep, with innumerable side gorges, all of which are nearly impassable for wagons and very difficult for horses. The Santa Fe Trail could not cross the Canadian any farther south than near the Cimarron River's junction, and even the Jicarilla east-west trail did not go north of Trementina. The hundred-mile intervening section was no place for white travelers, ranchers, or farmers. But the area also contained fine grasses for stock grazing, which would lead to innumerable troubles in the future.

Edmonson's statement that raiding had ceased was tenuous, and Colonel Price was not thrilled with his efforts, calling the May 26 fight "desultory" and the attempt to recapture the stolen horses "unsuccessful," having only "emboldened the Mexicans and Indians to commit further acts of aggression." In late June Mexicans stole horses at Las Vegas. Lt. Robert Brown and Lt. John A. Boarman of the 2nd Missouri, accompanied by two mounted volunteers and a Mexican guide, went in pursuit. In hindsight, sending such a small party seemed to be inviting disaster, and one might wonder if Edmonson's forces were so depleted that two lieutenants had to take up the hunt. They followed the trail south along the Gallinas River about fifteen miles until they reached the village of Las Valles on June 27. The track ended in town and the inhabitants were in a foul mood. In Price's words, "the Mexicans resisted and murdered the whole party."[32] In response, Major Edmonson had to scrounge together a larger party and ride right back to Las Valles, where they surprised the town, "shot down a few who attempted to escape, and took about forty prisoners." All were incarcerated in Santa Fe.

Capt. Jesse Morris (Morin?) of the Battalion of Missouri Mounted Volunteers had a grazing camp north of Las Vegas. Outlaws, perhaps from Cortés's band, attacked it on July 6 and killed Lt. John Larkin and four men, wounded nine, and captured all the horses and property. The Battalion's Lt. Col. David Willock immediately left Taos in pursuit, failed to catch up to them, and returned empty-handed.

Colonel Price reported that his forces were so diminished by enlistment expirations and attrition that he felt it necessary to concentrate all his remaining men in Santa Fe. "Rumors of insurrection are rife," he wrote, "and it is said that a large force is approaching from the direction of Chihuahua." He did not know if the rumors were true, but "it is certain that the New Mexican's entertain deadly hatred against the Americans, and that they will cut off small parties of the latter whenever they think they can escape detection." Price also hoped that a few companies of men could be formed from those whose enlistment was up and planned to stay in New Mexico.[33]

The situation improved in September 1847, when Col. Edward W. B. Newby and his Regiment of Illinois Volunteers arrived in New Mexico, after escorting another merchant caravan across the plains and never seeing one Indian.[34] With Newby's 1,000 infantry, one company of mounted men, plus the Santa Fe Battalion, Price's 2nd Missouri, the Battalion of Missouri Volunteers, and three companies of dragoons, about 3,300 soldiers were available. It should have been plenty if Indians were the only concern, but 50,000 New Mexicans also loomed as a threat. The *Santa Fe Republican* was pleased that "[m]arketing of all kinds has greatly increased in value since this country was occupied by the American troops, and must continue to yield remunerating prices while they remain." But the newspaper cautioned citizens to "be careful whilst large bodies of troops are in town, and remember that excitements are more easily raised than suppressed . . . and the only way to restore confidence between themselves and the Americans is to show by their acts that they have the peace and prosperity of the country at heart."[35]

At the same time the *Republican* warned that Judge Charles Beaubien at Taos reported that "the Indians, and disaffected Mexicans connected with them, threatened to commit depredations on the citizens of that place." We might wonder which Indians or outlaws were informing Beaubien of their plans, but a military response was a foregone conclusion. "The men of property and character have requested troops to be sent up, and we hear that several companies will go." The *Republican* blamed the unrest on "Apaches or Jicarillas" who "must be punished severely, and until it is done, we cannot expect peace in that neighbor-hood." Beaubien would cry wolf a number of times, seeking military protection for his property.[36]

More trouble came from the soldiers. In mid-October Lt. Col. Alton R. Easton, with another of the numerous Battalions of Missouri Volunteers, an artillery battalion, six companies of Col. John Ralls's 3rd Missouri Regiment, and five companies of the 5th Illinois began packing for the march to Mexico. Maj. Israel B. Donaldson led the Illinois companies, while Colonel Newby remained in command in Santa Fe. The move was said to be "hailed with delight," but the anticipation of getting into action soon changed to frustration and anger. By mid-December, after seven weeks of desultory marching, the units had only gone about 175 miles to the vicinity of Valverde, where they waited. The march was not without incidents. Traveling through the Rio Abajo area, the troops "were guilty of many unjust and uncalled for acts of violence upon the citizens of the lower part of the Territory," reported the *Republican*. There were "great complaints about the manner in which they passed through the country. It is no more proper for a soldier to commit acts of aggression or depredation upon a people" than for a citizen to commit the same, especially as the people had been promised military protection. The editors stated they hoped the depredations were "without the knowledge or sanction of the officers." Soldiers in Ralls's regiment shot a Pueblo Indian near Albuquerque. At first it was said the Indian was killed, but he "was only slightly wounded."[37]

The possibility of soldiers committing depredations was intolerable at any time but was especially aggravating while Indians were still raiding. Navajos allegedly attacked several places that fall. Ramón Luna gathered a party of New Mexicans in Socorro and went after one band. He successfully returned with prisoners, seventy-five horses, and about fifteen hundred sheep. It was also said that Luna's men had killed ten Indians, while having one of their own killed and five wounded. Ramón Luna filed a depredation claim with the U.S. government, stating that Navajos had stolen his stock on October 25, for a loss of $250. With sheep selling for about $1 a head and horses for about $70 each, one might consider the motive behind Luna's retaliation. If he had really lost $250 in stock and came back with animals worth $6,750, retaliatory raids had great profit potential. In effect these were not retaliations as much as pure thefts. And if the government reimbursed his initial claimed loss, Luna made an extra $250 to boot.[38]

A major point of the Trade and Intercourse Acts, however, was to approve depredation claims only if the injured party did not retaliate. Luna did, of course, but he had only to say that he did not. If neighbors supported his statements, chances are that they would get reimbursed. In fact it appears that the New Mexicans were becoming adept at using the Trade and Intercourse Acts. This gringo government might not be all bad. Americans and Nuevomexicanos began filing claims as early as January 1847, increasing in February and increasing more in March. These were claims against "Indians," mostly Navajos, but during a time when the insurrectionists were active and the outlaws were in full operation. While Major Edmonson was chasing Mexican thieves, other thieves were filing claims against Indians. One could not tell one crook from another without a scorecard. In May Juan Andrés Contreras claimed that Apaches had stolen 2,130 sheep and other property in the amount of $4,610. In June Antonio Sandoval claimed that the Navajos had stolen 15,000 sheep and other property from him for a loss of $38,435. These were the two largest claims filed in May and June, but there were eight more, with the total claimed losses amounting to about $58,000. As American soldiers marched south through the Rio Abajo in the fall of 1847, Nuevomexicanos filed more depredation claims—thirteen of them in September and October for about $29,000 in losses.[39]

Inactive and frustrated soldiers waited, scattered throughout the Rio Abajo, dying of disease and deserting, and getting into trouble until mid-winter, when most of them marched back to Albuquerque and Santa Fe. Rumor was that the war with Mexico was almost over, but the bandit war was still ongoing.

Soldiers and Bandits Behaving Badly

Throughout 1847 and 1848 there were more problems from New Mexican bandits and rebellious civilians still angry since the failed insurrection in January 1847. The association of the outlaws with the Jicarillas and Utes was tenuous to the point of insignificance—Nuevomexicanos did not partner with Apaches to fight Americans. But the United States had promised protection against the Indians, not against refractory, militant New Mexicans. To most people it was always the Indians who were the scoundrels, but they blamed even innocent Indians anyway, turning a significant portion of them into the marauders that they never were.

Manuel Cortés and his band were still riding the plains east of the Sangre de Cristo, attacking traffic on the Santa Fe Trail at the close of the year. Prior to this time the Jicarillas were seldom mentioned in depredation reports. But in November the *Santa Fe Republican* reported that Maj. William W. Reynolds, 3rd Missouri, had left Taos and was in pursuit of Jicarillas, "who have for some time been committing depredations on the frontier." The editors hoped that Reynolds would catch "this lawless set of Indians and give them a chastising which will restore quiet." Reynolds, they said, was active and efficient, "and we expect him to reduce to subjection a tribe which richly deserves the epithet of Arabs."[40]

On November 27 the paper reported that fifty or sixty Indians, "the same Apaches or Jicarillas which have been infesting the road," attacked a wagon train of Bullard, Hogh and Company east of Las Vegas. They claimed to have killed six of the attackers, while no one in their company was hurt. In late December Herman Grolman and two other Americans in Las Vegas arrived in Santa Fe, complaining that Cortés was in the area "committing all kinds of depredations, running off, killing and tying up the stock, and shutting off small parties that chance to pass." Grolman said that the civilians in Las Vegas were "inclined to be friendly" and wished that troops would be sent there for their protection. At the same time, other locals advised the Americans to leave town immediately, "as their lives were in danger." Cortés, the paper said, had "two or three hundred Mexicans and a large party of Indians, making in all some six or seven hundred," and were determined to expel the Americans. Cortés, with a bit of panache, stole thirty-one sheep from one New Mexican herder and gave him a receipt for them, telling the man that he could collect the cash from the Mexican government, which "would be good in a few days."[41]

Americans were frightened by new rumors that rebels would attack the placer gold diggings south of Santa Fe. Soldiers arrested six men who were "to be tried by a court-martial as conspirators, where they will have a fair trial and meet their just deserts." In this tense atmosphere, Don Miguel Sánchez, an influential man and representative to the legislature from San Miguel County, made the mistake of imbibing too much "aguardiente" with some Americans. Lost in the translation was a statement that Sánchez made, which the Americans understood as an admission that he was the bandit Cortés. Sánchez was arrested, but after questioning the Americans realized their mistake and freed him.[42]

In early November Capt. William Armstrong left Socorro with about forty men of Maj. Robert Walker's Santa Fe Battalion of Mounted Volunteers to hunt for Cortés. The bandit was said to have been commissioned a captain in the Mexican army by Governor Ángel Trias of Chihuahua. Armstrong tracked Cortés for nearly three weeks, as far as fifty miles south of Anton Chico. After one march of nearly two days without water, Armstrong surprised one of Cortés's camps of about sixty men, wounding a few men and capturing horses, blankets, saddles, bridles, and some well cooked beef that they hungrily devoured. Major Walker wrote to General Price: "Had we horses that could even trot, Cortes would have been ours." The banditry did not stop. On the first day of the New Year in 1848 the *Republican* reported that Cortés was raiding near Las Vegas, where he stole fifteen cows from one ranch and quickly butchered them to feed his men.[43]

Cortés was reported almost everywhere. At the same time he was hitting Las Vegas, he (or other outlaws) attacked government trains near Dona Ana. Capt. Washington L. McNair, 3rd Missouri, took a company north from El Paso in a fruitless search. At one time, Dona Ana only had a garrison of twenty-five men and even fewer when two soldiers stole horses and deserted. Five soldiers chased them but were themselves attacked by other bandits or Indians, who killed one of their number while the others escaped.

On December 10, Lt. Col. Richard H. Lane, 3rd Missouri, took fifty men to Dona Ana to protect the citizens, but he mistakenly barreled into friendly Apaches who had been trading in town. Lane chased them for miles but gave up at nightfall. The *Republican* admitted that the "Rough and Ready" boys were too "hell bent on getting some hair." In El Paso two soldiers of Ralls's 3rd Missouri killed a local Mexican and were jailed. In January bandits stole nearly fifty horses near El Paso. The paper reported: "Two or three Mexicans have been publicly whipped for these crimes, but none of the horses have been recovered." Lieutenant Colonel Lane complained that Mexicans constantly robbed his troops and that he had "adopted rigorous measures" to prevent it.[44]

Few could distinguish the good guys from the bad guys, and it is clear that New Mexican bandits, local Americans, and possibly even a few soldiers contributed to the turmoil. Regardless, in January and February 1848 civilians filed six depredation claims, all listing Navajos as the culprits. The largest claim was filed by José Antonio Montoya, for $8,855 in losses that he said occurred on February 14. Eight claims were filed in March, one of them by José de Jesús Luján of Las Vegas. He claimed that on March 25 Navajos stole 3,850 sheep, plus mares, mules, and a gun, all worth $8,200. The depredation was said to have occurred at "Agua del Corral" about 6 miles south of San Miguel. A local padre ordered one Rafael Baca to take forty "warriors" (Pueblo Indians?) in pursuit. After following the trail all day they caught the thieves, said to be three hundred Indians, supping on sheep at a place called Sierra Blanca. That was too many for them to fight, so they rode back home.

A 300-man raid was massive, more likely to have been formed during a war than for a sheep hunt. Perhaps the number was inflated so that the pursuers could save face. Perhaps they were Cortés's men, who had the ability to assemble such large numbers. In any event a plaintiff had to swear the robbers were Indians if he wanted to get paid. In addition the plaintiff would have to claim that Navajos were the culprits, because there was not yet a valid treaty with the Apaches in 1848. A claimant had to blame the "right" tribe.

The claim was not adjudicated for years. As late as 1884 Navajo agent John H. Bowman was still unable to learn anything about the claim or get an admission of guilt from the tribe. Even so, Luján did eventually receive $4,240 in compensation.[45]

Col. Edward Newby believed that New Mexicans were stealing immense numbers of cattle and sheep from the Navajos. When the Navajos retaliated, Newby was bombarded with so many civilian complaints that he felt he had to make a punitive expedition. The *Republican* reported that Newby was not going to make peace, "but to give them a good flogging which they richly deserve for their many depredations."[46]

On March 27 Newby issued a statement in which he lamented that many locals were still illegally trading with the Indians and that three-quarters of his forces were infantry and "utterly powerless" against mounted men. He returned all the weapons confiscated during the revolt and authorized the New Mexicans to go after the Indians—again, what the Trade and Intercourse Acts sought to prevent. The *Republican* commented: "Never were the towns garrisoned by better disciplined forces." Yet a page later it also called the conduct of a few 3rd Missouri soldiers under Major Reynolds "outrageous." Reynolds left Santa Fe for Taos and "most barbarously, and without provocation, murdered an old Mexican by shooting him dead in front of his own house and then beating his two sons in a most horrible manner." The editors concluded: "This is not the first outrage that has been committed upon poor and innocent Mexicans, but we hope it will be the last."[47]

Shortly after Colonel Newby left Santa Fe on May 1, 1848, one of his soldiers shot another Mexican dead in Albuquerque. Newby was aware that his own men were part of the problem, but he felt compelled to placate the civilians and go after the Indians. He had 150 men of the 3rd Missouri (Colonel Ralls had been ill for several weeks) and 50 Illinois infantry, for which he had secured horses. They traveled to northwest New Mexico and after a few skirmishes convinced the Navajos to come in to talk. Newby, who was supposedly going to give them a good flogging, decided that perhaps peace was the better alternative. By May 20 enough chiefs had arrived to make a deal. The treaty was not unlike Doniphan's. Peace was to exist among the Navajos, the United States, and the people of New Mexico, trade could be carried on between all parties and no one would be molested, all prisoners held by both sides would be restored, and the Navajos would deliver 300 sheep and 100 mules and horses as an indemnity for the expenses incurred by the United States in the campaign. Whereas the New Mexicans used retaliatory raids to steal stock, the army used extortion. The treaty was never ratified by the U.S. Senate.[48]

Fewer Soldiers, Fewer Depredations

The rumors of an end to the Mexican War had finally come true. Peace negotiations had begun in September 1847, and the final draft of the Treaty of Guadalupe Hidalgo was signed in February 1848, even though it was not ratified and exchanged until May 30, 1848. Gen. Antonio López de Santa Anna, negotiating for Mexico, said he did not want to give up New Mexico, because the people there had no desire to become part of the United States. It mattered little. Americans believed that it was their destiny to occupy the whole of the Southwest all the way to the Pacific. In the end Santa Anna capitulated. The United States, however, made some changes to the treaty. The Senate changed article 9, which granted citizenship to all Mexicans in what then became U.S. territory, into leaving them as Mexican citizens unless they specifically chose to become U.S. citizens. The Senate deleted article 10, which would have left the old Spanish and Mexican land grants in place, and made them valid only if proven so in a U.S. court. Americans wanted land, and this was a way to dispossess the old landowners.[49]

Manuel Rejón, who had served as Mexican foreign minister, believed that the treaty would mean Mexico's economic subordination to the United States and would be his country's "sentence of death." Many shared his opinion. Considering the opposition to the Treaty of Guadalupe Hidalgo, the Americans included article 11 as salve for Mexico's wounds, stating that all Indians within its new borders will be "forcibly restrained" from incursions into Mexico; when they could not be controlled, they would be punished. The article stated that no inhabitant of the United States could purchase or acquire any Mexican captured by the Indians or purchase any horses, mules, cattle, or any other property stolen in Mexico. Buying captured people and property would only lead to more plundering, so the military was to obtain the contraband "through the faithful exercise of its influence and power." In addition, the United States was to pass laws to facilitate the "sacredness of this obligation." Finally, the United States was to take "special care" not to drive the Indians out of its territory, leaving them no option but to invade Mexico.[50]

What this article promised was that the U.S. army would protect Mexican citizens as it would protect its own citizens. To do that, the army would need more soldiers and more posts along the border, which would take faithfulness and money—neither of which America had or cared to spend in order to honor its obligations.

The war was over. Thousands of troops marched home from Mexico and New Mexico. Conventional wisdom dictates that Indian raids and depredations should have increased. After all, the soldiers were supposed to be there to provide protection and quash Indian marauding. But a funny thing happened on the way to peace. As the war ended and the soldiers left, depredations decreased. Perhaps it was because Cortés disappeared and some of the organized banditry diminished. Civilians filed sixteen depredation claims in four months up to April—about the time that Cortés vanished—and only seven more during the next five months. Certainly the demise of many desperado bands made a difference, but the Nuevomexicanos may have also breathed a sigh of relief when the American volunteers vacated the territory.[51]

Fewer troops signified less fighting in New Mexico. That condition was also perceived in Texas in the 1860s, where some of the lowest numbers of settlers' deaths occurred while the lowest numbers of troops were on the frontier and some of the highest numbers of deaths occurred while troop levels were at their peaks. Placing more soldiers in harm's way was a self-fulfilling prophecy in one respect, although it was generally not the soldiers who did the dying. The civilians looked to the soldiers and rangers for protection, but to little avail. "Short of saturating every square yard of territory with an armed soldier, the number of troops protecting them did not make a significant difference, and troop increases—surges—were many times self-defeating."[52]

In New Mexico the number of Indians stayed the same, but there were fewer bandits, fewer American volunteer soldiers, and fewer depredation claims. We can never be sure whether this was coincidence, correlation, or cause and effect. Yet the fifty claims filed in 1847 dropped to thirty-four in 1848, twenty in 1849, and nineteen in 1850. Troop strength also dropped consecutively in these years from more than 3,000 to about 800. In 1851 troop strength went up to about 1,450 and depredation claims jumped to fifty-five, a new high. Circumstances other than an increase in troop strength may have contributed to the sharp increase in claims in 1851 (as considered later), but a pattern does emerge.[53] What was happening? It seems counterintuitive that fewer soldiers meant fewer depredations or that more soldiers caused more raiding. Perhaps the soldiers' presence simply furnished more opportunities for the locals to defraud the government.

In June 1848 a number of Navajos approached Santa Fe, bringing the captives and livestock that Colonel Newby had demanded. Unfortunately, armed Mexicans rode after them, so they turned back. A messenger brought them assurances that they would be safe. The *Santa Fe Republican* bemoaned the incident: "There can be no doubt from the disposition already shown by the Navajos that they sincerely desire a permanent peace, and should this be frustrated, the fault will not be theirs.... The blame lies with the Mexicans, who at the very moment when the Indians are coming in with stock and a number of prisoners, which they themselves (the Mexicans) could never have retaken, are getting up murdering and thieving expeditions, let them never complain hereafter of Indian depredations." The editors believed that the accord would work, except they also believed that "the Mexicans will be the first to break the treaty."[54]

The *Republican*, it should be noted, began as a small press owned by the Army Quartermaster's Department. Its publishers/editors, Oliver P. Hovey and Edward T. Davies, were privates in the 1st Missouri. They ran the paper until about November 1849, when the *Santa Fe New Mexican* took over, using the same equipment. The *Republican* expressed views that may have been considered typical of the triumphant Americans. While Hovey and Davies complained of Mexicans breaking the treaty, they praised the arrival of some American women in a rough land that had few such specimens of "the fair and superior race of the human family," whose "eye Beams with the radiant light of charity, We love to look upon woman when her face Glows with religion's pure and perfect grace ... which thrills the heart of man like dreams of Heaven." The editors looked forward to a time when the "country will be thickly settled by Americans" and the Mexican customs will fade away and they will come to "have also pride and ambition. At present, how can we expect to see a people, who as a majority of them have been brought up in ignorance, without respect for virtue or chastity, where both classes have mingled together, how can we expect to see them possessed of the same self respect that we have."[55]

2

The First Conflict

U p to this point the Jicarillas had rarely been in the news. New Mexicans had made many complaints about Navajos, but the Jicarillas, although sometimes implicated in raids, were not named in many depredation claims and were not the targets of major military efforts. For years the Spanish, and later the Mexicans, had not considered them much of a threat. That changed somewhat in 1839, when Irishman James Kirker, one-time privateer, trapper, trader, and miner, found a lucrative new way to make a profit working for the Chihuahua government by killing and scalping Apaches.

Kirker and his band of American, Shawnee, Creek, and Delaware cutthroats were supposed to hunt Apaches in Chihuahua, but he went north to Taos—no one would know the difference between a Jicarilla and a Chiricahua scalp. On September 4, 1839, Kirker and fifty men were camped near Taos when a few Jicarillas stole some of their horses. Kirker's vengeance was way beyond what the theft of a few horses would warrant. The Jicarillas had never seen men such as these before. Kirker attacked them in camp and blasted them with fifty guns. The survivors fled to the outskirts of Taos, but Kirker's men chased them through the streets, even killing some who took sanctuary in a church. Townsfolk were caught in the gunfire. According to one witness, "Shouts of the pursuers and screams of children within the dwellings mingled with the reports of firearms and the fiendish yells from the victims," and over all "echoed the hurrahs of the Americans, cheers as savage as the war whoops of the Indians." After half an hour the remaining Jicarillas begged for mercy. Kirker, his vengeance apparently satiated, let them go. He had lost one American and one mixed-blood man from his force, but he had killed forty Indians. Besides recovering his stolen horses, he took every animal and possession that the Indians owned, leaving them destitute.[1]

The Jicarillas had dealt many years with the Spanish and Mexicans but had never encountered people like this. In 1846 General Kearny invited the Jicarillas and Utes to talk and promised them peace, while the two tribes promised not to harm Mexicans or take their property. The Jicarillas also had expectations. They said that it was becoming increasingly difficult for them to farm and game was becoming scarce in the mountains. "You must, therefore, if you wish us to be peaceable, speak a good word to the Comanches, the Yutas, the Navajos, and the Arapahoes, our enemies, that they will allow us to kill buffalo on the Great Plains."[2]

No one's hopes were fulfilled. The Plains tribes continued to make war and the Jicarillas were right in the pathway of the arriving Americans. As their land and game disappeared, they had little other recourse but to steal or starve. In October 1847 Jicarillas attacked traders along the Santa Fe Trail in eastern New Mexico and ran off some of Beaubien's and Maxwell's cattle.

The American occupation had effectively ruined the trading operations of a small number of Americans and New Mexicans with the Utes along the Arkansas River. In the spring of 1848 a good number of them packed up and headed south to New Mexico, where they would be closer to the army and its potential contracts. Among them, Alexander Barclay, Joseph Doyle, and George Simpson were heading to the Mora River near Las Vegas to build a fort, as Bent had on the Arkansas, and start up what they hoped would be a lucrative business. All these emigrants, plus the usual traders and merchants, passed through Jicarilla and Ute land. On the south side of the Raton Mountains, Utes stopped an American trader named Munday and his six wagons, claiming that they were keeping him safe from the Jicarillas. They released him after pilfering some of his goods. When word reached Taos, who should come to rescue Munday from the Utes but James Kirker, James H. Quinn, and a few others. The presence of Kirker was guaranteed to anger the Indians.[3]

In May 1848 Lucien Maxwell was at Greenhorn, just east of the Wet Mountains in territory that would later become Colorado. Maxwell, Charles Town, the mixed blood Pascual Riviere, and several associates had been trading with the Utes and had about four hundred deerskins, which Maxwell packed on his sixty horses and mules. On June 1 they headed south for Taos, but Jicarillas blocked their path near the Raton Mountains. Maxwell corralled the wagons and waited; but as he sarcastically wrote on June 4 to his father-in-law, Charles Beaubien,

"[T]hey were too brave to attack us while at our corral." Maxwell, perhaps not considering his own bravery, turned back to Greenhorn. On the way the Indians approached again, calling out that they were friendly but taking about thirty horses and mules, with "several animals packed with deer-skins." Maxwell corralled again and waited. The Indians approached once more, insisted they were friendly, and asked the whites to come to their village. Maxwell refused. That night they hurried to Greenhorn, where Maxwell recruited eighteen more men to bolster his firepower. This time about 150 Jicarillas and Utes met them on the trail. The Indians again told the traders to come to the village if they wanted their animals back, but Maxwell insisted that they deliver the property then and there. The impasse ended with gunfire, which did no damage but sent Maxwell back to Greenhorn again.[4]

Maxwell later filed a depredation claim for the losses, and the incident illustrates what might occur in the process. The letter that Maxwell wrote to Beaubien on June 4 was very likely the truth about what happened. He had sixty horses and mules and four hundred deerskins. He said that he lost thirty animals and four hundred skins. Although only "several animals" were loaded with skins and could hardly have been carrying all four hundred, we will give him the benefit of the doubt. In Maxwell's claim however, which was filed in 1854, he said the attack happened on June 12 (eight days after he wrote Beaubien about it) and that he lost thirty mules, fifty horses, and six hundred buckskins, for a total amount of $7,200.

Did Maxwell simply misremember the date and number of animals and skins stolen, and if so why didn't he err on the low side instead? Did he just combine several incidents, including one a few weeks later at Manco Burro Pass, under a single date? Did he figure that he could easily dupe the government and purposely inflate the losses? This type of discrepancy appears common in a great number of claims filed. It cannot be dismissed as human nature to blame the Indians and embellish the losses, any more than filing false insurance claims or cheating on taxes. It is fraud, pure and simple.

The story does not end with Maxwell's second return to Greenhorn. When Maxwell wrote his letter to Beaubien, he sent it by courier to Taos. With this report and the news about Indians harassing the trader Munday, Capt. Samuel A. Boake, 3rd Missouri, took fifty men and went after the Jicarillas. Riding with Boake was James Kirker, who had been on the army payroll as an interpreter. Kirker had just returned from trying to assist Munday, and Boake assigned him as guide and spy. Boake's command found a Jicarilla village at the north side of Raton Pass near present Trinidad, Colorado. They charged into it, shot a few Indians, and captured about thirty horses and mules. If these animals were the ones stolen from Maxwell and they were returned to him, then Maxwell had even less reason to file a depredation claim. Boake did not follow up on his success but pleaded illness and returned to Taos. The Jicarillas were enraged and sought revenge.[5]

In the meantime Maxwell and company went from Greenhorn to Pueblo to recruit more men. The Delaware Indian Little Beaver joined up as well as a man named Piles. Maxwell took with him two orphaned children, James and Mary Tharp, whose father, William Tharp, had been killed by Indians on the Santa Fe Trail in Kansas the previous year. He hoped to take them to relatives in Taos. Maxwell continued east to Bent's Fort, where more wagons joined him. This westbound merchant train left Missouri for Santa Fe in May 1848 and included the traders Elliott Lee, Peter Joseph de Tevis, and Smith Town, Charles Town's brother. The combined parties left Bent's Fort about June 16, but they would not try Raton Pass. Instead they headed for Manco Burro Pass, about twelve miles east of Raton Pass, which Charles Town described as "a perfectly easy route" through the mountains.[6]

At noon on June 19 they stopped for lunch in a little valley at the top of the pass at 8,430 feet in elevation, just inside the Colorado line. While the stock grazed and they sat down to eat, about 150 Jicarillas and Utes attacked. The Indians ran off the animals and swept by the camp, firing as they went. The defenders drove them away, but they returned and fired the grass. The flames failed to drive the defenders away: they fought for about four hours. By that time one had been killed and five were wounded, and they decided that they had to break out of the circle and climb the mountain walls. As they broke out, Elliott Lee was hit in the hand and thigh but continued on. When a bullet broke Charles Town's leg, said Lee, he "was left to the mercy of the Indians."[7]

By nightfall eight wounded people had escaped the trap. They traveled through the night and at daylight they hid, covering themselves with dirt and rocks to ward off the cold. Lee's wound slowed him down, so the party left him behind. Lee walked and crawled toward Taos, eating some food that he found in an abandoned Indian camp. On the seventh day he met up with a small party of miners, one of whom was Thomas Boggs, who had been with Lee's original train but split off from it at the Middle Crossing of the Arkansas to take the Dry Route. Boggs took Lee to Mora, where he recuperated for a time before making his way to Taos. Four of the party were killed: Charles Town, José Cortez, José Carnuel, and Pascual Riviere.

Of the rest, only Tevis was not wounded and went ahead for help. Dick Wootton guided forty soldiers to bring the rest of them to Taos, much the worse for wear. In Taos Andrés Fernández died of his wounds. Lucien Maxwell was badly wounded but survived after having a musket ball removed. Mary and James Tharp never made it back. They were captured early in the escape attempt. Word of their capture was not reported at first. About three months later Taos merchants ransomed the children for $160, but Mary Tharp died shortly afterward.[8]

After this latest attack the troops at Taos hit the trail again. This time Major Reynolds took 150 men of the 3rd Missouri, with James Kirker and mountain men Robert Fisher, Levin Mitchell, and Bill Williams as guides. They left on July 18 and headed to the Raton Mountains. Reynolds divided the command into three detachments to cover more ground. At the headwaters of the Purgatoire they found a large trail made by what they estimated to be four hundred Jicarillas and Utes. The trail led back into New Mexico, where they attacked the Indians, on the headwaters of the Rio Chama. After a short skirmish the Indians fled north, but Kirker and the others tracked them to a strong defensive position at Cumbres Pass, just inside the present Colorado border in southwest Conejos County. The battle on July 23 lasted almost three hours, with "the Indians fighting like a set of desperadoes, and the Americans with an equal spirit." Reynolds was in the forefront of this hot affair. The soldiers claimed to have killed anywhere from twenty to thirty-six warriors, but not without cost, losing three killed and six wounded. Capt. Benjamin Salmon received a mortal wound, and old Bill Williams took a ball in the arm, "shattering it most horrible." The remaining Indians escaped and Reynolds returned to Taos.[9]

By then almost all of the volunteer troops had received orders to return to the United States. The fears of the remaining Americans and New Mexicans peaked with that news. In August General Price ordered Colonel Newby's Illinois Regiment to concentrate at Las Vegas for its march home, followed by Price with his 2nd Missouri, while four companies of dragoons would go to California. Coming north from Mexico to take command in New Mexico was Lt. Col. John M. Washington, 3rd Artillery, who had been breveted from major for gallantry at the February 23, 1847, Battle of Buena Vista. But the people wondered if several companies of artillery and a few companies of dragoons would be enough to protect the territory. The *Republican* thought not. "Can it be possible," the editors asked, "as Rumor says, that the Troops are all to be withdrawn from this Territory" with the exception of a few? "Can it be possible that our Government, after paying the fifteen millions of money for this country, be so imprudent as to leave it unprotected? Can it be possible that we are left exposed to ravages of the merciless tribes of savages by which we are surrounded?"[10]

It would not be as bad as all that. Most newspapers lived on sensationalism, after all, and fear is a big seller. In actuality, as the soldiers dwindled, so did reports of depredations. The numbers dropped throughout the rest of 1848. While there were upward of three thousand soldiers in New Mexico, about twenty-two depredation claims were filed; when the troop level dropped to about nine hundred after Price, Newby, Ralls, and most of the others marched home, twelve depredation claims were filed for the rest of the year. In 1849 and 1850, with fewer soldiers, fewer depredations were reported; when more troops arrived in 1851, up went the depredation claims (see appendix A).

Almost all the people in New Mexico, however, would have sworn that they were in great danger. Only Colonel Newby seemed to have a different opinion, saying that he had many more troops than he needed. In late August the *Republican* reported that "there is a large party of Indians in Taos, awaiting the departure of the troops. Whether it is their intention to enter Taos and massacre what few souls chance to be left there . . . we do not know, but much danger is apprehended in that vicinity." At the same time the paper mentioned that a large party of Navajos peacefully came in to return more captives as they had promised under their treaty with Newby. The inhabitants predicted disaster, but little happened.[11]

On October 10 Lt. Col. John M. Washington arrived with about 250 men of the 3rd Artillery. With a similar number of dragoons remaining under Maj. Benjamin Lloyd Beall, 1st Dragoons, there were only five hundred soldiers to protect New Mexico. Still, perhaps Beall was too aggressive in clamping down on potential troublemakers. The *Republican* said that he was instructing young Mexicans accused of theft or misdemeanors "by learning them the Cannon Waltz": they were tied to the mouth of a cannon and shown that "forty lashes is the first lesson." Washington distributed his companies to the districts he deemed most in need, but the people still complained that it was not enough. The *Republican*, however, reported several times during the fall that "the Indians have been very quiet" and that "we have not heard of any late depredations being committed by the Indians." Washington also wrote in a proclamation on November 23 that "peace, quiet and good order now exists in the Territory of New Mexico."[12]

Truly, it appeared that fewer soldiers correlated with fewer depredations, but that also meant fewer government dollars for the local economy. For a time, instead of worrying about being massacred, the citizens turned their energy toward political discussions about territorial or statehood status. President James K. Polk was anxious to organize the new territories; but while New Mexico's status was unresolved, he urged the people to continue to obey the temporary de facto military government.

The people, however, including Donaciano Vigil, who had been acting governor since Charles Bent was murdered, were not thrilled to be governed by military men. The citizens held a convention in October to determine their political status, an initiative disapproved by Lieutenant Colonel Washington. Among the petitioners were Padre Antonio J. Martínez, Francisco Sarracino, James H. Quinn, Charles Beaubien, Joab Houghton, Manuel A. Otero, Ramón Luna, José Pley, and Juan Perea. They asked to become a territory and not be divided up in favor of Texas, which also claimed much of New Mexico as its own. The petitioners stated that they "do not desire to have domestic slavery within our borders" and that, until they were considered for statehood, they wanted congressional protection against introducing slaves among them.[13]

The exclusion of slaves was not based on any altruistic, moral high ground; they simply figured that the local peons effectively were slaves, that black slaves would compete with cheap native labor, and that the land itself was not conducive to plantation-type slave operations. Besides that, the majority of Americans and New Mexicans did not want blacks around for racial reasons. Their attitude was not very different from that of the whites in other territorial communities, where nonslaveowners despised slavery but despised slaves even more.[14]

The petition was presented in Congress in December but met with great opposition. Texas protested against the banning of slavery, while South Carolina's senator John C. Calhoun branded the petition as insolent and said that the territory belonged to South Carolina and Virginia as much as it did to Massachusetts or New York and that any Southerners had a right to go there with their slaves. He claimed that the New Mexicans were trying to exclude Southerners, the very people who had fought for and conquered the area during the Mexican War. No one was willing to compromise. The slavery issue, along with racial and religious prejudices, would keep New Mexico from statehood for another sixty-four years.[15]

In any event, the political scene in New Mexico in the fall of 1848 caused far more uproar than did the Indians. The citizens wanted more soldiers around, for protection as well as for the dollars that they had to spend. Washington wanted more troops too but was told to manage with the force he had: he could not expect additional soldiers until the following June.[16] The trouble was that when he got them they served mostly as an accelerant in the start of a war. The coming turmoil also had some of its origins in the arrival of more Americans. John C. Frémont and his entourage were back in New Mexico. The Utes, who had been little problem so far, were drawn into the cauldron.

Frémont and the Utes

The Muache Utes were in a predicament not unlike that of the Jicarillas, with American trails of commerce and emigration crossing their lands. Where the Cimarron or Dry Route of the Santa Fe Trail traversed much of the Jicarilla land, the Mountain or Wet Route crossed a portion of Muache land. As the Jicarillas were an eastern branch of Apaches, the Muaches were an eastern branch of Utes. In northeast Utah were the Uintahs, in northwest Colorado the Yampas, in west central Colorado the Uncompahgres, and south of them the Weeminuches. The Muaches and Capotes roamed Colorado's Front Range down into the San Luis Valley and down the Sangre de Cristo into northern New Mexico. In the 1840s the Muaches were the farthest to the southeast, with the Capotes to the west of them.

The Muaches were hunter-gatherers, living in conical willow or pine wickiups or hide-covered tipis. They lived on a diet of fresh or dried meat, wild roots, fruits, and vegetables. They snared rabbits, quail, grouse, or sage hen in makeshift nets. In the mountain lakes and streams they caught fish with spears or by using weirs and nets. They also harvested wild potatoes and onions. The Muaches hunted elk, antelope, bear, mountain sheep, and wild turkey and ventured out onto the plains to hunt bison. They were organized in extended, multigenerational family bands, with leaders selected for their wisdom and courage. As among the Jicarillas, one band did not have any authority over another. Another similarity was in the fact that the Muache tried and succeeded in peaceful accommodation with the Spanish settlers. They would try peace with the Americans too.[17]

The Muaches, sometime enemies of the Apaches, were often Jicarilla allies. By the 1840s there had been significant intermarriage among them. Of late Jicarillas and Muaches had fought common enemy Plains tribes. The waves of arriving Americans were a problem for all of them. Certainly men like the Bents and Ceran St. Vrain developed business relations and brought products that the Utes could not manufacture themselves, but they also brought the devastating alcohol, used up the precious resources, and tore up the soil. The Utes also found that the Mexicans had given away large amounts of their land without their consent. Both tribes were being squeezed out but, remarkably, held themselves in check until the "steal or starve" equation was writ large and indelible.[18]

Into the center of the Muache homeland in late fall 1848 came John C. Frémont on his fourth exploration expedition. Georgia-born Frémont was educated in the Scientific Department of the College of Charleston and in 1838 was commissioned a second lieutenant in the United States Corps of Topographical Engineers. Frémont married Jessie Benton, the daughter of Missouri senator Thomas Hart Benton, and found the alliance extremely valuable to his coming career in exploration and politics. During the next twelve years, Frémont led five expeditions into the West, gaining fame as the "pathfinder." His fourth expedition was backed by father-in-law Benton and railroad interests. He was to learn whether or not the winter snows would be severe enough to prevent a route through the central Rocky Mountains.[19]

It was a crazy enterprise in retrospect, and not all that sane to some contemporary skeptics. Frémont and thirty-three companions reached Bent's Fort on November 16, long after most people would have been holing up for the winter. Storms had already hit and Indians were reporting deeper snow in the mountains than they had seen in years. Frémont asked old Tom Fitzpatrick to guide them, but the mountain man declined. Others warned Frémont not to continue, but he talked Richens Lacey "Uncle Dick" Wootton into guiding them. Wootton, only thirty-two years old, had worked for the Bents and as a trapper, trader, and occasional army scout. He was familiar with the mountains and agreed to go. Only a few days later, however, when the sky cleared and he saw the thick white peaks of the Sangre de Cristo, he turned back, saying: "There is too much snow ahead for me."[20]

Frémont got provisions in Pueblo and learned that many of the old inhabitants had left the area for New Mexico. After much argument about the expedition's chances of success, the old mountain man William S. Williams, born in North Carolina back in 1787, agreed to show them the way. "Old Bill," now sixty-one years old, figured that they "could manage to get through, though not without considerable suffering."[21]

Climbing Mosca Pass over the Sangre de Cristo in blizzard conditions with the temperatures falling below zero, more men gave up. Bill Williams told Frémont that "the snow was deeper and the weather more severe than he had ever known it to be before" and advised that they go south around the San Juan Mountains at the west end of the San Luis Valley. Frémont disagreed, as that would defeat the purpose of his expedition. He discharged Williams and made Alexis Godey the guide. Blizzards, frigid temperatures, wrong turns, backtracks, and hunger consumed them. Some froze to death and others starved. On Christmas day four men, including Williams, tried to get to Taos for supplies but became trapped themselves. Frémont finally realized that it was hopeless, cached some of his supplies and equipment, and made a desperate journey to Taos to save his men. On January 11, 1849, Utes found them, fed them, and gave them food and horses. Somewhat recovered, they pushed on, located Williams's party, and crawled back to Taos on January 20. Eleven men had died.[22]

Frémont's tragic expedition had serious ramifications. Williams took a lot of blame for the disaster. It was said that he purposely misled Frémont so that he would drop his baggage, leaving Williams free to salvage it the next spring. Three brothers who had been on the expedition (Edward M. Kern, Richard H. Kern, and Dr. Benjamin J. Kern) had acted as artist, topographer, and doctor, as well as being friends of Frémont. After the fiasco they found it best to part company with him. When Frémont headed for California after the weather eased, the Kerns tried to recover their instruments and natural history specimens that they had left behind. On the last day of February, Benjamin Kern, Bill Williams, and a few Mexican packers retraced their route up the Rio Grande without notifying the military of their journey.[23]

At the same time, locals were once more complaining about raiding Indians, but who were they and where were they raiding in this horrendous weather? Lt. Joseph H. Whittlesey, 1st Dragoons, stationed at Taos, recently had been in peace talks with the Utes, while Lieutenant Colonel Washington, as well as the newspaper, had remarked that the New Mexico Territory was tranquil. Why the sudden round of citizen complaints? It turns out that in December at least seven locals (Antonio Sandoval, Raphael Lema, José Armijo, Manuel Trujillo, Mariano Silva, Sylvester Abieta, and Juan Contreras) said that Indians had stolen cattle or sheep from them. Abieta's claim included the loss of 105 cattle and other property worth $2,100, and Sandoval claimed losses of $2,800.[24]

It might be well to question these claims. The alleged dates of theft stretched from December 15 to 27, 1849, with five of them supposedly occurring on December 24. Very oddly, five of the claims were all filed on the same day, August 23, 1854, more than five years after the events. Why such a long delay, and why so many filed at the same time? Did the claimants not know that they could file for losses until years later? Did they really lose stock, and if so what were the causes? It could have been Indians, but it could also have been white thieves. It could have been natural predators or, most likely, deaths due to the blizzard. It was well documented in the blizzard of 1886–87 that stock losses on the Great Plains reached 50 percent and higher. It was also known that stock, particularly cattle, would put their tails to the wind and walk, some of them later being found, dead and alive, a hundred miles from their home ranges. Perhaps many of these alleged losses in December 1848 were due to the blizzard, but losses due to bad weather could not be reimbursed. The claimants would have to say that Indians did it. When five claims were filed on the same day half a decade later, one might very well suspect collusion to support each other's allegations.

What harm would be done in blaming Indians? Lieutenant Colonel Washington directed Major Beall to take "active and vigilant measures" against all the hostile Indians who "have been such an annoyance to the inhabitants" of the Territory so that they "may be speedily brought either to a good and permanent understanding or receive such a chastisement as will for the further deter them from committing their daring and wanton depredations."[25]

Beall would have to wait for better weather to go after the Utes. In the meantime, word was received that Kiowas were camped at Bent's Fort holding a number of Mexican captives. Weather conditions were not as severe there, and the United States did promise to rescue Mexicans held by the Indians. In late January Washington directed Major Beall with Lieutenant Whittlesey, Company I, 1st Dragoons, and Lt. Alfred Pleasanton, Company H, 2nd Dragoons, to ride to Bent's Fort and "have these captives peaceably restored," leaving future compensation for the Indians to the Congress. "Peaceably or otherwise, the prisoners must be given up." Learning of the planned expedition, folks living along the upper Arkansas were worried. One of them was Lancaster Lupton, an ex-dragoon and now a trader and merchant. He wrote to Major Beall on February 20 that the Americans settled in the area "will be left in a very precarious situation in case you should have a fight with the Indians on account of the Spanish prisoners." Therefore he requested that Beall "leave us all the protection in your power in case you have a fight with the Indians." Everyone wanted the army, but there were never enough soldiers to ease their fears.[26]

Major Beall and his two companies arrived at Bent's, where agent Tom Fitzpatrick handed him a letter of caution. Arapahos, Cheyennes, Comanches, and Kiowas attended the council, mediated by Fitzpatrick. In his letter he told Beall that only the Kiowas had captives and that "they will never surrender them without ransom, or by force of arms," which Fitzpatrick believed would only lead to the deaths of the prisoners. He said that the Indian camps were intermixed and that if Beall tried to attack the Kiowas it would lead to disastrous retaliation. The agent could not believe that Congress would demand return of the prisoners and not allow payment of money or goods to ransom them, for force would never work. Fitzpatrick told Beall that his command was not "sufficiently strong" even to attempt to rescue the captives. If he did, and war broke out, all Americans using the Santa Fe Trail would suffer. Beall took Fitzpatrick's words to heart, for in council on February 26 he Beall did not make an issue about the captives at all. Beall said that he had heard that Indians had stolen some animals, "but I have since understood that the report is false." The war had ended, so all Mexicans living in New Mexico were not to be molested, and any Indians who committed depredations on the road to Santa Fe would be punished. He said that more traders would be bringing goods and "will deal fairly with them and not cheat them." Everything was going to be fine: "The President their great father will see it all, and see that it is good."[27]

Beall did not make an issue about the captives, the very purpose of his visit. Only diplomacy would let him escape alive. He headed back to Taos, where the weather had abated and Beall could more easily chastise alleged Ute and Jicarilla raiders. The settlers at Rio Colorado (present Cuesta on Red River), about twenty miles north of Taos, were complaining of Utes who were stealing stock. Recently they had been badly defeated in battle by the Arapahos and lost much of their own stock. Starving, in the midst of a horrific winter, they took some animals, promising that they would make amends in the spring. They had no time to do so, however, for on March 9 Major Beall ordered Lieutenant Whittlesey to take his company, find the Ute village, and "chastise them in the severest manner possible," at a time "while they are so hemmed in by their enemies and the snow that they cannot escape."[28]

Whittlesey left on March 11 with fifty-seven men of Company I, 1st Dragoons, ten men of Company G, 1st Dragoons, and a mountain howitzer and rode to Rio Colorado. He spoke to the alcalde (mayor), who claimed he had been threatened by a Ute chief. Whittlesey had ridden north about fifteen miles when he saw a small party of Indians on the opposite (west) bank of the Rio Grande. The river runs through a deep canyon there. Whittlesey had a rough crossing, having to dismantle the howitzer and pack it across on horses. He left a platoon under Sergeant Batty to get the equipment across, while hurrying on with only twenty-three men. He followed the Utes for ten miles "across a prairie heavy with mud, snow, and rocks" until he found a small village in the pines at the foot of Cerro de la Olla (Hill of the Pot). A half mile from the village, five Utes approached and asked Whittlesey what he wanted.[29]

"I came to fight," the major said.

"It is well," one of them answered, and they turned and ran. Whittlesey said that he "gave them fair starting space" and then charged after them. As he neared, he saw that the village was larger than he had believed, estimating that he was facing 100 warriors. Whittlesey wanted Company I bugler Otto Akerman to sound recall, but his horse had spooked and carried him among the Utes. Whittlesey halted and re-formed his men at the edge of the hill and made a flanking move to the right to try to turn the Ute position. They got into the pines but found the snow so deep that the horses, "being much blown and fatigued by the pursuit," could not proceed. The Utes angled their left back and swung around so that they again faced the soldiers square on. Whittlesey deemed any further attack "imprudent" and dismounted in a defensive position in a point of timber. The Utes climbed the hills above him and fired sporadically but seemed to be in no mood to press an attack either and after fifteen minutes abandoned their camp and fled, taking only their animals.

Whittlesey assessed his options. He discovered that one more man was missing. Pvt. John Beady of Company I had apparently missed the flanking maneuver and was cut off and killed. The major believed that he had killed five Utes and wounded about seven more. When the other soldiers arrived, Whittlesey decided to camp in the village for the night and pursue the next morning. Just then they saw more Indians approaching from the north, not suspecting the army presence and apparently hoping to join the band that had just fled. As the dragoons approached, the Utes turned and fled. Whittlesey charged again, chasing them for six miles through mud and snow. He complained that the Indian horses, "being much stronger than mine," enabled them to get away. Nevertheless, they claimed to have killed five Utes and captured two women and a boy, "a son of one of the chiefs." The soldiers killed several horses, captured ten more, took all the provisions and camp equipage, and destroyed the Indians' "bales of meat." Whittlesey reported that overall he had killed ten warriors and "from the blood on the snow" had wounded many more. He had destroyed a village of fifty lodges and killed twenty horses. The ten captured horses he gave to the citizens who had joined him as guides: Antoine Leroux, brothers Thomas and Charles Autobees, and Lucien Maxwell.

If the Utes had been destitute and starving before, they were worse off now. They fled north and scattered. On the morning of March 14 about a dozen of them stumbled across two Americans and a few New Mexicans camped near the Rio Grande. Doctor Kern, Bill Williams, and their packers had been on the trail for two weeks already, locating and gathering up the supplies, specimens, and equipment that they had cached more than two months ago while trying to escape from the frigid wilderness. They had not alerted the military about their journey; but as events transpired, it probably would not have made any difference. The two Americans sat at their campfire, packed up and ready to head back to Taos, unaware that these Utes had just fled from soldiers who had killed many of their people and destroyed their possessions. Without a hint of their intentions, two Utes raised their guns and fired, one bullet slamming into Bill Williams's forehead and another into Benjamin Kern's heart. The Mexican packers tried to flee, but the Utes indicated that they intended them no harm, for it was only the Americans they were at war with.[30]

Frémont's expedition was over, but its ramifications were long lasting. When the Mexicans who had been with Kern and Williams arrived at Rio Colorado and told the alcalde what had happened, a courier rode to Taos and reported it to Major Beall on March 25. The same evening Charles Beaubien brought Beall a letter from Abiquiu, about fifty miles southwest of Taos. Word was that Utes were converging on that town and desirous of making peace. Beall suspected that they were merely buying time to gather their forces and requested civilian assistance. Lieutenant Colonel Washington authorized four companies of volunteers, under Henry Dodge, John Chapman, José M. Valdez, and A. L. Papin, to enlist for six months and help strike down a coalition of Indians that had formed against them. Just who was in that coalition was not mentioned. In early April Capt. Henry B. Judd, Company C, 3rd Artillery, was in command at Taos. He received information from Abiquiu that Utes were selling Williams's and Kern's property to the locals. Judd said that if the New Mexicans, who had always begged the army to protect them from the Indians, were caught with property from Frémont's expedition they would be arrested as traitors that "are in correspondence with our enemies." In the meantime Edward and Richard Kern went to Abiquiu to identify the property and found a horse, a mule, and a California saddle that belonged to their murdered brother.[31]

On April 5 Dickerson wrote to Beall that the Utes were in the Abiquiu area seeking peace and wanting to return stolen property. "This is believed to be a subterfuge," he said, so that they could spy on the military and obtain "munitions of war." The only way for peace was for the Utes to return all stolen animals, surrender the murderers of the "American citizens," and give up the property taken from Frémont. Five days later militia captain John Chapman was posted at Abiquiu and heard that more of Frémont's property was concealed in the neighborhood. It was hard to get information, he said, because the prefect "is more of a friend to the Eautaws, than he is to the Americans," and he may himself have purchased some of the stolen property. Chapman found a young informant and rode to a village nearby where he "found three Mexicans who were recognized by the young man as being with Dr. Kern at the time he was murdered." Chapman searched the house and "found the villains with some of the clothing of the deceased on them, which they gave up." They informed him that the rest of Kern's property was being held in Mora. He arrested them but worried about holding them because "[t]he conduct of a great many of the Mexicans in this valley is very suspicious." A few of his men went to a Ute camp fifty miles away dressed as Mexican traders with a small amount of tobacco and trinkets to swap. They returned saying that they had seen Otto Akerman's bugle and brought back a dragoon saddle and a pistol belonging to either Akerman or John Beady, who had been killed at Cerro de la Olla.[32]

Later in the month a suspicious Captain Judd went to Abiquiu and remarked that "the presence of the Americans is more obnoxious to most of the people residing in the valley of Abiquiu than that of the Utes." He considered the prefect "a dangerous man." Judd was disheartened by a people who begged protection but seemed to work against the Americans whenever they could. There seemed no end to the civilians' "spirit of disaffection." Major Beall was of the same mind. "The Mexican prisoners who were suspected of having been concerned in the murder of Dr. Kern and Mr. Williams have been turned over to the civil authority," he wrote, but they "have since been bailed out." He also arrested two other Mexicans accused of stealing Frémont's property, but he figured it was useless, because "if such persons are turned over to the civil authority of this place justice will never be executed upon the guilty." Were the murderers of Kern and Williams Mexicans or Utes? We may never know for certain, but in November 1849 Indian agent James S. Calhoun was in communication with the Utes and heard that Frémont's property was long ago "parceled out to those who found it" and most of it was "consumed." In addition, "the murders, with which they are charged, was [sic] subsequent to the murders which *they* charge upon Lt. Whittlesey, and thus, they balance that account current."[33]

Arrival of the 49ers

Lieutenant Colonel Washington and most of the people of New Mexico wanted more soldiers, but not necessarily for the same reasons. Despite all the dire predictions of Indian massacre, little had happened, and the murders of Kern and Williams were the biggest stories of the winter and spring of 1849. Instead of Indian depredations, what made the news in April was a report of a man named "Capt. Bill Snooks" who raided Laguna Pueblo west of Albuquerque and "made requisitions" on the Indians for a number of horses and mules. Snooks, in "the presence of rather a formidable force of Americans," took a page out of Manuel Cortés's book, threatened to levy a fine of five hundred dollars on the Indians if they did not comply, took their animals, and gave them a receipt indicating that they could get compensation from the Quartermaster Department. The *Republican* stated that "Snooks" was an alias and that he was really a Spanish-speaking American lawyer from Santa Fe. It was an outrage, the paper said: "What is most astonishing, is that men calling themselves Americans should engage in so disgraceful an affair." It was certain that this man, whoever he was, could not have been an American, because real Americans would be loath to bring on such "disgrace and infamy" upon fellow countrymen.[34]

The newspaper noted that citizens should have no fear, however, for more real American soldiers were on their way, both to protect them and to protect Mexico by keeping "American" Indians from making hostile incursions. If the United States was unable to do so, the Mexican government by the Treaty of Guadalupe Hidalgo would "have a right to claim compensation for all the losses that her citizens may sustain." Congress was treaty and honor bound to fill the land with soldiers.

Nevertheless, the spring additions did not increase the troop count to anywhere near the numbers available during the Mexican War. If Washington had 500 men on hand during the winter and spring of 1849, the summer surge only brought the total up to 885. Leaving Fort Leavenworth in mid-May, Lt. Col. Edmund B. Alexander led four companies of the 3rd Infantry, two companies of the 2nd Artillery, and Company K, 2nd Dragoons, under Capt. Croghan Ker on the trail to New Mexico.[35]

Washington anxiously awaited their arrival so that he could pay and discharge the volunteers. He believed that they provided good service that "produced a most salutary effect upon the interests of this Territory," such as giving confidence to the inhabitants while showing the "hostile Indians" that they could not depredate at will. Washington, with much exaggeration, said that without the volunteers the settlements "must have been partially if not wholly destroyed."[36] In time, succeeding department commanders would come to have a more jaundiced opinion of the usefulness of the volunteers.

The regulars arrived in Santa Fe on July 22, 1849, and Washington distributed them among the various posts. Riding with them was the new Indian agent, James S. Calhoun. Born in South Carolina about 1802, James may have been a half-brother or cousin of the fiery Carolina senator John C. Calhoun. James married, moved to Georgia, and was in the shipping and banking business. He was also involved with the Columbus (Georgia) Land Company, a group of speculators who defrauded the Creeks out of thousands of acres of land. He became a lieutenant colonel in a unit of Georgia volunteers during the Mexican War and was a staunch Whig and supporter of Gen. Zachary Taylor. When Taylor became president, he rewarded Calhoun with an appointment as Indian agent for New Mexico. It was a political position, but Calhoun never seemed to understand that and always appeared surprised at what he saw as a lack of support and a constant conflict between him and the military. The money allotted to him by commissioner of Indian Affairs, William Medill, at the start of his journey might have given him a clue. He was given a draft for $3,800: $1,500 for his yearly salary; $300 as a year's salary for an interpreter; $200 for additional interpreters; $1,500 to pay for his rent, fuel, stationery, travel expenses, and presents to Indians; and $300 "for the release of Mexican captives."[37] The last stipulation was rather strange, given that the Treaty of Guadalupe Hidalgo expressly forbade Americans to purchase Mexican captives. In any event, the amount allotted to Calhoun was a pittance.

Calhoun may have been financially strapped, but he perceived the problem right off. In his first letter to Commissioner Medill after reaching Santa Fe, Calhoun said that Washington understood that the Indians would never be tamed "until they are properly chastised." Calhoun was comfortable with that sentiment, but he also stated that annihilating the Indians was out of the question. He pronounced that the tribes have never cultivated the soil and depredating was "the only labor known to them." They would never take to farming on their own, and "no earthly power can prevent robberies and murders, unless the hungry wants of these people are provided for, both physically and mentally."[38]

That belief that the Indians would have to steal or starve was often expressed by officials, but Calhoun and Washington would learn that sometimes the Indians could be the least of their worries. They had a near-constant concern that the Nuevomexicanos were always at the edge of rebellion. After Captain Judd had his difficulties with "dangerous" Mexicans in Abiquiu, he was sent to take command of the post at Las Vegas, for the locals were also a threat east of the mountains. Judd had hardly arrived when he imposed martial law on May 3, 1849, because the civil authority was "without force" and the same men who were behind the rebellion of 1847 were engaged in another conspiracy, duping the lower classes into following them. "The most intelligent, influential and wealthy of this region are without doubt implicated," he wrote, "but so secretly and subtly have affairs been

conducted that no proof can be fixed where suspicions amount to a certainty."
Judd saw a conspiracy so secret that there was no proof of it. The next day Judd
found everything quiet at San Miguel, and a few days later Washington directed
him to end martial law.[39]

In the ongoing search for scoundrels, Washington directed Judd to inspect
traders for contraband. In the meantime Major Beall in Taos received word that
Apaches were stealing horses and sheep in the neighborhood of Santa Barbara, a
little village southeast of Picuris Pueblo. He detailed Sgt. James Batty, Company
I, and twelve dragoons to find the thieves. Washington said that Batty was to
"force them to deliver up the property of every description to the proper owners"
and remind them of their promises not to molest the Mexicans. Batty should not
use "harsh measures unless absolutely necessary" and simply have them vacate
the area by going "to their own people at the Rita or form another settlement."
The initial report said that the raiders were Apaches, but Washington's reference
to "Rita" was confusing. Did he mean El Rito, which was a Ute village about ten
miles from Abiquiu, or the Rito de la Olla, a creek about ten miles south of Taos?
Who were the soldiers really targeting?[40]

It turned out they were chasing phantoms. Batty went to Santa Barbara and
met the Ollero Jicarilla leader Francisco Chacón, who told him there were sixteen
Jicarilla lodges under Fleche Rayada located at a hot springs four miles away.
Batty sent for the chief and the alcalde of Santa Barbara and questioned them.
Rayada told him that his people "had not in a single instance taken anything from
the Mexicans." When Batty asked the alcalde and other locals if the Indians had
molested them, they "all replied they had not and apparently were well satisfied
that the Indians should remain in that vicinity." Assured, Batty went with Rayada
and Chacón to Ojo Sarco, a small settlement west of Santa Barbara, where he
found another Jicarilla camp. More questioning elicited the same answers: no
one had any problems or heard about any thievery. Batty told them that they were
to keep clear of the Mexican villages. He reported to Beall: "Finding the Indians
living peaceable and following their own occupations believing that to force them
to leave immediately would result unfavorably and as the chiefs promised to
come to Taos very shortly to talk with the Col. commanding, I concluded to let
them remain as they were." Beall then reported to Washington that the reports
of raiding were "greatly exaggerated," the Apaches were abiding with the treaty,
and "they have not committed the depredations" that they were charged with.[41]

If everyone had Batty's attitude, much fighting and bloodshed might have
been prevented. The military was slowly learning that many of the reports of

marauding Jicarillas and Utes in New Mexico were often more smoke than fire
or like a morning fog in a Sangre de Cristo valley, dissipating in the sunlight.

Events likely would have worked out differently if affairs had proceeded in a
slow, orderly fashion, so that the military and the citizens might come to know
the Indians as beings other than "savages." Reports of depredations were down
from 1848, and the army was learning that a number of those reports were false
in any case. Still, most people saw it the other way around—it was the Indians
who had to learn the white way. Washington wrote to the adjutant general: "It
will take some considerable time for the various Indian tribes inhabiting and
adjacent to New Mexico . . . to become acquainted with our national strength,
and to learn the American character."[42] The irony in that assessment was soon
apparent, because hundreds of soldiers and thousands of American civilians were
converging like a swarm of locusts on the territory, most of them demonstrating
that the American character was much sculpted by a lust for gold.

Rumors of a great gold discovery in California began filtering east in 1848,
and some people returned carrying gold dust or nuggets as proof. President Polk
trumpeted the news in his fourth annual message to Congress on December
5, 1848. Thousands of people began preparations for their journeys, by sea and
land, as soon as practicable the next year.

Thus came the forty-niners. One of the first groups to converge on New Mexico
outfitted in Fort Smith, Arkansas. As we have seen, the winter had been a bad
one. In early April 1849 more than two thousand emigrants with nine hundred
wagons were eager to get rolling. They had been buying all the supplies in town
at high prices because of the great demand. The merchants and liquor dealers
loved it. Assigned to assist them on their journey was 5th Infantry Capt. Randolph
B. Marcy, with fifty of his infantrymen and twenty-six men of Company F, 1st
Dragoons. Their orders were to lead a military expedition along the Canadian
River to New Mexico, seeking the shortest and best wagon route from Fort Smith
to Santa Fe, to assist and protect the emigrants who would follow along with
him and to conciliate the Indians.

The ground had still been frozen in February, and in March the rains had
saturated the area and made it a bog. Through most of April the emigrants moved
in fits and starts, trailing out of Fort Smith in a line fifty miles long. Some of the
worst part of the journey was in eastern Oklahoma, as the struggling and cursing
emigrants tried to get their heavy wagons through the mud. The Shawnees in
the area appeared amazed at the white emigrants' travails and happily picked
up hundreds of discarded articles along the way. "You would laugh to see some

of the Indians here," wrote one of the locals. Many thought it would be different when they reached the lands of the Kiowas and Comanches, but the trip was uneventful, at least in regard to a feared Indian attack.[43]

Marcy reached Tucumcari Butte in eastern New Mexico on June 18, where at last he met some Comanches. His attitude is revealed in his journal. An old chief embraced him, "a la Mexicaine," which, Marcy said, "for the good of the service, I forced myself to submit to." The chief seized "me in his brawny arms . . . and laying his greasy head upon my shoulder, he gave me a most bruin-like squeeze." Marcy hoped that the introduction was over, "but in this I was mistaken, and was doomed to suffer another similar torture, with the savage's head upon my other shoulder, at the same time rubbing his greasy face against mine," all the time uttering his great love of the Americans, which Marcy, as their representative, "had the honor 'pour amor patria' to receive." When the uncomfortable hugging was over, Marcy told the Comanches of the Great Father's desire to be at peace with his "red children" and that the emigrants passing through the lands should not be molested. The Comanches insisted on their friendship, Marcy gave them gifts of pipes and tobacco, "and they went off well pleased."[44]

Captain Judd in Las Vegas was aware of the approaching forty-niners because five Comanches had been to see him in late May and told him that they were coming. This was more to worry about, but Judd was still trying to stop the trade between the locals and the Indians, "satisfied that the licenses granted to Mexican traders have in general been very much abused." Judd was referring to the Comancheros, Mexicans who traded, bought, and sold various goods and stock to the Indians living on the eastern plains. This trade was often the reason why New Mexicans' animals trickled out of the territory—not necessarily stolen by raiding Indians but traded or sold by Comanchero entrepreneurs.[45]

The Comanches were talking peace and trying to get out of the Americans' way, so it was surprising when Judd reported that Lucien Maxwell, James H. Quinn, and Christopher "Kit" Carson said that Indians had attacked Rayado twice and drove them out "with the loss of all their stock." Even more surprising, two weeks later Judd wrote to Washington: "The cattle on the Rayado are beyond comparison the finest I have seen in this country," so he "has engaged Kit Carson to furnish his company with fresh meat"—quite a bizarre statement considering that Carson had allegedly lost all of his stock. A couple of days later Judd wrote that the Indians were raiding the area, but the locals were not doing enough to defend themselves. "Ten thousand soldiers could not protect such people," he complained.[46]

Early in June a New Mexican went to Washington's headquarters in Santa Fe and reported that three hundred Comanches and Apaches had united and were raiding below Albuquerque between Chilili and Peralta and in the Manzano Mountains. Washington said that "the unreliable nature of Mexican reports" made it impossible to know just what action to take, but he felt duty-bound to investigate. Washington directed volunteer Captain Chapman, Lt. Oliver H. P. Taylor, now commanding Company I, 1st Dragoons, and Lieutenant Whittlesey, now in command of Company G, 1st Dragoons, to scour the area and find the marauders. The likelihood that Comanches and Apaches, who were mortal enemies, would have united was very slim. When the soldiers combed the area for marauders, they found none. Captain Judd, at Las Vegas, thought that he knew where some of the rumors originated. Citizens of Mora brought thirteen barrels of liquor from Santa Fe and deposited them at San Miguel, which were then taken and traded or sold to the Comanches in their camp down the Pecos at Bosque Redondo. Judd said that drunken Indians were making "the most violent expressions of rage and enmity against the Americans," who, after their drinking, "broke up into large parties and commenced their depredations."[47]

The Comanches were said to be depredating around Albuquerque, which proved false. Judd said that four hundred Apaches, an implausibly large number, were on the way past Tecolote and Mora, heading north to Rayado and Red River to raid. When the army scouted the areas, however, everything appeared peaceful. Lieutenant Whittlesey located Chacón in the vicinity of Cieneguilla on the Rio Grande, not far from where Batty had talked with him. He had not moved out of the area because he believed Navajos were raiding west of the river and he did not want his band implicated. About the same time Whittlesey learned that chief José Antonio had died, leaving Lobo Blanco the head man of the Llaneros. His band was in the area and accused of stealing stock, and the lieutenant wanted to "pursue and chastise them." Lobo's son Chino, however, met Whittlesey and explained that his father was coming to seek peace. It was true that some of José Antonio's men had taken stock, but Lobo promised to return all stolen animals and "hold himself responsible to cause full restitution of any depredations which might be hereafter committed." Lobo met Whittlesey on June 16, reiterated his son's message, and gave Whittlesey's Pueblo interpreter one of his own riding mules "as a mark of his sincerity." Whittlesey then "carefully examined the whole country and ranches and could find no sign of depredations other than the killing of two cows and the driving off of three or four." He claimed that his investigation could "hardly be erroneous." But, he added, "the Mexicans and major domos (as is their custom in such cases) represented the loss of more than fifty [animals]."⁴⁸

Swindling was widespread. In the same report in which Judd complained of Mexicans selling liquor to the Comanches, he also wrote that he had uncovered "a double fraud." He had seized unlicensed traders' goods and animals near Barclay's Fort north of Las Vegas, but they swore that their partners had the license and that they would get it and show it to him on their return. Judd let them go. But instead of returning they hurried to Santa Fe, finagled a license from Washington, and went back to the Las Vegas area, where they showed Captain Papin the license. He released all their goods. Only when Judd and Papin compared notes did they realize that they had been duped. Judd was convinced that most of their difficulties stemmed from the liquor trade. He believed that "the Indians have all been tampered with and excited by men who have taken advantage of their trading licenses to gain their own ends." Judd also predicted that the large parties of emigrants then arriving would doubtless frustrate and aggravate the Indians to an even greater extent.⁴⁹

On June 22, 1849, Captain Marcy and the first emigrant wagons neared the Gallinas River south of Las Vegas. He found cottonwoods and good water, but the grass was cropped short, due to the large flocks of sheep. Topographer Lt. J. H. Simpson heard a strange noise after breaking camp the next morning and rode over a hill to discover that he "was in the midst of the largest flock of sheep I had ever beheld." He watched a ragged young Mexican shepherd and his mule and dogs, slowly driving them in a spirit of "meekness, resignation, and patience." He estimated that he saw six thousand sheep on what Marcy called a great pasture ground. That one shepherd and a few dogs could lazily tend to so many sheep miles from the nearest towns showed that there was little fear of Indian raiders.⁵⁰

Marcy continued west to where the road forked north to San Miguel and south to Anton Chico. He turned south and reached Anton Chico on the Pecos River on June 23. The town of about five hundred people was the first settlement that he had seen since eastern Oklahoma, but Marcy was not impressed. He noted "running horses, fighting chickens, dancing," and the peons, who were "degraded to a condition worse than slavery." Marcy went up the Pecos to La Cuesta (present-day Villanueva) then went west around the southern end of the Sangre de Cristo to Galisteo and reached Santa Fe on June 28. Many of the emigrants who had been following Marcy decided to take the right fork into San Miguel. There a traveler recorded that one of their party was killed in a fight "on account of a canteen of whiskey." The murderer "will be hung on the 10th of July at San Miguel."⁵¹

The Americans had arrived, but many were not pleased. They found prices as high as or higher than in Fort Smith. The New Mexicans were not averse to making a profit either. The emigrants were not happy when they learned that the wagon and ox teams that they had so dearly bought in the east were a liability in the mountains on the second half of the journey, and they would need to sell them for mule teams. The locals paid little for the wagons but sold their mules at exorbitant prices. One emigrant complained of getting only fifty dollars for his wagon but having to pay from sixty to more than one hundred dollars for a mule. In Albuquerque another man had to sell a wagon and all his gear for only forty dollars. In July 1849 H. M. T. Powell stopped at Barclay's Fort. He called Barclay "a very sinister looking man," who told him that it was impossible to get to California with ox teams and wagons and that they must sell them and buy mules instead. Powell was certain that there was "a conspiracy in the country to cheat the Emigrants."[52]

Some were so disheartened and broke that they decided to give up on California and hunt for gold at the Placer Mine south of Santa Fe. Many left with poor impressions. One said that Socorro, "like all Mexican towns, is a dirty, filthy place." George K. Pattison, from New Jersey and a member of the Havilah Mining Association, hoped to make a killing in the goldfields. But when stuck for a month at the Pecos River repairing broken wagons he complained: "We have been grossly deceived as regards to roads, time, distance, and in fact everything else by a band of interested land pirates who wished the route opened for their benefit." Americans, who had fully bought into their system of capitalism, nevertheless often seemed shocked when that system operated at full throttle against them. Many emigrants did not have the cash or enough property to trade for mules and had to go home. One company of three hundred people from New York turned back. Others, who had the wherewithal to continue, were angry when they learned that Captain Marcy was not continuing on to California as they had believed but was returning to Fort Smith. The emigrants expressed their ire at the army, the government, the merchants of Fort Smith, and the merchants and locals of New Mexico. The locals were glad to make money off the forty-niners, but were probably just as happy when they finally moved out.[53]

Complaints about marauding Indians are significantly lacking from the emigrant journals. They were not stealing stock and were not killing emigrants. To the contrary, in late July a small party of Kiowas approached a California-bound wagon train on the Santa Fe Trail. According to Major Beall, the forty-niners had lost some of their horses a few day earlier, so even when the Kiowas rode into their camp "in a friendly manner" the emigrants accused them of theft. He said that the Kiowas "protested by signs that they had not done it, that the Indians seeing that the whites were mad attempted to leave the camp in haste and in doing so were shot." Four or five Kiowas were dead, including one supposed to be the son of Satank, a prominent Kiowa chief. If that proved to be true, Beall said, "I am apprehensive that many of the emigrants will lose their lives in crossing the plains next fall."[54]

Captain Judd Starts a War

Kiowas were not the main problem in New Mexico, but people still clamored for more army protection against real or phantom villains. With an increased army presence in the summer of 1849, the 9th Military Department commander, Lieutenant Colonel Washington, apparently believed that he finally had enough men to chastise the Indians. Strangely enough, he went after the Navajos again, with whom treaties had been made in 1846 and 1848. Although they had been peaceful, citizens still blamed them for depredations more than they did other tribes. Washington had been calling for more soldiers and, now that he had them, apparently felt that he could not end his tenure as department commander without getting at least one good expedition under his belt.[55]

In mid-August 1849 Washington left Santa Fe with about 350 men of the 2nd Artillery, 3rd Infantry, 1st Dragoons, and New Mexican volunteers to "over awe" the Navajos. Five weeks of hard marching led to the deaths of several Indians and another forced treaty that once again promised "perpetual peace and friendship."[56]

The Navajos had been returning captives and stock as per the agreements in the previous treaties. Although some individuals still raided, from this time on the local Nuevomexicanos and Americans made fewer complaints against them. From 1849 on the number of depredation claims filed against the Navajos fell each year as a percentage of claims as compared to those filed against other tribes.[57] Perhaps the Navajos curbed their raiding, but it is possible that after the 1849 treaty was ratified by the Senate the locals felt that they needed villains other than Navajos to blame for alleged property losses. Also, more complaints against the Jicarillas and Utes meant more military operations, contracts, and money in an area where many of the settlements were located.

Citizens living in and around the Sangre de Cristo never ended their grumbling about Indian marauders, real or imagined. Judge Charles Beaubien continuously requested military escorts to get him to his various district courts. Lieutenant Whittlesey at Taos complained that he did not have enough soldiers to act on the many complaints he received. He had been on the abortive mission near Albuquerque looking for nonexistent Comanche raiders, and now more reports of horse thefts came from Taos. On July 13 Whittlesey wrote: "The number of Indians in this region is supposed to be large," adding: "Many rumors are afloat, but not one worth mentioning." He said that the people of Taos valley "are anxious to make a United campaign against these Apaches . . . if the Governor would give the order," and they wanted "a free right to property captured," which may more accurately explain their motives.[58]

In mid-July Captain Judd responded to an order from Washington to catch a reported band of Mexican robbers in the mountains near San Miguel. Judd had been in a lather chasing Comancheros, outlaws, and whiskey peddlers, while buying cattle from American stock raisers who had supposedly lost all their cattle and wringing his hands over what he believed were four hundred Indians hiding in the mountains ready to pounce. In early August Lobo Blanco had finally come out of the mountains south of Taos after his talks with Whittlesey, where the lieutenant had found him peaceful and innocent of committing depredations. When the band came to Las Vegas to trade, however, Judd was skeptical. The Jicarillas, with their women and children, camped half a mile from town when the suspicious captain sent Lieutenant Burnside after them and precipitated a battle that resulted in the killing of several warriors and the capture of a number of people, including one of Lobo Blanco's daughters, as detailed below.[59]

Lobo was furious. His people fled back into the mountains then circled out and went east into the vastness of the plains, with many likely hiding in the canyons of the Canadian River. Judd sent out patrols to find them, unsuccessfully. On September 8 Apaches robbed a rancho at Chaparito about ten miles below the lower village of Las Valles. Capt. A. L. Papin, who had a company of Mexican volunteers stationed at Las Valles, took forty men and chased them. Fifteen miles out of town the trail divided. Papin and half the volunteers took one fork, while Sergeant Miller and twenty men followed the other. Six miles beyond the fork, about midnight, Miller came upon a camp. He had his men dismount and crawl up close, "his party delivering two fires in rapid succession, rushed upon the camp with the bayonet, routing the Indians in complete confusion and taking possession of their position." They found five bodies and captured two horses, several weapons, and articles of clothing, reporting that "one hundred and fifty head of cattle, fell into the hands of the victors." They believed that they had killed "the noted Chief Petrillo," and Judd boasted that he had in his possession, Petrillo's horse, lance, and shield, as well as his wife.[60]

Judd called the action "a brilliant little affair" and praised Papin and his Mexican volunteers for their "determination and gallantry." As a reward he told Papin to let the men keep any captured property that did not belong to the government but added: "The cattle will doubtless be claimed by Mexican herders." Judd ordered all civilians in the area to enroll in a patrol system to guard their villages but said that two American traders, W. H. Moore and Charles W. Kitchen, who profited most from Indian troubles and military occupation, refused to do their part.[61]

About this time, Lieutenant Colonel Washington returned from his Navajo campaign and echoed Judd's praise of the troops, stating that their efforts were unceasing and largely successful. Washington's assessment of the merits of cavalry and infantry are worth noting, in light of what future department commander, Col. Edwin V. Sumner, would have to say. Washington said: "A mounted force is much more efficient to operate against the Indians of this country than any other description of troops. Comparatively, Infantry is but of little use. One thousand men well armed and properly mounted would soon put an end to Indian difficulties in this quarter."[62]

Not all the mounted pursuit, however, was successful. To follow up Burnside's attack on the Jicarillas near Las Vegas, Judd sent the lieutenant on an expedition to find out where they had fled. During the last half of September Burnside marched to the Gallinas Mountains, then down Canyon Largo, crossed the Canadian, and went into La Cinta Canyon to the east, all in vain. After traveling more than three hundred miles, the exhausted command returned to Las Vegas, not knowing where the Jicarillas were.

The situation may have been too much for Judd to handle. He asked for a leave of absence, but his request was denied. The explanation was that "[t]he exposed state of the frontier renders your presence necessary," an exposure no doubt rendered by some of Judd's own actions.[63]

Agent Calhoun also got more than he had bargained for when he accepted the job. He believed that rumors of Indian troubles were increasing and noted that Ceran St. Vrain, who had been in the area for nearly three decades, "says a worse state of things has not existed in this country since he has been an inhabitant of it." Calhoun said that there were a number of discontented Indians in the New Mexico Territory but, "I regret to add, they are not the only evil people in it." He also grumbled of the "crafty misrepresentations of *wicked* priests" who circulate "falsehoods of every line" for the purpose of alienating the Nuevomexicanos against the American oppressors who were here only to rob them. He heard that

New Mexican traders were telling the Indians that the Pueblos and the American soldiers were coming "for the purpose of exterminating them" and taking their land. He heard of alcaldes committing fraud against their charges; if he had to choose who was lying, he said, the "Indians have not given me one reason to question their Veracity." Calhoun was deluged by complaints of Pueblo Indians against the New Mexicans and "wild" Indians, "wild" Indians against the New Mexicans, New Mexicans against all the Indians, New Mexicans against the Americans, and Americans against all parties.[64]

Amid the chaos, Lieutenant Burnside, a cousin of Calhoun's son-in-law, had been soliciting Calhoun to put a kind word in for him to secretary of war George W. Crawford, about obtaining a promotion. Calhoun tried but was frustrated by the slow mail service between Santa Fe and the States. In a letter to Commissioner Medill on October 27, he complained that unless they could get prompt, reliable mail and more direct supervision, "nothing of a highly reputable character may be expected to transpire in this territory."[65]

On October 23 Brevet Col. John Munroe, 2nd Artillery, took over from John Washington as commander of the 9th Military Department. The outgoing Washington remarked: "At the present time the aspect of Indian affairs in this Territory is more favorable than usual." The Comanches had disappeared and the Utes and Apaches had asked for peace. Washington briefed Munroe on the situation, which precipitated the latter's comment to headquarters: "The condition of things having complications which require knowledge and infinite caution to unravel or adjust." Perhaps the new regime would begin with a fresh outlook; however, the new commander immediately appropriated the title of "civil and military governor," which assuredly aggravated the already hard feelings among the civilians and army, the statehood proponents and the territorials.[66]

Calhoun, a statehood advocate, clashed almost instantly with Munroe—much of it developing from an incident that illuminated one reason why there was so much trouble with the mail. The day after Munroe arrived in Santa Fe, Lobo Blanco attacked the James White party at Point of Rocks. Hunted since Judd and Burnside had attacked him at Las Vegas in mid-August, Lobo hid and dodged expeditions sent after him. He disappeared until October 24, when he made his presence known in dramatic fashion by killing five men and capturing Mrs. White, her daughter, and their black servant. Now Lobo had captives, just as the army had taken captives from his family.

When word of the attack reached Santa Fe, Calhoun rushed another letter to Commissioner Medill, bemoaning his lack of money and troops to rescue the

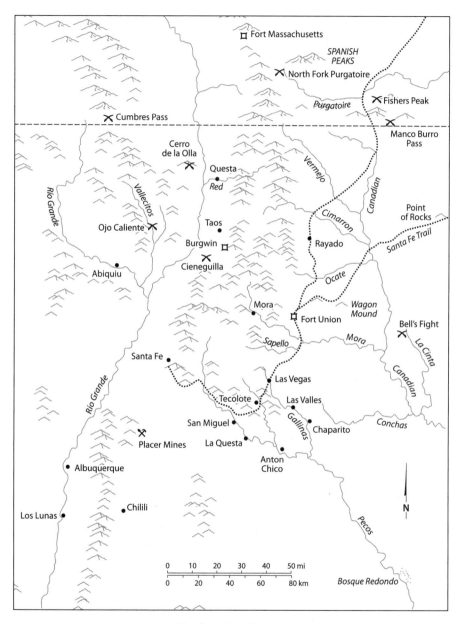

Northern New Mexico.

Map by Bill Nelson. Copyright © 2017 by the University of Oklahoma Press.

captives. He hoped to give Mexican traders money to ransom them, which was not allowed by the Guadalupe Hidalgo Treaty, but he did not believe Munroe was acting fast enough or that a military solution was the answer. Munroe had already stopped the latest mail for the states, so Calhoun's letters would be further delayed. The attack also stopped delegate Hugh N. Smith and his party from going to Washington to make a plea for New Mexico's territorial status. As he approached the attack site heading east, he met Alexander Barclay and others, who had just passed the site heading west and rescued a badly wounded Mexican boy who had been with the buffalo hunters that Lobo had also attacked. Barclay told Smith what he had just seen, and they all rushed to Santa Fe. The road was blocked. Calhoun wrung his hands in frustration. He wrote to Medill: "What Col. Munroe has done, if anything; or what he may design to do, I know not—nor is it my *privilege* to know."[67]

Munroe did something. Upon receipt of the news, he directed Capt. William N. Grier, now commanding at Taos, to organize an expedition and give "full protection" to that that section of the country. Grier took his Company I, 1st Dragoons, and forty men of Capt. J. M. Valdez's volunteers and rode out on November 4. With Antoine Leroux and Robert Fisher as guides, Grier crossed the mountains and stopped in Rayado to pick up Dick Wootton, James Quinn, and Kit Carson for added measure. They went east to Point of Rocks and about eight miles beyond it, where on November 9 they found wreckage, letters, broken trunks, cut harnesses, and other debris on Palo Blanco Creek. Grier wrote that this was "conclusive evidence that here had been the hiding place of those Indians" who had murdered Mr. White.[68]

Grier followed the trail cautiously, seeing evidence of Indian campsites every day. Carson said: "We tracked them for ten or twelve days [actually eight days] over the most difficult trail that I have ever followed." The Indians broke up into groups of two or three and then met again at appointed places. At almost every camp Carson found some of Mrs. White's clothing. On November 16 they marched forty miles and found a recently vacated camp with the fires still burning. They stopped for the night and the next morning moved out at a gallop.[69]

Grier said they saw the Indian camp about four miles away, "which lay on Red River [the Canadian] fifteen miles south [north] of 'Too-koon-karre Butte.'" Carson said he saw the camp first and motioned for Grier to follow him with the dragoons. Carson rode ahead, but no one followed. Antoine Leroux, Carson's rival, thought that the Indians would want to parley and convinced Captain Grier to halt until they could make contact. The Jicarillas saw the soldiers hesitate and began to leave as fast as they could. Grier realized his mistake and moved forward. The retreating Indians sent a few long-range rifle shots in his direction, and one struck him in the chest, but the nearly spent ball hit his heavy coat and folded up gauntlets, merely knocking the wind out of him. When he recovered his senses, Grier ordered a charge. They pursued the Indians for five miles, but, "[o]ur horses being completely jaded and blown, were reluctantly compelled to give up the chase." They had killed six Indians and wounded several more.[70]

Grier returned to the river and bivouacked that night near the Indian camp. "Here we found the dead body of Mrs. J. M. White," he wrote, "whom they had killed no doubt as soon as they saw us approaching their camp." Carson said that he found her body about two hundred yards beyond the campsite, "still perfectly warm. She had been shot through the heart with an arrow not five minutes before." He thought she had seen them coming and tried to escape. "I am certain that if the Indians had been charged immediately on our arrival she would have been saved." When he looked at Mrs. White's face, he saw the effects captivity could produce. She was "wasted, emaciated, the victim of a foul disease, and bore the sorrows of a life-long agony on her face." Her treatment "was so brutal and horrible that she could not possibly have lived very long."[71]

Soldiers found a book in the camp and showed it to Carson. It was a dime novel thriller of the later Ned Buntline type, and the hero was none other than Kit Carson. The famous scout was illiterate, and a soldier read him some passages. It was, he said, "the first of the kind I had ever seen" and represented him as "slaying Indians by the hundred." Sadly, Carson later thought that Mrs. White must have read it and imagined that someday soon he would come to rescue her, just as in the novel. Instead he had failed her, and the knowledge of that forever weighed on his mind. He had wanted to attack sooner and lamented: "They would not listen to me and they failed. I will say no more regarding this matter, nor attach any blame to any particular person, for I presume the consciences of those who were the cause of this tragedy have severely punished them ere this."[72]

The next morning Grier gave two captured Indian children to two Mexican volunteers who took them to Rayado and gave about seventy Indian ponies to the other volunteers. They burned the camp and headed for Barclay's Fort, but on November 23 they were overtaken "by a storm of sleet and snow, driven by the wind, which blinded my guides." They became scattered, "and but for remarkably good fortune, many would have perished of cold." Carson called it "the severest snow storm I ever experienced." Somewhere in the whiteout near Las Vegas they found a patch of timber and took shelter, but one man froze to death—Grier's own black servant. A few men made it to Barclay's and expected to find Grier, but, Barclay said, "he had been compelled to make for the Vegas and take it [the wind] on his back, but did not arrive there till this day [24th]." That day, Barclay recorded, "[James] Quinn & party here with all the Apache plunder passing—some of his men slept in the courtyard." The next day Grier, Carson, and Leroux arrived, and Quinn and the packers went up to Rayado. Back in Taos on December 3, Grier made a disability list for ten men of his company, while nine others were still in the hospital, "occasioned by the extreme hardships of winter campaigns, and by the vices of this country."[73]

Grier's scout was hardly a success. He had killed a few Jicarillas, but Ann White was dead and Virginia White and the servant girl were never found, dead or alive. In Santa Fe Agent Calhoun contracted with Encarnación García and Auguste Lacome to find the Apaches and rescue the captives. García was gone for two months, traveling as far south as the Guadalupe Mountains. He talked to Mescaleros who heard that the child had been killed with the mother. Lacome went north to talk to the Utes and heard a similar story: the child was killed during the attack and her body thrown in the river. The black servant was unable to keep up with the fast traveling Jicarillas and was killed shortly after leaving Point of Rocks.[74]

Rewards were offered. Mrs. White's brother, Isaac B. Dunn, offered one thousand dollars for Virginia's safe return. In 1850 Congress authorized agent Calhoun to offer the Indians $1,500 for the safe delivery of the girl, promising chastisement by the soldiers if they would not release her. As late as 1858, Brig. Gen. John Garland declared that he had been trying to locate and recover the child for five years, but all the information he received was that the child was dead. As agent to the Jicarillas and Utes, Carson could never learn what happened to her. Two years after her capture, a girl matching Virginia's description was seen living with the Comanches, but her ultimate fate remains unknown.[75]

The White killings and captures were big news and roused an even greater clamor for retribution. The *Santa Fe Republican*, which had become the *New Mexican* in the fall of 1849, reported on November 28: "We have now to record what is perfectly obvious to every reflecting mind in this Territory. 1st. There ought to be, at this moment, two thousand well mounted troops in this Territory." It also recommended that soldiers be placed at Point of Rocks, that the Indian tribes should be confined within "fixed limits," and that the entire land had to be "thoroughly scoured, and every Indian, and other robbers, driven from it." It was folly "to think of securing peace and quiet by making treaties with these

Indians. They must be thoroughly chastised and forced to a complete and entire submission to the mandates of our Government."[76]

Here was the familiar call for more troops and punishment of the Indians. Judd, Burnside, and others had stirred up a miniwar with the Jicarillas, but it seemed to fizzle out as quickly as it had begun. Lobo Blanco had disappeared, but he would be heard from again, especially after the latest fiasco. In late November Captain Judd sent out an army escort for an eastbound mail party. Lobo's daughter accompanied the soldiers on the chance that they would come across some Jicarillas and she could help negotiate with them for the release of Mrs. White. Unfortunately, along the trail she reportedly tried to kill two men, "ripped open two mules, and rushing through the camp with her blanket extended and with yells of defiance came very near causing a stampede of the whole concern amidst which she might have escaped. She was shot down and thus her mission ended." Lobo's daughter was dead and the Indians seemed to have vanished. The year ended with Captain Judd arresting fifteen citizens of San Miguel, "principals and accessories of a band of robbers who have infested the road to Santa Fe. One American, William Ireland, among them. Trial begins today."[77]

Incident at Wagon Mound

Some of the Jicarillas were now "hostile," but the military would increasingly learn that many of the civilian reports of Indian depredations were fraudulent. The Utes were making peace overtures, as they had been doing since they had been implicated in the deaths of Bill Williams and Ben Kern one year ago. Agent Calhoun said that they were a moderating influence on the Navajos and Jicarillas and deserved a treaty. Calhoun, with Lieutenant Whittlesey, his dragoons, and several witnesses, including Edward Kern, met with the Utes at Abiquiu and signed a treaty on December 30, 1849. Twenty-eight Utes put their marks on the document, with much the same articles as in all the previous treaties. Calhoun said that the Utes *"reluctantly agreed"* to article 7, which restricted them to a definite territory and indicated that they must build pueblos, cultivate the soil, and cease their roaming. For good measure, the treaty affirmed that the Utes would be directed "by the wisdom, justice, and humanity of the American People."[78]

As befitted the prejudices of the era, American officials always included treaty stipulations that called for the Indians to alter their lifestyles completely. A dwindling number of assimilationists still believed that the Indians could become part of American society if they would abandon their traditions and become "civilized." Did they not realize this was impossible, or were the conditions inserted because they could not be kept and would give further cause for punishment? Only a few days after the treaty was signed there was trouble around Abiquiu—too many Utes and Mexicans too close together. A Ute apparently stole A. M. García's hat, and a scuffle ensued. The Indian chased him, but the argument was ended when García split the Ute's skull with his ax. Utes retaliated by killing seven Mexicans and stealing their stock. Calhoun heard only that there was an unwarranted attack by the Utes but after investigating wrote: "From the various conflicting statements afloat, I have come to the conclusion, the Indians were *less* to blame, (if blamable at all), than the Mexicans." The only stock taken was that of Garcia and his confederates. Calhoun believed that a "very mischievous band of traders" in the area "caused the outbreak mentioned. I entertain not the slightest doubt."[79]

Calhoun distrusted the traders but had been sending some of them out to make contact with the Indians. In late January the alcalde of Rio Colorado notified the military that Ute chief Miguel Gallegos had come into town to request peace. He had heard that a peace was made, but "what has occurred in Abiquiu they knew nothing about," and they wanted to have peace and trade like the other bands. Major Beall in Taos sent the Utes word that the prior treaty included "the whole Utah nation" but said he would send Lieutenant Whittlesey there to explain it. Nevertheless, Whittlesey was to "be quick to notice and chastise anything which may appear to be a fair breach of the peace by them." Still finding alarm everywhere, Beall also wrote that Lucien Maxwell at Rayado had informed him that Apaches and Utes "are in large force on that frontier, and I fear are meditating some signal blow." Beall requested that Munroe pull troops from southern New Mexico to reinforce him.[80]

After some reflection, Beall admitted that the Utes had made "no hostile demonstrations" but said that his men had gone to arrest a Frenchman named Lacome who had been caught taking contraband to them. Lacome stated that he was authorized by Calhoun to trade, but this seemed "so absurd" to Beall, because Lacome and his partners were "men utterly devoid of all character & principal," having been punished for illicit trading previously. Beall demanded an explanation and got one. On February 26 Calhoun had authorized Lacome to meet the Utes to test their disposition and seek information on the whereabouts of Virginia White. He was allowed to take trade goods.[81]

Lacome reported to Calhoun that eight Ute chiefs who had never known about the treaty wanted one of their own. They said that the chiefs who signed the one in December were not authorized to do so. They claimed that only one of their own, Chico Velásquez (his signature does not appear on the treaty), signed it, but he would never act in good faith, because he was a sworn enemy of Americans and Mexicans. Further, they told Lacome that Velásquez was with the Jicarillas when they massacred the White party and when Grier attacked. The Utes told Lacome that Virginia White had been killed shortly after her mother was murdered during Grier's attack.[82]

Calhoun's other man, Encarnación García, who had gone south to hunt for Virginia White, heard the same story: the girl had been killed in Grier's attack. García did recover four other captives from Mexicans who bought them from either Comanches or Apaches in violation of the 1848 treaty. What was Calhoun to do? He could leave them with the Indians or leave them with the Mexicans, in which case they would be no more than slaves. He could not make war on the Mexicans, so he had to buy them. The problem, Calhoun wrote, was that "[t]he Mexicans from whom I received the captives will claim to have paid more than is stated above, and without doubt, *can prove any statement that they may make.*"[83]

Although Calhoun suspected that many of the alarms about depredating Indians were stories concocted by Mexicans or Americans for their own gain, he nevertheless joined in a petition addressed to the president of the United States, asking for more money and soldiers. He said that Indians had stolen twelve thousand sheep from around San Miguel and were alienating the Pueblo Indians from the Americans. The Apaches were going to the Utes "to unite with them in their savage warfare against the American people," and the Navajos were about to join the confederation. None of this was substantiated. Calhoun said that their troubles were "more terrible, and alarming, than we have ever known them before." The only remedy was more military posts, roads, and mounted troops. The letter was signed by fifty-two citizens, most of whom had much to gain from heightened fears and an increased military presence.[84]

Munroe wanted more troops too. In March 1850 he wrote that no fewer than ten cavalry companies of at least sixty men each were needed, with ten more companies of infantry to occupy the posts. In addition, he said the horses brought from the States the previous summer were still not fit for service and suggested that troops leaving New Mexico Territory should leave their horses behind and be remounted in the States. Munroe's letter went to the secretary of war and was answered by general-in-chief Winfield Scott. There was a bill before Congress to increase the size of the army, but until it was approved no "additional companies can be found to re-inforce the 9th Department." If Munroe actually got all the troops he wanted and still could not control the Indians, he already had an alibi: "It will be impossible with any number of troops to prevent the depredations of the Indians." The best result might be simply to make them more apprehensive.[85]

Commanding in El Paso, Capt. Jefferson Van Horne, 3rd Infantry, contradictorily believed that there was "great expense and difficulty keeping the animals in this country, especially during winter," and thought it better to remove them from the territory. If left in New Mexico there was a "great risk, too, of having the animals stolen, by Indians, Mexicans, and renegade Americans." His suggestion was to contract with private transportation and supply outfits that would do the job "on moderate terms" better than the army and would also free up more troops for field operations.[86] Without realizing it, Munroe and Van Horne were both saying that additional soldiers would not be the solution.

Although Indians, Mexicans, and renegade Americans may have committed depredations, the main targets of white reprisal were the Indians. Jicarillas, possibly of Lobo Blanco's band, were still playing hide and seek along the trails east of the mountains. On April 5, 1850, someone attacked Lucien Maxwell's stock only three miles from Rayado, wounding two herders and driving off horses and mules. Sgt. William C. Holbrook of Grier's Company I, 1st Dragoons, took about ten men and went in pursuit, with the assistance of Kit Carson, Robert Newell, William New, and Robert Fisher. On April 6 they followed the tracks east for nearly thirty miles to the vicinity of the Santa Fe Trail crossing of the Canadian. When they caught up, said Holbrook, "a charge was immediately made which resulted in the loss, on our side, of one horse, (that of Pvt. Richards shot from under him). We killed five Indians, (the scalps of which we have as a voucher), and wounded one or two others, and recovered all the animals but four, which, four Indians made their escape on."[87]

Grier added that "two of the Indians were killed with the Sabre—the contest having become so close." He also tried to explain the scalping: the scalps were not taken by Holbrook but "by two or three Mexican herders, who came up after the fight was over." As a result, Munroe ordered Grier to take his command and move from Taos to Rayado, to scour the area and also to see if the reports of fine wood, water, and grass nearby made it a good site to establish a military post.[88]

While Sergeant Holbrook was chasing Indians east of Rayado, a mail party that had left Santa Fe in late March had already cleared the area beyond Point of Rocks and was heading safely to Fort Leavenworth, Kansas. On April 18 the mail carriers, James Clay and Frank Hendrickson, joined a man named Branton and began the return journey to Santa Fe. On the way they met a relief train headed by Thomas W.

Flournoy, who was going out to help a stranded wagon train. That train, under James Brown of Missouri, consisted of about twenty wagons loaded with merchandise headed for Santa Fe. Brown had left Independence in early October 1849. Forty miles beyond the Arkansas on the Dry Route, about November 17, they got caught in a three-day snow storm. All of Brown's oxen perished. The storm may have been part of the frigid weather system that also caught Grier on the New Mexico plains several days later. Some of the men went back to Missouri to get more oxen, while the rest waited out the winter trying to protect their wagons. When the mail carriers and Flournoy's train found them, a few of them ditched Brown's wagons and joined them. Ten men continued west: Clay, Hendrickson, Branton, Flournoy, Benjamin Shaw, John Freeman, John Duty, John Williams, Moses Goldstein, who had wintered with the stranded wagons, and a German teamster.[89]

They probably felt safer when they camped near Wagon Mound, only about forty-four miles from Las Vegas, about May 8. It was their last night alive. A band of attackers, probably Jicarillas and possibly Utes and other allies, swept down on them from behind the hill and killed them all. The bodies lay decomposing or dined on by wolves for about ten days before a party of traders heading east stumbled upon them. They grabbed some of the mail bags and quickly returned to Las Vegas on May 20. The next day Lt. Col. Edmund B. Alexander, 3rd Infantry, commanding the post, sent out Lieutenant Burnside with a detachment of mounted artillery to bury the dead and collect whatever mail he could find. Burnside arrived at Wagon Mound on May 22, found the remains of ten people, and had Mexican laborers brought for that purpose dig the graves.

Burnside, Lt. Peter W. L. Plympton, 7th Infantry, and Alexander Barclay scouted the area to try to determine what had happened. Clay and Hendrickson's mail wagon was half a mile from the foot of Wagon Mound with the tongue broken and a dead mule still in harness. Two bodies were still in the wagon "in a complete state of putrifaction [*sic*]" and the other eight "very much eaten by the wolves."[90]

The farthest body was seventy-five yards away. One horse and two mules were killed near the wagon and two horses were dead near the foot of the mound. Burnside believed that some of the party had first camped about a mile from where the wagon was found and had been sitting around a fire when the Indians charged them. They ran or rode back to try to assemble but were all ridden down and killed within seventy-five yards of the wagon. The two men in the wagon were wounded in the thighs—which Burnside believed meant that they were mounted when they were hit—and crawled into the wagon for cover. Barclay believed that one of the dead was James Brown from the stranded wagon train. All the bodies were stripped but only two of them scalped. The bodies were buried in a common grave. A great number of arrows were found, some of which Barclay recognized as Ute, while one of the Mexicans recognized both Ute and Apache arrows. Nearly two weeks or more after the attack, there was no trail to follow. Burnside said that he had no clue as to which way the Indians might have gone. He made one ominous comment: "So large a party of Americans have never before been entirely destroyed by the Indians of that portion of the territory; and in fact ten Americans have heretofore been considered comparatively safe in traveling over the road, with proper care."[91]

Burnside collected all the mail he could find and rode back to Las Vegas. Colonel Munroe wrote that the attackers were Jicarillas and maybe some Utes and even Comanches. "On this occasion it is not improbable that they were joined with Mexicans and even whites, as the appearance of many of the letters which were collected indicate that they had been opened, torn and replaced in the envelopes."[92]

It was clear that a war of sorts had been ongoing on since the previous August, one that Burnside had helped initiate with his attack on friendly Jicarillas at Las Vegas. On May 27, 1850, Burnside, Plympton and twenty-two soldiers left Las Vegas as escorts for another mail party heading east. Just beyond Rabbit Ears Creek they found a blank muster roll of the type stolen in the mail attack, weighted down with two stones. On it was drawn a map showing "the manner in which the murders were committed near the 'Waggon Mound.'" A fresh trail convinced Burnside that the murderers were in the vicinity watching them. Proceeding cautiously about two miles, they came across a party of nearly two hundred Mexicans, "who represented themselves as being 'buffalo hunters,'" but they had more than three hundred pack animals and "no buffalo meat." One Mexican explained that a few days before they had fought with Arapahos and Cheyennes on the Cimarron, losing one man and killing three Indians. A short time later, however, a Pueblo Indian riding with them told Burnside that they had not fought or even seen any Indians. Another said that they had met the mail party near Point of Rocks about May 5 and traded with them, while still others said that they had not seen them at all.[93]

The meeting left Burnside supposing that "they might in some way be connected with the murder." He was convinced when they had ridden on and passed the last camp of the buffalo hunters, where they found a letter written by Ben Shaw, one of those killed, to a lady in Santa Fe. Burnside, with too few men to do anything, kept riding with the mail carriers to the Cimarron River before turning back.

3

Smoke and Fog

If people had been asked what was the major problem besetting New Mexico at this time, most would probably have answered "Indians." But that response was becoming hollow. Munroe and Burnside had suspicions that the attack at Wagon Mound might have been perpetrated by Mexicans: Burnside learned that many of the buffalo hunting party lived in the Taos area. Captain Grier stated: "I have not the slightest confidence in the honesty, patriotism, or fidelity of the people of Taos Valley. On those three points I regard them as but slightly superior to the Apaches."[1] Others (civilian and military) surmised that many of the reported property thefts were done by Indians but a significant portion may have been committed by Mexican or American bandits, while some of the allegations may even have been completely fabricated. More problems were likely caused by the locals in their conflict over who was to control the government.

Hugh Smith, who had been prevented from getting to Washington in October of 1849 because of the attack at Point of Rocks, eventually made it but had a tough time even getting seated as a delegate. Finally, in April 1850, the House of Representatives considered his bid to establish New Mexico as a territory. The proposal may have had a chance, but Smith, hoping to keep out slavery, wrote an inflammatory pamphlet in which he criticized a "decaying" South and a few "selfish, venal" Northern supporters of trying to obtain more power for the South in the Senate. Trashing members of Congress was not a smart idea. In addition, Smith's legitimacy was questioned because he was said to represent a government that was military rather than civilian in origin. The territorial bid was rejected. Munroe was still the boss until Congress said otherwise.[2]

73

In New Mexico the Staters and Territorials fought for power. Calhoun, a pro-State man, wrote to Commissioner Brown on June 19 that "no human minds can appreciate, or understand, the character and extent of the disorder in this territory." There were too many people, "who, if they can counteract honest efforts to advance the public good, are perfectly content to do so" and still more people "who are so recklessly bent, to accomplish their ends neither life or character would be regarded for a moment." Calhoun said that the Pueblos and Mexicans were excited, "and a *certain class* of Americans are greatly excited. The most unimaginable incongruities have combined, and are divided into two parties, neither possessing the characteristics of a national party." The contest between the military/territorial party and a civil/state party "is extremely violent."[3]

Among the issues were the New Mexico–Texas boundary, the approval or banning of slavery, citizenship and voting rights, peonage, racial and religious conflicts, land claims, property ownership, and government contracts, but most important was the question of power control and with it the means to adjudicate all the other issues.

By the spring of 1850 the factions were hardening. Among the Staters were Manuel Álvarez, F. Tomás Cabeza de Baca, Richard H. Weightman, William Z. Angney, William S. Messervy, James D. Robinson, Francisco Otero, and Vincente Martínez. Among the Territorials were Joab Houghton, Charles Beaubien, Lucien Maxwell, James Quinn, Donaciano Vigil, Ceran St. Vrain, Alexander Duvall, and Henry Connelly.[4]

It was no secret that a good number of the Territorials wanted a military government; some of them held or sought army contracts, and they wanted an army presence. Staters also wanted the army around but wanted local government control over it. One way to achieve their ends was to make sure that reports of murdering Indians and rebellious New Mexicans were always in the news. Fostering fear is an excellent way to hold power.

When the army arrived there were few surplus agricultural products to sell, but with the increased demand the Mexicans began planting whatever crops the army wished to purchase. They could sell high, because the transportation costs of hauling in supplies was not cost-effective. The locals made money on the army, and getting lucrative contracts was an extra boon. They certainly knew how to price gouge the forty-niners. If the New Mexicans had a dearth of crops at first, they did have an excess of sheep, which were not used much for their wool but for their meat. Again the army was a large consumer.[5]

It was good for the economy to have the army around. Businesspeople also believed that the taxes would be lower if New Mexico remained a territory. Some, however, such as President Taylor and secretary of war George Crawford, believed that the military should not be involved in government. They sent Maj. George A. McCall to assist Staters in their efforts to form a civilian government. On the day McCall arrived, March 11, 1850, he met with agent Calhoun and some of the leading statehood men "and enlisted them in the cause I desired to advance." The pressure for another convention had results. In April Colonel Munroe complied, seeing that Congress apparently wished the territory to become a state.[6]

The convention met from May 15 to 25. Joab Houghton was one of the leaders of the Territorials but softened his stance when McCall pressured him. An outspoken Stater was the abrasive Richard H. Weightman, a graduate of West Point and an ex-captain in the Battalion of Missouri Volunteers. Weightman, Angney, Álvarez, Calhoun, and several others were exasperatingly vocal. McCall noted that Territorials outnumbered Staters at the convention, but the Staters were still able to get most of what they wanted, mainly because of some key New Mexican support and because they wielded the club of presidential approval.[7]

The constitution that they hammered out defied Texas claims to eastern New Mexico, subordinated the military to the civil government, and challenged the dominance of the Roman Catholic Church, stating that freedom of conscience was guaranteed and that no one religion would have preference. But the most controversial item was still the hard stand against slavery. It was described as "a moral, social, and political evil," and the people of New Mexico unanimously agreed to reject it forever. This stand, used by delegate Hugh Smith, was what had gotten the prior territorial request rejected by the Southern faction in Congress. McCall was alarmed. He wrote to Secretary Crawford for instructions, but the letter was delayed by the attack at Wagon Mound. As time went on, the Staters, in trying to tone down the rabid antislavery rhetoric of the Territorials, began to be labeled proslavery.[8]

The final vote was to be on June 20. It would not only be a vote for or against the constitution but a vote to choose a governor, lieutenant governor, congressional representatives, and members of the state legislature. It was assumed that the Territorials, who had a majority, would get all their men elected, but not if Weightman had anything to say about it. His party had been appealing to the New Mexicans as being the true friends of the people and painted itself as antiauthority. Staters charged that the judges, sheriffs, alcaldes, prefects, civil officers, and army all favored the Territorials for their own selfish interests. The army provided jobs and contracts and even owned the press. How would the little people have a chance?

Weightman even wrote a letter to Munroe, accusing Judge Joab Houghton of taking bribes, being guilty of business fraud, judging cases concerning his own affairs, and announcing people's guilt even before the trials. Munroe declined to take any action, but Houghton, protesting that he had been secretly slandered, demanded satisfaction. Weightman, writing to James H. Quinn, an attorney in Houghton's court, said that he had not secretly said anything about Houghton—his scorn was public knowledge and he would gladly accept the challenge. The two men met near Santa Fe for a duel. At the command "fire," Weightman shot a pistol ball close by Houghton's ear. Houghton, who was somewhat deaf, said that he had not heard the command. Weightman lifted his hands and bade the judge to fire, but the seconds interposed and hurried both men off the field of honor.[9]

In the late spring of 1850 Weightman accused Judges Houghton and Antonio José Otero of spreading "persistent rumors of revolution, assassination, and other disturbances" in order "to intimidate the people into voting for a continuance in office of those then exercising civil authority." The two judges and prefect Ramón Luna of Sabinal allegedly threw one hundred protesters in jail so they could note vote on June 20, election day.[10]

The Houghton Territorial faction ran Dr. Henry Connelly for governor, a Kentuckian who for years had businesses in Chihuahua and New Mexico. Ceran St. Vrain was their choice for lieutenant governor. Hugh Smith, still in Washington, was the candidate for the House of Representatives. Weightman's State faction ran Tomás Cabeza de Baca and Manuel Álvarez for governor and lieutenant governor and William S. Messervy as congressional delegate. McCall, although he pushed for statehood, believed that the "Houghton party would carry all before them."[11]

The constitution was overwhelmingly approved, 8,371 to 39, but the offices were split. Connelly won as governor, but Álvarez became lieutenant governor and Messervy was the delegate. When members of the new state legislature met, they selected the two senators. Houghton had hoped for this office, but Weightman beat him, while Maj. Francis A. Cunningham, still a paymaster in the army, became the compromise choice as the second senator. It was quite a shock to many. Calhoun wrote to Commissioner Brown that the Territorials supported by Munroe "submitted to an overwhelming defeat, and the party who commenced the agitation . . . triumphed." Weightman could not help crow about his party's victory "despite the partisan acts of the military commander, despite the almost unanimous opposition of the judges, prefectos, alcaldes . . . who held their offices at the will and pleasure of the military commander."[12]

As a result of the election, Munroe wrote to the secretary of war that the newly elected government "has assumed to supersede the actual government, and go at once into operation." Munroe did not believe he should bow to their wishes but "await the determination of congress" for approval. He did not trust "the general ignorance of the people" and their "manifest dislike" of Americans. Munroe asked for further instructions. When Gen. Winfield Scott was informed, he wrote: "It will be seen that Col. Munroe does not mean to allow the new government to go into effect."[13]

It turns out that all the electioneering, slander, accusations, and recriminations were for naught. On July 9, 1850, Zachary Taylor died, and with him went much of the support for statehood. Millard Fillmore became the president, and on August 15 George Crawford was replaced by Charles M. Conrad as secretary of war. Congress debated the state or territory question for New Mexico and California all summer. On September 9, in what became known as the Compromise of 1850, the Texas boundary was settled, Utah and New Mexico became territories, California became a state, and "popular sovereignty" became the law for determining future statehood. Senator-elect Richard Weightman, who had just arrived in Washington, left in frustration.

Colonel Munroe was not feeling very well either. He had written to Secretary Crawford, but Secretary Conrad answered. In a letter penned the day after the law passed, Conrad stated that the president regretted any misunderstandings between Munroe and the people of New Mexico, but "[i]t is at all times desirable that the civil and military departments of the government should be kept entirely distinct." Conrad believed that the country was tranquil: the people had not rebelled and did not need military suppression. Munroe was "directed to abstain from all further interference in the civil or political affairs of that country."[14]

The reprimand did not greatly alter Munroe's conduct. He did not tell anyone about the Conrad letter and kept acting as civil and military governor until the territorial government was officially installed, with James Calhoun as the new governor, on March 3, 1851. Richard Weightman continued to paint Munroe as a tyrant who oppressed the people, interfered with their religious worship, arbitrarily taxed them, and then embezzled the taxes. Weightman believed that Munroe viewed Mexicans as degraded and vicious, always on the verge of rebellion, and seeking only to vex the authorities.[15]

Was Munroe really such a bad apple? If so, it may have been a function of the company that he kept. The Territorial party wanted the army around for reasons that we have seen. People of all political alignments wanted the best deal for themselves, and some were not averse to bending the rules. Members of both factions filed Indian depredation claims. Some of them were legitimate claims for property losses actually caused by raiding Indians. Many times the losses were exaggerated. Sometimes there were no such raids: the losses were concocted solely to collect from the government.

The Territorials, who had most to gain by inciting an atmosphere of turmoil and fear, were also the ones who filed the most Indian depredation claims and had the most army contracts. Of the eighty-three men whose preference for State or Territory has come down to us in the historical record, nineteen filed depredation claims (23 percent). Of those nineteen, fourteen were filed by Territory proponents (74 percent). All of the army contracts went to Territorial men (see appendix B). Coincidence or correlation? Perhaps the percentages would change if we knew the political preferences of the hundreds of other depredation claimants and those who had army contracts, but it is telling that the Territorials, who had most to gain from an army presence, were the ones who most often raised the alarm about alleged rebellions and Indian raids.

Depredation and Retaliation

After Sergeant Holbrook's fight and the killing at Wagon Mound in May 1850, Colonel Munroe ordered Captain Grier to move to Rayado. Grier, hearing a rumor that there were three hundred Indians in the vicinity, asked for an additional dragoon company and marched from Taos to Rayado. Today Highway 64 generally follows most of his trail, but it is a winding, difficult drive. Grier tried to get there with wagons. Making only twelve miles in two days, with three out of his four wagons broken, he gave up and sent back to Taos for pack mules. When he reached Rayado, he reported that the area was excellent for a post. It was centrally located forty miles from Taos, forty-five miles from Point of Rocks, forty-five miles from Raton Pass, twenty-five miles from Wagon Mound, and forty miles from Mora. It had good wood, water, and grass, and little snowfall. Grier believed only half rations of corn would be needed because of the fine grazing and hay-making possibilities. The Indians could not pass easily through the mountains with a post at Rayado. Besides, Lucien Maxwell just happened to have two well-built houses that he agreed to rent to the army, for only $1,440 per year.[16]

Grier had hardly sent his letter off to Munroe when Lieutenant Whittlesey warned that it was unsafe to leave Taos "without military protection" because "it is feared by intelligent citizens that outrages may be committed." On June 18 Grier sent Lt. Oliver Taylor with a detachment of Company G back to Taos to keep the peace during the upcoming election.[17]

Calhoun was getting mixed signals. The Utes at Abiquiu declared that they were friendly. He said that "they have committed no acts of hostility, or depredations against the people of this territory and I am inclined to credit the declaration." The Pueblos wanted stricter enforcement of the laws "so that they may be protected from improper intrusions of the whites." Calhoun was more concerned about the Jicarillas. East of the mountains people were still envisioning dangerous Indians and rebellious Mexicans. On June 21 in Mora Dr. John M. Whitlock, a physician, farmer, and merchant who had once been hired by Lieutenant Colonel Washington as his private doctor, wrote an urgent letter to "Dear Judge" (Houghton or Beaubien?). He said that all the Americans in town were forted up because of news that the Mexicans at Agua Negra, about five miles up the Mora River, "will be down tonight for the purpose of exterminating such white men as they may find." They had been holed up for three nights. Ceran St. Vrain and José Pley had gone to Taos for help. Whitlock wrote: "Judge, I really think from my own observations that if troops are not here very soon the American population of this place and their friends of Mexicans will be killed off." The leaders of the insurrection, he said, were a group of buffalo hunters who had already captured Santa Fe.[18]

With this latest fright, the army was on high alert, but in Taos Capt. Henry L. Kendrick, 2nd Artillery, said that "[n]o plan of insurrection [had been] discovered" and that "[t]he Apaches have disappeared." Regardless, Lt. John Adams and Company K, 2nd Dragoons, was hurriedly sent to Mora. Despite Whitlock's dire predictions, Adams and the local sheriff only arrested "three offenders against the Civil Law." Adams "[c]ould find no revolutionary movement, merely a little excitement against the Alcalde, a Spaniard, by those opposed to him in politics."[19]

While soldiers hurried to Mora for another false alarm, Rayado was actually attacked. On June 26 Grier reported that three hundred Apaches and Comanches struck the herd at noon. Grier said he had his hands full just saving the company's horses because he only had twenty men, while the Indians had free run of the place, "driving off all stock." They killed a Mexican shepherd and Bill New, who rode with Grier in the fight the previous November on the Canadian, as well as Company I bugler Rengel, who for some reason was alone and unarmed one mile from camp. Grier called for Lieutenant Taylor to return from Taos and asked for dragoon reinforcements from Las Vegas plus more pack mules and supplies before he could chase after the raiders.[20]

Several people at Rayado filed claims for losses, including Lucien Maxwell and James Quinn. As we have seen, Maxwell had once exaggerated his losses in an alleged stock theft in June 1848, and twice in 1849 he and Quinn were supposedly robbed of all their stock. Nonetheless, the two had gotten a contract beginning in April 1849 to supply the army with beef at eight cents a pound, most all of it coming from their holdings near Rayado.[21]

The men had a good deal going. Even with all the thefts that allegedly wiped them out, they always had cattle to sell to the army. If the cattle really were stolen they could file a claim and get reimbursed. The problem was that the thieves had to be of the right tribe. Grier and other witnesses said that the raiders were Apaches and Comanches, however unlikely it was that those tribes were working together. Claimants could be compensated only if there were valid peace treaties with the tribes doing the raiding (the tribe had to be in "amity") and cash annuities were available from which the losses could be deducted. Quinn and Maxwell must have talked over their options. They did not file a claim until May 1853, for the theft of 175 cattle and 10 horses and mules, for losses of $5,175. Since neither Jicarillas nor Comanches were in amity at the time of the raid, the claimants had to finger a different tribe—they said that the Utes did it.

Manuel Abreu allegedly owned stock in the Rayado area. He filed a claim for losses and also said that the perpetrators were Utes. His case was not finally adjudicated until 1902, but the government attorneys used Grier's report to show that the raiders were probably Jicarillas, not Utes. As there was no treaty with the Jicarillas, they were not in amity and were not liable for damages. Abreu lost the case, as did Maxwell and Quinn.[22] No treaty, no liability. The tendency of claimants to exaggerate losses or even concoct them and to blame innocent people was a real problem, but not for the accusers. If they got away with it, they made money; if they did not, they faced no repercussions.

As usual, the Indians took the heat. Grier was duty bound to chase and punish someone. Lieutenant Whittlesey in Taos responded to Grier's call for help and said that he would leave for Rayado on June 29 with every available man but was worried because he had to leave behind quartermaster and subsistence stores, plus arms and ammunition "without the slightest protection beyond what is afforded by locks and bolts." He reminded Munroe that there were Utes at Rio Colorado, Apaches "lurking" in the mountains, and Mexicans, "influenced by the efforts of unprincipled politicians," who were "ripe for disorder."[23]

The day of the Rayado raid, reports came from Abiquiu that Utes had stolen forty animals from El Rito, about ten miles to the north. This sent the troops scurrying about as usual until a week or so later, when several Utes visited the post at Abiquiu with the stock in tow, declaring, in Calhoun's words, that they were still "in favor of a peaceable and quiet life." "The Utah chiefs have secured the animals, sent word to the owners, they were ready to deliver them up, and had severely chastised the thieves." While the Utes were returning stock at Abiquiu, an American in Santa Fe was trying to steal some. Caught clambering over a corral wall where the government animals were kept, the thief was discovered by a sentry and promptly "was Shot through the head, and died immediately thereafter."[24]

Captain Grier was still trying to organize a punitive expedition against whoever attacked Rayado when another distraction delayed it. The Comanches implicated in the Rayado attack turned up near the Old Placer gold mines in the Ortiz Mountains south of Santa Fe. They were only passing through to make a treaty with the Santo Domingo Pueblo about fifteen miles northwest of the mines. The rumor was that when they made their treaty they would continue west and go after the Navajos. Munroe hurried troops to that area "so as to defeat any combination between the Pueblo and Comanche Indians or put down any war between tribes."[25]

The idea that Pueblos would ally with Comanches was preposterous. Nevertheless, troops investigated, only to find that the Comanche foray was a will-o'-the-wisp. Citizens, however, were still complaining of depredations. West of the mountains, Auguste Lacome had an encounter with the Muache Utes. Acting with Calhoun's approval, the trader was still seeking information on the whereabouts of Mrs. White's daughter. On July 23 Lacome came upon a twenty-lodge camp on Culebra Creek in the San Luis Valley. The Muaches were not pleased to see him, had not participated in the peace talks, and roughed him up a bit, filling his rifle with water and stealing about $690 worth of his trade goods. After telling Lacome to tell Colonel Munroe that they were not afraid of him, strangely enough, they returned some of his goods, gave his rifle back, let him take home four of his mules, and even gave him two oxen and two cows. Regardless, Lacome filed a depredation claim.[26]

From what Lacome gathered during his meeting, the Muaches were camped along the west side of the Sangre de Cristo to steal from traders coming down from Kiowa and Cheyenne territory, while the Jicarillas were watching the trails east of the mountains in the vicinity of the Spanish Peaks. It was likely the latter group that Grier soon encountered.

Munroe was besieged with requests for war. Citizens of Taos County wrote a petition saying the Apaches near Rio Colorado "are daily becoming bolder in their depredations. We therefore pray Your Excellency to issue an order for a campaign of the People of this County." It was signed by eighteen men, many of them the usual Territorials who constantly stirred up fears of rebellion and raids, including James Quinn, Lucien Maxwell, Charles Beaubien, Charles Autobees, William Kronig, and William White.[27]

Munroe ordered Grier to organize volunteers at Rayado, but he considered them more trouble than they were worth. When Lieutenant Adams and Company K, 2nd Dragoons, finally arrived, Grier was ready to go. On July 23, 1850, Grier, with seventy-eight men of Companies G and I, 1st Dragoons, Company K, 2nd Dragoons, and "one hundred Mexicans who have volunteered," rode after the Indians who had attacked Rayado almost one month earlier. They were not "hot" on any trail.

They rode north, roughly following the course of the Vermejo River to its headwaters, and crossed what would become the Colorado border in the vicinity of San Francisco Pass. According to Grier: "Having traveled two days and nights, we struck the Indian trail leading over mountains and difficult canyons." On July 25 the Mexican "spies reported a small party of the enemy in sight." How Grier could have known they were "enemy," beyond the fact that they were Indians, is questionable—one month after the raid they had struck a trail made by someone fifty miles from Rayado. Regardless, Lieutenant Adams with the advance guard attacked: "by a rapid and well-executed movement, he killed or wounded the whole party, and captured the animals which they were driving." Later in the evening a party of volunteers surprised another small band of Indians, killed one or two, and captured several animals.[28]

With only a short rest, the command marched that night and through the next morning. About one in the afternoon of July 26, possibly along the North Fork Purgatoire River in present southwestern Las Animas County, Colorado, they found the "main village, situated on the edge of a mountain in a thick and almost impenetrable growth of Aspens." The Indians saw them and fled. Grier called for a charge, but the attack bogged down in extremely marshy ground around the village, which "rendered further pursuit useless." The Indians fled north, descending the mountain in the direction of the Spanish Peaks. Nevertheless, Grier kept up the chase, believing that he had killed or wounded half a dozen, while his only loss was Sgt. Lewis V. Guthrie, who was mortally wounded and died the next day. Adams said that they captured all the Indians' cattle and a portion of their stock, but his horses were completely broken down. The Indians, whether they were Jicarillas or Utes or of another tribe, managed to outpace the troops and the exhausted soldiers let them go.[29]

Grier said that they killed six and wounded five or six more, capturing sixty horses and mules, eighty cattle, and one hundred and fifty sheep, plus a quantity of provisions and camp material. On July 27 they went south across the mountains, down Costilla Creek, up Comanche Creek, over the mountains again, and down Moreno Creek to the Eagle's Nest area, where they picked up the Taos to Rayado Trail. They arrived at Rayado on July 30, after traveling nearly two hundred miles. Lieutenant Adams credited the Mexican spies for finding and surprising the Indians twice, but Grier complained that he wished "to decline any further assistance from or cooperation with Mexican Volunteers. Their utter want of anything like order and discipline (to say nothing of their general want of courage) will disconcert and render unavailing, the best arranged plans for surprising an enemy."[30]

Some military officers still held the Nuevomexicanos in contempt, deigning them beneath American standards of manliness and military prowess—at least until they needed them in an emergency. Grier gave the captured horses, mules, and sheep to the Mexican volunteers, which is likely what they wanted when they joined the expedition. He gave the captured cattle to Maxwell and Quinn, believing that they were the same ones allegedly stolen. Surely the men appreciated it—but they still filed a depredation claim in spite of getting back the cattle, even blaming the wrong tribe.[31]

Humo y Niebla

After Captain Grier's expedition to attack unknown Indians who may or may not have been guilty of raiding, the "war" begun by Judd and Burnside the previous August had sputtered out. Only about nineteen depredation claims were filed for alleged thefts in 1850, but a number of them proved to be false. The army wanted to chastise warring Indians but often found itself chasing down spurious reports. There was much *humo y niebla* (smoke and fog) enveloping the Sangre de Cristo for a prolonged period.

Shortly after Grier returned, Lieutenant Colonel Alexander at Las Vegas complained that Grier was holding Lieutenant Adams at Rayado when he was supposed to send him back to Las Vegas. "A robber band of Indians, Spaniards, and Americans are near us," Alexander said, "and his services are needed." But Grier said that he needed Adams until his command returned from escorting supplies over from Taos, due to fear of an "attack from the Indians who are constantly hovering around us." To the contrary, Alexander said: "Fears of raids at the Rayado have been allayed."[32] Grier had just gone two hundred miles to find Indians to attack but there were none "hovering" around him. When Alexander looked for the robbers, they too were nothing but *humo.*

Calhoun was out of money and begged for more funds in August. Even though he was unable to purchase the usual gifts and supplies for the Indians, they remained comparatively quiet. The Pueblos of Zuni were afraid of the Navajos and unable to farm their fields. They complained to Calhoun of the deceits they "had been subjected to since Gen. Kearny entered the country, and pledged to them the protection of the Government of the United States." They also wanted more soldiers. At Abiquiu agent Cyrus Choice had approved several men to trade with the Utes. Since he forbade them taking powder and lead, the traders were angry and concocted a story that the Utes captured them and their freighters and employees, about thirty men. The story was that if Choice would get the ammunition it could be used to trade to the Indians for the release of the captives. Shortly afterward several of the allegedly guilty Utes visited Choice and "expressed their utmost surprise at the story of the thirty traders retained as prisoners." The traders were unharmed and the yarn exposed. "The entire statement," said Calhoun, "was a base fabrication for base purposes."[33]

In August the Pueblos of San Ildefonso, Santa Clara, and Cochiti complained to Calhoun that Mexicans were committing depredations on their fields. In September two New Mexicans rushed to Calhoun's office in Santa Fe to report that they had been with a party under Lucien Maxwell carrying merchandise and money from Santa Fe. Somewhere east of the mountains Apaches attacked them, killed Maxwell, and stole his property. The two of them escaped. The tale caused more alarm, but it did not happen. Calhoun later learned that the report "was not true" and that Maxwell was alive and well.[34]

In early October about fifteen Jicarilla men, women, and children were headed to Abiquiu to ask permission to live near the post. On the way they stopped at Ojo Caliente to ask the Nuevomexicanos for something to eat. After they were fed, several were induced to look around the area. While they were separated from the rest, as Calhoun reported, "four of them, one man and three small boys, were murdered upon the spot," while one man, a girl, and two boys ran off and were still missing. One Mexican was arrested and placed in jail in Santa Fe. Calhoun was worried that he would be set free with a small bond, which would please the locals but infuriate the Indians. Justice could not be served said Calhoun. "A considerable sum of money has been subscribed to procure a gold medal to be presented to this cold-blooded murderer, and this is done, chiefly, by Americans."[35]

About the same time Calhoun was writing his news to Commissioner Brown, assistant quartermaster Capt. Thomas L. Brent was making an inspection. One of his recommendations was to arm the "defenseless inhabitants of New Mexico" so that it "could be protected from the savages who have laid it waste."[36]

The "defenseless inhabitants," meanwhile, were protecting themselves. The Territorial proponent and prefect of Pajarito, Francisco Sarracino, wrote to Calhoun in January 1851 of past Indian raids, including one in June 1850 when Navajos were accused of stealing stock along the Puerco River from José Antonio Chavis, José Rafael Sánchez, Manuel Padillos, and Felipe Herrera. They gathered some locals and chased the Indians, while Francisco Chávez went to Cebolleta to demand assistance from the troops, which he said "were of no use." The Indians were too strong. Several civilians were wounded. José Chavis alone later filed a claim stating he had lost 6,700 sheep worth $17,440.[37]

In October 1850 Navajos were said to have stolen stock from Juan García and Rafael Mejicano near Pajarito. Troops chased the raiders but came back after one day with "no reason assigned" for their quick return. On October 24 Navajos were accused of stealing 3,869 sheep from José Antonio Sarracino at Agua Salada and killing two shepherds. On December 7 Navajos at Rincon de Concha were said to have run off 5,822 sheep from José and Jesús Apodaca. Jesús demanded help from the troops at Cebolleta, but said only seven men looked for the trail, determined that recent snow had covered the tracks, and returned to the post. Sarracino said that on December 31 Apaches stole 100 cattle from the town of Isleta. He gathered forty men, trailed and caught the thieves in the mountains, recovered the cattle, wounded two Indians, and "took from them four saddled animals and other spoil."[38]

The locals were not pleased with American protection. Alcalde J. A. Pino wrote to Ramón Luna, prefect of Valencia County, about his recent experience with American soldiers. Pino believed that Apaches had stolen his stock in early January 1851 and went to the military at Socorro for help. The chase, said Pino, "proved fruitless, on account of the manner in which the Americans and their officers wished to travel, their days march was to be exactly five leagues, and [it] was necessary that they should have an abundance of water." They trailed east of the Rio Grande, but the officer refused to go beyond thirty leagues (about ninety miles). At one point Pino saw smoke and sent a detachment to investigate but was "abandoned by the men who accompanied me," which he blamed on recalcitrant Americans who wanted to sabotage the expedition because Pino did not "furnish them with everything necessary for their transportation." Pino told Luna "not to trouble your Honor too much, suffice it to say that it lacked but little that I should go to the Devil in company with the Americans."[39]

Perhaps the army was not thrilled about chasing Indians because many reports turned out to be *humo y niebla*. On January 20, at almost the same time and place when Pino was guiding soldiers east of the Manzano Mountains, Jicarillas arrived in the town of Manzano to trade. Territorial man William C. Skinner of Peralta, who had candle contracts with the army, wrote to Maj. Marshall S. Howe, 2nd Dragoons, commanding in Albuquerque, that along with trading goods "[t]hey brought with them a large number of the mules stolen from Dr. Connelly and myself by this tribe in the month of August last." Jicarillas were returning mules supposedly stolen from Skinner, but he represented them as dangerous "savages" within striking distance of Manzano. Connelly, who had three corn contracts with the army, filed claims for losses of sixty-five mules, along with twenty belonging to Skinner, for incidents alleged to have occurred in July 1850. Forgotten was the fact that the Jicarillas had returned to them "a large number" of those mules.[40]

At the same time when Sarracino, Pino, Skinner, and others were complaining of depredations, Colonel Munroe reported that he had "heard of no depredations committed" by the Gila Apaches and that "[t]he Utahs, and Jicarilla Apaches, have been perfectly quiet."[41]

Indians were allegedly back raiding in the Pajarito area in February. American Sidney A. Hubbell said that on February 9 Navajos stole stock from him, Ramón Gutirres, José Chavis, and Francisco Sarracino, right near their homes, only a few miles from the Rio Grande. Their total losses were sixty-five cattle, ten mules, one horse, and three oxen. While Sarracino rode to Albuquerque to get army help, Hubbell and ten men started in pursuit northwest to the Puerco River. Seeing that they were being pursued, the Indians, said Hubbell, "herded all of the cattle, and lanced all except one cow and three calves, which they did not have time to do for our near approach." Hubbell's party continued to gain on the Indians, who stopped again to lance six mules and horses. Hubbell had gone thirty-five miles in five hours until his horses "were so much blown," that he gave up.[42]

When Sarracino arrived in Albuquerque, Lt. Alfred Pleasanton, with men of Company K, 2nd Dragoons, rode to the rescue. Sarracino said he had guides who would lead them to the Indian trail, but when they crossed the Rio Grande the guides pointed the way and told Pleasanton that "their mission was ended." Sarracino said that more than 100 warriors had taken 1,000 sheep and a large number of horses, mules, and oxen. Pleasanton was skeptical. "From the deplorable picture drawn by these worthy citizens . . . I was induced to believe that all the stock in the Rio Abajo, had been driven off, and could not reconcile the small trail pointed out to me as having been trampled by hundreds of herds."[43]

Nevertheless, Pleasanton followed the trail but "soon observed that there were no sheep tracks, and very few of either horses or mules; I further perceived that the Indians were on foot." They camped on the Rio Puerco. The next morning Sidney Hubbell and his men rode in to inform Pleasanton that Hubbell had lost all his stock and had also been chasing the marauders, who had killed almost all the animals and gotten away. Besides, he added, "there were only *nine Indians, two with guns*." Pleasanton was perturbed by the "greatest discrepancy between the real state of things and the reports of Don Francisco Sarracino . . . both as to the number of Indians and the amount of property stolen." The lieutenant wrote that Sarracino was dilatory in reporting the raid, did not tell him about Hubbell, and exhibited "cowardice in permitting *nine Indians with but two guns*, to run off his stock with impunity, without daring to defend himself." To Pleasanton, this was "sufficient to prove he [Sarracino] is neither worthy of his office, or of protection from the government." In addition, Pleasanton asserted that the Rio Abajo had sufficient men to repel any raiders. "But the name of Indian, like that of *Richard of England among the Saracens*, seems to them a spell of terror from which they cannot recover."[44]

Pleasanton may have misread the citizens' intentions: for many of them the idea was purposely to feign helplessness, exaggerate the Indian menace, and force the army to remain in the area to hunt Indians, in order to promote business. Hubbell admitted that only seventy-nine animals were taken and that Chavis lost only one horse and Sarracino only three oxen. But for good measure Sarracino claimed that a thousand sheep were taken, while Chavis filed a depredation claim in which his one stolen horse suddenly became forty cows worth $1,000 (see appendix A).

Indians may have been the main culprits, but apparently some men of the 2nd Dragoons were involved in the thefts. They formed a secret society known as the "Dark Riders," which engaged in "robbing and desertion" and committed some minor mayhem for a time. After they were caught and in February 1851, a general court-martial in Santa Fe found several of them guilty. Their sentences included time in the guardhouse, loss of pay, hard labor, head shaving, and wearing a ball and chain. A few had to carry the weights all the way back to Leavenworth, where they were drummed out of service.[45]

Marcelino Vigil complained in Taos about one of Capt. William H. Gordon's 3rd Infantryman, a Private Dougherty, who broke some windows and entered Vigil's house one night and tried to rape his wife—she escaped only because she paid him eight dollars to leave her alone. Vigil also reported that two soldiers knifed a Mexican boy at a fandango. Gordon's response was that the private appeared to have been "in a state of derangement," while the stabbing occurred because the soldiers had been evicted from the fandango. Gordon brushed off the incident, saying that Vigil and his brother "are men of the most dubious character."[46]

Around this time an incident on the east side of the Sangre de Cristo, perhaps seemingly unimportant at the time, illuminated the character of another American, Samuel B. Watrous, who left his name on a little town at the junction of the Sapello and Mora Rivers about twenty miles northeast of Las Vegas. Watrous and Alexander Barclay built residences/forts within a mile of each other and were important in the early development of the area. About March 4, 1851, Watrous wrote in a note to Lieutenant Colonel Alexander at Las Vegas that Indians had killed the "major domo of Don Juan Vaca, and taken off four or five thousand sheep" about eight miles below Watrous's place. His stock and much of the stock owned by other citizens were grazing nearby and were "very likely gone also." Watrous said they had no weapons and expected army assistance.[47]

On March 5 Alexander directed Lt. John Adams to take thirty men to the scene of the "outrage." Adams rode to "the Junta," which was the junction of the Sapello and Mora, attempting "to ascertain the truth of a report from a Mr. Waters [sic]." Three miles short of Watrous's house and only half a mile off the main road, Adams saw five thousand or more sheep. He asked the shepherd who owned the sheep. "I was greatly surprised by his answer, which was that 'they were Juan Baca's,' the same sheep which Mr. Waters reports to have been stolen." The herder told Adams that the previous day he had been driving the sheep to the grazing area when he found "the dead body of a Mexican" but did not find any Indian trail. Adams did not believe there was "a single sheep missing." His guide, a Mr. Donaldson, said that "[t]here is no truth in this report" and believed that "the Mexicans have had a quarrel with the man and murdered him. This was also my opinion."[48]

In order to confirm his suspicion, Adams rode to Watrous's house. Sam was not home, but his wife said that Indians at Baca's ranch had "taken *some* of the sheep," a story that did not agree with the shepherd's. Just then "Water's son-in-law (an American I am sorry to add) came out and not having heard Mrs. Water's statement, told me that *every one* of Juan Baca's sheep had been run off." Adams "proved strongly to him the fallacy of his statement" and said that in the future Watrous ought to be "more careful" in the stories he reported.

Not content, Adams rode a mile to Barclay's Fort to further confirm or deny the allegations. Barclay was not there, so Adams wrote a letter to Levin Mitchell, a trader, farmer, and rancher, who had once been partners with Barclay and Doyle and was supposed to be with Watrous. Adams asked Mitchell to come in and explain what happened. Mitchell "did neither, but sent me word that at his camp there had been six Cheyennes . . . he pursued them, took back what they had taken, which was 100 of his sheep and three horses." The Indians "escaped" and Mitchell indicated "it was useless for me to go on any further." Adams returned to Las Vegas "with the conviction that the Indians reported by Mr. Waters were never at Juan Baca's ranch, that the murder was committed by Mexicans, and that Mr. Waters or others who have perhaps influenced him, sent in the report for some other object, such as selling corn, getting the loan of fire arms, etc."

On March 11 Judge Herman Grolman of Las Vegas, whose cry of "wolf" had stirred up problems back in 1849, wrote to newly installed Governor Calhoun for more troops. Unaware of Adams's investigation, Grolman wrote that more soldiers were needed to "drive the Indians out of the settlement." Apparently they were there "with no other object than to supply themselves with powder and lead and reconnoiter and will commit depredations at their departure according to their custom."[49] This was the same story used against visiting Jicarillas in August 1849, which led to Burnside's attack and the beginning of the first Jicarilla "war."

In addition, Colonel Munroe heard that Apaches and Comanches had been raiding at Anton Chico and were currently camped near the Pecos about forty miles southeast of that place. He directed Alexander to investigate, because in addition to reports of theft came the strange report that Apaches had come in to Anton Chico "with several hundred sheep which they assert were found strolling about without a Pastor." He told Alexander to watch them and "hold your command in readiness to punish any depredations."[50]

Reports were arriving from all over. On March 15, James Cumming, alcalde at New Placer, wrote to Calhoun that two days earlier Navajos killed José María Baca and wounded his peon within five miles of the mines. Cumming hoped that Calhoun "will be able to afford the necessary protection in the premises, and to exterminate or expel the Indians," who were not far from Manzano.[51]

Munroe's adjutant, Lafayette McLaws, passed on information from Grolman, Watrous, Cumming, and Calhoun to Alexander, who was supposed to investigate all these reports. Alexander replied that he had already sent Lt. Orren Chapman, Company F, 1st Dragoons, to Anton Chico, not because of Indian problems but simply to obtain forage for his horses. Alexander sent a note to Chapman telling him to investigate, because "quite an excitement has been got up in relation to the Indians in that quarter." Chapman's understanding was different. He reported that Quentas Azules (Blue Bead), a Mescalero, and about 115 of his people were camped forty miles south of Anton Chico. They were coming in to make peace and brought with them three hundred sheep as an offer of goodwill. Chapman said that "no complaints have as yet been made against them by the citizens," but the Mescaleros were in the grazing grounds and could run off many cattle and sheep if they wanted to.[52]

Mescaleros, with some Jicarillas, came to Anton Chico to trade and were peacefully doing so between March 9 and 15. Herman Grolman was there, prodding Chapman to expel the Indians, when Benjamin F. Latz, an agent of Governor Calhoun, arrived to negotiate peace with the Indians and, keeping up the forlorn hope, attempt to recover the captured Virginia White. Chapman moved north to La Cuesta to await the results of Latz's meeting, saying: "I do not think that any additional force will be required in this quarter." He knew nothing of the alleged killing of José Baca. After hearing from Chapman, Alexander reported that all appeared peaceful. He had never heard of any Mexican being killed at New Placer before Cumming's letter arrived and as far as he knew the Indians were actually bringing in sheep, not stealing them. There were never more than fourteen Indians in Anton Chico, and four of them were women. "I never believed that any additional troops were required," he concluded.[53]

Distortions in the reports were rife. The story Calhoun heard was that Jicarillas stole one thousand sheep, "slaughtered seven hundred, and returned to the owner near Anton Chico, three hundred of the poorest, and demanded pay for their honesty." He also wrote of increased depredations, mentioning Baca's murder, a stock raid fifteen miles from Santa Fe, and another one near San Ysidro. Calhoun decided that it was again time to call out volunteers "to pursue and attack any hostile tribe of Indians." Their pay would be whatever they could capture, but he had to warn them not to depredate upon or injure their own fellow citizens.[54]

The army searched for the perpetrators in vain. Munroe directed Major Howe at Albuquerque to investigate New Placer and the raids around Santa Fe and San Ysidro. Lt. William D. Smith, Company H, 2nd Dragoons, rode out of Ceboletta to Jemez Pueblo and then down the Puerco River. He searched near San Ysidro and east to San Domingo, then southwest toward Albuquerque, crossing "every trail which the Navajoes make when they pass or repass" through the area. He examined the country "most faithfully," talked to the local inhabitants, and concluded that "I have every reason to believe that there has not been a single Navajoe through this section of the country for three weeks, at least, I am sure that none passed out in this direction while I was in the saddle." Smith's superior, Capt. Daniel T. Chandler, 3rd Infantry, wrote: "The depredations said to have been committed near New Placer, I believe to be utterly without foundation in truth."[55]

Captain Henry L. Kendrick, 2nd Artillery, rode out of Santa Fe with orders "to proceed to the New Placer and destroy a band of Navajoe Indians," but had no more success than Smith. He talked to the locals, all of whom gave him conflicting reports: ten Indians were said to be riding in different directions; there were three Indians in another place; five Mexicans said that they had seen Indians steal their stock; and all insisted that the Indians had gone into a nearby canyon. Kendrick, with the help of those "professed to know perfectly the ground," blocked the canyon and entered, only to return "without having seen anything to warrant the conclusion that Indians had ever been on the ground that we traversed." They went to the spot Baca was said to have been murdered and found only "the track of one man and a mule." Next the locals told Kendrick that the Indians had actually gotten away to different mountains and that some San Domingo Pueblos would arrive the next day to help search. The Pueblos and Mexicans, however, said that the search might take up to six days and the guides seemed reluctant. Kendrick said: "[W]e obviated one excuse after another until it was pretty plainly intimated that money was wanted. We thought to pay people for aiding in defending themselves against what we believed to be entirely an imaginary danger, would be an unsafe precedent to make in New Mexico."[56]

With additional searchers, Kendrick and the Mexicans split up to investigate various leads. No Indian signs were seen at New Placer or Old Placer or on the roads. Kendrick learned from one Pueblo that the alleged raiding Navajos were probably a band trading at San Domingo and suggested that Pedro Ortiz could illuminate the confusion. Kendrick and Lt. Charles Griffin confronted him. Ortiz told Griffin that he had seen three Indians but told Kendrick that he had seen six. When Kendrick challenged him with the inconsistencies, he "admitted that he had, at no time, seen any at all," only tracks. Ortiz also said that the Indians had killed a beef just the day before and took them to the spot.

But upon examination they found that the carcass "had been dead at least five days." Kendrick believed Ortiz had killed it for his own consumption. Ortiz was the man who made the initial depredation report to Cumming, which started the entire uproar. Kendrick concluded that any Navajos who were stealing stock must be poor raiders, because "the mule ridden by Baca comprises the whole" of the theft. Kendrick perceived one likely reason for the false alarm: the locals desired "the loan of arms" from the government.[57]

Another expedition under Lt. Jonas P. Holliday, Company K, 2nd Dragoons, left Albuquerque for New Placer and Chilili to investigate the Baca murder "and follow up and exterminate said band." With forty-four men and twenty days' rations, Holliday crossed the area for six days before reaching the small Mexican town of Manzano. The son of Ollero Jicarilla chief Francisco Chacón rode up to Holliday and asked the reason for his visit. When Holliday said that he wanted to talk to his father, the boy took him to their camp of about two hundred people. Chacón had remained at peace even during the troubles in 1849 and told Holliday he still wanted peace. He said that he had been in the area the entire winter, trading with Americans and Mexicans and no one had any complaints. Holliday confirmed his story with the local citizens and was satisfied that any depredations committed were probably done by Navajos, although Lieutenant Smith and Captain Kendrick could find no evidence of Navajo raiding. The story Holliday got was that Navajos had taken three thousand sheep, but nine Jicarillas chased them and recovered them all. On the way back, Holliday stopped at Peralta and talked to William Skinner, who, two months earlier, had complained of Indian raiders who were actually returning some of his and Henry Connelly's mules. This time Skinner confirmed that Chacón's Jicarillas "had been protecting the flocks of the inhabitants of the neighborhood for a number of months past."[58]

What was going on? Indians who were supposedly inveterate thieves and murderers were protecting the local livestock and assisting Americans and Nuevomexicanos. As the citizens rang the alarm bells the military was trying to calm their anxieties, if, indeed, this was not more posturing than panic. Munroe reported that Governor Calhoun had been continuously asking for the Indians to be expelled or exterminated, but over the past months he had found that the dire warnings were mostly smoke. He enclosed Kendrick's, Holliday's, and Adams's reports showing that the depredation allegations were false. He mentioned Skinner's letter noting that the Indians had been protecting the flocks and Watrous's complaint, which he believed was made so he could make "a claim on the government." Munroe said that the incidents were "typical of the character of a large proportion" of the people involved, who showed "a disregard for facts from motives of self-interest." He told Jones that the portrayals were made

> having in view to disparage the military force . . . with direct violation
> of truth, or with gross misrepresentation intentionally made. The objects
> mainly to be attained being, to prepare the public mind and the Congress
> of the United States to consider favorably the claim proposed to be set up
> for the payment of all stock which has been, or which they will represent, to
> have been driven off by the various bands of surrounding Indians, through
> the supposed neglect of the government to give that protection which
> has been guaranteed to the people of the Territory, and by deprecating
> the services of the regular army, expect that Congress will authorize the
> creation of a local force as a substitute or partial substitute for it.[59]

In other words, the peoples' protestations were more façade than fear, made only to misappropriate government money, obtain weapons, and be allowed to raise their own volunteers to steal from the Indians.

Of those "depredating" Indians east of the Rio Grande, the chiefs Chacón, Lobo, Guero, and Josecito came into Santa Fe and signed a peace treaty on April 2, 1851. It stipulated that these Mescalero and Jicarilla bands declared submission to the government; they would abstain from all murders and depredations, return all stolen property and captives, stay fifty miles outside of the settlements, and receive farming implements so that they could begin to cultivate the soil. Only licensed traders would be allowed to enter their territory to do business.[60]

The treaty was very nice on paper just like all the other treaties, but all the bands were not party to it, the conditions were impossible to comply with, and it was never ratified by the Senate. Besides that, even if the treaty had been ratified, nothing in it would prevent the Americans and Mexicans from depredations against the Indians or filing false claims against them.

Las Ovejas

The people of New Mexico were beginning to learn the feasibly lucrative practice of filing Indian depredation claims, just as they already knew ways to swindle in the *partidario* system (see below). In both schemes sheep were the great majority of things most often reported stolen. Sheep had been the mainstay of the area for centuries. Either French king Louis XIII or Cardinal Richelieu supposedly said that without beavers Canada was hardly worth the trouble. The same could be said of the sheep in New Mexico. The first domesticated sheep were brought into the area by Francisco Coronado in 1540, where they found almost perfect conditions to be fruitful and multiply. By the mid-seventeenth century the Spanish were realizing great economic opportunities in breeding sheep in the high plains and deserts and driving them to markets hundreds of miles south down the Camino Real. When the Spanish were expelled during the Pueblo Revolt of 1680, the Indians realized that they too could make a living from breeding and selling sheep. Pueblos, Hopis, and Navajos in particular seized the opportunity. Spain reconquered the area, however, and it took several decades before the sheep industry was productive again. By the eighteenth-century *las ovejas* (sheep) had become worth more than the plentiful cheap land. There were many thefts by the Spanish, the Indians, and the rustler bands, plus the usual losses due to drought, blizzard, and the open range, where livestock could just wander off and disappear. But it had already become an "all-too-familiar theme" for the Spanish governors to blame stock losses on the Indians.[61]

One element that facilitated the revival of New Mexico's stock industry was the *partido* system. The practice had been around for centuries. As it developed in New Mexico, a region virtually without hard cash, the owner turned over a number of sheep to the *partidario*, who took responsibility for their care. As the sheep reproduced, the *partidario* would make payments of agreed-upon amounts of lambs or wool to the lender, usually about 20 percent annually. At the end of the contract period, from three to five years, the *partidarios* would return all the loaned sheep; the owners got their stock back plus some of the increase without having to expend the time and labor in caring for them, and the borrowers got some of the natural increase to start up their own herds.

It seemed to be a good deal for everyone, but it could be a great deal for the borrower. Because sheep could be lost while in the *partidario*'s care, a sort of "escape clause" was added to the contracts. Sheep were bound to die from disease or be lost in droughts and blizzards or wander off or be eaten by wolves, and the parties agreed to divide the losses due to those "acts of God" equally. The kicker came in case of Indian theft: in that event, the *partidario* was free from obligation to repay. In one case in 1740 Francisco Saís did not pay back 114 lambs that were due as interest after one year. He claimed that the missing sheep were eaten by wolves or perhaps were stolen by Indians. After a few days in jail, Saís admitted to having gambled away some of the sheep and sold others to pay off his debts. As one historian of the system explained, the inherent fraud and deception "between sheep owners and their *partidarios* filled New Mexico's court dockets for the next two hundred years."[62]

Sheep had been bred, bought, sold, and stolen in New Mexico ever since Coronado introduced them. Numbers can be notoriously inaccurate, but there are some estimates. In 1757 Spaniards were said to have owned about 2,500 horses, 7,800 cattle, and 47,600 sheep, while the Pueblos and Hopis owned 4,800 horses, 8,300 cattle, and 64,500 sheep. When the church began collecting tithes on stock, the numbers owned suddenly dropped dramatically. People hid or undercounted their stock or claimed that the Indians took them. Tax evasion is no new phenomenon. A census in 1779 showed that the numbers of sheep had declined almost 40 percent.

Sheep were legitimately disappearing too, as trail drives increased, with most stock flowing south. In 1794 nearly 20,000 sheep left the territory, and in 1803 about 25,000 were driven out for sale, while Indian attacks on these southern caravans were few. In 1832 alone 30,000 sheep were driven to Durango. So many sheep were driven into Old Mexico in 1835 (80,000) that the following year only 6,000 sheep were left for sale. It took a few years to build up stock again for larger trail drives. Another 13,000 sheep were sold in 1838 and 3,000 sheep per year in 1839 and 1840. By then the market in Old Mexico was saturated, and low prices meant that the New Mexicans began sending their sheep to the United States. In 1845, the last year before the American conquest, about 15,000 sheep went south.[63]

A substantial sheep business had been in operation for decades before the Americans arrived, and Indians were not stealing sheep in substantial numbers. In fact, events conspired to keep sheep theft at minimal levels. Spanish, Mexican, and Indian bonds grew through trade as well as in trafficking in human captives. As the traders found more connections with the Indians to the east, they dealt less with Mexico City. When the American traders arrived in the 1820s, imposing their conventions and interfering with the old customs, guns and whiskey began to be introduced into the equation. Prices went up. Indians were induced to steal stock in Mexico and Texas. The Mexicans were not very happy with the meddling Americans, yet the money that they paid to buy stolen horses or rescue captives only gave more incentive for the Comancheros and Indians to continue the cycle. Captured humans and livestock moved north out of Mexico and Texas, and manufactured goods, weapons, ammunition, and whiskey passed to the Indians.[64]

It did not take the Comanches long to realize that peace with the tribes migrating from the east and with the Cheyennes and Arapahos to the north would open up new markets for them. Instead of having to fight their northern neighbors and guard their villages, leaving fewer warriors to raid in Mexico, peace would allow them to concentrate fully on stealing tens of thousands of horses and become the brokers and main suppliers for customers across the length and breadth of the plains.

The game changer came in 1840 when the Comanches and Kiowas made peace with the Cheyennes and Arapahos in a great ceremony on the Arkansas River. The peace had far-reaching consequences. The contested plains east of the Rockies, which had been a no-man's land because of the incessant intertribal warfare, had been a bison haven. After 1840 the land was open to all, which resulted in the exploitation of the bison. Bison robes became the hot new trade item. The Bent Brothers became prime beneficiaries as middlemen for the Cheyennes and Arapahos as those tribes began the remarkably quick process of hunting the animals toward extinction. The Comanches and Kiowas, in contrast, cared less about the bison as a marketable item but could now turn their full attention south into the rich horse regions of northern Mexico. "Peace" sent the buffalo on the road to extinction in one region and led to increased conflict in another.[65]

Much of the fighting in New Mexico between the Indians and the Spaniards, and later the Mexicans, was really a business war over turf and control of scarce resources. New Mexicans and Comanches had experienced long-established kinship and trade ties since the peace they made in 1786. One reason why the Comanches and Kiowas generally left the New Mexicans alone was because they owned few horses. There were only several thousand horses, but hundreds of thousands of sheep grazed the New Mexican plains. The Cheyennes and Arapahos wanted bison robes and generally left the New Mexicans alone; the Comanches were not shepherds, did not want sheep, and consequently used New Mexicans as trade partners. In contrast, the department of Durango was said to possess about 150,000 horses and mules. Comanches, Kiowas, and Apaches would devastate Texas and Old Mexico, scouring them of their horseflesh; but New Mexico was comparatively safe, at least as long as the economics of the deal suited the Indians' needs.[66]

If the idea of massive thefts of livestock by Indians in New Mexico was somewhat of a chimera, what, if anything, was happening to the New Mexican sheep? Listening to some of the citizens and officials, one might think that the Indians had unleashed an assault upon the territory such as had never been experienced before. Governor Calhoun often wrote to the Indian commissioners, complaining, for instance, that "[t]he Wild Indians of this country have been so much more successful in their robberies since Genl Kearney took possession of the country" and that "our Indian troubles at this moment are of a more terrible, and alarming character, than we have ever known before, and many of us have lived in this territory from five to fifty years." Ceran St. Vrain was said to have pronounced the conditions "to be worse than any they have ever witnessed before."[67]

William W. H. Davis, territorial district attorney in the 1850s, got the same idea. He said that fifteen or twenty years earlier (1830s) the sheep business had been much more prosperous, because at present it was "greatly retarded by the hostile incursions of the numerous bands of Indians." As for the farmers who have lost their flocks, "in but few instances have they received any remuneration from the government, although there is a law to that effect." Davis believed, incorrectly, that in the 1830s half a million sheep were annually driven to the markets of Mexico.[68]

In 1850 George McCall reported that back in 1825 or 1830 New Mexicans had exported as many as 200,000 sheep per year (also an exaggerated number), but that was "before the hand of the Redman had fallen so heavily upon them." He said that now barely one thousand sheep were sent from the districts: "such has been the rapacity and the relentless spirit of hostility of the Navajoes and Apaches." Counting up individual cases, McCall said that in the eighteen months before September 1850 Indians stole 47,300 sheep.[69]

Members of the Territorial Legislature petitioned Calhoun for redress in July 1851, stating that back in 1830 to 1834 "the country presented a wonderful state of prosperity." They estimated that 1.5 million sheep roamed the lands free from molestation back then, contrasting that with the "present miserable condition," with prosperity "swept away as by an impetuous torrent" of Indian marauders, who have "carried off nearly all the property owned in New Mexico." Their remedy was "to raise volunteer companies against the invaders."[70]

Governor Calhoun calculated that in 1850 alone 58,399 sheep were stolen and that in 1846 to 1850 losses were 150,231.[71] Using various sources, author James Brooks compiled sheep losses in the years from 1830 to 1844 at 20,000; from 1846 to 1850 at about 49,000; and from 1851 to 1860 at about 77,000. In addition, commissioner George W. Manypenny reported that 80,000 sheep were stolen from 1846 to 1854.[72]

John Russell Bartlett, appointed the boundary commissioner in 1850, gave the staggering number of 453,293 sheep lost to the Indians between 1846 and 1850.[73] One might compare the reported numbers of stolen sheep with the 1850 Census Bureau record, which totaled the entire number of sheep in the territory at 377,000.

In October 1850 U.S. assistant quartermaster Thomas L. Brent wrote in his assessment of New Mexico: "The country was once celebrated for its flocks of sheep and herds of cattle. These have nearly all disappeared, from the constant forays of the Indians."[74] If the heyday of sheep production and drives was in the 1820s and 1830s, when 80,000 sheep were sent south (so many that only 6,000 were left for sale the next year), then the reported sheep losses from 1846 to 1850 were possibly more sheep than existed in the territory. No one actually counted all the sheep, and official record keepers had to rely on civilian declarations. Certainly some of them gave the most accurate estimates they could, while those less scrupulous may have adjusted the numbers for their own benefit.

In truth, by 1850 the market for sheep had never been better. Few of the Plains tribes to the east wanted sheep, except for the occasional meal. The southern market stagnated during the Mexican War, but by 1850 that market was open for business, plus California was clamoring for sheep. The miners had to be fed, and mutton was as good as gold. It started in August 1849, when two hundred men, known as the "Peoria Company," trudged across the plains following their infamous guide, James Kirker. They stopped in Galisteo to recuperate and there one of the group known only as "Old Roberts," bought five hundred sheep for $250. His companions complained and figured that the sheep were nothing but a nuisance, but Roberts got them to Los Angeles, where he sold them for about $15 a head, making more than $8,000 on a $250 investment.[75]

Word quickly spread of the great demand for sheep in California. Among the first to exploit the situation were Anglo businesspeople, many of whom began buying up all the New Mexican sheep that they could get. In 1850 William Z. Angney put away his law books and drove six thousand sheep to San Francisco. He was so excited that on the way he wrote to the lieutenant governor and Santa Fe merchant Manuel Álvarez about the prospects: "Sheep are the first article of merchandise in California and the market cannot be glutted . . . business brisk and prices high." Angney convinced Álvarez to partner with him. Álvarez begin buying all the sheep he could in the Rio Abajo, from the Pereas, Sandovals, and Oteros, paying up to two dollars a head.[76]

With all that money to be made, however, Álvarez decided that he did not need Angney and went into business himself, buying about 4,600 sheep for a trail drive in 1851. The idea caught on. In 1852 three or four drives headed to California, one with nine thousand sheep led by Dick Wootton and Jesse B. Turley. They assembled the flock in Watrous and sold them in San Francisco for about nine dollars a head. Hispano families began to get involved. Antonio José Luna, his brother Rafael, Miguel Antonio Otero, and Ambrosio Armijo from the Rio Abajo drove twenty-five thousand head. Another drive took fourteen thousand sheep. In 1852 Álvarez partnered with Francis X. Aubrey to take five thousand sheep to the coast. Kit Carson, Lucien Maxwell, and John L. Hatcher gathered a flock in the Rayado area to drive to California. Heading back east in 1853, they passed a herd of thirty-five thousand sheep near Los Angeles. Farther east they passed Nicolás Pino and his herd of fifteen thousand. By the Pima villages in Arizona, Carson found Aubrey with sixteen thousand sheep, Francisco Perea with ten thousand, Judge Antonio Otero with eight thousand, and J. Francisco Chávez and several others with an additional sixteen thousand. In May 1853 Carson had been appointed Indian agent, but Governor William Carr Lane could not assign him duties; he wrote to commissioner George W. Manypenny: "Unfortunately for the public service, Mr. Carson is now in California and cannot be expected to return until next Autumn." He told Manypenny to imagine his difficulties in governing when his agents were continually running around the country when they ought to be with their assigned tribes. He tried to correct the "scandalous" situation, and hoped his "worthy successor" would have more luck.[77]

Sheep were streaming out of the New Mexico Territory. José Luna and his brother Rafael filed at least a dozen depredation claims for losses, a number of them denied for lack of evidence. Were they truly losses due to Indian theft as claimed or bogus accusations to compensate for the money that they spent in purchasing the sheep, or maybe a little of both? A person did not actually have to drive the sheep to claim losses. A number of people bought their sheep from the owners of huge flocks, such as Antonio Sandoval, Antonio Ortiz, and Santiago Ulibarri. These three men alone filed at least eighteen claims for losses. Were they truly losses to Indians as claimed or simply a way to partially make up for the sheep that they had sold to the dealers (see appendix A)?

The numbers of sheep being driven out of New Mexico to markets in the 1850s far exceeded the numbers of the supposed peak years of the 1820s and 1830s. It is clear that before mutton prices in California collapsed after 1854 there were plenty of sheep around in New Mexico to sell, while even later in the decade James Quinn drove 15,000 sheep in 1855 and Sidney Hubbell, Joaquín Perea, and José Jaramillo drove 39,000 head in 1857.[78]

Census records list the numbers of cattle and sheep in 1850 as 9,185 and 377,231, respectively. Yet in 1860 the numbers went up to 28,829 and 769,416. Hundreds of thousands of sheep were still available, but prices had declined so much that a broker's time and effort were not paying off as well as they used to.

The Indians were not stealing all that many sheep; what they took to keep from starving was but a tiny percentage of what was being driven for sale to outside markets and what was being reported as being lost. Actual stock theft by Indians never increased after the Americans arrived; what increased tenfold were the fraudulent theft reports. The least perspicacious entrepreneur could see the profits to be made by selling sheep in California or selling to buyers taking sheep to California and then reporting them as stolen by the Indians.

"More Cattle Killed Than Belonged to the Whole Valley"

Despite another peace treaty and the army's inability to substantiate many civilian complaints of raids, the robbery reports kept coming in. After Lieutenant Chapman had investigated at Anton Chico in March and found no evidence of raiding Indians, he waited while agent Benjamin F. Latz initiated a peace council. In his report he commented on the locals, saying that "they do not appear to be of the most thrifty class, and evidently depend more on their flocks and herds . . . and frequent traffic with the Indians, than upon the tilling of the earth for subsistence." They were too friendly with the Indians in Chapman's estimation. Local unlicensed traders sold the Indians illegal whiskey and warned them whenever troops were in the area. They were false friends, however, for they coaxed the Indians into the settlements, only to get them "traded out of all they possess," so that they were then forced to steal "from the herds to prevent starvation." Chapman had a special dislike of Antonio Baca, "the most obnoxious of these traders," who sold the Jicarillas whiskey for mules and kept them apprised when soldiers approached. Baca had also filed a depredation claim.[79]

Two weeks later Chapman received news from "reliable sources" that some of the warriors of Cuentas Azules were still in the neighborhood of Las Valles and La Cuesta. Although the treaty stipulated that they must remain fifty miles outside the settlements, it had been signed less than a fortnight before, so news of it certainly could not have been disseminated to all the bands. Chapman went to investigate, although "[n]o complaint has been made against them by the citizens and none will be so long as their trade is profitable." He asked for advice and was told that the treaty said that the Indians must leave, but Chapman was only to advise them of the stipulation to vacate the settlements and "in the event of a non-compliance, treat them as enemies."[80]

Chapman was reluctant to start anything with peaceful Indians. It was true that several small bands were crossing through the area, but most appeared to be heading down the Pecos toward Bosque Redondo. One group still in the Mora

Valley consisted of fourteen lodges, with seventy men, women, and children. Chapman wrote that their business "at present appears to be the manufacture and barter of earthen vessels, dressed skins, etc., for corn and provisions."[81]

Unfortunately, about this time at Barclay's Fort, Joe Doyle claimed that Apaches had stolen fourteen of their cattle. Seven of his employees followed the trail to the Canadian River and found a campsite where the Indians had allegedly butchered four of the cattle. The Indians, only about seven or eight lodges, moved about ten miles downriver, but Doyle's trailers figured that they were too few to do anything and returned to the fort.

Then Herman Grolman got into the act again. The judge and prefect of Las Vegas was constantly agitating for the removal of the Indians. This time he complained to Lieutenant Colonel Alexander that Jicarillas were "scattered over a large portion of the settlements." The treaty had banned them, so the "article has been grossly violated." Grolman said that it "appears injudicious" to chase the small band that took Doyle's cattle, but the army should not "leave the main body of the tribe in the heart of the settlements to take reprisals on the life and property of the citizens, wherefore I request the assistance of the troops under your command to remove the said Indians from the settlements and force them to respect the limits prescribed by the treaty."[82]

Colonel Munroe was not impressed and told Alexander: "It is not desired at this time to press those Indians." Apparently Lieutenant Chapman took ill for a few days, and Lt. James N. Ward, 3rd Infantry, took charge of Chapman's company. He understood that he was to push the Indians out of the settlements but "was enjoined to be mild with them and exercise my discretion in my treatment of them." In late April he met Benjamin Latz at San Miguel, who gave him the news that more Indians were coming in to talk peace. While waiting, Ward met Chief Chacón, a signatory of the April 2 treaty. Ward asked him why he was there. Chacón replied: "I and my family are starving to death, we have made peace, we do not want to do harm, as you see from bringing women and children with us, we want to go to the clay bank at San Jose and make vessels to sell so as to procure an honest living, we can't steal and must do something to earn a living." Ward told him to wait at San Miguel while he asked for further instructions. At this time Lieutenant Chapman returned and took back command of his company. Before he left, Ward also learned that Cuentas Azules was also coming with his family, noting: "No outrage of any kind has been committed by the Indians."[83]

Next Chapman accompanied Latz to Chacón's camp, where they found the chief and about fifty men, women, and children engaged in making pottery.

Chapman said that Chacón was in violation of the treaty. But Chacón, as he told Ward, was starving, and "if we forced him to move out on the plains, his tribe must either starve or steal." Chacón said he would be responsible for his people, who would not harm anyone in the neighborhood. According to Chapman: "[h]e seemed to have as much idea of the articles of the treaty as the man in the moon." Chapman wanted to leave the Indians alone, stating that they did not understand the treaty, had brought along their families, and had not committed any depredations. He figured that occasionally a young warrior would steal a horse without the chief knowing about it, but Indians were not the main problem. "On the other hand, when thieves and rascals are as plentiful as they are in this territory, the presence of Apaches will furnish a most convenient cloak for their misdoings, and keep the government and troops continually annoyed by groundless complaints against the Indians." Chapman said that trying to remove the Indians forcefully "would amount to a declaration of war with them."[84]

On May 7, a few days after Chapman made his report, Governor Calhoun wrote to Munroe: "If these Indians remain in their present localities we must anticipate bloodshed & depredations." Calhoun depicted the handful of Jicarillas and Mescaleros in San Miguel County at the time as "from two to five thousand Indians characterized by the worst possible passions of man within our Borders," with hundreds of innocent people in their clutches. Thus "many of these citizens must be butchered" or driven out. The military, said Calhoun, "is wholly inadequate to prevent serious disorders." What was needed was "a much more augmented force to preserve the Lives & Property of the people in this Territory."[85]

Munroe, perhaps in frustration, accompanied Governor Calhoun to investigate. Cognizant of the situation, Munroe ordered that fifty fanegas of corn be delivered to Anton Chico to distribute among the starving Apaches. The Indians, however, likely concerned for their safety, had already vacated the area. Munroe and Calhoun arrived at Anton Chico on May 16 "but found no Indians." Lieutenant Chapman informed them that there had been no Apaches in the area for days.[86]

Lieutenant Whittlesey was also out hunting Indians. In late May he left Rayado with a detachment of Company I, 1st Dragoons, to Point of Rocks to protect the mail and search for reported Apaches. They found a trail in the vicinity of the Canadian crossing headed north toward the Raton Mountains, but upon following it they met a party of Utes under Chico Velásquez. They had passed through the area a month earlier on a hunt and were "begging not to be molested."

Whittlesey said that the Utes were friendly and wanted to catch "the little wagon" (the mail) to ask for tobacco, but it had passed them too quickly. They had not seen any Apaches in the area. Whittlesey only hoped that the next party of "citizens leaving Santa Fe for the States may know how to act if they meet them."[87]

Captain Richard S. Ewell, 1st Dragoons, located Chacón in the Mora area and told him the treaty stipulated that he was to keep fifty miles out of the settlements. Chacón showed Ewell a pass signed by Governor Calhoun that allowed him to be there. Civil and military seemed to be working at cross purposes; Calhoun let them in and then complained to the army. Chacón said that he did not know that he was supposed to meet Munroe and Calhoun in Anton Chico and expressed the same surprise that Chapman had mentioned, adding that his people could not leave, for if they were forced out onto the plains they would starve. Ewell told them that there was corn waiting for them at Anton Chico. He questioned the locals about the Indians' behavior. "All the citizens agreed in stating that the Indians had been perfectly quiet and had committed no offense." In fact Chacón had been to see the alcalde of Mora to complain that Mexicans and Americans had been molesting his people and even tried to get the alcalde to take measures to stop the citizens from selling his people whiskey. Regardless of any provocation, Ewell said, if "the Mexicans or Americans molested them, they, the Indians, would stand with folded arms and submit."[88]

Benjamin Latz had gone to Bosque Redondo and brought the Comanche Eagle Feathers to Anton Chico, with five men and five women, a small child, and one captive Mexican boy. Chapman directed them to Santa Fe. On May 28 they met Calhoun and Munroe and professed their friendship, while Munroe ensured their safety. The Comanches were given quarters in town. But about one o'clock the next morning "some evil disposed persons" crept up to their room and informed them that the governor "was only waiting a favorable moment to have them murdered." The Comanches fled, leaving their property and animals behind. When Calhoun and Munroe learned what had happened they wanted to find the Comanches, tell them that it was a mistake, and return their property. Alexander at Las Vegas, Lieutenant Chapman at Anton Chico, and Lieutenant Pleasanton at Tecolote were told to spare no efforts to locate them and assure them that they had been "under a Safe Guard which is considered sacred with us." Thus occurred the one-in-a-million scene of dragoons looking for Indians to restore their property and say that they were sorry.[89]

The incident was resolved. Munroe ordered the Comanches' property to be taken to Anton Chico. Chapman had two Mexicans search for the fleeing

Comanches, but on the night of May 30 San Miguel County sheriff Jesús Lucero met Chapman and said that he had talked to Eagle Feathers. The Comanches had circled south of the mountains and arrived at La Cuesta to ask Lucero for help. They explained their situation, said that they were running from the Americans "who wished to kill them," and admitted having stolen five animals as they fled. Lucero advised them to wait until he could inform the lieutenant, but the Comanches were afraid and wanted to hurry to Bosque Redondo. Lucero even gave them one of his horses. Chapman understood that the reason Eagle Feathers fled was that "some vile scoundrel (and there are plenty of such in the land) had frightened them by willful misrepresentation." The sheriff, whom Chapman described as "somewhat flurried with the duties of his new office," requested that Chapman take all responsibility for the affair, and he agreed.[90]

Chapman said that he could have caught the Comanches. They seemed peaceful and were frightened, however, so any confrontation meant that he might have to kill them. He figured that he would "let them go unmolested, particularly as the animals which they left behind were better and more numerous than those they carried off." Then Ma-chee-ma-va arrived, an old man who had not fled with Eagle Feathers but rode with the escort bringing the Indian property to Chapman. He also said that they had meant no harm but were frightened off when a Mexican came to their quarters at night and said that the Americans were going to kill them. Chapman restored Ma-chee-ma-va's horse, mule, and whatever other property he said was his and left to find Eagle Feathers to tell him all was well and to chide him for being afraid. Chapman concluded his report by stating that the Mexicans hated and feared the Americans more than they did the Indians and "had rather see us involved in a war with these tribes than not, and if secretly, by misrepresentations they can effect that object they will do it."[91]

As a follow-up, Chapman sent two Mexican traders to Bosque Redondo to see what the Comanches were up to. For a cover, he gave them two mules to return to Eagle Feathers that he had abandoned during his flight. A day later Ma-chee-ma-va rode in to Anton Chico. The Comanches had accepted the two mules and returned seven more. Chapman said that the animals were poor, but the number of animals that the Indians gave was more than they had stolen, so he figured that all was square. He believed that all of this could have been resolved much faster if Sheriff Lucero had just stopped Eagle Feathers when they met. They were friends, so he could have insisted that the Comanches go directly to exchange animals with Chapman at Anton Chico. Instead he gave them his own horse and let them ride away. This reinforced Chapman's distrust of Mexicans. He wrote: "If one was to believe, however, in all the losses reported by the Mexicans, those twelve Indians must have carried off something like a *hundred* horses & mules, & *all of the best quality.*"[92]

Chapman had misgivings but was levelheaded and dispassionate. Certain civilians were another story. Charles Beaubien wrote to Calhoun from Taos that unspecified "indications" had convinced him that "a rebellion against the constituted United States authorities is in contemplation among the lower class of the inhabitants of the County of Taos." Beaubien said he had information from "reliable sources [that] secret meetings have been held under various pretenses for the purpose of organizing an insurrection, its object the extermination of the Americans and the robbery of their property." Ever since the Taos uprising in January 1847 Americans of property had lived in fear—what Beaubien described as "absolute suspicion" of the Mexicans, Apaches, and Pueblos. He said that the Mexicans sold the Indians whiskey, which made them belligerent, and the operators at St. Vrain's mill south of town had been "threatened with massacre by drunken Jicarillas." The nearby Utes were getting "insolent" and had also held secret meetings about massacring all the Americans. Beaubien wanted more soldiers.[93]

With Governor Calhoun also adding a warning that it would require the utmost vigilance to prevent an outbreak, Munroe sent Captain Kendrick with a detachment of 2nd Artillery to Taos. When he arrived on June 18, however, he "found everything perfectly quiet" and only succeeded in creating hard feelings with Captain Gordon, Company H, 3rd Infantry, who took umbrage that the arrival of Kendrick was somehow an indication that he was unable to protect the town. From what Kendrick could learn, the dire alarms of insurrection were no more than the usual griping done by some of the local laborers. It was "highly improbable that anything like an organized plan of insurrection has been entertained by anyone." Kendrick said that there was no need for his men to be there.[94]

Just as things cooled down in San Miguel County after the alarms sent by Herman Grolman and Joe Doyle, Isidor Samson heated it up again. No sooner had Lieutenant Chapman returned to Las Vegas than Samson wrote to Alexander on June 28 that Comanches were raiding at Anton Chico. Then he reported to Chapman that the Indians "espouse great feelings towards the American government" so there was no need of troops. Two days later he wrote to Munroe that Comanches were depredating at La Cuesta, "cutting up" and stealing cattle from Jesús Lucero and José Antonio Flores, and had "killed everything they could find on the road in La Cuesta." He requested that Munroe station troops at La Cuesta and Anton Chico.[95]

This time Alexander sent Lt. John Adams with men of Company K, 2nd Dragoons, "to give protection to the inhabitants and to punish the Indians." Adams arrived in Anton Chico on the evening of June 28 and "saw the herds belonging to the place grazing as usual & the inhabitants laboring in their fields without the slightest apprehension of danger." The alcalde told Adams that Indians had been there earlier but were "perfectly quiet & harmless," except for a few who had gotten whiskey from trader Antonio Baca and killed a couple of goats. Adams was tired of the fruitless chases. "[T]o have listened to the Mexican complaints," he wrote, "you would have found more cattle killed than belonged to the whole valley." Adams rode to La Cuesta the next day, where the alcalde told him that "the Indians had done nothing." The lieutenant was annoyed by people who sold the Indians whiskey: when "they become excited & wound an ox or kill a goat . . . the Mexicans call upon us for protection." Adams met Comanches at La Cuesta, talked peacefully with them, and gave them corn. They left town "perfectly satisfied." He waited until ten that night before riding back to Las Vegas. At the very time that Samson said Comanches were "cutting up" Sheriff Lucero's cattle, Adams was on the spot proving that his accusation was a lie.[96]

On July 2 the alcalde of Galisteo reported to Munroe that Comanches had come to his village for supplies then headed westward to attack the Navajos. Munroe notified Major Howe at Albuquerque to send troops to prevent their crossing the Rio Grande and "treat them as enemies if they had committed depredations." He scrambled the troops at Ceboletta to find the Comanches and force them to return. Capt. Horace Brooks, with all the available men of two companies of 2nd Artillery, left Santa Fe and found the Comanches near Santo Domingo Pueblo and learned that they had contemplated an excursion against the Navajos, but poor grass and scarce water changed their minds. They were already heading east for home. "As the Indians had behaved peaceably," Munroe ordered Brooks back to Santa Fe.[97]

Lieutenant Adams, back in La Cuesta on July 4, learned as much. After talking with more Mexicans, he said that "neither man, woman or child or horse or mule have been killed, wounded, or taken." The Comanches who had supposedly wanted to raid the Navajos only wanted to trade with the Pueblos and were now going home. Fourteen of them passed through, Adams said. "They asked for nothing and what is very strange for such 'very bad Indians' they nor any of them . . . have done any damage at all, not even killed a goat."[98]

Two days later Adams was in San Miguel, where he exasperatingly reported that the Mexicans wailed: "'The Indians . . . have run off all our cattle.' There were about 100 Mexican men in the plaza. Says I, 'Why don't *you* go and bring them back, there are only 14 Indians?' They shrugged their shoulders and said, 'No!'" Adams took ten of his men to pursue the Indians, forcing the prefect to accompany him and promising "to whip the person bringing in the report *if not true.*" The Mexicans immediately "reported the truth, which was, 'the Indians have done no harm.'" By now Adams was infuriated. After "abusing pretty strongly" the prefect and the townsfolk, the prefect replied that the people were uneducated and "were given to lying." Adams countered that they were indeed educated in one respect, "and that is to lie." He then lumped Samson in with the lot of them, saying that he too was a liar or had been duped by Mexican reports, "of which I am confident more than half are lies."[99]

Munroe could not sort it all out. Why did Samson write to him in Santa Fe sixty miles from the alleged incidents and not tell Lieutenant Adams, who was only eighteen miles away, that Indians were supposed to be depredating and then change his mind a minute later? Alexander figured that it was done "to create a false impression." Munroe concluded that the army would never get the truth, because for the most part the Indians had never been depredating, and the people along the Pecos River carried on a friendly trade with them. Munroe dismissed the constant alarms, even by such prominent men as Judge Beaubien, saying that "he is entirely under a misapprehension" about rebellion threats. Beaubien's complaint illustrated "the peculiar position of the Army in this country," having to protect the inhabitants from Indian incursions while "the inhabitants themselves are in league with those Indians." In fact, Munroe wrote to Adjutant General Roger Jones that the Indians "have not committed depredations and have seemed inclined to provide and have been providing for their wants by following peaceful pursuits." Munroe only knew of one proven depredation out of the entire business. When Eagle Feathers fled Santa Fe and headed back into the mountains, his band killed one cow to eat. He considered it a fair trade for the Mexican captive he left behind who was taken in by Governor Calhoun.[100]

Calhoun was beginning to realize that much of the turmoil was caused by Americans of the Territorial Party—at least as he saw it—although he, a Statehood man, had done more to spread false rumors than Territorial man Munroe. The factions had hardened after the latest elections. On June 3, 1851, the first territorial legislature met, with thirteen senators and twenty-six representatives. According to Calhoun, his Statehood men had the great majority, but the recalcitrant "minority party damn everybody but themselves" and caused great turmoil. In a letter to secretary of state Daniel Webster, Calhoun named quartermaster Capt. Alexander W. Reynolds, who ran as a delegate in the Territorial Party, and Charles Beaubien as the chief conspirators, blaming those who had lost in the last election as those most involved in sowing discontent. Calhoun said that these reports "were fabricated and put in circulation of collisions, the destruction of property, and the approach of Wild Indians," which left the public mind "in a very fevered condition." Calhoun wanted to "ferret out the dark doings of traitors" and needed more money to do it. All the while bemoaning false alarms, he still insisted: "We need munitions of war, and authority to call out the militia to preserve internal quiet and to repel aggressions at Points which cannot be supported by the troops."[101]

While Calhoun wrote to Daniel Webster, other pro-Staters in the House of Representatives wrote to President Millard Fillmore. They needed more protection, because "the masterly inactivity of the Government troops does not afford that protection from the foray and rapine" of the "lawless savages upon our frontiers and roaming banditti in our midst." They wanted a militia that would "fight for their altars and their firesides" and not have to rely on the army. Soldiers, it seemed, were "disposed to recline upon the glory of past triumphs, and are reluctant to tarnish by petty skirmishes with hordes of half naked savages, or scattered bandits, the laurels which they have so freshly won upon the tented field."[102]

Not to be outshouted, the Territorial proponents wrote their own manifesto "To the People of New Mexico," which Calhoun called an "inflammatory article . . . abounding in falsehoods," serving only to prove their motto, which was "rule or ruin." The Territorials accused Calhoun of abusing his power to keep in office his party and friends, while removing from office all those who were not "a tool of the Governor." They accused him of disenfranchising the Pueblos from their voting rights as guaranteed in the Organic Law. The Territorials demanded equal and just taxation, separation of the executive branch from the legislative and judicial branches, modification of the governor's veto power, and direct election of officials by the people and stated their opposition to any state government "on account of the heavy burden of Taxation." The manifesto was signed by twenty-nine men, including Antonio Sandoval, Antonio Otero, Ceran St. Vrain, Robert T. Brent, Tomás Ortiz, Alexander Duvall, Rafael Armijo, Juan Sánchez, and James Giddings, who all had army contracts and/or had filed Indian depredation claims.[103]

What seems most striking is that both factions thrived on turmoil and that both wanted either an increased number of soldiers or volunteer militia. Whether in government blue or in homespun, more men with guns were better able to take and secure land and property belonging to others. Both sides were willing to twist the "facts" for their own ends. They fabricated tales of robbery and rapine out of whole cloth if it served their purpose. Each side had its own truth, which was all relative and resided only in the confirmatory biases of the competing parties. Seeing was not believing; whatever you believed, you saw. And they certainly understood that the more fear they could engender, the better chance they had to gain and hold power.

Very likely unaware that the discontent and fear that he had strewn propagated an atmosphere ripe for filing false depredation claims, Calhoun wrote to Commissioner Lea of his concerns. Unless the system for filing claims was properly administered, "unjust demands will be admitted and paid." He believed that all the claims for depredations should be taken before Indian agents or the superintendent so they could be properly overseen and regulated, because "there are persons now engaged in preparing such claims whose interests will be advanced by increasing their amounts, and witnesses are easily obtained. This is deemed sufficient to put you on your guard."[104]

Although Calhoun probably had realized it for some time, he finally made it official that people were filing false depredation claims and that the numbers of filings only increased as more Americans engulfed the Indian lands. A capitalist economy born under a suspicion of authority, America was a natural Petri dish for the acculturation of fraud. As noted above, the several Trade and Intercourse Acts opened up the government purse to those inclined to take advantage of the loopholes.[105]

Becoming an actual victim of an Indian attack was less real than the perceived threat. Sam Watrous made false theft claims. His neighbor from only a mile away, Alex Barclay, kept a near-daily diary from 1846 to 1850. It contains virtually no entries about Indians stealing his stock but many entries about animal predators killing his cattle and his stock freezing to death, being stolen by neighbors, or wandering off in storms. In one entry on March 30, 1849, he noted: "Wolves killing cattle like the devil every night."[106]

But depredation claims could not be filed against wolves. The military had been responding to the allegations of theft and mayhem, but in sundry instances they found the claims without merit. Governor Calhoun was coming to realize this, while a number of army officers were definitely aware of it. Perhaps the new department commander, Col. Edwin V. Sumner, would remedy the situation.

Stephen Watts Kearny led the "Army of the West" into New Mexico in 1846.
Courtesy of the Center for Southwest Research, University Libraries, University of New Mexico.

The high cliffs along a 100-mile stretch of the
Canadian River made it very difficult to cross.
From the author's collection.

Las Valles (La Liendre), now a ghost town on the Gallinas River.
From the author's collection.

Lucien Maxwell, who owned a land grant of more than 1.6 million acres,
was not averse to filing fraudulent depredation claims.
Courtesy of the Center for Southwest Research, University Libraries, University of New Mexico.

At Cerro de la Olla, Lt. Joseph H. Whittlesey battled the Utes on March 11, 1849.
From the author's collection.

Indian agent James S. Calhoun arrived in New Mexico Territory
in July 1849 and became territorial governor in 1851.
Courtesy of the Center for Southwest Research, University Libraries, University of New Mexico.

Anton Chico, a Mexican village on the Pecos River,
was the location of several army and Indian confrontations.
From the author's collection.

Wagon Mound, on the Santa Fe Trail between Fort Union and Rayado, was prime Jicarilla country and the scene of several confrontations.

From the author's collection.

Lt. Col. Edwin V. Sumner, 1st Dragoons, took over as Ninth Military Department commander in July 1851.

Courtesy of the Center for Southwest Research, University Libraries, University of New Mexico.

William Carr Lane arrived in September 1852
as the third governor of New Mexico Territory.
Courtesy of the Center for Southwest Research, University Libraries, University of New Mexico.

Cantonment Burgwin, named for Capt. John Burgwin, killed during the
1847 Taos Rebellion, was constructed south of Taos in August 1852.
From the author's collection.

David Meriwether became the second territorial governor
of New Mexico in August 1853.

Courtesy of the Center for Southwest Research, University Libraries, University of New Mexico.

The upper reaches of La Cinta Creek, the likely spot where Lt. David Bell
had his confrontation with Lobo Blanco on March 5, 1854.

From the author's collection.

Gen. John Garland joined his friend Meriwether
to pledge to protect New Mexicans' "life, liberty, and happiness."
*Civil War Glass Negative Collection, Prints and Photographs Division,
Library of Congress, LC-DIG-cwpb-04797.*

118

Lt. Col. Philip St. George Cooke caught the Jicarillas at Ojo Caliente on April 8, 1854.
The soldiers came down the mountain on the right and attacked the village in the
trees in the foreground. The Rio Vallecitos runs through the center.

From the author's collection.

(opposite top)
Lt. John W. Davidson attacked the Jicarillas at Cieneguilla on March 30, 1854.
Photo shows the area of the dragoons' farthest southern approach to
the village (they held horses to the left downslope).

From the author's collection.

(opposite bottom)
View from the Jicarilla village at Cieneguilla. Davidson approached from
the low ground in the center and retreated back to the ridge in
the central background, then to the left and down.

From the author's collection.

119

Major James H. Carleton attacked the Jicarillas at Fishers Peak on June 4, 1854, in the high, bowl-shaped valley in the center background.
From the author's collection.

(*opposite top*)
Col. Thomas T. Fauntleroy led dragoons and volunteers against the Jicarillas and Utes in several fights in the spring of 1855, in this area of Saguache "Pass."
From the author's collection.

(*opposite bottom*)
Often called the Battle of Poncha Pass, the April 29, 1855, fight probably took place along Chalk Creek, near the foot of Mt. Princeton in the Sawatch Range.
From the author's collection.

4

"State to Me the Scenes of Desolation"

The people of New Mexico Territory were pleased that Colonel Munroe was on his way out and certainly figured that the new commander would be easier to work with. Edwin V. Sumner, however, did not get the nickname "Bull Head" for no reason. Born in Boston in 1797, he joined the army as a second lieutenant in 1819. Legend says that a musket ball once bounced off his forehead without harming him, but his temperament may really have been the reason for the nickname. Sumner, who had been in New Mexico briefly with Kearny in 1846, arrived in Santa Fe on July 19, 1851, as lieutenant colonel of the 1st Dragoons and the new 9th Military Department commander.

In the spring Sumner received orders from Adjutant General Jones, telling him to proceed to New Mexico to take over. Jones told Sumner that "[t]here is reason to believe that the stations at present occupied by the troops in the 9th Department are not the best for the protection of the frontiers against the inroads of the Indians" and that he would have discretion to change their locations. He was to take with him 642 recruits for the 3rd Infantry, 2nd Artillery, and 1st and 2nd Dragoons. Sumner was also to be addressed by his brevet rank of colonel.[1]

Secretary of war Charles Conrad had other reasons for the change. There were civilian complaints that Munroe interfered too much with the civilian government, but most damaging was the charge that "the Indians had become so bold as to commit their depredations within a few miles of the military posts." Conrad regretted that "in no instance was their audacity challenged."[2]

The allegation was unfair, for Munroe had investigated the alleged raids but most often found them to be phantasms. On April 1 Secretary Conrad ordered

Sumner to "revise the whole system of defence" and to take troops from the towns for "both economy and efficiency" and station them on the frontier nearer to the Indians for better protection, forage, and fuel. Sumner was to make "every effort to reduce the enormous expenditures of the army in New Mexico" and "rigidly enforce" all cost-conscious measures. Sumner brought with him farmers and machinists who were supposed to teach the army how to raise its own crops, using methods more attuned with the well-watered East. No more lazy soldiers hanging around the posts gambling and drinking: they would work for their keep, which would promote their health and reduce expenses, while building their own posts far from the towns would save on rent and remove the soldiers from lure of prostitution and whiskey.[3]

Almost everyone besides Sumner hated the idea. What the civilian government could expect was illustrated only one day after Sumner's arrival. Calhoun, strapped for funds as usual, asked the colonel for food supplies to help feed the territorial prisoners. Sumner quickly responded, thanking Calhoun for his offer of cooperation, but denying his request: "I regret that I do not feel authorized to issue any rations to the civil prisoners of this territory."[4]

Economy was Sumner's watchword. Sumner's orders were to brook no insolence from the Indians, for they would never keep a treaty "until they have been made to feel the power of our Arms." Sumner was to campaign against the Navajos, Utes, and Apaches "and inflict upon them a severe chastisement."[5]

Munroe's army had been unsuccessfully looking for raiding Indians for a year, discovering that most of the reports were false alarms. Calhoun complained to Commissioner Luke Lea that it was the Americans and Mexicans who kept trying to excite the Indians "by misrepresentations and outrages upon their rights." He said that St. Vrain had recently come in from Taos, telling him that the Jicarillas "are entirely quiet" and have made no depredations since the treaty. The Utes had been patient and submissive. The Comanches crossed the Rio Grande as if to attack the Navajos, but they returned home "without committing outrages of any kind." The only problems that he knew of were reports of raiding Navajos. In July Robert Nesbitt and Hiram Parker, who had an army hay contract, told Calhoun that Indians had run off their mules, along with some that belonged to Capt. A. W. Reynolds, at Valle Grande.[6]

Calhoun was an enigma; he could cry wolf with the best of them, but he often saw through the false alarms. The great majority of the Indians were at peace, and Calhoun wanted to caution Lea "in relation to claims for depredations. Many of them are heavy, and should be paid. But there are others that will be greatly exaggerated, and the weakest proof will be couched in terms that will seem to establish losses beyond all doubt. The loose way of preparing affidavits and going through the country in search of the witnesses, may not, always, elicit the truth." Calhoun was talking about the plethora of attorneys who seemed to appear out of nowhere, akin to today's "ambulance chasers," looking for people supposedly injured or harmed in some way so they could bring suit.[7]

Calhoun cautioned about false reports of marauding Indians yet wanted the army to chastise them. But when Sumner made plans to go after them, Calhoun had second thoughts. The townspeople needed protection while the army was away chasing Indians. His agents were supposed to communicate with the tribes, so they also needed protection and supplies to go to and from the Indian villages. Would Sumner be so kind as to escort the agents and leave sufficient force in the cities? Sumner, however, was proving to be a tougher bird than Munroe. The colonel would provide sufficient protection for the cities but would not divulge his plans to Calhoun. As for the usual troubles with malcontents and criminals, Sumner regretted the territorial laws were not strong enough "to repress such people." In regard to assisting Calhoun's agents, Sumner said no allowances could be made "to any person from army supplies," because he assumed that Calhoun's boss in the Indian Department had already given him whatever "is deemed suitable."[8]

Given the few tentative reports of raiding Navajos, it seems inexplicable that Sumner felt such a need to "chastise" them, unless it was simply because of Conrad's words that the previous commander had not sufficiently challenged the Indians. Nevertheless, he set out on August 17 with about 350 men to chase Navajos in northwestern New Mexico. Sumner entered their stronghold in Canyon de Chelly. One night the canyon rim appeared to be ablaze with hundreds of small campfires, which apparently spooked Sumner enough that he roused the troops in the middle of the night and quietly marched back out. By this time they had lost three hundred horses and pack mules. Sumner headed for home and tried to place blame for the fiasco. "This expedition was not as decisive as I could wish," he wrote, but he offered a reason. It was the horses' fault. Sumner stated that in any future expeditions "against Indians, the main body must be foot." Horses, he said, break down too quickly in rough country; by the time they are ready to chase the Indians the horses are useless and "are a great embarrassment," requiring men to be detached to take care of them. Effective cavalry must be supplied with well-trained men and superb horseflesh only in small numbers, used more as scouts than as fighters. He recommended that four dragoon companies be withdrawn from the territory and that the Mounted Rifle Regiment (minus the mounts) or an infantry regiment be sent out in their place.[9]

Sumner wrote that "it will not be necessary to replace with any other troops, the four companies of horse that I have asked to have withdrawn. There will be troops enough here without them. It seems to me that it would be sound policy to reduce the force in this territory gradually, and then oblige the Mexicans to aid in their own defense." He added: "There is nothing whatever to apprehend from these Mexicans."[10]

The recommendations seemed incredible to the War Department. While other army officers and civilians knew of the near impossibility of foot soldiers catching Indians, here was a dragoon colonel stating that horses were fairly useless. Sumner had reasons: he could blame his campaign debacle on poor horses and then economize by getting rid of the dragoons. Yet perhaps Sumner was less "mad" than astute. Conceivably he intuited that many frontier problems were the result of too great an army presence. Surprisingly, Winfield Scott agreed. He wrote: "This is a very interesting report. I shall propose, next spring, that we withdraw the cavalry as suggested within. I ought to add that I highly approve the views & measures of Colonel Sumner."[11]

Before Sumner went chasing Navajos, he began the process of getting the army out of the cities and into frontier posts—another one of his mandates. "My first step was to break up the post at Santa Fe, that sink of vice and extravagance, and to remove the troops and public property to this place." The place was Fort Union. For many months this change was in the offing, and several officers had scouted east of the Sangre de Cristo for the perfect site to build a new headquarters fort. Mora, Las Vegas, and Rayado were considered. Rayado was probably the best choice, but Lucien Maxwell already owned the land and was charging high rent if the army wanted to use his dwellings and land. The site finally selected was on Wolf Creek, southeast of the Turkey Mountains, about eight miles above the junction of the Mora and Sapello Rivers and about halfway between Wagon Mound and Las Vegas. The choice proved questionable.[12]

Sumner nevertheless was more concerned with getting his men out—a move wanted neither by his men nor by the townsfolk. They petitioned to the government to bring the army back, mostly for protection reasons, but Sumner was certain that their pleas came "from those who have hitherto managed to live, in some way, from the extravagant expenditures of the Government" and hoped that their entreaties would not be heeded.

Sumner withdrew troops from Las Vegas, Rayado, Albuquerque, Ceboletta, Socorro, Dona Ana, San Elizario, and El Paso. He established Fort Union on the Santa Fe Trail, Fort Fillmore near El Paso, Fort Conrad south of Socorro, and Fort Defiance in Navajo country and would build Fort Massachusetts in what would become Colorado. Sumner said that he selected all the new posts with a view to cultivation as well as defense. Because the soldiers would build them, they would be labor and rent free. He considered it imperative to get the troops to places where discipline and economy would be facilitated, because the soldiers had been demoralized "by the vicious associations in those towns." Sumner was so intent on economizing that in October he sent 71 wagons and 473 mules back to Fort Leavenworth so he did not have the expense of wintering them in New Mexico.

There could be a number of problems associated with building new posts. One was that very soon after moving the army would find that the civilians had followed. Topographical engineer Capt. John Pope, who surveyed the territory from 1851 to 1853, clearly stated what would happen: "The establishment of a military post in Indian country brings with it the inevitable consequence of gradually but certainly driving the Indians to the side opposite the white settlements and, at the same time, of attracting the white to occupy and cultivate the country in its vicinity." He concluded that "these effects are well understood and common to every post."[13]

Sumner could not totally escape what he saw as the pernicious influence of civilians on his soldiers. He may have believed that he was getting ahead in the game by building new posts, but some of the sites selected were already taken. The area he chose for Fort Union was already "owned" by several people. It was most likely in the John Scolly or La Junta Land Grant, given by Governor Armijo in 1843, although the area was never surveyed accurately. The day Sumner arrived in Santa Fe he was approached by no less than eight men who had claims to the area and sought to sell or lease him the land: Robert T. Brent, Donaciano Vigil, James Giddings, George H. Estes, Herman Grolman, Henry O'Neil, Samuel Watrous, and Alexander Barclay. They were not all original grantees, as some had bought or sold their portions later. Barclay supposedly purchased his part from Giddings and William T. Smith. The deal was made purely in anticipation of this moment. In 1847 agent Tom Fitzpatrick had written to Barclay that the army would be looking for land to build new posts and that the area near the Sapello and Mora was a prime location—"This you may rely on." Barclay had pulled up stakes along the Arkansas and built his fort near the junction of those rivers, as did Sam Watrous. Barclay said to his sister: "I am building that fort under the expectation of selling it to the government." Now the army had come. Both men looked to cash in, but it would not be easy. "Owners" were approaching from everywhere in anticipation, but no one seemed to have clear title.[14]

Barclay promoted his land as the best anywhere for a post and said that he would sell it for twenty thousand dollars or rent it for two thousand dollars annually. Sumner would have none of it. He was there to save, not to spend. Later in 1851 Barclay conceded: "I shall never be able to sell out to [the] government, for after all my endeavors to give the impression of the importance of the site it has only had the effect of inducing them to come and establish a post themselves on the confines of our grant."[15]

Sumner would build his fort and not pay anyone. The new department commander quickly wore out his welcome, mainly because of his attitude toward the civilians and their government, plus his charge to save the army money. "[I]f I do nothing else in this Territory," he said, "I will certainly effect a great reduction in expenses but I hope to do more." As the troops left the towns the civilians howled their displeasure. It started when Sumner went after the Navajos. Calhoun crowed: just as he had predicted, the "Navajos are in his [Sumner's] rear" raiding the settlements, killing, and driving off stock. Three agents, A. R. Woolley, Edward H. Wingfield, and John Greiner, were hired to set up shop near Sumner's new posts but soon learned that they were not wanted. Sumner "refused to afford any *facilities* whatever" to them. They said that the "want of comity and cooperation" between the Military and Indian Departments made it impossible for them to do their jobs.[16]

Calhoun repeated the same litany to secretary of state Daniel Webster. The local "agitators are hourly exciting the passions of the ignorant, and those whom they control. The people are persuaded that they are not properly cared for—they know that wild Indians roam in every direction in this Territory, and commit depredations without being chastised." In mid-September Calhoun approved a trip by agent Wingfield to Washington "for the purpose of explaining the embarrassments under which we labor in this Territory." At the same time Theodore D. Wheaton of Taos, the Speaker of the Territorial House of Representatives, wrote to Calhoun complaining that Indians were back raiding since all the troops had been moved out of the towns and that the only way to remedy it was to call out volunteer companies, "equiped [sic] and paid by the genl Government," who could do more in one year to protect them from the Indians "than the regular army could do in three." By October Calhoun was again writing: "We can not do with less than two (new) Mounted regiments—and the Governor must have authority to call out the militia" as well as have control of war munitions and the payroll. He asked how he would distribute Indian appropriations when Sumner would not give him military escort. "The want of harmony between the military and civil authorities, is well understood." An exasperated Calhoun concluded that the executive and military offices could not harmonize, so "I am not certain that the public interests would not be promoted by relieving us all from duty in this Territory." He told Webster that Sumner's actions were "productive of no good." They needed volunteers because the Indians were still active, while "our troops seem to be in winter quarters." Calhoun said to Lea that "the Indians are not the worst people in this Territory, and increasing efforts are daily made to drive them to desperation."[17]

In October agent Greiner informed the governor that Kiowas and Arapahos had attacked a Ute village on the Red River north of Taos, driving the Utes southwest near Ojo Caliente, where they were said to be preparing a retaliatory raid. In addition, Taos citizens were organizing to move north into the San Luis Valley along the Conejos River, to settle in lands that the Utes claimed were their winter hunting grounds, where their ancestors were buried. They "will not give it up quietly," Greiner said.[18]

Calhoun was assailed from all sides. People bombarded him with reports of raiding, most of which were never borne out. Mexicans, Americans, and Indians were constantly complaining about rebellion threats, transgressions, insults, robberies, murders, encroachments, voter tampering, family feuds, requests to raise militia companies, and the like. The army had moved away, ostensibly to protect the frontier better, but the townsfolk only saw the move as a way to avoid Indians. Sumner would not arm volunteers or provide supplies or protection for the Indian agents. Local settlers sought to invade Ute lands. Calhoun was deteriorating mentally and physically. He was on a downward spiral that led to his abandoning New Mexico the next spring.

"State to Me the Scenes of Desolation"

The problem of Indian raids may have been one of the major issues between the civilians and the army, but not the only one. Very high on the list of grievances was Sumner's cost-cutting. The years 1850 and 1851 were a period of drought, which increased the cost of field crops and limited the growth of grasses. In the summer of 1851 John Greiner said that there had hardly been any rain all year "and the whole face of the country is dried up." Corn that sold for about four dollars a fanega (about one and-a-half bushels) the year before was now approaching fifteen dollars. Grass near the towns had long ago been consumed, and grazing camps had to be established in several places east of the Sangre de Cristo, in places like Galisteo, San Miguel, Las Vegas, and Rayado. Placing the stock there kept them better fed but also made them more tempting for thieves.[19]

Few army contracts for subsistence supplies were made in New Mexico before 1849 simply because so few were available. Most of what was grown was for local consumption only. Soon enough, however, people realized that money could be made in supplying the army. The army liked pork, but it was almost nonexistent at first. Cattle were not numerous, and goats rather than cows were used for dairy products. During the American occupation period some quartermaster contracts were given out to Americans to herd cattle for one dollar per head per month. The *Santa Fe Republican* carried ads for offers to graze stock with full responsibility, "unless it should be run off by Indians." The *partido* system was alive and well.[20]

Those who had been making money off the army were badly jolted when the Mexican War ended and the army went home, but they were relieved to learn that other troops would soon take their place. Hence the ongoing struggle to stir up enough trouble to keep troops levels as high as possible. After Ceran St. Vrain and William Bent dissolved their partnership in 1849, St. Vrain partnered with Isaac McCarty to supply wheat flour to the army. They had never done it before but figured that it was a good way to make money. They built gristmills south of Taos and at Mora and agreed to furnish the army with 1 million pounds per year for three years. Simeon Hart built similar mills at El Paso and Santa Cruz de Rosales to supply the southern half of the territory. St. Vrain and Hart also had army corn contracts.[21]

Army contracts were awarded more frequently by 1851. Philip Shoaff got a hay contract at Socorro; Edward Ownby got a hay contract to deliver at Cebolleta; Robert Nesbitt and Hiram Parker got one to furnish hay at Santa Fe and Abiquiu; Tomás Ortiz and Domingo Baca got hay contracts to supply several locations between Santa Fe and Albuquerque. The Ortiz and Baca contracts were some of the first that Sumner canceled. He claimed it was "the worst transaction in New Mexico," possibly because of short deliveries and possibly because it was one of the few contracts made with Spanish Americans.[22]

Beef was in short supply, but Lucien Maxwell and James Quinn got a contract to supply it for eight cents per pound, while Alex Duvall got a beef contract for fourteen cents per pound. As we have seen, Maxwell and Quinn claimed that the Indians had stolen all their cattle, yet they kept supplying the army without a break. Sheep were always available, however, even during the drought, so the army soon acquired a taste for mutton. Numerous mutton contracts were made. When the locals began driving the sheep to California where they could make more money than by selling to the penurious army, the strange practice of driving sheep into New Mexico from as far away as Ohio developed.

The army gave contracts for salt and vinegar, and William Skinner of Peralta got a contract to supply tallow candles at thirty cents per pound, while Sam Ellison and William Davy got a contract for one thousand bushels of beans. The army purchased molasses, lard, peaches, pickles, apples, sauerkraut (as an antiscorbutic), and occasionally whiskey for medicinal purposes. Contracts were given to freighters. The first was to James Brown in 1848, who hauled in goods from the east for less money than the government could. By 1850 much of the freighting was by contract. In that year 266 government wagons freighted more than a half million pounds of supplies, while private contractors with 658 wagons hauled in more than 3 million pounds.[23]

Things were looking good for business until Sumner began cutting contracts. While President Taylor supported spending money on the army, President Fillmore was more concerned with economy, and Sumner's orders reflected that. Secretary of war Charles Conrad wanted to turn soldiers into farmers. They could grow their own food, build their own forts, and theoretically promote the health and well-being of the men while saving money.

It did not turn out that way. The cost-cutting led to hampered efficiency, shoddy results, and increased costs in the long run. For example, while Fort Union was being constructed, Sumner found more suitable farming land about twenty-three miles north on Ocate Creek. He sent his soldiers there to break ground, but unfortunately the land was owned by Manuel Álvarez, who hired an attorney to oust the soldiers from his property. Barclay and Doyle claimed that Sumner was building his fort on their land and after much litigation won a lawsuit against the army for trespassing. Their award was only $100, but the army thereafter had to pay them rent of $1,200 annually, although it was too late to save Barclay and Doyle from bankruptcy.

The farming experiment never worked out. First, Sumner refused to use the Mexicans' "miserable method of cultivation," certain that the eastern methods he was familiar with worked the best. None of the soldiers wanted to be farmers, and they only made a half-hearted effort. Even the officers were unenthusiastic. It got to the point where Sumner said that he would not entrust a man to command a post who did not "manifest zeal and ability" in carrying out his agricultural program.[24]

Sumner saw waste everywhere and began canceling contracts. He wrote to the department quartermaster that his cost-cutting measures were having an immediate effect. He believed that they had enough pork, beef, beans, coffee, sugar, vinegar, candles, soap, and salt in the stores that "we shall not *require any contract train next year.*" Sumner stated that "we are safe in the subsistence department for some time beyond the 1st of August 1853." "[T]his surplus of subsistence, arises from the discharge of the citizens, [and] laborers"; if he needed supplies in the future, he would ask for them.[25]

Sumner would not pay for corn "where there is grass and nothing for the horses to do." When he found three contractors bidding with similar prices, he suspected collusion and price-fixing. A horse was only expected to survive three years in New Mexico and Sumner proposed using infantry instead of dragoons, possibly because he never fed his horses an ample diet. They could not live on prairie grass as an Indian pony could. When Gen. John Garland took over in 1853, he found poor horses and deficient supplies and had to make unusually large requisitions of all stores. He believed that many horses "perished for want of forage." The *Santa Fe Weekly Gazette* remarked that many of the department horses had "died of *economy.*"[26]

In the end the frugality was counterproductive. Col. Joseph K. F. Mansfield made an inspection of the territory in 1853 and reported that the farming program was "a failure generally." In 1853 Lt. Col. Philip St. George Cooke, later in command at Fort Union, said that the corn they grew at the post cost four times what it could be purchased for on the open market. In the same year adjutant general Samuel Cooper said that the farm program across the West was more than eighteen thousand dollars in debt. Winfield Scott, general in chief of the army, also believed that farming was a waste because it saved little, infringed upon soldiers' duties, hurt military discipline, and discouraged civilian settlement.[27]

Contractors were losing their jobs and locals made dire predictions of destruction when the army moved out, but they still lobbied for favors. In October St. Vrain and a number of merchants in Taos wrote a letter to Sumner, saying that they believed it "would be advantageous to your sending one or two companies of dragoons to this place to winter, as well as to render such protection to the people as the circumstances may require." Why? It just so happened that St. Vrain had a mill near Taos to produce flour, plus he could provide two thousand sacks of corn to be delivered anywhere in Taos Valley, provided army officers did not try to buy their own on the open market, for that would drive up prices. Zero competition was good for St. Vrain. He may have thought the tone of the letter smacked of cupidity, so he assured Sumner that "it is not for any speculations that may arise from the presence of those troops but the general safety of the citizens are more or less involved and I believe for it will be much to the advantage as to the health of your men and animals."[28]

St. Vrain was only one of a handful who kept their contracts and continued to make money. As much as they complained about Washington or Munroe, most of the locals probably wished that they were back, because Sumner seemed the worst of the lot. Capt. Isaac Bowen of the subsistence department, along with his wife, Kittie, had arrived in New Mexico with Sumner. Stationed at Fort Union, both were disillusioned and displeased with the situation. By October Captain Bowen wanted to go home with Sumner's mules. "I wish we were to accompany the train to the states," he said, "for, if there ever was a country which our creator had deserted, that country must be New Mexico." Kittie wrote to her father. She claimed that "I will not say anything" of Colonel Sumner but then continued: the folks would soon "hear enough of Colonel Sumner's doings." If she could get them a few Santa Fe papers they would "read in full the contempt the inhabitants have for him. . . . He is very unpopular in his command and throughout the country, and his excessive economy with regard to troops and animals has just the same effect as meanness in a household." At some of the posts "troops are on half rations because the cattle for the trains of supplies are so poorly fed that they die on the way. . . . Economy won't work in such a poor country as this."[29]

It was good that the Bowens did not make that trip. Sumner's hope to save a few dollars by sending 473 mules to winter at Leavenworth proved to be a disaster. In mid-November the train was hit by a great rain, sleet, and snow storm about sixty miles west of Council Grove, Kansas. One man and 275 mules died.[30]

At Fort Union Kittie kept writing candid letters to her father. There were several companies around, although Sumner sent some to Galisteo, ostensibly to protect the inhabitants there but mainly because forage was being used at too great a rate at Fort Union. Kittie believed that it was all fuss and feathers and could not care less whether soldiers were around at all. "We do not need much protection in this out-of-the-way place," she wrote. "We never think of Indians and have not heard that any were near." Daily existence was only punctuated by the occasional "Mexicans who come in with donkey loads of vegetables and fruit for sale; and we are so quiet that no sentinels are posted except over the provision and clothing tents." The only invasion that she dreaded were the cattle that roamed in and nosed about the house.[31]

If the rest of the citizens had shared Kittie's level-headed practicality there would have been less trouble. On November 9 Preston Beck Jr. and several others wrote to Governor Calhoun that they had organized a volunteer company in Santa Fe to protect them "from frequent incursions and depredations of the Wild Indians who surround us" and that they wanted weapons. Calhoun wrote to Sumner, asking for arms and accoutrements for seventy-five men. Perhaps not wanting to be depicted as totally uncooperative, Sumner ordered that seventy-five flintlock muskets with a like amount of cartridge boxes, bayonet scabbards, belts, and so on be given to Calhoun to be entrusted to Captain Beck.[32]

Sumner was beginning to question the need for the militia and weapons and began to wonder if the Indians were depredating at all, for as far as he knew they had all made treaties and were at peace. His predecessor had already gone through the learning curve, having legitimate qualms about the attack claims. In fact about this time Munroe arrived in Virginia and wrote to the adjutant general, stating that he felt it is "my duty even at this late date" to report on events that he did not have time to convey during the summer. He wrote of a July 1851 Indian attack on hay contractors Robert Nesbitt and Hiram Parker and said that the allegation of a depredation near Ceboletta had been "since found to be false." In regard to the investigation by Lt. Beverly H. Robertson, 2nd Dragoons, he noted "a wide discrepancy" in the stories of Nesbitt and Parker and Robertson, plus the two civilians never furnished any written affidavits. Munroe wanted to alert headquarters because he believed "it to be the intention of Nesbitt to petition Congress for a remuneration for their losses." Munroe felt that "little reliance" should "be placed upon the reports of citizens of that country—exaggerating their losses—when there is a prospect that government may recognize their claims."[33]

Sumner too, was seeing the light. If these latest reports of raids referred to the Apaches, he said, "I know of no depredations that have been committed by that band since I have been in the Territory." Still, he agreed to give Calhoun weapons under two conditions: that they would be returned when requested and they would never be used "in making hostile incursions into the Indian Country." Sumner's suspicion of their motives was illuminated by his question to Calhoun as to exactly what the "marauding parties" had planned. During one of their strained conversations, Sumner also told Calhoun that if the volunteers went into Indian country he would have the army stop them and punish them.[34]

Calhoun was incensed. He wrote to Sumner repeating the formulaic line about "numerous murders and depredations." "The winter is at hand, and ruthless invaders are in our midst, and, unless adequate protection is afforded, our firesides must be rendered desolate" before next spring. Calhoun disparaged Sumner's troop dispositions and the conditions of his horses, which rendered military help "impracticable." Thus the people had to defend themselves, so Sumner's conditions were "untenable." How could the militia operate if Sumner drew some invisible line between the settlements and Indian country and forbade the volunteers to cross it? The army was sent to New Mexico "to chastise the blood thirsty [*sic*] Indians because of their depredations upon our people." Now the soldiers "were to become the defenders of the Indians and chastise New Mexican troops because they are authorized to seek and attempt redress and secure the protection due the people, but which has not as yet been afforded to them by that power from whence it should come." Calhoun insisted that Indians were at the very moment "in our settlements committing murders, seizing and carrying off captives, and committing every species of depredations."[35]

The verbal and written battles continued. Like two petulant children on a middle school playground they battled it out until they could not even bear to speak to each other. But they certainly kept the messengers busy: fifteen letters passed between their Santa Fe offices in three days. It was Sumner's turn. He was fed up with Calhoun's constant wailing about depredations and asked: "Will you please state to me the scenes of desolation that have been recently witnessed in this territory before I reply to your letter of this date?" Calhoun shot back that he had been talking about depredations for months: in particular there was a murder at Greenhorn (more than two hundred miles from Santa Fe); six Ute women and children were captured near Taos (by Kiowas or Arapahos); a Pueblo and an Apache were killed near Taos; a Mexican was killed near Anton Chico; two men were killed on the Jornada del Muerto (more than two hundred miles from Santa Fe); a Mexican killed three Indians in the Rio Abajo; a girl was killed at Pena Blanca when Sumner was off on his Navajo expedition; and two hay camps were attacked.[36]

Calhoun offered these examples as scenes of desolation, but they included incidents from the past summer, some from far away, and more of the alleged crimes were committed against Indians than by them. Sumner was not impressed. He told Calhoun that he did not want to block attempts by the people to defend themselves, but it was "a very different matter from organizing marauding parties to traverse the Indian Country. This is not the kind of warfare that our government has hitherto condescended to engage in."[37]

Calhoun replied that he would leave it to others to decide just what type of warfare "our government has not 'condescended to engage in'" and asked why Sumner had not "condescended" to answer Calhoun's replies about "scenes of desolation." Sumner did not believe that the incidents Calhoun outlined were worthy of the term "desolation." Calhoun snapped back that if he was wrong about the word "desolation," then "the fault is properly chargeable to the learned Noah Webster, L. L. D." Then he asked if Sumner still planned to use troops to expel and punish the volunteers. Sumner said that after "mature reflection" he had decided that he would not use his troops to expel the "marauding parties" from Indian Country, "as it will not be their fault." But he warned Calhoun not to interfere with his duties as per the orders of the War Department. Calhoun asked why Sumner kept referring to the volunteers as "marauding parties," because that was "an epithet of opprobrium." It would not deter him from the discharge of his duties. Sumner said that he had not much more to say, except that "we differ widely" as to the meaning of the term "scenes of desolation." Also, did Calhoun still want to receive the weapons for his volunteers on the terms he imposed? Calhoun said that he did not, because Captain Beck refused those terms and wanted to operate as an independent company.[38]

Sumner finally quit, stating: "I have given it all the consideration that I think it is entitled to." Still, Sumner had to report to his boss. He prefaced his report: "I regret to trouble the Genl. in-chief with a voluminous correspondence with Governor Calhoun." He said that he had tried to avoid the confrontation, but it was too important to prevent "Mexican marauding parties" from killing Indians in their homelands. "This predatory war has been carried on for two hundred years," he wrote, with both sides stealing captives and cattle from each other "like two Indian nations." He asked that explicit orders be sent to Calhoun to prevent him from sending war parties against the Indians.[39]

The military commanders on the New Mexican frontier struggled to limit the rampant militarism of the civilians, tried to be a calming influence, and expended much effort protecting the Indians. Department commanders Washington, Munroe, and Sumner were skeptical about civilian complaints against Indians. They did their best to tamp down the false alarms and calm the fears, but it was nearly an impossible task, because it was in the civilians' self-interest to keep all in high dudgeon. They showed it by filing increased numbers of depredation claims in 1851. The record is replete with military reports dismissing depredation complaints as false, yet claim filing went from a low of nineteen in 1850 to a high of fifty-five in 1851. In addition, troop strength climbed from a low of about 800 in 1850 to a new postwar high of about 1,450 in 1851.

It seems as if we are again confronted with a paradox: more soldiers correlated with more raiding, fighting, and killing. Did an increased soldier presence really cause the Indians to raid more? That is unlikely, because much of the purported raiding was more fantasy than reality. Depredation filings likely increased because more troops meant that civilians had a better chance of eliciting a response—there is no point in crying wolf when there is no one to hear you. People were angry when Sumner moved the soldiers away from the towns and cut into their profits and when Sumner cut contracts. Crying wolf was a way to prove that Sumner was wrong and rub his face in it. The military repeatedly went on wild goose chases and found little evidence of raids. What we see in 1851 was another chapter of false reporting and filing to portray the army as insufficient and inept and to justify raising militia companies to raid and steal from the Indians. It is probably not a coincidence that twenty depredation claims were filed for the first six months of 1851 and thirty-five were filed in the second half of the year—after Sumner brought in 642 more soldiers, moved the troops out of the towns, and cut civilian contracts. While the army tried to curb militarist civilians, the civilians tried to impede a peacekeeping army.

"Much Depends on Keeping Everything Dark"

President Fillmore gave his annual message to Congress in December 1851, blaming it for "having failed" to adopt his recommendation to raise an additional mounted regiment for use in New Mexico. He mentioned the "new arrangement of the military posts . . . whereby the troops are brought nearer to the Mexican frontier and to the tribes they are intended to overawe." Fillmore hoped that the new posts would check the Indians' "marauding expeditions"—a view in line with the civilian perspective but not so much with his own military. He cited the Treaty of Guadalupe Hidalgo, which stated that America was bound to protect Mexico against incursions by Indians within our borders "with equal diligence and energy" as we would protect our own citizens. Nevertheless, Fillmore said, Mexico has suffered from depredations by American Indians. One exacerbating condition was that few if any Mexican troops were stationed in the northern reaches of Sonora and Chihuahua. When U.S. soldiers attacked Indians in New Mexico, they simply crossed into Mexico. Fillmore knew the conundrum of an escalation—a surge: "[T]he number and activity of our troops will rather increase than diminish the evil, as the Indians will naturally turn towards that country where they encounter the least resistance."[40]

The Mexican citizens knew this very well. Francisco G. Palacio, an attorney representing Mexican plaintiffs seeking redress and a member of the Joint Claims Commission, argued that Indians driven out of American territory were wantonly depredating in Mexico. Palacio claimed that per the treaty Mexican citizens were to be indemnified the same as U.S. citizens. In addition to driving the Indians into Mexico, the people north of the border continued to purchase captives, stock, and property stolen in Mexico, fueling the raids instead of stemming them. Palacio said that Americans destabilized the situation when they showed up in 1846, for Indians had never raided in Mexico as much as they did afterward. He said that 1848 was the year when the great devastation, depopulation, and poverty had begun. American Indians were moving to Mexico and raiding there and were stealing and selling in New Mexico, but the U.S. Army did nothing about it. Indeed, Palacio claimed, America had made quite a profit in not honoring the treaty. He estimated that the United States "has saved thirty or forty millions of dollars which would have cost the faithful fulfillment of this treaty." He also said that "the towns on the American frontier have not suffered much in consequence of the depredations of the Indians, because these had the vast territory of Mexico where to rob and murder with impunity."[41]

Palacio was saying what some army officers were coming to understand: depredations on the American frontier were more hype than genuine. But the same question arises on the Mexican side. Depredation claims are underlain by the quest for monetary gain: if so many American claims were mendacious, how many Mexican claims were too?

In his 1851 report Secretary Conrad also spoke of these issues. He too wanted a new mounted regiment to be used in the southwest, contrary to Sumner's recommendation, because it would help protect the border area and fulfill the treaty obligations. Congress had ratified the treaty but now refused to appropriate the funds to enforce it. Conrad chose Sumner to head the department, to be aggressive and "overawe the Indians by a constant display of military force." Moving the posts to the frontiers was part of that plan.[42]

Conrad said, however, that it was never the intent of the treaty for the United States to take over complete responsibility for protecting Mexico. He did concede that vigorous U.S. actions had the effect of driving the Indians into Mexico, but Mexico ought to make an effort to protect itself. Embracing the stereotypes of the time, Conrad said that the difficulty stemmed from the "difference in character" of the people of the two countries. Americans were familiar with weapons and readily formed themselves into militia companies. This, "joined with a native hardihood of character," enabled American pioneers to subdue much more formidable Indian tribes "than the robber bands that infest the frontiers of Mexico." Conrad said that Mexicans, on the contrary, "have little skill in fire-arms—nothing that deserves the name of a militia, and little of that daring intrepidity which distinguished the early settlers of our own country." As a result the Indians are not afraid of the Mexicans.

Conrad spoke of depredations, saying that he believed that "vague rumors" of Indian ravages in Mexico "have been grossly exaggerated, and sometimes entirely fabricated." Probably unaware of or dismissing the same propensities of his own people, Conrad stated that "tales of depredations have been invented with a view of bringing fictitious claims for damages against the Government." Still, Conrad was not totally naive; he did recognize that in some conflicts "the Indians have been goaded on to these acts of hostility by the conduct of our own people."

Realizing that getting a penny-pinching Congress to approve more troops would be difficult, Conrad suggested the alternative of arming the citizens and forming militia companies. It would be cheaper and perhaps the Indians would be less likely to raid if they knew that everyone was armed. In a suggestion that seems a bit topsy-turvy but consonant with the frontier myth of shooting first and asking questions later, Conrad said that the first choice to end depredations was through "the terror of our arms," but if that did not work "we should try the effect of conciliatory measures." But he realized that the Indians "are frequently impelled to commit depredations by despair and hunger." They had been driven from their lands and had lost their resources, "and the circle of white population seems rapidly closing around them." Conrad recommended that the Indians be given enough food and supplies to wean them from their nomadic lifestyle and teach them the ways of white society, an idea that had been around for centuries. With a logic that should have been embraced by Congress, he said that "it would be far less expensive to feed than to fight them."

In a classic example of one hand not working in cooperation with the other, quartermaster general Thomas S. Jesup also completed his year-end summary. He believed that the military expenses were enormous and had to be reduced and also said that the budget allowed by Congress for the next year was too low. It was completely insufficient "unless an entire change be made in our Indian as well as our military policy." The numbers of "wild" Indians in the territory were "by no means so numerous as they have been represented." Whereas Charles Bent estimated about thirty-seven thousand in 1846, and the 1850 census reported forty-five thousand, Jesup said that "they do not exceed ten thousand souls." Even so, the United States would have to pay the bill for the depredations committed by Indians on both sides of the border. To prevent depredations, the United States needed an all-mounted force in Texas and New Mexico harassing the Indians so much that they would never be able to bother the Americans. Soldiers might not be good farmers, so Jesup suggested that half of them be detailed to work in the mines and give half of the proceeds of their labor to the government. (How to make soldiers into semislaves in the mines while they were all supposed to be on offensive expeditions is not explained.) Jesup stated that the troops should not "be dispersed in small frontier garrisons," because it cost more money that way and it made a better impression on the Indians that the soldiers should "always be shown in large bodies."[43]

The war-makers' and peacekeepers' theories were often mismatched. It did not appear that moving the soldiers to frontier posts would save money and decrease depredations, because depredation reports were on the increase. Raiding reports did not abate as 1852 began, and even Colonel Sumner had second thoughts about the feasibility of his post locations. While he continued to praise the new forts and planned on building yet another one in Ute country (Fort Massachusetts), he acknowledged that he found it "indispensably necessary to remove my headquarters" from Fort Union to Albuquerque, because it was more centrally located and was in easier "striking distance" of the new posts. Sumner was coming to see the advantage of the central towns just as had Washington and Munroe.[44]

The *Santa Fe Weekly Gazette* was puzzled. Why did Sumner move the troops out and then move them back as in the nursery rhyme: "The noble Duke of York, he had ten thousand men; he marched them up to the top of the hill and he marched them down again." The editor wrote that Sumner "was cocked and primed" to build a post at "Holes in the Prairie" (Fort Union). That was when "the first explosion of his genius took place," but "[t]he walls of Jericho were doomed to fall." The paper proclaimed that "[m]en who leap in the dark are very liable to break a bone." It said that Sumner's common sense was damaged, for "[t]he military stores that went one hundred miles to the Holes in the Prairie, soon after went . . . several hundred miles westward to the Navajo Country." Why, the paper asked, did Sumner have "a particular animosity to Santa Fe?" "If it be true that our merchants and farmers received the public money; it is equally true that they did not disburse it."[45]

Sumner's seemingly confusing troop shuffling and post building were not understood or appreciated by the people. But at least some of the Calhoun-Sumner animosity had been defused by January 1852, mainly because of the unwarranted action of Major Electus Backus, 3rd Infantry, at Fort Defiance.

Sumner and Calhoun had both been wanting to chastise the Navajos further, especially Sumner after his summer fiasco. Backus, however, entered into a preliminary treaty arrangement with Navajo chief Zarcillos Largos and others while Calhoun and Sumner sparred verbally in Santa Fe. Presented with a fait accompli, Sumner and Calhoun could do little but meet with the Navajos and formalize the treaty at Jemez Pueblo on December 25, 1851. The usual articles were agreed upon, including an end to raiding and the return of in all captives. The colonel and the governor still could not agree on everything, however, for Calhoun distributed presents worth more than two thousand dollars, while Sumner said he would not have given them a penny until after they had been on probation for good behavior for six months "with a rod of iron over their heads." Sumner called it a great mistake, believing that "these Indians will undoubtedly feel that their submission has been purchased."[46]

As a result of the treaty, Navajos came to Santa Fe to parley. Calhoun was sick, laid up because of the "continuous and severe services to which I have been subjected for months," plus catarrh and jaundice, and had just gotten word of the death of his youngest daughter back in Georgia. He temporarily turned over duties to agent John Greiner and went to his sick-bed. The visitors included Armijo, Águila Negra, Barboncito, and a tall, young chief whom Greiner and others impishly gave the name "Winfield Scott." The meeting was not a joke to the Navajos, however. Armijo told how the drought had ruined the crops and his people used their own fingers and toenails to dig the soil. He said that they greatly appreciated the hoes given to them: "*We are struck dead with gratitude.*" The comment may have been barbed with the same sarcasm that the whites applied in naming their new chief.[47]

Armijo got to the heart of the matter. He was returning three captive Mexican boys as directed, but he wondered who would pay for the deaths of his grandfather and two other members of his family, killed by Mexicans. Greiner countered that the people of Rio Abajo complained of Navajos capturing their children and stealing their stock. Armijo replied, "*My people are all crying in the same way.*" "More than 200 of our children have been carried off and we know not where they are—the Mexicans have lost but few children in comparison with what they have stolen from us." Two years ago Mexicans had stolen seven hundred animals from his brother. Since Colonel Newby first made a peace with them they had been returning captives. "Eleven times have we given up our captives—only once have they given us ours." Armijo then asked: "*Is it American justice that we must give up everything and receive nothing?*"[48]

Greiner could not dispute the argument. He promised that the Great Father would look into it, gave the Navajos some flannel shirts, and (absurdly) a few hoes and told them to go home. Still, Greiner was affected by the talk. He said that the Navajos were already what the government insisted that it wanted Indians to become—industrious farmers, stock-raisers, and manufacturers. Like Sumner, he called the New Mexican forays "marauding expeditions." More people were coming to see that the "savage" tribes were more sinned against than sinners.[49]

Agent Edward Wingfield, who had gone to Washington to explain the difficulties they labored under, gave similar explanations of how the Indians had been wronged, particularly the Pueblos. Americans, he said, "make constant trespasses on their domain." The government should "compensate in some measure, for the frequent depredations and injuries which they have sustained."[50]

If the civilians opposed Sumner's post construction as wasteful and likely to increase depredations, the colonel was much more sanguine. He wrote that he was greatly satisfied that "the new posts that have been established in this territory are already exercising a favorable influence in our Indian relations." He said the Utes, Jicarillas, and Navajos were all at peace and the Gilas had not raided since Fort Webster was built. The surest way to subdue Indians, he said, was to build posts "in the heart of their country," which would make them reluctant to raid because they would be constantly worried about soldiers being so close to their villages. Military conquest had a more sinister side, however. If the Indians "are brought into contact with us, and their wants are multiplied, and as we only can supply them, it makes them directly dependent upon us."[51] Indians needed to embrace American capitalism to become compliant consumers.

In the meantime additional transgressions were being committed against the Indians, which brought the usual retaliations. In the fall of 1851 in the little town of San Antonio south of Socorro a Nuevomexicano was playing "a friendly game of chance" with three Gila Apaches. As the story goes, the New Mexican was angry that one Apache had a pair of queens to top his pair of jacks. When a fight broke out, he and his friends killed two Apaches. The third one, wounded, escaped to tell his tribe. The next day the Apaches came to town and demanded that the guilty man be brought to trial, following white law. The alcalde placed the killer in jail. But when the Indians were gone, he was set free. Sumner said that "when the Indians heard of it they became furious." The result was that on January 25, 1852, Apaches attacked eleven men of the 2nd Dragoons escorting wagons across the Jornada del Muerto, killing three soldiers and wounding one. The soldiers believed that they had killed up to nine Indians. The corporal in charge was sure there were white men among them, "as they had large whiskers and curly hair" and cursed the soldiers in English. Sumner blamed the incident on "the remissness of the civil authority in this Territory."[52]

Citizens of Socorro immediately petitioned Calhoun for weapons and more protection, stating that they were continuously "insulted by the presence of the savages," their lives and property were constantly sacrificed and despoiled, and the soldiers were worthless because they could not even protect "their *own* lives and property." Calhoun then petitioned Sumner for the use of five hundred weapons to form volunteer companies for an immediate expedition into Indian country. In addition, on February 25, Calhoun appointed Charles Overman as special Indian agent to reside in Socorro to watch the Apaches and, incredibly, to "report to me at every convenient opportunity, the movements of the United States troops, and their successes against the aforesaid Apache Indians and the probability of their chastising and subduing them." Calhoun employed a spy to watch the military. A few days later he wrote a letter to secretary of state Daniel Webster continuing the familiar litany of grievances against the soldiers, calling them "totally useless" and insisting that murders and robberies by the Indians were increasing daily. The same day he shot off a similar letter to Commissioner Lea, adding that if Sumner would only give him the weapons he wanted, Calhoun would take the field himself and see that "the hostile Indians were chastised into obedience or have them entirely exterminated."[53]

Calhoun mentioned an alleged incident involving Antonio Constante, a merchant taking stores to Fort Webster. Apaches were said to have attacked him in January 1852, stealing his supplies and killing or stealing his mules. Constante said that his losses amounted to $5,000, but like so many others his claimed losses seemed to have a way of growing. The congressional adjudication stated that "in 1853 this claimant presented a petition, under oath, estimating the value of the property at about $5,000, and now he, (claimant,) swears it was worth $7,418." The claim was denied.[54]

Interestingly enough, shortly after the Constante incident, 3rd Infantry Capt. Israel B. Richardson, who had been chasing Apaches in the area, alleged that four horses and a mule of his own were lost in the campaigning. He filed a claim for $400 in 1858. It was approved for only $60 but barred for being filed beyond the three-year statute of limitations.[55] Even the army officers tried to get in on the action.

For all Calhoun's bellicosity and insistence that Indians were attacking from every point of the compass, there was often a disparate reality. Lt. Beverly H. Robertson received word that three hundred Gila Apaches were encamped and committing "numerous depredations" near San Antonio, less than twenty miles north of Fort Conrad. On March 18 he marched to investigate with thirty-four dragoons—on foot because their horses were unfit for service. They found no Indians or sign of them. Robertson circled the town, talked with the locals, and met the alcalde, who "seemed surprised" at Robertson's information. Three days earlier several Apaches had been reported in the area, and it was said a herder and a few oxen had been killed, but little was substantiated. Back at the fort, an irritated Robertson wrote: "I would respectfully recommend that immediate measures be adopted to bring before justice, if any exists in this territory, the base perpetrator of such an unmitigated falsehood, as an example to those who have heretofore been too prone to make similar reports."[56]

If Calhoun was concerned by the army skepticism, it would have mattered little by that point. He continued to sicken and was in no shape to deal with the army or the Indians. Perhaps Sumner regretted their many disagreements, for in March he decided to give Calhoun one hundred flintlock muskets, with ammunition, to be used by the people of San Antonio, "where this war originated," and ordered Capt. Horace Brooks at Santa Fe to release the weapons. Calhoun accepted the offer and requested that Brooks deliver the arms to San Antonio. Brooks, also in a querulous vein, replied that his orders did not require him to deliver the arms anywhere. Calhoun—by now so ill that his assistant scribe David V. Whiting was composing all his correspondence—wrote to Sumner that Brooks had refused to comply with the requisition. Sumner said that he never expected Brooks to ship the arms but told Calhoun to pick them up himself. Calhoun then wrote to Secretary Webster, enclosing all the above correspondence, "for your consideration without further comments."[57]

Sumner wrote his own version to secretary of war Charles Conrad, explaining that the locals wanted weapons but, even "banded together in large numbers, have not the manliness to defend themselves from small parties of roving Indians, [and] they deserve to suffer." He added that it was not that Mexicans lived in fear "so much as their cupidity": they begged for more troops because "they want the government money."[58]

Sumner blamed the latest mess on the Mexicans who had murdered the Apaches at San Antonio, forcing him to make another campaign. He told Maj. Gouverneur Morris, 3rd Infantry, commanding at Fort Webster, that white men among them "are at the bottom of all the mischief." Although he had few troops, he stubbornly refused to use any volunteers. When Calhoun, who had been wailing for army action, heard of Sumner's proposed campaign, he shifted back to the old argument that the towns would be in danger if the troops left. Once again Calhoun had just heard that "plans are afoot to unite the several tribes of Wild Indians, by whom we are surrounded." It was more important to protect the citizens than to chase Apaches. Calhoun believed that he was dying and appointed John Greiner as acting superintendent during his incapacity. Even so, Calhoun had to get in another dig that Sumner could have done more to protect the people if he had selected a "Central position" to keep his soldiers, where all the animals could be watched and fed, and ready to move at a moment's notice to any point.[59]

Greiner got into the contest, writing that one thousand soldiers in New Mexico could not manage the Indians: "Our troops are of no earthly account. They cannot catch a single Indian. A dragoon mounted will weigh 225 pounds. Their horses are all as poor as carrion. The Indians have nothing but their bows and arrows and their ponies are as fleet as deer. Cipher it up." For all the army expeditions, "not a single Indian had been caught!" The Indians "laugh at their pursuers." The governor could not get arms for the people to defend themselves. "You may think it strange," he wrote, "but I have more fears of Mexicans and some *Americans* here than I have of any of the Indians." At another time, Greiner wrote: "If traveling on the road, you meet an American, you put your hand on your pistol for fear of accidents."[60]

A few days later Greiner wrote to Sumner that a suspicious Mexican, Juan Antonio Baca, was up to "some devilment" in stirring up the Pueblos, while Don Carlos, a Tesuque Pueblo, reported that he had just come from Comanche country and learned that a "League" was being made between the Comanches and Mexicans to unite with the other wild tribes to attack New Mexico. Greiner went so far as to implicate the "President of Mexico," who supposedly had a document from a priest inviting them all to join in the rebellion. "Be on the alert," Greiner warned Sumner. Greiner also wrote a letter to Spruce M. Baird, whom Calhoun had recently appointed as Navajo agent: should anything spark a fight, "blame must not be at our doors." Responsibility for any disaster must not lie with the Indian Department. Greiner asked Baird to "talk around" the wild Indians to learn of any conspiracies, "But say nothing—do nothing—to excite suspicion in the breast of anyone. Much depends on keeping everything dark."[61]

Darkness and fear, smoke and fog, were the tools of power, but very likely few of the men who used the tools were even aware of what they were doing. Sumner, however, very likely wondered if this nonsense was ever going to end and responded: "I am much surprised" at the information received, but "I can not think that we should give full credence to it." Nevertheless, he postponed his planned Apache campaign to concentrate his units to wait for another full-blown rebellion that never came.[62]

On April 9 Sumner related that Calhoun was near death. He had heard from officials that if he died "the government should devolve upon me." Noting that "I have no desire to do this," he said that he would take over "from a sense of imperative necessity" if an emergency should arise during the interregnum. That emergency, Sumner told Adjutant Jones, was another of the "constant rumors" about Mexican and Indian rebellion. Sumner said that there was nothing to be feared from the Mexicans and that most of the "stories originate with some unprincipled Americans, or if they do not create them, they distort and exaggerate them for the purpose of keeping up this excitement. It is my deliberate opinion that there are some men in this Territory who would stick at nothing to increase the expenditures of the government." The alarms served only "to alienate the different classes from each other."[63]

Calhoun's paranoia increased as his life ebbed. He recommended that "every American female" should leave the country. Because he had no more money even to feed the prisoners, he had to turn them loose. Some of them were thought to have run to the frontiers and to be terrorizing the settlements, disguised as Indians. Calhoun was positive that a rebellion was waiting to happen. He told Captain Brooks in Santa Fe that the capital must be defended. Brooks complied, moving all his stores and ammunition into the Governor's Palace and placing it "in a complete state of defence." But that was not enough. As Calhoun prepared for an Alamo-like siege, he also asked Sumner for an additional artillery force to help shore up the bastions. Although Sumner "saw no appearance of disaffection," he brought in more men and set up "military police" to support the civil authorities. On April 21 Sumner and Calhoun issued a statement to the people, announcing that there would be no interregnum without a government. If Calhoun left the territory or died, Sumner would "take charge of the Executive Office to make the preservation of law and order, absolutely certain."[64]

On the last day of April acting superintendent John Greiner wrote to Commissioner Lea: "Not a single complaint has been entered against any of the Indians during the month just past, a remarkable fact." The Comanches were peacefully hunting buffalo, the Gila Apaches "are very quiet" and desirous of being on even friendlier terms, some Jicarillas had moved near Pecos where they intended to manufacture *tinajas* (water jars), the Navajos were on their farms "behaving like good people," and the Utes are "the easiest managed of any" and "can always be relied on." The Pueblos were attending to their farms as usual and were very industrious. "Could they be protected from the depredations of the Mexicans," said Greiner, "they would not only be examples for their *red* brethren—but for some people of a lighter complexion."[65]

Before Governor Calhoun could leave, however, the rebellion scare reached east of the mountains. Maj. James H. Carleton, 1st Dragoons, had replaced Lieutenant Colonel Alexander in command at Fort Union in April. His first order of business was to go after the whiskey sellers surrounding the fort, where he believed rebels and thieves congregated to "lay schemes for carrying on further depredations." Alexander Barclay was a suspect. But when he and William Bransford, who ran St. Vrain's mill at Mora, passed on their suspicions of an uprising, Carleton issued arms to the American citizens at Mora. Sumner was not pleased and laid the blame for rebellion talk on "designing Mexicans."[66]

The situation was in its usual turmoil when Calhoun, in a mule-drawn army ambulance, and his entourage arrived at Fort Union on May 11. The dying man had employed a local carpenter to build him a coffin, which accompanied him on his journey. Sumner told Carleton to let Calhoun rest in his house at the fort for as long as necessary, to provide what he needed, and to furnish him an escort across the plains. The caravan continued its slow journey east on May 26. About June 30, somewhere east of Council Grove, Calhoun died. His body was placed in his coffin, and the caravan went on. Calhoun's secretary David Whiting simply wrote that his remains were "interred at Kansas [City], Mo."[67]

It would be fair to say that Calhoun tried his best and had the interests of his country in mind, but he had a dark side. There is truth in the old adage that power corrupts. When someone seeking to gain or hold power exploits public anxieties, we get much more than we bargained for. Powerbrokers know that fear is a powerful weapon. In this instance the military was often the calming influence, trying to inject rationality into an electrically charged atmosphere. Without the army investigating and disarming wild rumors of raiding, rebellion, and murder, New Mexico Territory might have degenerated into a state of chaotic warfare. Sumner, although possibly bull-headed, tried to put a damper on the panics, as did Washington and Munroe. They succeeded for the most part but were generally seen as appropriating power that belonged to the citizens.

Perhaps not unexpectedly, talk of rebellions and raids diminished when Calhoun left. About the time of the governor's death, Greiner wrote: "*Not a single depredation has been committed by any of the Indians in New Mexico for three months. The 'oldest inhabitant' cannot recollect the time when this could have been said with truth before.*"[68]

The Indians were quiet and at peace. There were no depredations. Yet this did not stop at least seventeen people from filing depredation claims for alleged robberies in the spring and summer of 1852. At least they claimed that the depredations were during that spring and summer, but they may simply have "confused" the actual dates, because the claims were filed from two to (incredibly) twenty-two years later. Or maybe the depredations never happened at all.

A New Governor

The day after Governor Calhoun pulled out of Fort Union on his last journey, Colonel Sumner wrote a long letter to secretary of war Conrad. It appeared that he too was heartily sick of the Territory and recommended giving it up. Sumner could see no light at the end of the tunnel, only more money being thrown away. "Withdraw all the troops and the civil officers," he said, "and let the people elect their own civil officers, and conduct their government in their own way, under the general supervision of the government." The United States kept pumping money in, but that only made the people "more idle and worthless." "Speculators, adventurers, and the like, are all that will come, and their example is pernicious rather than beneficial." All civilian branches of the government had failed and the military was the only thing preventing complete collapse. "The truth is," Sumner wrote, "the only resource of this country is the government money. All classes depend upon it, from the professional man and trader down to the beggar." The military should pull out, give the people arms, and let them defend themselves. "If the Mexicans should act justly by the Indians, I think there would be no difficulty; but if they did not, and war should ensue, the Mexicans would always steal from the Indians quite as much as the Indians would steal from them, and thus they would be no losers in the end." All the American adventurers "when they can no longer make money . . . will soon leave." A few posts along the Rio Grande would suffice for treaty compliance. Secretary Conrad believed that Sumner's recommendations had merit, but his manifesto did little beyond giving pause to his superiors over what to do with a department commander who did not want to be there.[69]

John Greiner tried to avoid Sumner. His daily diary from April through September 1852 is replete with seemingly mundane matters but is also very revealing of the territory's problems, recording numerous visits from Indians begging for food and assistance and complaining about trespasses or robberies by New Mexicans and Americans. Pueblos complained of "unjust treatment" from the Mexicans. Captain Ewell said that the Apaches "were not as hostile as reported." The Pueblo Don Carlos related that he had been hunting with Eagle Feathers, the Comanche who had fled from Santa Fe the previous year under threat of murder. Carlos said when they were in the mountains a party of Americans accosted and took from them a number of captives, and "they are angry about it." On April 12 Pablo Romero of Taos visited Greiner, telling of his meeting with Apache chiefs who vowed that they would not be the first to break any peace. Lobo Blanco, who had not been heard from much since he signed a treaty in 1851, complained that his people were not getting the presents that other tribes were getting, but Romero told him to be patient and he would not be forgotten. Romero considered Lobo "a very good man and reliable." One Ute chief was keeping his band away from Abiquiu because the local Mexicans told him that "the Americans would take his head."[70]

That same month Picuris Pueblos told Greiner that Mexicans from Mora were stealing their water supply, while Santa Clara Pueblos protested that an American named Rudolph had settled on their property and was stealing their water. Utes voluntarily turned in some stolen animals to agent Baird at Jemez. Sixty-five Jicarillas visited Greiner; while some sought whiskey, there was "no trouble at all with them." Their women stayed behind to manufacture *tinajas*. A San Ildefonso man reported that his pueblo had not lost any stock as was alleged. The Jicarilla Chacón wanted to bring in his people and begin to farm. Greiner had not heard one complaint about Indians for the month of April.

In May Greiner wrote that the Navajos were busily working on their farms, but a Pueblo from San Juan complained of a Mexican who had claimed some of his land, while others arrived to report Mexicans stealing water from the arroyos at San Ildefonso. Mr. Rudolph came to see Greiner and said that he would abandon the land he claimed at Santa Clara but also brought word that some Mexicans near Pojoaque Pueblo "were trying to excite the Indians by telling them that the Americans were about sending more troops here for the purpose of destroying the pueblos." Armijo and a few other Navajos told Greiner that Mexicans had stolen seven of their horses. Two Nambe Pueblos reported Mexicans trying to sell them a stolen mule. Jicarillas were accused of killing six sheep at Bosque Redondo. Greiner called in Chacón to answer for it. He did so, but Greiner only said that his people would be punished "if they did not quit it." Chacón agreed. In the meantime Lobo was engaged in planting near Mora.

In June Greiner learned that a complaint about Chacón was a "made up story." A Pueblo from Cochiti told Greiner that two Mexicans had stolen some of his animals. Greiner also learned that agent Latz was involved in a scheme to "catch what presents they suppose the Indians will get" and told Latz that he would be held responsible if such conduct continued. Gila Apaches tried to see Greiner, but some men told them that "a trap was laid for them, to get them in here and kill them off." Late in the month Greiner had one of his first brushes with Colonel Sumner. Greiner had given a pass to hunt buffalo to a Pueblo, who was accosted by soldiers who claimed that he could not hunt. Greiner said that Sumner "has no right to interfere with the Indian Department" and continued to issue passes. Sumner claimed that he was head of the department by virtue of Calhoun's absence. Greiner said that they should let the judiciary decide who was in charge, but Sumner objected.

Thus it went the rest of the summer. Sumner insisted he would make peace with the Indians, not Greiner. Trader Lacome was caught whipping an Apache. Cochiti Pueblos were in looking for a Mexican who had stolen their mules. There was great trouble on July 22 in Santa Fe when a brawl and shooting broke out between Mexicans and American soldiers. The governor of Santo Domingo complained that Mexicans kept running stock in their planted fields, while people of San Ildefonso protested that soldiers' animals were destroying their gardens. Tesuque Indians protested against troops who were stealing their mules. In August a frustrated Greiner wrote: "If the Mexicans will only give the Indians a fair chance, we will have but little trouble with them."[71]

On September 9 the new governor, William Carr Lane, arrived. Greiner had recently taken an oath to become the secretary of the territory but helped with the superintendent job until Lane could get situated. Lane was inaugurated on September 13 and was promptly visited by several Indians, who entered a complaint about an American who had stolen one of their mules. A few days later three Picuris Pueblos arrived to complain that the land they had been farming all year had been confiscated by a Mexican. On the last day of the month fourteen Jicarillas protested that Mexicans had taken their horses and mules. Greiner made the last entry in his diary on that day, writing that he now "gives up all the duties of Indian affairs to the governor."[72] He probably wanted to add "Thank goodness" and wash his hands of the whole mess.

When President Fillmore offered the governorship of New Mexico Territory to William Carr Lane, he cheerfully accepted the appointment but soon questioned his decision. Lane, born in Pennsylvania in 1789, was a successful physician, an eight-time mayor of St. Louis, Missouri, and could have been elected to the U.S. Senate, but he declined the office. For some reason he jumped at the chance of being a frontier governor, although he was sixty-three years old and had to leave his family behind. In Lane's inaugural address he promised the people that he came not to improve his private fortune or advance any political views but simply to serve honorably and do what was best for the territory. The task, he said, "is to build up that which has been torn down by revolutions, to harmonize conflicting laws, and to reconcile conventionalities in social life, so as to produce civity of action and goodwill throughout the land."[73]

Just what goodwill Lane would encounter was immediately shown at the inauguration. Sumner, likely feeling good about governing the territory with no James Calhoun to torment him, was not pleased. Two days before the ceremony he pulled most of his troops out of Santa Fe and retired to Albuquerque. When Captain Brooks's soldiers simply fired a salute to the governor at the inauguration, Sumner reprimanded him, saying that "the civil government . . . is not to depend in any way upon the military authority." Sumner then ordered the American flag, which had floated in the plaza since 1846, to be removed. When Lane courteously asked for the flag to be replaced, Sumner responded: "I regret that I cannot furnish you with military supplies, not provided by law without an order from the war department."[74]

Lane, often called high-tempered, did not take kindly to the rebuff. The exchange nearly led to a duel. When Lane later requested five hundred volunteers to fight the Indians, Sumner refused. Lane actually challenged him to a duel, although Sumner declined to fight.

"Never was an executive officer in a more pitiable plight," Lane wrote to Sumner. He was an utter stranger to official duties, without legal advice, with scarcely an official document to direct him, he had no money and no credit, the judges and attorney general were absent in the States, and only two agents were stationed in the territory. They had no militia there to protect them, no muskets available, and no police. "[A]nd you, Colonel Sumner, must have been, from your official position, duly informed of these things."[75]

On September 26 Lane wrote to his family that nine out of ten Americans in Santa Fe "go around constantly armed; and I do not know anybody, that does not sleep with pistols under, or near their pillows." The reason was a fear not of the Indians but of the New Mexicans. Lane said the "palace" was nothing but a white-washed mud-house, and his daily routine consisted of "one eternal round of appeals, written & verbal, from Mexicans & Indians, & sometimes Americans, for reparations, of every description of wrongs . . . every 5 minutes—besides getting at least 50 embraces, from Indians & sometimes from Mexicans, daily." Calhoun and Greiner could have told him that. It did not take long before Lane wrote to his wife, Mary: "I had the blues dreadfully, at first, and would have made an immediate retreat, if I could have done it with honor."[76] Welcome to New Mexico Territory.

Lane had a rough start, but he quickly adjusted to the situation. Unlike Calhoun, Lane actually seemed to like the people he governed. He wrote to his wife that he wished the New Mexicans would not change one bit of their "beneficial or praiseworthy customs": to remember their heritage and to keep "their beautiful language," their "dignified manners," and their "Christian customs." He hoped that so-called progress would not destroy them as a people. He thought the climate was excellent and the land strikingly beautiful. Even when he later ran for Congress and realized that the people would rather support a local man, he said: "God bless them."[77]

Lane relished traveling. Very soon after arriving, he visited seven counties and began talks with the Indians. He made more treaties, none of which were ratified, and spent twenty thousand dollars, liberally distributing supplies and gifts with the idea that it was cheaper to make friends than enemies. When his expenditures were later curtailed, the Indians felt that the United States had broken the treaties again.[78]

That was in the future. In the fall of 1852 Lane was settling in and welcoming Indian visitors as Greiner did on a near-daily basis. Lane's secretary, John Ward, also kept a journal, although without the details that Greiner had provided. On October 1 Jicarillas and Pueblos visited their new "Tata" (the governor) and left highly pleased with him. But, Ward recorded, it cost $4.25 to feed them. There was a rumor that the Utes were planning a retaliatory raid on the Cheyennes, Kiowas, and Comanches, and Lane hoped to prevent it. Greiner tried to arrange a meeting in Taos in early November. When other bands heard of this they all wanted to attend. Lane had to buy extra supplies from the Lacome Brothers. The $2,500 that Lane had on hand was not enough. He had to request more funds. Agent Baird had to make a trip to Navajo country with presents to placate them.[79]

Greiner assisted Lane by meeting the Indians, but at Abiquiu, not Taos, because of hostile Plains Indians supposedly still prowling in the mountains. About 400 Utes and 150 Jicarillas attended. Greiner quickly went through about $3,000 in gifts. He was proud to report that they did not need one soldier around, for the Indians were all "on the most friendly terms," and had behaved well for the past two years. Greiner said that "the Great Father" was "well pleased with his red children" and wished to make them happy.[80]

Chief Coniache spoke for the Utes and said that they were pleased with the gifts and friendship but that the whites needed to heed other things. His people did not live, work, or play like white people. They did not live in houses and had to burn down a dwelling and move whenever someone died. The women already had too much work to do and did not need more. It seemed that the Americans cared more for the Plains Tribes than for the Utes, "for many of them are married to and have children upon the Prairies, but the Utahs have no pale faced children." The Americans gave their enemies guns and ammunition, while no such gifts were given to the Utes. "The Prairie Indians have committed many depredations upon our people, and we have been told we must not make war," Coniache said. They got flour and meat but no weapons and felt the Great Father "had not the confidence in us he should have, or he would give us some powder and lead." "We do not wish to have our hands bound together, when our enemies are permitted to steal our stock and murder our wives and children." If the Utes cannot make war, Coniache said, "we shall expect the Americans at the fort to protect us and our property."

The post referred to, Fort Massachusetts, was constructed by Maj. George Blake, under Sumner's orders, beginning in June 1852, on Ute Creek about six miles north of the present town of Fort Garland, Colorado, and about eighty-five miles north of Taos. It was supposed to guard the passes leading from the Plains into the San Luis Valley. "But the fort does us no good," Coniache said. "There are five passes through the mountains . . . and it is not near any of them."

How helpless the soldiers at Fort Massachusetts were to prevent incursions was demonstrated in February 1853, when Arapahos and Cheyennes crossed the mountains and attacked the Utes, killing many, stealing their horses, and leaving forty families starving in the valley. Nevertheless, Greiner and Ward returned to Santa Fe after the Abiquiu meeting, convinced that the council had "been a fine one," certain that all were happy and that the new fort would protect them. Only three days later a disgruntled American employee at John J. Lease's sawmill near Las Vegas shot and killed one Apache and wounded two more. Governor Lane quickly dispatched Greiner to talk to the Indians and "spare no means in order to have them pacified and the injured families rewarded as much as possible" so as to prevent a retaliation.[81]

What the army commanders had been saying for years was still true: if the Americans and New Mexicans would simply leave the Indians alone, there would be much less trouble. In a message to the Legislative Assembly on December 7, 1852, Lane summed up what he had seen in his brief stint as governor: "It cannot be denied that the first aspect of things in this Territory is discouraging." The territory was far from the States, "surrounded by barbarians of doubtful faith."

Water was scarce and some of the land was sterile. The population of about sixty thousand was so scattered that twenty companies of soldiers could not protect it. The locals were badly armed and could not protect themselves. The mines were not productive and agriculture and stock-raising were "depressed, for want of protection for flocks and herds." The roads were bad, and education was nearly nonexistent. "The country is run over with red and white thieves and robbers." The prisons were insecure and the laws imperfectly administered, with little money to enforce them. "[U]nreasonable jealousies and bickerings exist between the natives of the country and immigrants," creating discontent and insecurity in business.[82]

But Lane said that "time, perseverance, mutual forbearance, and the exercise of wisdom and justice will assuredly correct all these evils." Some of the country was fertile and could be made productive with irrigation and the good artesian water. The stock-raising potential was unlimited. An organized militia would "protect your stock from *red* thieves, and a penitentiary will rid you of *white* thieves." Roads, railroads, and telegraph would arrive and bring modernity with them. Lane questioned continuing the practice of conducting affairs in English and Spanish, which doubled the necessary work. He recommended repealing the law that authorized licensing of gambling houses. Lane told them that he had asked the War Department to treat New Mexico not as a conquered land but as a place whose people voluntarily joined the United States in peace. Admittedly, he said, "insecurity of property from Indian depredations" might still cause disturbances of the peace. But overall this was exaggerated, while the idea of revolution "was a chimera of heated imaginations only."[83]

Dr. Michael Steck came to New Mexico as an army contract surgeon but accepted a job as Indian agent to bring his tubercular wife to a healthier dry climate. At Anton Chico he met with Mescaleros Josecito, Santa Ana, and Cuentas Azules and Jicarillas Lobo and San Pablo. His findings were similar to Lane's: "In all my intercourse with them the most perfect good feeling seemed to prevail." All of them "have been behaving unusually well."[84]

In spite of all the talk of tranquillity, citizens continued to file depredation claims in the fall of 1852—even Jicarilla agent Michael Steck filed a claim (unproven) for $1,440 in property losses. But the military made few excursions after "raiders" who had been exposed as phantoms so many times before. Much of the army's latest concern was with the civilians and its own soldiers. Sumner had tried to get his men away from the dens of iniquities in the towns, but the "vice" followed him, just as Captain Pope had written it would. Prostitutes set up shop just off the military reservation at Fort Union and even made themselves homes in the caves in the hills to ply their trade, while other civilians sold liquor all around the reserve. In order to buy women and whiskey, soldiers often stole government stores to sell or trade. Captain Bowen, in charge of stores, recorded that for the first six months of 1852 the items on the "Wastage or Stolen" list included 9,379 pounds of bacon, 3,400 pounds of flour, 4,303 pounds of coffee, 1,313 candles, 1,191 pounds of ham, and 5,254 pounds of sugar—sweets for their sweets, apparently. Bowen reported that the great majority of these items were stolen by enlisted men "and sold to the grog shops and bawdy houses in the neighborhood."[85]

Major Carleton was incensed, saying that he had never seen such alarming "intoxication and crime" among any other troops. Most of the area "raids" were conducted by Carleton, who constantly hectored the hookers and hooch-sellers. Kittie Bowen wrote: "All the shanties and groggeries around this post occupied by miserable Americans, have, by order of the chief in Santa Fe, been burned down and the keepers put in irons and sent to town for trial." The people were "very bitter" toward Carleton. Alex Barclay and Joe Doyle showed it by filing suits against him to the tune of $15,000. Carleton had civilians whipped, and several hookers ran to Barclay for protection. On the night of December 11, 1852, Carleton broke up "a whiskey establishment" on the military reserve. Apparently the neighbors were not so friendly with each other either, for Carleton said: "Mr. Doyle informed me that [José] Pley was at the bottom of the whiskey business." Barclay and Doyle sold liquor too, but Barclay blamed the situation on others. He complained that his laborers and servants were untrustworthy: "The Americans generally found rambling about Mexico are of the most worthless class. The Mexicans, by nature and education idle and dishonest, rob us yearly to an unknown amount of implements and other loose things." Americans Barclay, Doyle, and their neighbor Sam Watrous, who illegally sold whiskey and filed fraudulent depredation claims, apparently believed that they were of a better class.[86]

When Carleton heard that José Pley was among the whiskey sellers, he reprimanded Captain Bowen for buying corn from him: "I did not learn until these 110 fanegas of corn had been delivered that you had made . . . such a bargain, or I should have disapproved of it throughout." Carleton said that the civilians were suing him for breaking up their establishments and promised that "any man who shall directly or indirectly be engaged in this degrading business, shall under no circumstances be allowed . . . to sell one dollar's worth of produce for government purposes at this post."[87]

With Indian alarms on the wane, there was conflict between soldiers and civilians instead. Lt. Robert Ransom, 1st Dragoons, also had problems. He had constructed Cantonment Burgwin in August 1852, which was named after Capt. John Burgwin, who was killed during the Taos Rebellion in 1847. Built on the Rio Grande del Rancho about ten miles south of Taos, it was never officially designated as a fort but was occupied by troops for eight years to ease the continuous cries from citizens in Taos Valley for protection from Indians. Ransom drew his flour from nearby St. Vrain's mill, his corn from the people of the valley, and his beef from Maxwell and Quinn at Rayado, calling it "the very best I have seen since I left the states."[88]

When Ransom first arrived, he took over land on which Juan Martínez was herding his sheep and goats. Martínez reluctantly moved, with "no violence of force" used to remove him. In early 1853, however, the nearby Nuevomexicanos began complaining of "depredations committed by the soldiers" of Ransom's company, in particular killing cattle. Ransom investigated and reported that "the whole is a total falsehood of Mexican fabrications." They found one spot where an ox was killed. They could not find "the track of an American," only the track of moccasins and saw one Mexican carrying a side of beef. If any cattle were killed, they were government cattle. Ransom said that "it is much more probable that if such offences [*sic*] were committed a half starved Mexican population was the perpetrator [rather] than the troops who always have the abundance." He maintained that his men never committed any depredations.[89]

In mid-January the civilians at Fort Union got a great scare when suddenly, as Kittie Bowen recorded, "the garrison was full of Apaches." She considered them to be "the most frightful beings the sun ever shown upon." One peeked into a window at Major Carleton's quarters and scared his four-year-old daughter so badly that "she fell backwards from the chair and went into a fit." Kittie said that "they look savage enough for cannibals"; but when she saw that their frightful faces seemed to be sunken "a foot through the cheeks," she realized that they were starving and had come to the fort only to beg for food. Kittie joined with others to feed them turkey, ham, jelly, and even cake and ice cream, and "they all enjoyed it very much."[90]

For someone who looked a little more closely, the scary savages suddenly became hungry human beings. Since Governor Lane had arrived it seemed that he had exerted a calming influence over the territory, with fewer Indian alarms, or at least was not so prone to jump at rumors and fan the flames as was Governor Calhoun. Colonel Sumner had always believed most of the trouble came not from the Indians but from scalawag New Mexicans and Americans. Of late the turmoil centered more on civilian and soldier confrontations than on Indians. The Indians occasionally raided, but the civilians sporadically killed a neighbor's cow or ran off government stock and filed depredation claims, while the soldiers continued to get drunk and visit prostitutes. One month Fort Union reported treating sixty cases of venereal disease.[91] Harlots and hooch were more harmful than Jicarillas.

A Tentative Peace, 1853

The new year started well. Sumner wrote that he had "the pleasure to report that the Indians of the Territory all continue peaceable." There had been a few "trifling thefts" but no hostile acts "for some time past."[92] With fewer Indian tocsins of late, it seemed as if the Americans needed to stir up something to keep the kettle boiling. The boundary between New Mexico Territory and Old Mexico was never exactly drawn out in the Guadalupe Hidalgo Treaty, and people of the Mesilla Valley and the area around El Paso were never certain exactly where the border was. After the Mexican War, the people living on the east bank of the Rio Grande were being harassed by Americans moving in and claiming property that had been in Spanish-Mexican families for hundreds of years. When Sumner built Fort Fillmore in the fall of 1851, speculators poured in to gobble up the nearby land. The situation was made worse when Texas began issuing "headrights," one mile square land grants to veterans who had served Texas in its wars. Disgruntled Mexicans began crossing to the west side of the Rio Grande and filling up the Mesilla Valley, believing that they were in Mexico and could no longer be bothered by the land-hungry Yankees. That move was to no avail either: as American railroaders began to see that stretch of territory as one of the best routes to build a railroad to the Pacific, the Mesilla Valley was predestined to become American territory. Manifest Destiny had a strange way of preempting the best land, roads, watercourses, and ports.[93]

Governor Calhoun, who stood with the Whigs in general, had not pressed to resolve the issue and lobby for American property rights. Governor Lane, who was less belligerent with the Indians, was more vexed at what he saw as Mexican efforts to block American progress. He wrote to his wife in February 1853: "Be not surprised if I should take possession of the disputed territory." Lane traveled south to Dona Ana and on March 13 issued a proclamation: "I, William Carr Lane, Governor of the Territory of New Mexico (upon my own official responsibility and without orders from the cabinet at Washington) do hereby, in behalf of the

United States, retake possession of the said disputed territory" until the exact boundary could be determined. The unwarranted action of a territorial governor deciding the boundary between two countries dialed up the tension. Mexican president Santa Anna ordered Gen. Ángel Trías, governor of Chihuahua, to move Mexican troops into the disputed valley and resist American attempts to take over. The American minister to Mexico, Alfred Conkling, protested Lane's action. Lane wanted to fight and asked Sumner for federal troops. Sumner knew that this was a mess he definitely needed to stay out of and refused assistance. Lane wanted arms for volunteers, but again Sumner refused. Secretary of state William L. Marcy believed that Americans had a right to the region but disapproved forceful action on Lane's part. The situation became heated enough that it appeared another war with Mexico was possible.[94]

When Democrat Franklin Pierce became president in 1852 and was inaugurated on March 4, 1853, Lane knew that his days were numbered. The spoils system meant that he was certain to be ousted. As early as December 31, 1852, Lane wrote that unless Pierce should "expressly request that I remain here," he would send in his resignation. Pierce disapproved of Lane's conduct in agitating over the Mesilla Valley, so he made no such request. American agent James Gadsden, also a railroad man, stepped in and purchased the disputed land (plus more) for $10 million. Another crisis was averted.[95]

Governor Lane was not long in office but used much of his time trying to obtain treaties with the Indians and gave them many presents to prove his goodwill. That spring he agreed to furnish some Apache tribes with food for five years and spent between twenty thousand and forty thousand dollars on the project, without Senate approval.[96]

Sumner, in the meantime, was getting flak from secretary of war Conrad about interfering with the civil government and also getting lambasted by the civilians about being too lenient with the Indians. Sumner realized that peace was not likely to be achieved through unnecessary bloodshed. He had recently chastised Major Howe for allowing Capt. William Steele, 2nd Dragoons, to attack a possibly innocent Apache camp while chasing alleged stock thieves. Steele killed and wounded several Apaches and took cattle, thirty ponies, corn, powder, and other items. Howe awarded the property to the soldiers. Sumner was incensed. "I cannot approve of your order to Capt. Steele," he wrote to Howe. "A theft does not justify the infraction of a treaty." If Mexicans had stolen animals from peaceful Indians, Sumner explained, we would not consider that a justification for the Indians to attack a town. Steele should have chased the thieves and demanded the return of the stolen animals, not kill them indiscriminately and ransack their village. Sumner was astonished. "You surely do not mean, that the cattle belonging to the Mexicans were given to them [the soldiers], if so, they will immediately be restored to the owners."[97]

Many civilians had a different view of compassion and justice. A military commander needed to prove his mettle through war, not by returning property and handing out gifts. Sumner was even blamed for the food and presents that Lane gave away. True, the Indians were quiet. But as the *Weekly Gazette* contended, it was not Sumner but the "red cloths and calico shirts" that had placated the Indians. The paper called him "The Big Bug of Albuquerque," said that "his every official act for two years . . . [was] one series of blunders and absurdities," and concluded: "He is too stupid and dishonest to acknowledge himself wrong." Sumner "held himself impassible and aloof, as a superior being, from his fellow creatures around him." He was marginally indulgent of the people, "[b]ut toleration is not friendship; nor does politeness imply confidence."[98]

The *Gazette* said that Sumner had purchased peace rather than gain peace by military triumph. The paper made a joke of Secretary Conrad's statement that "[in] New Mexico the depredations of the Indians have been *entirely* arrested." Perhaps depredations were fewer, but how have the Indians been overawed? "In what bloody contest, with loss of how many of their braves, with what and how many scourgings, at the hands of the American forces, within the last year, has this 'complete overawing' been affected?" Maybe it was so in a War Department bulletin, but not in the territory. The overawing there "has consisted in a meagre donation of beef, bread, blankets, brass kettles, and tobacco."[99]

Sumner was at the exploding point. Did these constantly carping civilians only want peace when it was written in letters of blood? Sumner was convinced that the civilians were the cause of almost every problem; but if they wanted war, very well. On May 3 a Navajo killed Ramón Martín at his grazing camp south of Abiquiu. Sumner scrambled his soldiers in pursuit, and Lane sent Donaciano Vigil to demand that the chiefs surrender the murderer. Astonishingly, Lane told Vigil to tell the Indians that "failure, on the part of the tribe, to comply with these demands, will be considered a justifiable cause of war." Sumner was in full agreement and wrote to Lane that "the murderers must be given up, or a war will be commenced against the whole tribe."[100]

Americans censured Indians because they reportedly took vengeance on innocent people, but now the governor and department commander had just threatened to make war on an entire tribe because of a single crime. Águila Negra went to Santa Fe and begged Vigil and Lane to reconsider, because capturing the guilty man would result in war among his own people. They would not budge. The man must be delivered by July 1 or soldiers would invade. In the meantime Lieutenant Ransom was sent from Cantonment Burgwin to Abiquiu with forty dragoons to "overawe" the Indians and, if any raiders were found, to "pursue them and demand the instant surrender of the depredators and the chiefs of the party." He also received notice that if demands were not met "hostilities would be commenced against them and their country laid waste."[101]

The governor and the department commander met in Santa Fe on June 1 to decide on a course of action. Lane may have had kinder feelings toward the Mexicans than did Calhoun, but he was becoming a hard-liner toward the Indians. If they did not comply, the army would begin "hostilities against the whole of the Navajo tribe, by either laying waste their country, taking hostages, or destroying the whole race." Lane added that if Sumner did not do it, "he would do it himself." Before they crossed the point of no return, thankfully, Sumner had second thoughts "and questioned the propriety of holding the whole Navajo tribe responsible for the act of . . . ungovernable Indians," which "seemed an unjust and almost unjustifiable undertaking."[102]

Sumner saw the wisdom in caution but felt trapped. Certainly he was bothered by the howls from the people and press about his conciliatory attitude. On June 6 he issued orders for the campaign, mobilizing seven companies of infantry, dragoons, and artillery to converge on Navajo country. In keeping with his belief that horses would easily break down, the dragoons were to "walk and lead their horses" on the expedition.[103]

All the while, the colonel could not shake his conviction that most of the problems stemmed from New Mexicans and Americans. He was getting burned out, just like Governor Calhoun. Back in December 1852 he had requested to be relieved of departmental command by the summer of 1853 and if that was impossible to be given a leave of absence beginning in June; but approval was slow in coming. Then a possible way out of the war dilemma appeared. Navajos had spoken to Captain Kendrick and convinced him that the men responsible for killing Martin had left the tribe and had gone to live with the Utes. Also, Navajos who had taken no part in the killing contributed 433 sheep and 4 horses in reparations. Maybe there was no need to destroy the entire tribe.[104]

While Sumner and Lane contemplated wiping out the Navajos, agent Michael Steck had concluded a successful deal with the Jicarillas that the military and civilian officials had been trying to make for years. Steck went to meet the Ollero

Chief Chacón. Believing that he "expressed a willingness to attempt the cultivation of the soil," Steck convinced Chacón to move his people out of the Sangre de
Cristo. They went west of the Rio Grande and selected a suitable site on the Rio
Puerco twenty miles west of Abiquiu, with tillable soil, good grazing, and plentiful
water and timber. It was a good spot not claimed by either Utes or Navajos. The
first twenty-seven lodges of Chacón's people moved there in March and began
clearing the land and planting a hundred acres in corn, wheat, pumpkin, squash,
and melons. Steck believed that those who were still not convinced to move
would see their fellows prospering and would soon join them. He said it was
imperative that the Indians had clear title to the land so that they would not be
"hereafter disturbed by settlers," particularly after they harvested their crops,
for inevitably Americans or New Mexicans would be among them and "they
would waste or allow themselves to be swindled out of it in a single month."[105]

Relations with the Jicarillas appeared to be improving, if only the Americans and New Mexicans would leave them alone. Down at Fort Webster, agent
Edward Wingfield reached the same conclusion. The Apaches in his vicinity were
falling "under all the corrupting influences of Traders and other ill-disposed
persons." Since the incident at San Antonio when a Mexican shot three of their
people they had rarely come near an agency. Wingfield managed to convince
Chiefs Ponce and Negrito to bring their people to Fort Webster in February,
but the agent was shocked at their appearance: "I have never seen such squalid
wretchedness as was exhibited by these people on their first appearance at the
post. They were so long the victims of heartless and corrupt traders that they
were literally stripped of everything; men, women and children, almost in a
state of nudity without any means whatever of subsistence." Wingfield fed and
supplied them and wrote to Governor Lane that the present laws did not seem to
be working. The Trade and Intercourse Act, he said, is "altogether inapplicable
to the state of things in New Mexico." They had to stop making treaties that
were immediately broken by one side or the other and "adopt a kind and liberal
policy towards the Indians."[106]

Wingfield had only taken the job in December 1852, but by May he told
Lane "I can't think of holding office longer than the 30th of December." The job
drained him. He saw every other branch of service being supported by adequate
money and supplies, but with "the meagre appropriations for this Territory, it
looks as though New Mexico was considered a sort of excrescence or cancer on
the body politic." Treat the Apaches kindly and provide them with food and
you will have peace, he told Lane. Neglect them and you might as well abolish

all the agencies, for "as soon as we discontinue giving these Indians rations, hostilities will commence."[107]

A few days later Mangas Coloradas brought in his people to talk. Wingfield found them proud, well mannered, and civilized. It was true that they had robbed the Mexicans, but "the Mexicans have been pursuing the same game towards them." Wingfield said that he could detail one hundred examples of Indian amiability and good character "and a nice discrimination of right and wrong as exhibited by the Apaches that would put to the blush the conduct of many who have been raised under the teachings of the Decalogue and Christ's Sermon on the Mount."[108]

The Jicarillas and other Apaches were behaving. A number of civilian and military officials understood that they were not the major obstruction to peace. Even the war talk that flared up so quickly against the Navajos faded away, especially when Colonel Sumner's leave of absence was approved and Lane was supplanted by a new governor. The two replacements were on their way. In a hurry to get out, Sumner left Santa Fe on June 30. The next day, instead of beginning a war of extermination against the Navajos, departmental command was transferred to Lt. Col. Dixon Miles—he could figure out what to do. As Sumner passed Fort Union, his pet fort that had seen so much trouble, the few people who noted his passing were not sad. Kittie Bowen simply wrote that they "moved into the parched and yellow country . . . they will have a warm time, but will have home at the end of the journey to reward them."[109]

Edwin Sumner was gone and William Lane would be gone. The Pierce presidency meant that new officials would take over. After Lane resigned, he desired to represent New Mexico as a congressional candidate in Washington. As he campaigned in the Mora and Las Vegas area, he knew he would meet resistance. On August 30 he wrote to his wife: "I am thus far, upon an Electioneering tour, and I am in a Rabidly infected District. In point of fact, the opposition, to everything American, is so uncompromising that if this country should turn the scale against me, you must not be surprised." As he surmised, he was beaten by José Manuel Gallegos by about 500 votes. He contested the election because the Indian ballots were not counted, but Congress decided that the Indians did not have the right to vote. Lane dejectedly went to Washington to settle his accounts before going home to St. Louis. To his wife, Mary, he wrote: "I cannot say these 10 months have been happy."[110]

In March 1853 George W. Manypenny replaced Luke Lea as commissioner of Indian Affairs and Jefferson Davis replaced Charles Conrad as secretary of war. David Meriwether would be the new governor and Brevet Brig. Gen. John Garland would be the new department commander. When General Garland made his first public comments at Meriwether's inaugural ceremony on August 8, 1853, the *Gazette* commented: "It was gratifying to behold for the first time in this territory that mutual respect which should have always prevailed between the civil and military authorities."[111]

"Now My Troubles and Vexations Commenced"

The script was similar. Another governor took the oath of office. This time it was Virginia-born David Meriwether, who lived most of his fifty-three years in Kentucky, where he spent much time in the Kentucky General Assembly. In 1852 he was appointed United States senator to fill the vacancy caused by the death of Henry Clay, and the next year President Pierce appointed him governor of New Mexico Territory. Meriwether had been there before. As a nineteen-year-old trader he and a few others had been captured in 1820 while scouting a trade route to Santa Fe and imprisoned for a month in the dungeon attached to the Palace of Governors. Thirty-four years later, when Pierce asked Meriwether how soon he could leave for New Mexico, Meriwether said: "In five days." Pierce asked him how he could prepare so quickly. Meriwether answered that on his last visit the Mexicans robbed him of all his baggage and this time he would travel lighter.[112]

Meriwether may have been able to travel fast, but he was bogged down in Kansas waiting for everyone else involved in the regime change. He had secured the appointment of his son-in-law, Capt. Edward A. Graves, as a new Indian agent. They were also joined by another new agent, James M. Smith. The new chief justice of the territory, James J. Davenport, joined them, as did Capt. John W. Gunnison, with a party of surveyors and explorers bound for Utah. General Garland and his staff linked up at Council Grove, as did Col. Joseph K. H. Mansfield, going out to make an assessment of New Mexico for the inspector general. Maj. Electus Backus, 3rd Infantry, was bringing 212 new recruits. The large, slow caravan lumbered across the plains, giving time for Garland and Meriwether to become friends. Tradition has it that at the very moment of Meriwether's arrival in Santa Fe on August 8 the roof of the cell where he had been held thirty-four years earlier collapsed. This was supposedly taken as a good omen.[113]

Meriwether gave his short inaugural address on the plaza, interrupted after every sentence as territorial secretary William S. Messervy translated it into Spanish. Meriwether claimed that no discrimination would be practiced during his term: "The elevated and the lowly, the rich and the poor, the native-born citizen and the immigrant . . . are all alike entitled to the protection of the laws, and must be held answerable to their behests." To facilitate progress there had to be "a united and harmonious action on the part of the several departments of the territorial government, as well as the military power of the general government." Above all they needed the support of the community. At the feast held after the ceremony ex-governor Lane joined Meriwether, Garland, Davenport, and many others in numerous toasts to the civil, military, and judiciary, "to show that the three powers of the State would be a unit in order to protect 'the life, liberty, and happiness' of the people of the Territory."[114]

"Now my troubles and vexations commenced," Meriwether wrote in his auto-biography. Almost immediately he began finding fault with ex-governor Lane's policies, writing to Manypenny that Lane spent way too much money, leaving him with little to work with, and claiming that the territory "will be in a sad condition ere long." The Indians have been surviving "by the chase and by depredations upon the neighboring white settlements." Governor Lane had curtailed some of the raids by feeding them, but without more funds their rations would be cut off and they would again "either starve or subsist themselves by depredations."[115]

In addition, Meriwether had two new agents who "had probably never seen a wild Indian in their lives." Henry Dodge replaced Spruce Baird for the Navajos, and the two new agents argued over who would get the agency closest to the seat of government. Meriwether ended up assigning Graves to Abiquiu with the Utes, while Smith went to the Apaches at Fort Webster to replace Wingfield, who could not stomach the job even until December as he had hoped. Even so, Meriwether had no funds for their traveling expenses. He also approached Lane about the excess spending down at Fort Webster, but Lane defended Wingfield, saying that he might have spent more than was authorized, but "the amount of good" attained by the extra food "must not be forgotten."[116]

As usual, the incoming officials were regaled by the ubiquitous tales of dep-redating Indians. Earlier in the year James L. Collins, publisher of the *Gazette*, probably gave the truest assessment of the situation that could be printed without civilian protest: "Within the last year, the depredations of the Indians have not been frequent, nor of great value, it is true; but it is not true that they have been 'entirely arrested.'"[117]

John Ward continued to keep his journal as secretary to the superintendent, and it was replete with the same routine matters that he and Greiner had recorded before. In January 1853 came reports of hungry Jicarillas and Mescaleros at Anton Chico and many Indians who came in to see Lane and were given gifts of hoes, axes, and sickles. In February San Felipe Pueblos complained about Mexicans using their land without permission, while San Domingo Pueblos told Lane that the Mexicans were causing them trouble. In May four Cochiti Pueblos asked that authorities in the Mora–Las Vegas area assist them in their search for stolen stock, which they suspected were at Barclay's Fort. That same month San Ildefonso Pueblos arrived in Santa Fe to complain about the Mexicans forever grazing stock in their fields. On May 25 agent Steck learned that Mexicans had been among the Jicarillas in Rio Arriba country, spreading tales that smallpox was ravaging the area in order to chase them from the land and take over their fields. In early June the latest rumor in Santa Fe was that Navajos had just killed the preacher John Shaw and new agent, Henry L. Dodge, and that the tribe was about to unite with the Utes to form a league against the whites. It took nearly two weeks to learn that the men had not been killed and there was no tribal conspiracy. In June Steck reported that the Jicarillas and Utes were peaceful and the Utes had 150 acres under cultivation. In July special agent Lafayette Head reported that all was quiet at Abiquiu and Chacón's band was doing very well.[118]

The Indians were peaceful and common sense dictated that an entire tribe should not be punished for the act of one man, so the planned Navajo campaign rightfully died of entropy. Lieutenant Colonel Miles, left in command after Sumner's departure and once described by Lane as "a walking sponge" and martinet, had no heart for another fruitless chase. Garland later wrote to head-quarters, noting that "Col. Sumner, my predecessor, embarrassed me not a little, by placing an order on the books of the Department for a campaign against the Navajoes [*sic*] which he had not the means of carrying out, and in this state of things left the Department." To comply, Miles simply gave Captain Kendrick and Lieutenant Ransom orders to make a cursory ride into Navajo country, explore, and intimidate them "so that the Navajoes may believe we are in earnest in what we tell them." They were to round up stolen stock if they found any, "but in a gentle way," and remember to "treat all friendly."[119]

The campaign was a goodwill excursion to placate civilian complaints of army inaction. Its duty done, the military enjoyed another term of comparatively peaceful inactivity. But civilians kept moaning about marauding Indians, filing at least forty depredation claims in 1853. While claims against the Navajos dropped to only six (one of which elicited army action because it involved a murder), claims against the various Apache bands climbed to thirty-three. They did not provoke military response, probably because the claims were more of the usual *humo y niebla* and the army was tired of tilting at windmills.

Only in the territory a few weeks, Governor Meriwether nevertheless wrote a report that contained many of the same horror stories that Calhoun had spread. He said that "scarcely a day passes over without the commission of some theft, robbery, or murder," which could likely be said of any community in any year. Meriwether claimed that people were afraid to travel without armed escort and that sheep were constantly stolen, with the civilians chasing the robbers and only making the situation "worse than useless." These reports, said Meriwether, came from the "best informed portion of our citizens, and the well-authenticated complaints filed in this office; and if the picture is not reversed soon, a vast amount of claims against the government will have accumulated."[120]

Meriwether mouthed the same sentiment as his predecessors: "the government must either feed and clothe these Indians to a certain extent, or chastise them in a decisive manner." Ex-governor Lane, he said, thought that the feed and clothe solution would work, but it only served to spread disaffection among the tribes who are not included in the largesse. Meriwether believed the feeding program could cost up to $100,000 per year, an exorbitant sum, but it would only seem like a bribe to the Indians, because "every act of kindness and every concession on our part" serves only to make them think we are afraid of them. Meriwether did not like Lane's moving the Jicarillas west of the Rio Grande and feeding them while they were growing their crops because he thought that it would curtail sincere efforts at farming: when the contract ended and rations were cut off they would return to raiding. Meriwether proposed gradually cutting the rations, apparently believing that slow suffocation was better than a quick garroting. The governor said that he had only four agents, not enough to control fifty thousand Indians. He also made the somewhat puzzling remark that the farther removed from white civilization a tribe was, the better behaved it was, in particular the Navajos, who "rarely engage in predatory excursions within the white settlements."[121]

The Navajos were "rarely" raiding, and agent Graves said the Utes and Jicarillas were "on good terms." The Jicarillas were farming peaceably on the Rio Puerco and were "quiet and well disposed." Still, Graves found fault with the Trade and Intercourse Act. Depredation remuneration was too complicated: an agent has to investigate the claim; he reports to the superintendent, who investigates the claim; he determines that the Indians should be chastised and reports to the military; the military has the option whether to comply or not but often does nothing. Graves believed that having two authorities meant that there would be no action: "the Indians go scot free and the citizen obtains no redress." He thought that the entire process ought to be turned over to the army. The army had to take responsibility, because the citizens were denied the right "to retaliate upon the Indians." It was a matter of Mosaic Law, Graves said: "an eye for an eye, and a tooth for a tooth." Although Graves admitted that "the Mexicans are continually making encroachments" upon the Indians, he could not fathom the idea that the Indians also needed redress. Sharing many of the biases of the day, Graves wanted decisive action "not because of any unkind feelings I entertain towards the red man of the mountain; but, on the contrary, he has my profound sympathy on account of his savage and degraded condition. It is his acts of cruelty and inhumanity that I condemn, and for which I would have him punished."[122]

Many minorities have suffered from an overabundance of good intentions. Graves wanted army action, as did Meriwether. The governor's bellicosity was shown in an incident that developed shortly after his arrival when he made a political speech to a number of voters, extolling the virtues of the Democratic Party over the Whigs. Where the Whigs wanted a loose interpretation of the Constitution, the Democrats were strict constructionists; where the Whigs were in favor of excluding slavery from the territories, the Democrats wanted to allow slaveholders and nonslaveholders in while letting the voters decide the question of slavery. It was apparently lost on Meriwether that this probably would not favorably illuminate the Democratic ticket in a place that had abolished slavery in 1823. The next morning Meriwether's black servant "Wash" came to his room to inform him: "They have done hung you and Judge Davenport" on the plaza flagstaff. Meriwether investigated and saw effigies of the two men, stuffed with straw and hanging by the neck, with name placards on them. "Judge," Meriwether said to Davenport, "I wouldn't mind this thing, for I have no doubt in less than a year, you will have an opportunity of pronouncing sentence of death against its authors, and I will have the satisfaction of ordering their execution in reality. They can hang suits of clothes stuffed with straw, but you and I can cause them to be hung in reality."[123]

Execution for making straw men? The governor, his agents, and judges were out for blood. What was the military attitude?

Born in Virginia in 1792, and with a long army career beginning as a lieutenant in the War of 1812, John Garland had slowly risen in the ranks. He became colonel of the 8th Infantry in 1849, was brevetted brigadier general for his Mexican War service, and was always referred to as General Garland while serving as commander in New Mexico. When he reached Fort Union, he learned that

Alex Barclay had filed a suit against the government for trespass and realized that they might be ejected at any time. Garland ordered that all further building construction cease, decided that the post was "entirely out of position for a depot," and began to remove its stores to Albuquerque. Thus Sumner's plan for a large central headquarters away from the towns further deteriorated.[124]

Garland had hardly moved in when the locals began testing his resolve to chase Indians. Word arrived that merchant Peter Joseph had sent employee Pedro Barella to bring in his cattle that were grazing near Mora Creek. Barella, said to be "a reliable and trustworthy man," reported that four Utes robbed him of his horse, saddle, bridle, and provisions and spared his life only so he could relay the news that the Utes were forming "a plan to conduct a war against the Americans." They did not fear the Americans, who were "a set of deceitful rascals," and if the Mexicans did not keep out of the fight they would give them hell as well. Edward Graves said he talked with some Ute chiefs who admitted that four men had robbed Barella, but it was against their wishes and they did not know where the thieves were. If they could catch them they would punish them and return the property. A few days later Graves got a secondhand report that in mid-August Utes had taken five or six horses from a Mexican hunting party. He wrote: "There seems to be but little room to doubt, that the Utahs intend both robbery and murder against our citizens" and will likely continue so "until they are made to feel and know the power of the government." Several days later Meriwether wrote to Garland of "several depredations" and the great danger of a "serious outbreak" by the Utes.[125]

Garland was skeptical and wanted more evidence. He still hoped for a peaceful settlement, but it was difficult when some of his subordinates had the attitude of Major Carleton. When Utes were accused of stealing one government horse five miles from Fort Union, Carleton was furious and exclaimed: "Had I caught or killed these Indians, dead or alive I should have hung them upon the trees at the point where they stampeded the horses."[126]

Executions for stampeding horses was about as bad as executions for making an effigy. Word of these incidents quickly spread, and Major Blake at Fort Massachusetts and Lieutenant Ransom at Cantonment Burgwin were ordered to be on the alert for further depredators. If they were found, the officers were to "demand immediate restitution."[127]

In September Jicarillas visiting at Fort Union were accused of killing rancher Juan Silva and stealing his cattle. About the same time, these thieves or others reportedly stole twenty-two of the best government animals grazing near the

Ocate River. Capt. Nathaniel C. Macrae, 3rd Infantry, at Fort Union stated: "When I first heard of the Indian theft, I was rather incredulous," but he sent men to investigate. There were also about five hundred Comanches and Kiowas in the vicinity, so it was uncertain who the thieves might be. Kiowas were involved, but not as first believed. Utes had originally taken some stock and headed north, but Kiowas intercepted them and took all but four or five animals. The Utes who escaped made it to Abiquiu but were stopped by their own people and forced to return the animals to the agency.[128]

Certainly some stock thefts occurred, but the uproar was way out of proportion. In Meriwether's autobiography he makes no mention of any Indian depredations during the entire fall of 1853 and winter of 1854. He did succeed in recovering two Mexican children held by the Indians and per the Guadalupe Hidalgo Treaty sent them to the governor of Chihuahua at El Paso. He was also involved in the rescue of Jane Wilson, a white woman captured by the Comanches in Texas in late September 1853. With her husband and several family members killed, Jane and two young brothers-in-law were taken to the wilds of the Texas Panhandle. Jane escaped and was lost until discovered by New Mexican Comancheros. They took her to Pecos, where she met Major Carleton and received women's clothing from the army wives at Fort Union. The governor's son, Raymond Meriwether, escorted her to Santa Fe, where they arrived on December 3. The governor said: "On her arrival she presented the most pitiful spectacle I had ever seen. She was in rags, emaciated, and her mind was somewhat disordered." Meriwether wrote to Texas governor Elisha M. Pease, telling him that Jane Wilson had been recovered. He had paid the Comancheros forty dollars for her and spent about three hundred dollars for her care. With Pease's help, Jane was finally sent home in the spring of 1854. The "inhuman murders and robberies" hardened Meriwether, who hoped that they "may induce the government to adopt a more stringent policy towards the Indians of this country."[129]

Meriwether and Garland actually had more problems with Americans and New Mexicans than with Indians, and both still complained about the state of affairs left by the previous administration. In October Garland complained of Sumner: "It is never considered in good taste to attack one's predecessor, but I am forced to do it, else, the odium of bad management, extravagant expenditures, &c &c will fall upon me, however much my course may be blameless." Although Sumner "is an old friend," he had to say that "he has left the Department in an impoverished and crippled condition, wanting in many of the essentials for undertaking a successful enterprise." All of Sumner's efforts had failed, "his economy run into parsimony, the result of which, was the loss of a vast number of horses and mules." Garland would have to spend much more to build up the depleted stores, ordinance, granaries, wagons, and mules. Many dragoons had no horses. He would have to withdraw most of the garrison at Fort Massachusetts for the winter in order to feed them in Taos. The Navajos were peaceful, however, and the chiefs had made restitution for the few stock thefts.[130]

Sumner's farming program was a failure. Favored by secretary of war Conrad, it was essentially dumped by new secretary of war Davis, a military academy graduate, and President Pierce, a Mexican War veteran. Inspector Mansfield believed that it was a flop, and Gen. Winfield Scott was against it. Garland wrote: "The attempt to cultivate farms at the several military posts in New Mexico with one inconsiderable exception proved a failure." He recommended that "all further farming operations in this department be discontinued" and that all the equipment be sold to pay off other debts. An accounting showed that dispersion of the posts to the frontiers made transportation costs rise. Garland transferred the commissary, medical, and quartermaster stores back to Albuquerque. The next summer, however, he called Albuquerque "the dirtiest hole in New Mexico" and transferred his command to Santa Fe. The people in the towns centered along the Rio Grande were happy, as business picked up again. Of Sumner's nine new posts only two stayed active for more than a decade; even Fort Union was to have been abandoned in 1860 but was saved by the Civil War. Almost all of Sumner's measures enacted over the past few years were being undone.[131]

Where Garland complained about Sumner's parsimony, Meriwether blamed Governor Lane for extravagance. In November he stated: "The lavish expenditure of the public money made by my predecessor has caused the Indians of this Territory to expect much assistance from me whilst it has deprived me of the ability of assist them even to a very limited amount." Being unable to supply the Indians or comply "with the promises made by Governor Lane many depredations have been committed and I fear that many more will be committed before this reaches you." Unless the governor got more funds and supplies, the commissioner "may expect to hear of depredations and murder and consequently large claims against the government."[132]

Meanwhile the civilians constantly caused trouble. A number of people around Taos claimed to hold a land grant in the San Luis Valley and planned to begin a settlement, which Meriwether said was certain to result in "a serious collision" with the Utes. Also, because of the Territorial Court ruling earlier in the year declaring there was no "Indian Country" in New Mexico, whiskey sellers would no longer be restricted, making "the intercourse laws . . . inoperative." They always sold to the Pueblos, who were not considered part of "Indian Country," and now they could sell to the "wild" Indians. Agent Graves figured that the Trade and Intercourse Act "becomes a dead letter to all intents." He cited an incident in October, when a Jicarilla band under Subchief Tranchaya (Tanchua?) came to Mora and freely purchased liquor, after which a melee broke out and Tranchaya was killed. His son went to Graves and asked "to have vengeance inflicted upon the Mexicans in order to appease the death of his father." Graves said that drunken brawls would increase with the nullification of the Intercourse Act. It would inevitably result in the "bequeathment of an Indian war."[133]

Much of the theft and killing was preventable if only the Indians were not molested. Chief Cuentas Azules had visited Fort Fillmore at Major Backus's request. After an agreement to "live on amicable terms," Azules was on his way home when Mexicans from Mesilla attacked his party near Dona Ana on November 3. In Backus's words, Azules was "inveigled from his camp in the night, by men who had followed him the day previous, and his brains were beaten out with a club." The other Mescaleros fled but "threaten to be avenged on all Mexicans." Even so, some of Azules's band said they would give white people's justice a chance and wait to have the murderers apprehended and tried. Unfortunately, the citizens of Mesilla Valley, on the Mexican side of the Rio Grande, would not permit the marshal to make an arrest. When the Apaches learned that the Mexicans would not surrender the guilty men, "they left with threats of vengeance against all Mexicans." Governor Meriwether predicted more Indian depredations as a result, followed by more claims for compensation against the government. Major Backus saw the irony of the situation: the 11th article of the Guadalupe Hidalgo Treaty said that the United States guaranteed to protect the Mexicans from Indian incursions, but he believed that the treaty was annulled and abrogated by the Mexican attacks. Who was to protect the Indians from the Mexicans?[134]

Such instances were generally the case—more scare than substance. Eleven incidents of theft were alleged to have occurred between September and December 1853 inclusive, but none of these were filed during those months. They were filed from six months to eighteen months later, so Meriwether would not have known about them as he wrote his last letter of the year to the commissioner; he was simply infected by the territory's embellishment epidemic.[135]

Meriwether opened his missive with the old complaint that his precursor had spent too much money on the Indians. When he could not continue, they became dissatisfied and begged for food, "which I had not the means of affording," so some of the Indians might have "visited their white neighbors and helped them-selves." Perplexingly, in the very next sentence Meriwether stated: "In no recent instance so far as I am informed, have these Indians committed depredations to a very large amount." Who, then, was doing the daily depredating: Mexicans and Americans? Or was the occasional theft of a cow not really a transgression worthy of the label "depredation," but only more smoke and fog? Meriwether was buried by complaints, but the amounts hardly ever amounted to a hundred dollars, "and this would not more than pay some lawyer to prepare their claim." People asked him how long it would take to receive payment. When Meriwether said a year or two, they asked how they were supposed to feed their families in the meantime. Having no satisfactory answer, Meriwether asked Manypenny if Congress would allow him money so that he could settle and pay the claims. In conclusion, Meriwether called the depredations "petty" and said that they were confined to the bands that "Gov. Lane had been feeding during the last summer." Contradictorily, again, he asserted that the "large portion" of the Indians "appear to be peaceably disposed at this time."[136]

The *Gazette* voiced similar criticisms: "We hear almost daily, that the Indians are either committing depredations upon the whites, or are threatening to do so." The Utes were complaining that they did not receive as many presents as the other tribes. "This is the result of the ruinous policy of Gov. Lane," who "made them promises for the future which he ought to have known could not be fulfilled."[137]

Provoked by these constant attacks, Lane protested: "Old Merriwether has been writing, secretly and openly, gross libels against an ex-Indn. Agent [Wingfield] and indirectly attempting to implicate me." Lane also wrote to Manypenny in January 1854, stating that the commissioner knew why he had spent the money: to feed the Indians and keep the peace—and it had worked. He said that the department had no cause for complaint regarding expenditures because the guns he denied the Indians were commensurate with the cost of the rations he gave them. "The Indians made a peace, and as long as I remained in the country," they safeguarded the lives and property of our people, giving them "an immunity which had not been before enjoyed by our citizens, since the annexation of N. Mexico to the United States."[138]

Lane had a point. By the end of 1853 Indian depredation claims were decreas-ing. The previous high for claims filed was in 1847, when troop strength was at its highest and there was no Indian "war" in progress. Some fighting took place in 1848 and 1849, but depredation claims dropped as troop strength dropped. In 1851 Sumner arrived with more soldiers; there was no war; the posts were moved away from the towns; civilian-army contracts were cut; the people were unhappy; and depredation claims increased to a new high. As troop strength dropped in 1852 and 1853, depredation claims dropped. When Garland arrived and disassembled Sumner's programs, moving troops back to the cities and appeasing many, claims dropped even more. Claims continued to fall even during the war years of 1854 and 1855. What was happening? It was as if the claims filing process operated independently of the raiding and fighting, almost in an inverse proportion—more warfare seemed to result in fewer claims, while more claims were filed during times of peace. Additionally, we have the direct proportion puzzle of more troop strength resulting in more warfare. In any event, one contention in this study is that enough false cries of "wolf" would inevitably lead to war. Reports of raiding had caused numerous retaliatory excursions, but a skeptical military usually questioned the alarms and restrained civilian demands for harsh action against Indians who were very often innocent of the charges leveled against them. By 1854, with civilian and military administrations buttressing each other, it might only take one key false depredation claim to set off a series of events that could lead to war.

5

"The Long Wished for Crisis Is on Us"

In early January 1854 an agitated citizen came to see Judge José Gabriel Rivera in San Miguel. José Salazar told him that he and several others were with a small wagon train belonging to Pedro Gonzales on a trip to the eastern plains to hunt buffalo. On the Ocate River they joined another party of hunters from Tecolote and headed to the vicinity of Rabbit Ears Creek. Some of the hunters chased a small party of Indians there on December 22, killing one Mexican and two Indians. The remaining hunters, concerned about reprisals, abandoned their wagons and rode back to report the "attack."[1]

Judge Francisco López at Las Vegas received the news from one of the hunters, Manuel Gallegos, who added that when he returned to their campsite he found the burned body of a dead man. López ordered the coroner and six men to investigate. They found two more bodies nearby, said to be "two Americans known to have gone hunting." In quick succession, Jesús Gallegos reported that Jicarillas "had taken 27 Beeves from his Rancho," and two shepherds said that "the Indians had carried off all the sheep and 67 head of cattle" from Pablo Martín's ranch. On January 8, Damacio Salazar approached Judge López and asked for assistance in recovering the body of his brother, Luis, who was one of the hunters killed near Rabbit Ears Creek. Efforts to round up a posse failed, because "those who were called upon clearly declared that they would not give their services without pay." López reported the standard litany to Governor Meriwether: "I beg that your Excellency will provide means by which we may be protected, because if it is not done, this frontier will be inevitably ruined."[2]

Meriwether passed the news to Garland, who had doubts but ordered Major Blake at Cantonment Burgwin and Lt. Col. Philip St. George Cooke at Fort Union to investigate and punish the delinquents. The order came with a caveat, however, for Garland called "your Excellency's attention to the fact . . . that large armed parties of New Mexicans are in the habit of going into the Indian Country . . . where they kill off the very game upon which the Indians depend for subsistence." As a result the Indians would starve to death or, more likely, kill the hunters or commit depredations in the settlements.[3]

Garland gave more specifics to Cooke. The lieutenant colonel, now in the 2nd Dragoons and in command at Fort Union, had been in the army many years. Born in 1809, a graduate of the Military Academy and a career officer, Cooke had been traveling the West for decades, was with Kearny's Army in 1846, and led the Mormon Battalion to California. He was not about to chase after every red flag. Garland told him to escort the people of San Miguel to help them recover their wagons and goods. Cooke was also to go to Las Vegas and gather "correct information" on the two Americans said to have been killed in the vicinity of the attack on the buffalo hunters and determine the amount of property stolen.[4]

Cooke detailed Lt. Joseph E. Maxwell, 3rd Infantry, to investigate the "alleged depredations—which were never reported to me" and give notice to the hunt- ers, "who were probably intruders on Indian lands," that he wanted to know everything that transpired. James Giddings visited Cooke and related what he had learned. When Maxwell returned, they compared notes. The story was quite different from the one that the New Mexicans told. Cooke reported to Garland that Pedro Gonzales and the hunters often illegally traded with the Indians on Rabbit Ears Creek, more than sixty miles into Indian country. Two Americans were involved. The hunters' story was that Indians had taken several animals, a fight began, the hunters killed two Indians, and the Indians killed the two Americans, plus Luis Salazar. A third Indian was wounded and escaped but actually returned the animals that had been run off. Cooke, Giddings, and Maxwell learned that it was not Indians but the New Mexicans who had killed the two Americans during the fracas. Frightened, the Indians took what property they could and hurried back home.[5]

Cooke reported that "one of the Mexican murderers of the two white men whose bodies were found had been apprehended but let off on some trifling testimony of his relatives." In addition, he said that no one had lost any sheep. The Mexicans had not stayed west of the Canadian River where they belonged but intruded as far east as the Arkansas River, and "the white men were murdered by New Mexicans who are not punished." Cooke concluded: "It appears as the result of this investigation, that the complaints made to the governor, had but little color of truth."[6]

It was no surprise. The army had been learning this for the past six years: many of the civilians were lying. On the day Cooke reported the results of his investigation, Meriwether wrote to Manypenny that the depredations continued "with no diminution in the commission of such outrages." Yet he resumed his baffling inconsistencies, stating that "the main body of the Indians appear peaceably disposed."[7]

Sam Watrous and Lieutenant Bell Start a War

The scene was set for the next complaint, this one coming in early February from Sam Watrous. Watrous, previously accused of selling liquor to the Indians and to the soldiers at Fort Union, had complained of depredations before. In March 1851 his allegations of livestock theft had resulted in an army investigation that found his claim to be fraudulent—Lieutenant Adams proved to Watrous that his statements were untrue, and Colonel Munroe believed that Watrous wanted only to file a claim on the government. But he was at it again.

On February 12 Watrous reported to Cooke at Fort Union that Jicarillas had robbed him "of several of his cattle which were herded about 60 miles from this post." Given that Cooke had recently investigated the New Mexican complaints and found them almost entirely contrived, as well as Garland's realization that a great majority of these civilian complaints were bogus, Cooke's reaction seems odd. Perhaps he was unaware of Watrous's history or put more trust in "American" grievances than he did in New Mexican grievances. Or maybe it was because Watrous then held the beef contract to supply Fort Union. But in any event Cooke ordered Lt. David Bell, Company H, 2nd Dragoons, to the Canadian River to find the Indians who had "committed depredations, robbing Mr. Waters [Watrous] of cattle and maltreating his herdsmen." Cooke ordered Bell to surround the thieves, prevent their retreat, "demand the surrender of the actual marauders," and, if they were delivered, "have them severely whipped." Bell was to take a pony for Watrous as an indemnity. If the Indians would not deliver the guilty party, Bell was to "keep the chief in your power" and seize horses or ponies "double the amount in value of the stolen animals." If the Indians resisted, were insolent, or fled, Bell was to attack them.[8]

Bell could not find any Indians. They found a spot where it looked like some cattle had been killed and returned to the post. Unsatisfied, Cooke ordered Bell to try again. This time he was to get a better guide, take fifteen days of rations, cross the Canadian, and scout downriver as far as Cinto Mountain (La Cinta Mesa near present-day Conchas), which was about seventy miles southeast of the fort and much farther by trail. Cooke told Bell that "[r]epeated small depredations & insults to straggling citizens are reported—besides the robbery of Mr. Waters, which occasioned your last march, & which you did not succeed in settling with the Indians."[9]

Bell understood. He would have to catch and punish some Indians—any Indians. He left the fort on March 2 with thirty-five dragoons, accompanied by 3rd Infantry lieutenants George Sykes and Joseph Maxwell. The first night they camped near Wagon Mound. The next day they crossed the Canadian and turned southeast, roughly paralleling the river. The evening of March 4, after a twenty-two mile march, they found a good campsite. When a man accidentally shot himself in the thigh, Bell detached a wagon, a litter, and several men to accompany him back to the fort. On March 5 they continued southeast, crossing a series of arroyos that ran from the east to west, becoming increasingly deep and impassable as they approached the Canadian. About ten in the morning they found the remains of an old Indian camp. The guide picked up a fresh trail of about seven horses and mules, and Bell ordered them to pick up the pace. About one mile farther along they spotted several mounted Indians across a ravine "flying from pursuit."[10]

After crossing the ravine and ascending the next ridge, they saw a lone Indian watching them from a half-mile away. "We gave chase," said Bell. Several men cut the Indian off and caught him. He was "trembling violently and professing the most profound friendship for us" and said that his people were nearby. Within minutes a band of mounted warriors rounded a point of woods less than a mile away. Bell left the prisoner with a guard and galloped toward them. The warriors approached, and the two forces halted about 150 yards apart. The leader made "a series of most eccentric movements" on his horse, while beating his shield "and uttering hideous yells." Bell called out to him in Spanish that they had not come to fight but "to talk and be friends." The Indians approached and shook hands, apologizing that when they first saw the soldiers they "mistook us for Comanches."[11]

The speaker, whom Bell called the "orator," asked why the soldiers had taken one of their people prisoner. Bell said that he needed a guide, but the prisoner was freed because that was no longer necessary. Bell, apparently not knowing who he was looking for, asked if they knew where the Ute chief Chico Velásquez was. The orator said that "he knew no such person and was entirely ignorant of the whereabouts of the Utahs." Bell explained that three weeks ago three cattle had been taken from Watrous in Canon Largo. He followed that trail west of the river before losing it, but this time he found an Indian camp east of the river, believed it was an Apache camp, and "was perfectly well satisfied that the meat of the stolen animals had been conveyed to this camp."

When Bell finished his explanation, the orator acted surprised and said that his band had not been west of the river the entire season then laughed heartily and said: "Those Utahs were great thieves." When Bell asked again where the Utes were, the orator said that they had been in the area three weeks ago but had gone over the mountains toward Taos. Bell then said that he knew that Lobo was their chief and that he and his band had taken Watrous's cattle. "I was satisfied his people were the depredators," Bell said, and he reminded the orator of the treaty, which demanded that all thieves "should suffer for their breach of faith." The orator replied that their people were under several different chiefs. Without a council among all of them it was impossible to find the thieves and give them up. He asked Bell to bring his men into the canyon to meet with the rest of the band to discuss the matter.

"This I refused," Bell said, and the orator "became contemptuous."

"Why," the orator asked Bell, "if I already knew everything, I did not point out the thieves myself?"

Bell was losing his composure. "I now told him I would take his Chief [Lobo] who was present and hold him a prisoner until such time as they chose to surrender the thieves, adding that I would also take ponies to indemnify Mr. Waters." When Bell told his men to "take charge" of the ponies, the orator "utterly rejected" the attempt, while the other warriors stood firm. Two old men walked the line and harangued the young warriors to have courage. Just then the band's families came in sight on a hill about three miles away. Not wanting to fight with their people so close, the Indians edged off, sending a rider back to get the families out of harm's way. In ones and twos, the warriors slowly eased back out of sight into a ravine about two hundred yards away (very likely the upper reaches of La Cinta Creek, southwest of present-day Roy, New Mexico). Soon only about twenty warriors remained.

Bell said that "the Chief utterly refused compliance." Whether he meant the orator or another chief or had somehow divined that Lobo was indeed there and had identified him is uncertain. Bell figured that they were trying to draw him into the canyon for an ambush. He ordered two men to dismount and grab the

"Chief." The man ran back and placed himself in the middle of a semicircle of warriors, all on foot, and defied Bell.

"There was now but one course to pursue," Bell reported, "and I commanded 'draw pistols' and formed." Lieutenant Sykes rushed forward and called to the Indians in Spanish "not to force us to the last extremity." When the Indians answered with "a contemptuous gesture," Bell charged. As the dragoons rode right through the line, the Jicarillas sidestepped the horses and shot arrows into the dragoons' backs. Turning about, the dragoons charged again, passing through the intervals a second time. Not pressing their luck at dodging the horses a third time, the Indians fled toward the ravine, but the soldiers still had trouble connecting. "When closely pressed they would throw themselves under the very necks of the horses," Bell explained, "dexterously avoid being trampled upon and discharge their arrows with wonderful rapidity at the riders. The fight lasted but a few minutes."

Three Jicarillas were killed in the first two charges, and two more died at the edge of the ravine. Bell did not pursue, for he was sure they had an ambush waiting. "I take pleasure in stating," Bell said, that among the dead "was Lobo, a cruel, daring, and treacherous Chief, and who was leader in several massacres of whites."

Two dragoons were killed, Pvt. James Bell by an arrow and Pvt. W. A. Arnold by a spear, and four were wounded by gunshot. Bell captured six ponies, two being so poor that they were shot. Bell wished that his force was larger, for with more men he believed that "the families and property of the Indians would have been in our power." They buried their dead on the field and retreated with the wounded, taking a different return route to avoid the deep arroyos. Bell sent Cooke a note by a lone rider requesting an ambulance. They traveled until three in the morning of March 6, "our guide having lost his course." They crossed the Canadian the next morning and met the ambulance.

A few miles west of the Ocate River on the trail to the fort, a messenger overtook Bell with more news. On the morning of March 6, one day after Bell attacked the Jicarillas, that band crossed the Canadian and raided government cattle "at a ranch in the Red River Canyon," killed one herdsman, and drove off two hundred cattle. The unnamed messenger said that the Jicarillas almost killed him "but were prevented by a party of Utahs who defended him." He said that Chico Velásquez wanted to see Bell but was afraid to approach for fear he might be attacked. When Bell agreed to meet the chief, Velásquez, accompanied by fifteen men, explained that they had been going to Taos when they saw the

Jicarillas running off the cattle. His warriors not only prevented the loss of more cattle but protected the remaining herdsmen. He left five men with the herders to help round up the stray stock. An appreciative Bell hurried back to Fort Union, reaching there at seven in the evening.[12]

White justice resulted in seven dead men and four captured ponies. We might ask if this was a fair trade to indemnify Sam Watrous, who had previously made false depredation claims and may or may not have lost any cattle at all. In any case, Watrous and Bell had inadvertently started a war, one likely from greed and the other likely from bruised pride.

Whether the band that Bell attacked had actually taken three of Watrous's cattle is unknown. But it is certain that the day after the attack they retaliated by killing a herdsman and taking two hundred cattle. More trouble could be expected. Cooke reported to Garland that Bell did a fine job. If he only had his entire company, "his victory could have had more fruit & he had probably made an end of what is a mere beginning." As it was, the Indians attacked the government cattle "as their first revenge." Cooke announced the story that Bell slew Lobo and remarked that Velásquez's protection of the herdsmen "is extraordinary," given the prior reports that the Utes and Jicarillas were brothers in marauding. Still, Cooke stated that the hostile bands numbered three hundred warriors, who "are now, or speedily will be at open war with us." He said that it was for General Garland to decide how to meet the threat, "defensively or offensively, weakly or vigorously."[13]

The *Gazette* was ecstatic. The army had finally killed "the scoundrel Lobo," whose band has "caused more trouble, for the last three or four years, than all the other Indians in the Territory." The paper wanted to make Lieutenant Bell a captain, for "[h]e has given the first defeat to this daring band of outlaws" and freebooters of the plains. The newspaper complimented Garland: since he has been in command "his course has been marked by great activity in suppressing Indian depredations, and punishing the offenders. He has shown a desire to assist the civil authorities in every possible way, which is quite in contrast with the conduct of some previous commanders."[14]

This was not true, because Garland had not been pursuing Indian raiders and believed most of the trouble stemmed from Americans and Mexicans. Cooke also had been skeptical, but it was his insistence that Bell find some Indians to punish that had presented Garland with a fait accompli.

Governor Meriwether was not as pleased with the news. He wanted to go back east for some time and did not want an inconvenient war to interfere with his plans. He wrote to Manypenny that Bell had killed Lobo, a "head chief who is a notoriously bad man." Bell took four ponies, but Meriwether inflated the number to "between thirty and forty horses." He said that Chico Velásquez offered his services to the army, but the governor wondered about his sincerity, seeing it only as a ploy to get in his good graces. The chief "will probably recover a part of the cattle and return them and the remainder will be consumed by his people and the other Indians." All should work out fine, however, because Meriwether believed that the Jicarillas would escape with the cattle and would have plenty to eat for the season. "I do not anticipate any further difficulty as the whole tribe cannot muster over one hundred warriors."[15]

Meriwether, who had been trumpeting depredations and discontent for months, suddenly rationalized that everything would turn out peacefully, turned over the reins to secretary William Messervy, and hurried to get out of the territory.

Cooke called for reinforcements. Certain that a large combined Jicarilla-Ute force was heading north, bent on raiding, he sent Bell's overworked company to Rayado to protect the public cattle. Cooke then wrote to Major Blake at Cantonment Burgwin that four Apaches, two of them women, had been seen near Mora, heading in the direction of Taos. Perhaps realizing that four Indians were not much of a threat, he added that "the Utahs have been following the same conduct, perhaps with like results in your quarter & beyond."[16]

Blake already had his own problems before he received Cooke's message. Late in February he got word that Utes were allegedly raiding at Rio Colorado north of Taos. In what seems to be an overreaction, Blake sent Capt. Philip R. Thompson and Lt. Robert Johnston, 1st Dragoons, with sixty-five men of Companies F and I, in pursuit. Taking Kit Carson as a guide they rode north through the San Luis Valley and crossed east of the Sangre de Cristo into the Wet Mountain Valley. With bad weather and no new spring grass as yet, and figuring the raiders were two weeks ahead of them, they turned back, returning to Taos after eleven days and nearly three hundred miles traveled.[17]

Taos Valley was having another Indian scare. Garland said that they must "press these Jicarilla marauders to the last extremity; it is not advisable to patch up a hasty peace with them; talking in the present state of affairs will be no use." Thus Blake directed his men "to apprehend all Apaches that may be found in the vicinity of the post." By March 9, when Cooke had not yet heard anything about the two hundred stolen cattle, he sent out Lieutenant Bell again. He first headed toward Rayado, where Edward F. Mitchell, who had beef and corn contracts with the army, was concerned about his cattle and where Lieutenant Sykes was certain the Jicarilla "thieves" must have gone. On the road Bell received new information from local Mexicans that Mitchell's herd was grazing near the crossing of the Canadian. Not finding any cattle there, he headed downriver, much as he had on his other two trips. Finally spotting Indians, Bell gave chase. Thankfully, before "serious consequences" ensued, Bell realized that they had been mistakenly chasing Pueblos.[18]

On March 14 Cooke got news from the alcalde of Mora that forty-five lodges of Apaches had just arrived there "in great alarm." A few of the Indians were somehow recognized as having participated in the fight with Bell. Cooke did not know how to proceed without proof of their guilt or innocence. But even if they were guilty, he could not chase them, for "there were no American horses to be had in the territory" to mount his dragoons. At the same time a "vast number" of buffalo hunters came through with a fine load of skins, apparently unharmed and unconcerned. Said Cooke: "I suspect the Mexicans generally have too good an understanding with the wild Indians, to suffer *much* from them—but property holders, as far as I have heard are highly pleased with the course which was taken against the Apaches."[19]

As usual, the property holders were calling for action against the Indians. Cooke wanted to oblige them but was still skeptical of the reports. Everyone was getting frustrated. Cooke sent orders to Blake to send a mounted company to Mora to inspect the Apaches, who were "professing innocence & a desire for peace." Cooke may have wanted a concord, but Garland had already said that talk would be of no use. If the Apaches ran again, the dragoons should overtake them and "attack the males, if not quite submissive, & make prisoners of women."[20]

Blake had several concerns. He received a report that "Apaches were in the settlements on the Culebra" in the San Luis Valley, a place where the New Mexicans had been warned not to settle. He sent Captain Thompson and Lieutenant Johnston north with thirty-five dragoons of Company F to investigate. To assist Cooke he detailed Lt. John W. Davidson with Company I, 1st Dragoons, to Mora.[21]

Davidson, later known as "Black Jack" because of his black hair and beard and because he later commanded the black 10th Cavalry, was a questionable choice to send on a delicate mission. Said to be "literally, born with a sword in his hand" in Virginia in 1825, Davidson, with such an extraordinary appendage, was a natural for West Point, graduating in 1845 and being assigned to the saber-wielding 1st Dragoons.[22]

It seemed that Davidson, like George Armstrong Custer, was a character either loved or hated. His belligerence at times, however, did not present him in a good light. As Davidson marched south from Cantonment Burgwin, Cooke, still uncertain as to where all those "hostile" Jicarillas had gone, had ordered Lieutenant Bell to look for them south along the west side of the Canadian and directed Lieutenant Sturgis to travel down the east side of the Canadian as far south as La Cinta Mesa. Both commands were to cooperate when possible. While searching for the stolen cattle, "[t]he Apaches are to be pursued & attacked vigorously."[23]

Cooke was certain that stock-thieving Apaches were somewhere out on the eastern plains. He was not so sure about the group camping peacefully near Mora that Lieutenant Davidson was aiming at. Along the way Davidson ran into Capt. Horace Brooks, 2nd Artillery, on the road in the Sangre de Cristo. Brooks told him that he had just talked to these Apaches, who "were perfectly friendly and desired peace not war." Davidson went to see for himself, meeting them on March 22, with his fifty dragoons itching for battle. He said he counted 107 warriors and 150 women and children. They told him that they wanted to go to Taos and talk to their agent. Davidson told them to proceed but to keep together, because if they scattered "they would be chastised." He marched his men to Mora and rode to Fort Union to see Cooke, who "approved my measures."[24]

That evening at Fort Union Davidson met with several officers in Cooke's residence, which he shared with David Bell. Bell would be leaving on his scout the next morning. He joined the conversation in which Davidson related his meeting with the Apaches. Said Bell: "[H]e described them as being overwhelmed with fear and protesting that they desired peace, stating also that he had made advantageous dispositions for battle in case they exhibited any signs of insolence or hostility. He also commented on the miserable quality of their arms, and their mean shrinking deportment, at the same time averring that he was sorry they did not show some signs of hostility, for that if the[y] had he would have 'wiped them out.'" Bell, who had fought the Jicarillas just a few weeks earlier, had a different take, telling Davidson that they "evinced anything but a cowardly spirit." Davidson, however, "reiterated his assertion, or rather boast, as to what he would do with them."[25]

The next morning Bell went on his scout and Davidson headed back to Cantonment Burgwin. As he approached the post on March 24, he learned from locals that the Jicarillas had separated in two bodies, one heading north toward Taos and the other heading west toward the Cieneguilla crossing of the Rio Grande. They had disobeyed him. Davidson made a night march north, which one of his men, Pvt. James A. Bronson, described as a terrible ride through wind and sleet and "the darkest night I ever saw." The next morning at Rancho Taos the cold and wet dragoons captured ten Indians—the principal chiefs and men who were going to see the agent just as they had said. The women and children were in the group heading west. Davidson said that this "rendered future operations unnecessary," yet he was not satisfied, for had he not promised that if they separated "they would be chastised"?[26]

Cieneguilla

Kit Carson was finally installed as Ute agent. He had been appointed the previous year but was off on one of his sheep drives to California and did not even know that. He had returned to his family in Taos on Christmas Day in 1853. In some of Carson's first correspondence with Meriwether, he tried to dampen the governor's excitability, telling him that reported depredations were likely exaggerated, being only the work of a few who were "in a starving condition," and that the majority were "as well disposed as ever."[27]

The day that Davidson nabbed the Jicarillas heading to Taos, Carson went to meet with them at Cantonment Burgwin. He was reporting to Messervy now, who had been acting as governor since Meriwether left on March 20. Carson reported that the Jicarillas were friendly. "There are at present about one hundred warriors with their families stationed near Picuris engaged in making earthen vessels. They say they were not engaged in any of the depredations committed on the east of the mountains and that none of them were engaged in the fight with the Dragoons on Red River." Carson said that the Jicarillas came over the mountains to the settlements to show their friendship and make ollas to trade for provisions, "as they are in a starving condition."[28]

Messervy wanted to punish the guilty Indians as well as to protect the innocent. He directed Carson to go to Picuris and count the Jicarillas, discern their disposition, and get assurances that they had not participated in the fighting to the east and that they came to the mountains only to escape the soldiers who were "now in pursuit of the guilty." He told Carson to let the Jicarillas stay where they were and furnish them with sufficient wheat or corn to alleviate their hunger. He directed Lafayette Head to report to Carson and act as their special agent.[29]

Before Carson and Head could get to Picuris the situation drastically changed. Cooke had sent a note to Blake stating that the Indians near Taos were not to be held responsible for the fighting in the east. Cooke told Blake that all he had to do "is to be watchful of these Indians & the temper they show; & pursue & attack any warlike or depredating party that may be formed." Blake, however, got a different story from Davidson, who told him on March 29 that "the Apache had broken up their camp and were moving off." Perhaps this was a misunderstanding and Davidson was merely speaking of the two groups that they were already aware of: the one that went to Taos and the other that went to Picuris. In any event, Blake told Davidson to take sixty men "to watch and control this movement and not bring on a fight if possible."[30]

Davidson rode out on the evening of March 29 with sixty men of Companies F and I, 1st Dragoons, accompanied by assistant surgeon David L. Magruder. At eight o'clock in the morning of March 30 everything went haywire. Ten hours later the beaten remnants of his command straggled back to Burgwin, where Davidson scribbled a hasty report. He had encountered the Apaches near Cieneguilla, "who at once sounded the war whoop. There was but one thing to do, I dismounted my command and attacked their camp driving them from it. They rallied at once, however, and charged the command at close quarters seven times. After a desperate fight of three hours I was compelled to withdraw with my wounded, whom I succeeded in bringing to Taos." Davidson said that twenty-two of his men were killed and twenty-three were wounded and that he lost forty-five horses. He claimed that "upwards of three hundred Apache and Utah warriors" opposed him but said he had killed "not less than thirty to forty Indians" and wounded a great many more.[31]

Written on the facing of the report envelope was an endorsement by those who went out afterward to bring in the dead. They counted 93 lodges; supposedly, with 3 or 4 warriors to a lodge, this meant that Davidson had faced a minimum of 279 warriors. Davidson wrote that Judge Beaubien, Auguste Lacome, Kit Carson, and his guide, Jesús Silva, all told him that the Apaches "always scalp the dead unless they have lost more in action than their enemies. Now the Apaches did not scalp any one of my dead . . . so it is fair that their loss must have been much greater than ours."

The battle at Cieneguilla has generally been depicted much as in Davidson's report, but the addendum on the envelope indicates that Davidson was already looking to find an explanation for his poor showing. It had to be because he was jumped by an overwhelming force of warriors; but even so, he must have killed more than he lost. The rationalizations had begun.

Much of the truth of the matter might not have been revealed had it not been for Lieutenant Bell. He had completed his abortive scout for hostile Jicarillas on the plains and returned to Fort Union when a message from Blake arrived telling of a disastrous fight. Cooke, with Bell and his men, rushed to Cantonment Burgwin. On April 1 Cooke questioned Davidson in the presence of Bell. This time Davidson said that he "killed fifty or sixty Indians." Bell, greatly disturbed by Davidson's explanations and demeanor, later wrote of his qualms to his friend Lt. Robert Williams. Davidson, who was only supposed to watch and control the Indians, directly attacked them. He trailed them up a canyon, dismounted, divided the men into two platoons, and purposely assaulted a camp full of women and children to fulfill his boast about "wiping them out." It did not matter who fired first, according to Bell: "Was not the advance upon the Camp in a hostile attitude a *bona fide attack?*" Nobody would doubt that, especially the Indians. Bell said: "If he [Davidson] had been under the command of almost any officer other than Maj. Blake he would have been tried for disobedience of orders."[32]

Bell said Davidson's advance over rough, hilly ground "was the most unmilitary as well as the most exposed order possible." Any noncommissioned officer who could not have seen the impracticability of the approach would have been cashiered for incapacity. A mounted attack could not be made, and the steepness of terrain meant that the men could not lead and control their horses. Thus the horses were left behind, only to become the targets of Indians who had circled around and attacked them. With the situation falling apart, Davidson gave the order to "mount men and save yourselves," which "was calculated to strike terror to the heart of the bravest soldier." That order ruined the command, for every man sought to save himself "while he abandoned his wounded comrades to be butchered."

Bell continued with his understanding of events, telling Williams that only five soldiers' bodies were found on the hill where Davidson advanced, a few in the ravine below, and fourteen on the line of retreat. This proved, he said, that they "retreated without an attempt to preserve order when they had lost 5 of their number." In addition, Davidson said up to three hundred Apache and Ute warriors opposed him, but "there were no Utahs in the fight" and no more than 130 warriors in total. If Davidson really killed 50 or 60, then every one of the other warriors must have been incapacitated, given the usual proportions of killed to wounded. There would have been no one left to chase the dragoons away. Bell also said: "As to fighting three hours that is the most ridiculously absurd assertion in the whole report." A cavalry cartridge box holds thirty to fifty cartridges: "How long would it take a man to fire this number of Cartridges assuming that he fired all of them?" In addition, a man in a fight will lose some of his ammunition. Bell concluded that the fight "never lasted 30 minutes." During the follow-up campaign Bell said that they passed through numerous villages and talked to the locals, who said the Indians "lost only two men in the battle."

Bell told Williams that he could sympathize with Davidson's misfortune. But when Davidson attempted to "transform an unskilled attack, a feeble resistance, a disorderly and disastrous flight," which resulted in further toil and suffering, into a glorious triumph, then Bell could not "conceive it my duty longer to be silent." In addition, Bell said that before Cieneguilla Davidson had made charges of a "very grave nature" against Blake. But after the fight, when Blake supported Davidson's action, Davidson dropped the charges. That could only represent collusion. When Davidson heard snide gossip about his conduct, he demanded a court of inquiry to exonerate himself. Bell hoped that there would be an inquiry and told Williams that he was free to show the letter to anyone because it came not only from his convictions but was "also drawn from unmistakable facts."

Williams showed the letter to his superiors. A court of inquiry was held in Santa Fe, which began on March 10, 1856, and lasted twelve days. Presiding were Col. Benjamin L. E. Bonneville, 3rd Infantry, Major Carleton and Captain Grier, and Lt. Henry B. Clitz as recorder. From that record, and from the archaeological investigations on the field between 2000 and 2002, we can understand a little more clearly what may have happened at Cieneguilla.

Davidson marched out of Cantonment Burgwin with orders not to start a fight, but his boasting indicates that he may have been itching for a showdown. Private Bronson of Company I recorded in his diary that on March 29 Major Blake said that the Indians had just driven off 1,500 cattle, killed two herdsmen, and fled.[33] The report was completely false; but if Davidson heard it related in that way, it may have given him cause to believe that he was going after hostile Indians.

Before he left, Davidson asked Blake for reinforcements and received a detachment of fifteen men of Company F. The dragoons were armed with the .69 caliber Springfield musketoon, a percussion muzzle-loading, smoothbore weapon. For small arms they had .54 caliber single-shot Model 1842 percussion horse pistols or .44 caliber Colt Dragoon revolvers. None of the weapons were very accurate, and the difficulty of loading the musketoon was notorious. The previous fall Davidson had requested twelve rifles, because "I regard the musketoon as useless."[34]

Davidson camped that evening near Cieneguilla (now Pilar) where the steep Rio Grande canyon opens up to allow a crossing place. Early in the morning scouts saw campfire smoke in the Embudo Mountains to the east. Davidson turned his command up a narrow mountain trail that led between Cieneguilla and Picuris. Men on iron-shod horses with clanking canteens, weapons, and other implements struggling uphill through Agua Caliente Canyon must have

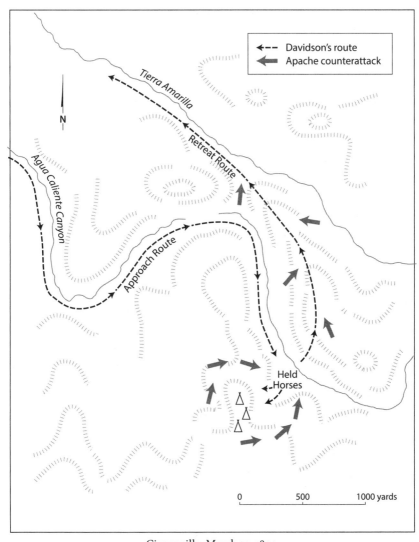

Cieneguilla, March 30, 1854.

Map by Bill Nelson. Copyright © 2017 by the University of Oklahoma Press.

made quite a racket, and the Apaches heard them coming. The Jicarillas had been promised peace and had no reason to believe that soldiers were coming after them, but they prepared and waited.

A detachment rode ahead and saw the camp on a high bluff about one hundred feet above them. About eight o'clock Davidson arrived and considered his options. The Jicarillas were not attacking, but they were not running. In fact, they were yelling down at them. Sgt. William Holbrook, who had killed and scalped Jicarillas four years ago when Captain Grier was in command, warned: "Look out men, that is a war whoop and we have got to fight." Company I Pvt. James Strowbridge heard a man on the hilltop call out in English: "Come on if you want to fight." Davidson believed that he had been challenged. As he wrote in his report, "There was but one thing to do, I dismounted my command and attacked."[35]

A mounted charge up the steep hill was impossible, so Davidson left his horses with fifteen men near the bottom of the canyon. He formed the rest into two platoons: Sergeant Holbrook took about twenty men uphill on the right, while Sgt. William Kent took a second platoon of about twenty men up to the left. The Jicarillas fired on them as they ascended, killing or wounding a few. Reaching the crest, the platoons tried to form up and advance through the village of domed, bark and thatch wickiups. The Jicarillas fell back but continued to fire, killing Sergeant Kent. As the dragoons got off a few rounds, the Indians pulled back and disappeared. It seemed like an easy victory. Then came the firing from behind.

The Jicarillas had not run away but circled around both flanks of the attacking soldiers and went after the horses. Only five minutes after they reached the hilltop the dragoons heard a bugle call—Pvt. James A. Bronson did not know if it was "the recall or retreat." Doctor Magruder and the men guarding the horses were hard pressed, and Davidson formed the returning soldiers in a semicircle around the horses. The Apaches seemed everywhere, firing from behind trees, bushes, and slopes. The dragoons took cover and returned fire. With the musketoon being slow and difficult to load and horribly inaccurate, however, it was an uneven contest.[36]

The Jicarillas made several charges, some from two and three sides at once. They came at intervals of twenty minutes or half an hour. Each time they were repulsed, but the dragoons were taking casualties, and their small ammunition supply was rapidly dwindling. The Jicarillas did best when they just stayed back out of musketoon range and sent showers of arrows plunging down among the men and horses. With the ground strewn with arrows, the hollow filling with dense smoke, and the Jicarillas dashing in to attack and disappear, the dragoons were getting rattled. Exaggerations of time and space were likely. Several men said that they were surrounded and attacked for several hours by overwhelming numbers of Indians. Davidson believed that there were three hundred. Private Bronson, succinctly recorded in his diary: "found ourselves . . . in ambush, surrounded by about 400 Indians; fought hard until 12 noon when we started to retreat."[37]

Davidson may have been involved in a scene similar to one on the Little Bighorn River in 1876 when Maj. Marcus Reno witnessed his scout Bloody Knife get shot in the head and immediately called for a retreat. This time Davidson and Holbrook were consulting about what to do when "a ball passed between their faces and struck a tree about two yards to the rear of them." Davidson quickly realized that he must get out. They scrambled to a new spot, but it was no better. He again called out to his men "to save what wounded they could and to retreat."[38]

The situation rapidly deteriorated. The dragoons crossed a shallow stream and headed uphill on the opposite side of the canyon. Private Strowbridge's horse was shot. He asked Holbrook if he should remove the saddle and put it on another horse, but the sergeant, trying to maintain a brave front, said: "Wait till we whip the Indians, and then it will be time enough to take the kit off the dead horse." Halfway up the slope Company F trooper George Breenwald was hit and cried out: "Please don't leave me." Davidson stopped to let the men catch their breath and reload. Magruder worked on Breenwald, but he bled to death in moments. Perhaps five soldiers were hit on the climb out.[39]

On the hilltop the retreat nearly became a rout. Silhouetted along an 800-yard ridgeline, the dragoons were nearly sitting ducks. The Jicarillas had ascended on both sides, came up in the rear, and circled to the front. The dragoons fought desperately to escape the trap. Davidson tried to rally them, but he fell when an arrow hit him in the shoulder. Corp. Benjamin Dempsey pulled the arrow out, but one musket ball smashed into his leg while another shot off his thumb. Two arrows hit Sergeant Holbrook, who said: "I am shot and cannot go any farther on foot." Strowbridge tried to get him on a horse, but the sergeant fell back and died. Bronson was hit by a ball that went through both thighs. He kept walking and running until he managed to get between two horses, grabbed their stirrups, and was dragged for half a mile. About forty-five out of their sixty horses were dead, but twenty-two men were also now dead or dying. The twenty-three wounded men either doubled up on the remaining horses or stumbled along, walking and running. They finally got off the deadly ridge and stumbled down the Tierra Amarilla that led toward Cieneguilla. Thankfully for them, the Jicarillas apparently had enough killing and let them go.[40]

When the stragglers reached Cieneguilla, Davidson sent one unwounded man on a good horse to ride for help. Blake, who had been spending the afternoon drinking at St. Vrain's Mill, hastily assembled twenty soldiers and a few civilians and Pueblos and hurried to the scene. One of the civilians was John M. Francisco, a merchant and one-time sutler at Fort Massachusetts who had filed depredation claims against the Indians. He said that they reached Cieneguilla the next day and retraced the flight route, finding seventeen bodies along the ridge, a few in the gorge defense spot, about five between the gorge and the Indian camp, and one in the camp. Francisco counted sixty lodges.[41]

Twenty-four soldiers died. Reports of Indian deaths varied widely: Davidson believed that perhaps sixty were killed; searchers said that they found nine Jicarilla bodies, while years later a Jicarilla participant told anthropologist Pliny Goddard that only four of their people were killed. It was first believed that it was the camp of Francisco Chacón, but both he and Chico Velásquez were camped at the time up near Fort Massachusetts. At least one chief, Pacheco, was killed in the fight. Recent historical and archaeological research shows that the numbers of Indians involved were fewer than the army estimated, perhaps 100 to 130 warriors at most. The Indians did not begin the attack or ambush the dragoons. Davidson was not forced to attack them and was not prepared for the counterattack by the unintimidated Jicarillas. They turned the tables on him and trapped him in a canyon. The fight may not have taken only thirty minutes as Lieutenant Bell contended, but it did not last several hours either. It may have involved moments of a hard-fought defense but also much semipanic, with the men being easily picked off as they ran. Some wounded certainly were left behind.[42]

When word of the episode got out, the army presented the initial military reports as the standard storyline. On April 1 General Garland wrote to Washington that a force of 250 Jicarillas and Utes "unexpectedly attacked a company of Dragoons" but that Lieutenant Davidson "succeeded, after a desperate conflict, in overwhelming it" in a three-hour contest, stating that his conduct "calls for the admiration of every true soldier."[43]

Something had to be done. Garland ordered Cooke, Brooks, Ewell, and Carleton to hurry to Taos for a retaliatory expedition. He also called for volunteers. Cooke learned that the Jicarillas had crossed the Rio Grande at Embudo, heading to the mountains north of Abiquiu. He directed troops from Santa Fe to march northwest while he left Taos on a similar axis before cutting obliquely southwest, hoping to trap the Indians between the columns.[44]

After the fight at Cieneguilla it became impossible to keep a lid on the conflict that began to boil with Bell's confrontation with Lobo. The army's competency and honor had been impugned. Someone had to pay.

"The Long Wished for Crisis Is on Us"

Acting governor William Messervy was in a hot spot. On the last day of March he twice wrote to Commissioner Manypenny. In the first letter he said that Governor Meriwether had departed from the territory on March 20, leaving him with many crises and little money. He believed about one-third of the Jicarillas were at war since Bell's fight, while the balance refused to fight and professed friendship. This put Messervy in a difficult position. "If their whole band would unite in their hostile movements, it would relieve the Superintendency of all responsibility" and the military could take over the entire problem. Messervy said: "I find myself perplexed, as to what course to pursue." The destitute Indians "must either steal or starve," but "I have not one dollar of funds." If they go out to hunt "they are in danger of being met by the Troops, who cannot distinguish the good from the bad." In addition, Messervy was losing agents: James Smith died at Dona Ana in December 1853, and Edward Graves was taking leave for the States in April. Things were not going well. Messervy had barely finished writing that missive when news about Davidson's disaster arrived—and in that tale the number of dead soldiers had already increased to thirty. His instructions to Carson about feeding and placating the Jicarillas were now useless. "It is my painful duty to inform you," Messervy wrote, "that my worst fears have been more than realized." "We are now at war with the whole tribe of Jicarillas, and apprehend the same may be said of the Utahs."[45]

As if on cue, reports began filtering in of increased Indian raiding. A band of one hundred Mescalero warriors was said to have passed east of Albuquerque heading north as the army assembled to go after the Jicarillas, the implication being that they were on their way to join the Jicarillas. Major Backus at Fort Fillmore was told to send three companies to catch the Mescaleros, "demand an account" for the reason of their move, and "in case no satisfactory reason should be given, to seize women and children, the chiefs, and all that can be reached and cripple them as much as possible."[46]

In Taos Captain Thompson believed the Jicarillas were headed west, but if pressed they would turn south for Mescalero country and the White Mountains, likely using the Mora Valley route. Thompson pleaded for help, for he only had twenty-five men after Cooke pulled out. If the Indians attacked it would have "disastrous consequences."[47]

On April 7 Garland sent Cooke an update, stating that "until these marauding Apaches have been well whipped, give them neither rest nor quarter until they are humbled to the dust." From special agent Head he heard that Fleche Rayada, said to be the successor of Lobo, was in command at Cieneguilla and that he only had lost three men. Head next heard that Rayada was near Ojo Caliente and would fight the soldiers if he had to but was willing to give up the captured horses and weapons if the soldiers would give him peace. The Jicarilla Chacón and the Ute Chico Velásquez were camped around Fort Massachusetts and would probably not join with Rayada. Nevertheless, Garland told Cooke, "they are the head devils who murdered the White Family, and the mail party at Wagon Mound, and I desire above all things connected with your campaign to hear they have been hung."[48]

Whether Garland realized it or not, during the past month the Jicarillas had not been raiding but had been accused by Watrous, attacked by Bell, and attacked by Davidson. They were still fleeing. Chacón and Velásquez likely had not been involved with the White kidnapping and Wagon Mound episodes. Chacón had been one of the friendliest and most cooperative chiefs, and Velásquez was even protecting the American and New Mexican sheep and herders. Now, with Lobo dead, new head devils needed to be installed as the objects of fear and hate. Garland had succumbed to the panic and joined with the civilians in the clarion call for death or destruction of the Indians.

On April 8, 1854, the *Gazette* ran a news story: "Terrible Slaughter by the Indians." From its source it learned that three or four days earlier a band of Indians had attacked Lucien Maxwell's ranch at Rayado and killed everyone: ten men, eight women, and two or three children, "not leaving a soul to bear witness to the terrible details." The Indians who had just fought Davidson at Cieneguilla and had crossed the Rio Grande heading west were blamed for massacring everyone at Rayado, forty miles east of Taos. The *Gazette* called it an "inhuman act" and "another outrage to add to their catalog of crimes." The paper said that it was high time for the government to change its Indian policy from the hopeless persuasive system. The government says to "give them presents and that perhaps will quiet them," while the people of the States respond, "[Y]es the poor red man, pity him, for he knows no better." It only resulted in more innocent deaths. "Presents and big talking will not remedy this state of things." The *Gazette* and the people wanted blood.[49]

While Cooke was chasing the Jicarillas, the remaining troops investigated the latest alleged depredations. One report claimed that Mescaleros were moving east of Albuquerque, but "[a]s no depredations have been heard of on their supposed route through the settlements, the truth of the rumor is very much doubted." The army disputed the *Gazette* editorial about the attack on Maxwell's ranch, "none of which is believed to be true. No reliable intelligence of the attack upon Rayado has reached us." It was the third or fourth time that Maxwell was supposed to have been killed.[50]

As Indian alarms rang at various points of the compass, Cooke had assembled his expedition at Cantonment Burgwin. On April 2 he was ready to go, with a detachment of 1st Dragoons under Lieutenant Samuel D. Sturgis; Company H, 2nd Dragoons, under Lieutenant Bell; and Company D, 2nd Artillery, under Lieutenant Sykes, all serving as riflemen. The next day Cooke marched to Taos, where he picked up twenty-two men of Company F, 1st Dragoons, thirty-two Mexicans and Pueblos in a "Spy Company" under James H. Quinn, and Kit Carson. Cooke left on April 4, "with 110 Sabres," fifty-seven "rifles," and thirty-two "spies." They marched northwest to the junction of the Rio Hondo and Rio Grande, about ten miles from Taos.[51]

On the morning of April 5 they traveled southwest "about twenty miles over a bad country" and camped at Serviletta on the Rio Tusas. The next day they went west five miles and discovered a deserted camp with broken army equipment. Assuming the articles to be from Davidson's men, they followed the trail, crossed the divide to the Rio Vallecitos, moved upriver to the village of Vallecitos, obtained grain, and camped about three miles north. On April 7 they followed the trail north in a twisting course, which Quinn called "a long and fatiguing march of about twenty-five miles up and down high mountains, the Indians trying to disguise their trail and evade pursuit." Two vacant campsites showed they were getting closer. On April 8 they discovered that the Indians had doubled back and were retreating south. They crossed mountains with snow two to three feet deep. It was rough travel, but they could easily follow the tracks. Cooke said that the route was "through a chaos of steep slopes, rock, snow and bog." They bypassed some deep canyons when suddenly, about two in the afternoon, the spies came out on top of a ridge looking down on the Jicarilla camp in the rugged valley of the Rio Vallecitos, about three miles above its junction with the Rio Tusas.[52]

Cooke described the physical layout: "The Agua Caliente comes to force its way from the right, into a vast ravine formed by two parallel mountains, and turns to the left, running by our left flank at the foot of the precipitous rocks."

Flowing down "between that point and the mountain to the left, a narrow defile, the passage of which is almost forbidden by the torrent, which in several channels amidst trees and thickets, rushes four feet deep over rolling rock. The crags, in front of us, being scaled we look down upon the river in a profound chasm."

The Jicarilla camp was below on the same bank inside one loop of the "S" bend. It would take hours to move up or downriver to turn the position, so Cooke ordered a direct attack. The Spy Company was ahead and to the left. Carson and the Mexicans started down, while Quinn with the Pueblos fell in on his right. With Cooke farther to the right, Lieutenant Sykes led downhill with the 2nd Artillery riflemen as skirmishers, while Lieutenant Bell moved the dragoons downhill "handsomely to the front, through the fire of the enemy, up into the angle of the cliffs and the mountains, dismounted his men, and seized a position below the mountain top, but on the flank of the enemy in the crags," according to Cooke.

Cooke came down in the center, supported by Major Blake and Lieutenant Sturgis and a squadron of 1st Dragoons. Cooke called the Jicarilla position "formidable," because after they had come down the cliffs the Indians were still in "a ridge of the rocks" above them. Quinn said that the Jicarillas took "possession of the rocks which surrounded the camp [in] three-fourths of a circle [and] returned our fire with spirit." Carson believed that the women and children would escape and tried to hurry the troops. Said Quinn: "Col. Cooke came up most beautifully and flanking the Indians on both sides they fled precipitately." Sykes, with some of Lieutenant Moore's dragoons, passed down a defile to the left, turned the Jicarillas' right flank, then crossed the river and entered the woods beyond. At the same time Bell's flanking fire from above and right, even with poor-ranged musketoons, was enough to worry them out of their position.

The Jicarillas' stand quickly turned to flight. Women and children splashed across the swirling river. Soldiers entered the camp in various spots, while others pursued across the river. Blake went across to the right to "push the enemy on the mountain beyond," while Cooke, with Bell's men, "galloped down to the left, plunged through the river" and followed along the canyon. Here Cooke saw a dragoon shot down, who then "rose, stood erect a moment, & then fell *quite dead.*"

Quinn said: "There was but one place the stream could be forded by horse and here it had a few logs for the convenience of the Indians in their retreat, but the infantry dragoons under Sturgis went bulging through it regardless of every danger. Some Indians were drowned in the stream, for I saw some go in whom I did not see on the other side though very close—not thirty yards." Quinn saw two Indian horses drown in what he called "a Mountain Torrent."

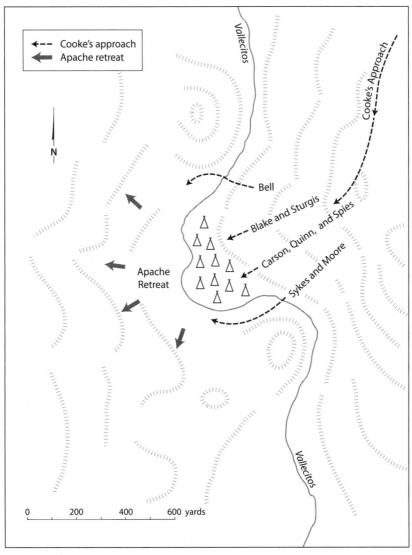

Ojo Caliente, April 8, 1854.

Map by Bill Nelson. Copyright © 2017 by the University of Oklahoma Press.

Some Jicarillas who had crossed the river made another stand in the rocks and trees on the western bank. Cooke said that the Indian position was "impracticable for a Cavalry charge—I dismounted the company, & with Lt. Bell, led a charge on foot—the enemy did not await it, but dispersed with a dropping fire, while we pursued a mile further in the pine forest, until there was no indication of his presence." Cooke sent the skirmishers to sweep the ridge. Lieutenant Maxwell led a small detachment uphill and into the forest, where he intercepted several fleeing Indians and captured three horses. With the Jicarillas dispersed in every direction, Cooke ordered everyone back to the abandoned camp. The men "being quite exhausted & it being late afternoon," said Cooke, "I reluctantly abandoned the idea of further immediate pursuit as impracticable."

Cooke said that he recovered four sabers, two carbines, and fifteen saddles that had belonged to Davidson's defeated dragoons, plus several "enemy" rifles and about twenty-two horses. Quinn said that they captured eighteen horses and burned all the camp equipage, robes, and provisions. Cooke burned seventy-seven lodges, estimated two warriors per lodge, and concluded he must have been fighting 150 men—more than his own force. Cooke said that two to five Indians were killed and five or six wounded. But Quinn said that there were "no dead Indians" on the field, although they wounded a number. Quinn said that seventeen women and children "perished by exposure by snow and hunger" after they fled. One woman carrying an infant was shot and drowned in the river, but her baby was saved and taken to Taos by a Mexican after a "large reward humanely offered by Major Blake." One soldier was killed and one wounded.

Cooke was proud of the victory, saying that "all the officers exhibited energy and gallantry," including Quinn and Carson and singling out "the handsome charge of Lieutenant Bell." Cooke believed that the Jicarillas intended to offer battle there and prepared their position accordingly, but it proved to be a mistake, because "ever before, and after, they were found on mountains and peaks."[53]

Cooke was not finished. On April 9 he sent his wounded man to the village of Vallecitos. The command searched for the Indian trail through forests and over the mountains where, in Cooke's words, "a world of blank snows spread unlimited to the west." Horses broke through icy streams and bogged down in deep drifts, but they kept to the trail even at night. "Such was the scene of the enemy's flight by moonlight; the tracks of bare and diminutive feet left a feeble memorial of its sufferings." After a march of eighteen miles they made a cold camp in the mountains. The next morning the trail turned southwest into the Canjilon Creek valley. Near the creek's junction with the Rio Chama they saw four Jicarillas, but, said Cooke, "the Indians, on foot, escaped like deer into the cover of their native fastnesses." Lieutenant Bell chased them across the Chama but gave up. The command camped. Quinn reported: "Hard day's work and a number of animals gave out and were shot." On April 12 the trail was worse. They climbed Mesa Prieta, which Cooke called "a most lofty table land," but found only rough going and no water. They saw butchered horses and smoke signals. When the trail died out on a ledge a thousand feet above the Chama River, they could go no farther. Cooke was reluctant to give up, but his officers concurred with the guides. "It was with much pain" that Cooke ordered them to turn back and head for Abiquiu about twenty miles to the southeast.[54]

Carson dictated a letter to Messervy. Tired and disillusioned, he said that the Jicarillas "were driven into the war, by the action of the officers & troops in that quarter." He noted that their privations were great: they had been attacked and some killed, their property had been destroyed, and they had been "pursued through the worst mountains I ever tracked through." But "thinking there will be no quarter or mercy shown them, they will resort to all desperate expedients to escape." The Jicarillas would not be caught, but Carson believed that they would gladly surrender if they were given a fair and just treaty.[55]

While Cooke waited for supplies, perhaps wishing that he had not destroyed so many at Ojo Caliente, he got a note from General Garland, who was not of the same mind as Carson. Garland "is not authorized, nor does he desire it, to make any peace, or treaty with these Indians, until they have been thoroughly chastised."[56]

Back in Taos at his Ute Agency, Carson sketched events for Messervy and added that Chico Velásquez had arrived to assert the Utes were "friendly disposed" and that none of them had been involved in the fighting. Some Apaches urged him to join in the war, but he refused. Velásquez said that Chacón was not at Cieneguilla, but his people were attacked, so "he supposed he must either fight or die." Chacón reached his people just in time for the Ojo Caliente fight.[57] One of the friendliest and most cooperative chiefs was now at war.

Having rested and resupplied, Cooke continued his chase on April 18. The spy company, this time supported by Major Carleton and his dragoons, went up the Rio Puerco and over the mountains to Coyote Creek and back, traveling about twenty-five miles. They crossed the raging Chama, which Quinn called "the most dangerous river in New Mexico." After struggling across a ford, they ascended up the Mesa de los Viejos, headed northeast, and camped at Canjilon Creek, where they had been nearly two weeks earlier. They woke up on April 23 to nearly a foot of snow on the valley floor, so they turned back to El Rito. Cooke became very ill with chills and fever, and they camped three days. On April 28 Cooke stayed behind while Quinn's spies and Carleton, Ransom, and Moore headed back to the Canjilon Valley, where they were to wait for another expedition converging from the east.[58]

That force, under Capt. William T. H. Brooks, sixty 3rd Infantrymen, and Capt. José M. Valdez with forty "spies," left Taos in the hope of driving the Jicarillas toward Cooke. While Cooke recovered, he wrote to Garland of his plan and ordered beef cattle sent to Fort Massachusetts in expectation that the army would pursue the Jicarillas to that quarter. Garland, apparently believing that Cooke was reluctant to continue the campaign, ordered him, "[i]n consideration of the present state of your command," to return either to Taos or to Fort Union and to continue offensive operations after resupplying. In the meantime Brooks "will keep the field."[59]

The cattle to feed the expedition came from Rayado. After supplying Brooks, Davidson needed more for himself. From Peter Joseph he bought sixty more cattle at twenty dollars per head. Joseph seemed eager to sell and used his own employees to drive the stock from Rayado to Taos. Davidson wrote: "I believe he sells them so cheap because the Indians have already run off some of his cattle and he is afraid of losing the rest."[60]

Brooks reached Vallecitos on May 3, joined with Quinn's spies, marched northeast to the Rio Tusas, and found a trail heading north to Rio San Antonio. Continuing downriver and into present-day Colorado, they reached the Conejos River and caught a half-blind Ute. He told them that his village was near but that he knew of no Apaches. At the village Brooks learned that Chacón had crossed the Rio Grande earlier. The spies were "perfectly confounded" by all the Ute trails and did not know which one to follow. The Rio Grande was running high, but Brooks forced them across. Quinn called it a "laughable scene," and they had to camp to dry out everything that they had just soaked. On May 11 Captain Valdez rode to the settlement on Culebra Creek and learned that the Apaches had gone in the direction of the Spanish Peaks. Brooks, for "great want of shoes and clothing and the indefiniteness of the true position of the trail," called it off and headed back to Taos.[61]

After the fights at Cieneguilla and Ojo Caliente and a long fruitless chase, Garland broadened his plans to "chastise" the Indians. On April 10 Messervy proclaimed that the Jicarillas "have made war upon, and commenced hostilities against the government of the United States," and everyone was prohibited from dealing with them. New Mexican citizens were in ecstasy. *Gazette* editor William Davis declared: "The long wished for crisis appears to be on us in all its glory and exciting circumstance—a regular war between the Indians and the U. S.—and that lesson and chastisement so long merited are about to be given them by a hand that will not spare the rod." Davis proclaimed that "[t]he war was begun by them, without the least provocation," as complete a misrepresentation as could possibly have been made. The Jicarillas were "human devils" who ran off stock and massacred defenseless people. Davis's "long catalogue" of bloody deeds perpetrated by "infernal demons" was merely the standard complaint of the attacks on the White party and the mail party at Wagon Mound—all occurring more than four years earlier. Davis's solution was "total extinction of the whole tribe of Jicarillas and their allies."[62]

The end result of all those false depredation claims, false reports of robberies and murders, the greed for Indian land, the quest for power, and an atmosphere of fear and hate was that the people finally got their Indian war.

Fishers Peak

General Garland wanted to attack all the tribes. Of the Jicarillas in the north he said that he desired to "crush this Band of *Pirates*," but he had not yet resolved the truth of the matter concerning Mescaleros who were supposed to be raiding in the south. To "divert the attention of the Mescaleros" he planned simultaneous campaigns against them as well.[63]

In the meantime the militia had some minor successes. About May 10 Apaches were said to be raiding around El Rito. Justice Felipe Martínez and twenty men surprised them and captured three men, three women, and two boys. "One of the men," the *Gazette* reported, "is a brother of Chief Chacon, the murderer of Mrs. White, and who commanded the massacre of the mail party, and La Cieneguilla." Editor Davis, like Garland, had deleted Lobo Blanco as the leader in the first two episodes and inserted Chacón as the leader in all three.[64]

About the same time near Serviletta Juan Martín y Peña and some others attacked four Apache men, five women, and a child, asleep in camp. The Indians fought bravely with sticks and rocks, but all were captured and taken to Taos, where they supposedly declared that they would continue to fight "as long as one of them is left alive." Several companies of Rio Arriba militia were hunting Apaches. About June 10 Captain Gerónimo Jaramillo and Lieutenant Maes surrounded and captured an eight-lodge camp—about forty people in all. One of the captured was said to be "the well-known chief, El Guero." A few weeks later Maes and his men took six of the captives to Santa Fe, where they allegedly tried to escape. Three were killed, the *Gazette* reported. "Their scalps were then taken off and brought in; which we saw dangling at the saddle of one of the men, in front of the people."[65]

The Jicarillas had been on the run since April. Probably every one of them who had been west of the Sangre de Cristo at the time of the Cieneguilla fight had fled north to the San Luis Valley and beyond. Nevertheless, the citizens figured that it was a good time to attack as well as to complain about depredations. Jicarillas were said to be stealing sheep and cattle throughout Rio Arriba County as well as east of the mountains. Messervy reported that Cheyennes, Arapahos, and Kiowas were robbing and killing in San Miguel County. He said that agent Tom Fitzpatrick had distributed powder, lead, rifles, and even Colt revolvers to the Indians, which "are now turned against the defenseless inhabitants of this Territory." Messervy claimed that the Indians hit the settlements around Las Vegas and "destroyed all they could lay their hands upon, in one week they murdered twenty-one of our citizens, took ten herder boys captive, & ran off a large number" of animals. He was in a state of high anxiety. A captive who had supposedly escaped from the Indians told him that "there will be a union of the Tribes" that wished to destroy the northern settlements. Messervy was "fully impressed" with the belief that the Plains tribes would combine with the Mescaleros "to devastate the whole frontier of our country extending from the mouth of the Rio Grande in Texas to the Mora near Fort Union." He called for two hundred more militia from Rio Arriba and two hundred from San Miguel, plus more help from "the arm of the General Government" to hold back the hordes.[66]

Back in Louisville, Kentucky, Governor Meriwether had finally heard the story of Lucien Maxwell and twenty of his family and employees supposedly killed by Indians in April. He rushed a letter to Manypenny, but by now the number of murdered had increased to thirty, they were in a general Indian war with the Apaches and Utes, and the entire frontier was about to be broken up and the inhabitants murdered. Meriwether strongly urged "the necessity of sending out additional troops" as soon as possible while authorizing an entire regiment of volunteers.[67]

The rumors were outrageous, but the fear was palpable. Twenty-one people had not been killed by Indians in San Miguel County, any more than twenty of Maxwell's people had been killed at Rayado. What else did the civilians want? Garland already had several columns in the field and Messervy called out the militia, although Garland believed that it was "much to be regretted." Garland

became more aggressive than his predecessors, but it was because he was forced
into war by a fait accompli of his own officers. Lieutenants Ransom and Bell
searched for raiding Mescaleros, leaving Fort Union on May 30. They went down
the Gallinas River to Alexander Hatch's ranch, where they heard that Indians
were killing herders and stealing sheep from Juan Paría near the Cuervo Hills
about forty miles to the southeast. Ransom hurried there to find about three
thousand sheep, roaming without herders. He simply rounded them up and sent
them back to the settlements. "After further examination," he wrote, "[I] could
find no signs of the Indians," possibly because of recent rains. Ransom returned to
Hatch's, where he found the herders with the rest of Paría's sheep. This time they
reported that Indians had stolen 6,500 of them! A skeptical Ransom nevertheless
turned back downriver, chased some Indians who were driving livestock, and
eventually went as far as the Bosque Redondo before turning back. He believed
that the Indians he chased south were Mescaleros, but those, if any, who stole
sheep "I think were *Prairie* Indians."[68]

Garland may have been fighting the Jicarillas, but he had doubts about other
depredations.[69] If Mescaleros were raiding in the Anton Chico vicinity and he
had to investigate, it would divert his efforts against the Jicarillas. Cooke had
similar misgivings, believed that the raiders were likely "Chians" (Cheyennes).
He acerbically wrote that talk of "serious depredations & bloodshed" must have
been "occasioned by a rather limited number of Indians." "That the 'prairie
Indians' should commit depredations on this frontier is reasonably to be expected
& in retaliation of serious depredations committed by the inhabitants of the
territory on them." Cooke believed that the militia would provide sufficient
protection against apprehended attacks. Meanwhile, he wrote, "I hear nothing
of the Jicarilla."[70]

While Garland was distracted by events in the south, his main objective was
still to find the Jicarillas who had fled north. Since Cooke's fight at Ojo Caliente,
they had spent nearly two months chasing scattered bands and trying to bring
them to battle. When Brooks returned empty-handed, it was Major Carleton's
turn. He readied 1st Dragoon Companies K and G, with a platoon of Company I
under Lieutenant Davidson, plus Quinn's Spy Company. They left Taos on May 25
and headed north toward Fort Massachusetts to search for the trail that Brooks
believed went east over the Sangre de Cristo. Captain Valdez's spies and a squad
of 2nd Dragoons went toward the Raton Mountains by a more easterly route.[71]

Quinn's spies crossed the range at Mosca Pass, while the main force used
Sangre de Cristo Pass, both converging in the Huerfano Valley. Quinn found

a trail estimated to be of thirty-three lodges, heading east down the Huerfano River. Traveling south toward the Spanish Peaks, they discovered "evidence" in an old campsite that showed the Indians had been those who had fought at Cieneguilla. That evening Carleton camped near "the eternal snows on the northernmost of the Spanish Peaks," where they located another abandoned Indian camp. The trail curved around the eastern base of the peaks and south twenty-five miles "over the most difficult country imaginable." Believing that they were gaining on the Indians, they hurried down Sarcillo Canyon to the Purgatoire River then turned east toward the Santa Fe Trail where it begins its climb over the Raton Mountains.[72]

On the morning of June 4 they reached the road six miles north of the summit and were on a "warm" trail—so warm that Carson told Carleton that "the command would be sure to overtake the Apaches by two o'clock that day." The trail went up the west side of Fishers Peak. Carleton used the tree-covered canyon of Clear Creek to make his approach unseen. They snaked up single file until they reached the summit, a "level table-land" barely one hundred yards in width. But on the other side a deep amphitheater cut in from the prairie on the north and east, "cutting this towering mesa nearly in sunder." The bowl-shaped area in front of them was of several thousand acres with San Miguel Creek running through the center while the right was covered by thick timber. Carleton said that you could look "toward the north upon the prairie as upon a stage."

Carson saw a horse herd grazing about four hundred yards below them and Indian lodges in the timber on the right. The only practical way down was by a narrow path right in front of them, but it was only wide enough for two horses abreast. The noise they made alerted the Jicarillas below. They fled "panic-stricken" as the Mexicans and Pueblos of the Spy Company fired, whooped, and "dashed furiously down over the rocks." Most of the Jicarillas disappeared into the woods. Quinn's spies rushed down the creek to round up the horses while Lieutenant Davidson and men of Company I, 1st Dragoons, took the same course to cut off any Indians who tried to escape in that quarter. Company G went to the right into the woods to try to capture the women and children. Lieutenant Isaiah Moore, with men of Company K, 1st Dragoons, moved along the mesa top to the right to cut off those who might try to climb back up and escape to the south and west.

The basin was wooded and boulder strewn and easily concealed the Indian fugitives. Davidson formed a skirmish line to beat the ground and advance toward the village, while Moore formed a skirmish line on the opposite side and four hundred feet above him and pushed downslope to meet Davidson. Moore's men had to use ropes tied to tree trunks to descend. When both commands met, they turned back uphill and swept toward the campsite. Lt. Robert Johnston kept a party of mounted men at the north edge closest to the prairie to catch anyone fleeing in that direction. "The woods were thus swept through," Carleton wrote, "but the Indians had concealed themselves so effectually, not one could be found." He had "assembly" sounded and everyone met at the camp.

The Jicarillas did leave almost everything behind, with hot food still cooking on the fires. Carleton destroyed meat, skins, and lodges and captured thirty-eight horses. This was not the blessing that it first appeared to be, for Carson and Quinn said that "not a sign" was left to follow. Carleton decided to recross Fishers Peak Mesa to the good grass and water on the southern slope. Perhaps not killing a single Indian rankled Carleton a bit. He left Quinn, Moore, and forty men behind to hide and wait for any Indians who returned. Two men and two women appeared before dark, and bullets flew in the ambush, but only one Indian, said to be the son of Chief Huero, was killed. A Pueblo Indian accompanying the party took his scalp. That night they held a scalp dance.

There was not much left to do. Carson said that the Jicarillas "are the most difficult of all Indians to pursue" because after an attack they always break up into small parties with no baggage and can travel for several days without food, making it "impossible for any body of regular troops to overtake them." No troops or spies were injured and only one Jicarilla was killed, so it was not a victory written in blood. Carleton rationalized that "the moral effect" of his fight had to be great because the Indians "lost everything; and have been taught the fact that with all their cunning the Americans can pursue and find them." Carson and Quinn received Carleton's praises, but Carson got an added bonus. When he told Carleton he would find the Indians by two o'clock on June 4, the major promised that if he did so "he would give me one of the finest hats that could be procured in New York." Carson got his hat, "and a fine one it was," he said.[73]

The offensive came to a standstill because there were no Jicarillas left to chase. Carson believed that most of them went west of the Rio Grande. They only trailed about thirty-three lodges to the east side. No one really knew if these were the "guilty" ones from Bell's fight or Cieneguilla. Cooke did not care for the services of Valdez's spies, believing that they were not as effective as Quinn's. He retained Quinn and paid off and discharged Valdez. Spy companies were expensive; Cooke estimated that from their initial employment to June 15 they had cost the government $6,325. Cooke was not as parsimonious as Sumner, but that was a lot of money.[74]

"I Didn't Know It Was Any Harm to Kill an Indian"

General Garland had achieved some results—at least enough to placate the civilians who believed that they had finally gotten their war of extermination. But he shut down the offensive. The Jicarillas had disappeared, he was receiving peace overtures, and other Indian alarms were proving to be the usual smoke and fog. Jesús M. Córdoba, alcalde at Culebra, complained that Apaches raided his settlement on June 14 and stole ten animals. Villagers chased the thieves but were not strong enough to do anything. Córdoba believed the Jicarillas and Utes were camped near the Huerfano River, just where Carleton's expedition had searched two weeks earlier. Copies of Córdoba's letter went to Carson and Davidson, who forwarded it to headquarters. Davidson commented: "To prevent exaggerated reports of rumors which may reach HQ," giving them a heads up.[75]

Garland was loath to send another expedition to cover the same territory again, but he did, reporting that "all has been done which was in the power of troops to do." He stated: "The Jicarilla Apaches have been most thoroughly humbled, and beg for peace. They are dispersed in small parties with the exception of one band, which is now hard pressed by about one hundred men under Major Blake and Captain Ewell, 1st Dragoons." To justify the lack of a great triumph in blood, Garland rationalized as did Carleton, stating that what the troops proved to the Indians "is worth more than a victory; that is, they are not safe from pursuit in the most inaccessible parts of the Rocky Mountains." Soldiers were chasing Mescaleros near El Paso, but the Jicarillas wanted peace and the Navajos "have remained quiet this year." Renegades stole some sheep, but "the nation has restored [them] to the proper owners."[76]

Garland acknowledged the good job done by the militia, particularly in capturing thirty-nine Jicarillas. Unfortunately, most of them escaped and "were shot in making the attempts." In any case, the volunteers could be disbanded. Garland thanked the acting governor, saying that "he has aided me with his influence and authority—in other words, we have acted in perfect harmony." Garland credited the Pueblo scouts, who could be "relied upon under all circumstances, not so with a part of the Mexican population, which is not only unreliable, but quite equal to the Indians in thieving and duplicity." To illustrate his point, Garland noted a recent report of fourteen Mexicans being killed by Cheyennes and Arapahos in San Miguel County. The previous winter Mexicans had gone to the Arkansas River and committed the "dastardly act" of killing three Cheyennes and stealing their horses. "These Indians," Garland concluded, "as is their custom, took their revenge."[77]

The war was not quite over, for one more fight took place near the Canadian River only about thirty-five miles from Fort Union. Lieutenants George Sykes and Joseph Maxwell, 3rd Infantry, left Fort Union on June 29 with fifty-eight men of Companies D and H, 2nd Dragoons, scouting along the Sapello River because of a report that Indians had attacked the village of Manuelitas north of Las Vegas. Meeting two small parties of New Mexican militia, Sykes took command of the whole party and followed a trail east toward the Canadian. At eight in the morning on June 30 they moved down "an almost impracticable canyon" where they came upon a dozen Indians believed to be Jicarillas. The Indians fled and Sykes and one detachment chased them while Maxwell and about twenty dragoons veered off to the right to try to intercept them.[78]

On the canyon's rim Maxwell abruptly confronted seven or eight Indians who turned to fight. With only four troopers who kept up with him they were momentarily outnumbered, and the Indians made their superiority count. As Maxwell attempted to saber the nearest warrior, another one shot him with two arrows, "almost instantaneously" killing him. Private Abraham Allen shot the warrior who had shot Maxwell, and the short but violent contest ended, Sykes alleged, with three Indians killed and five or six badly wounded (more casualties than they had in numbers engaged). Sgt. Francis Smith and Private Moore of Company H were wounded.

The remaining Indians fled. Sykes chased them for six miles until they reached the Mora River. When Sykes stopped to rest his men, the Indians disappeared into the deep Canadian canyons. They rode on. With the sun setting and the water low, however, Sykes ordered a return to the fort. Of Maxwell's death, he reported: "I have no words sir to express my feelings in making this announcement. A braver, gallant or more high toned gentleman and soldier never drew sword."

The last skirmish of the war may have been fitting. On the other side of the Canadian four months earlier Lieutenant Bell had attacked Indians who may or may not have been guilty of stealing stock. The soldiers killed Lobo Blanco and touched off a war. This time, as revealed in Sykes's "P.S." to his report, they may have also attacked innocent Indians who may not have been Jicarillas. The New Mexicans with Sykes "state confidently" that they found mescal in the Indian camp, which was not native to that part of the country. They believed that whoever the people that they had attacked were had not been raiding the settlements but "were on their return from the country of the Mescaleros."

Lieutenant Maxwell and three Indians had been killed in this latest aggression against people who were very likely innocent. Unwittingly, Cooke underscored what a number of people perceived but were reluctant to say, stating of Maxwell's death: "He fell fighting, with great bravery in a skirmish, of otherwise, no great importance." Some folks did not like that inference. Two months later Cooke had to explicate, saying that his unfortunate phrase was "misconstrued" and was not meant to be a poor reflection on their mission or on Lieutenant Sykes's "distinguished zeal and ability."[79]

The war was winding down. Major Blake returned to Fort Massachusetts empty-handed, "without meeting with the Apache or a sign." Lieutenant Davidson took his company to Rayado but encountered no Indians. Cooke scouted out of Fort Union but found no Indians.[80]

None of this stopped the locals from their usual complaints. The July 15 *Gazette* announced that Apaches near Anton Chico had run off 4,000 sheep belonging to Mariano Ylisario, and a few days later Apaches were said to have stolen five animals from Vicente Quintana and three from Rumaldo Archiveque near the Pecos River. The *Gazette* tried to tell the future, titling one report: "Contemplated depredations by the Jicarillas." It printed an extract of a July 6 letter from Judge Beaubien, who, true to his alarmist tendencies, stated: "I inform you that the Apaches are committing many depredations on all the mountain roads." He reported that some were seen along the Taos road near Laguna Negra, certainly gathering to attack a wagon train arriving from the States. As a result, Carson, Quinn, and twelve men rode out to strike the thieves preemptively before they struck the wagons. They found no marauding Indians.[81]

What General Garland thought about all this is revealed in his monthly report. He said that Fort Massachusetts was out of place, was difficult to access, commanded none of the mountain passes, and did not protect any Indians or settlers. Troops were investigating reports of raiding in the far south near El Paso. Elsewhere, however, Mescalero Chiefs Palanquito and Santos had met with Garland, told him where their bands were located, and said that they had never "committed any crime whatsoever." Garland nevertheless told them that "I would hold their whole nation accountable for the acts of any one of their bands." The Jicarillas, he reported, "are pretty thoroughly subdued." Some of them visited him with peace overtures, although "some evil disposed persons induced them to depart abruptly." Major Blake had gone north looking for Jicarillas and Utes, "but found the news of their depredations and hostility greatly exaggerated. I now have very little expectation of difficulty from that quarter."[82]

Believing there was a war raging, Governor Meriwether left Louisville on June 17 and returned to the territory on July 22, just in time, he claimed, to help a beleaguered General Garland by raising a regiment of volunteers to save the day. Facts do not bear this out. Meriwether knew of the troubles in May, but Garland had everything under control by July and did not want any volunteers causing more complications.[83]

Meriwether may have returned, but agent Edward Graves was gone. Being Meriwether's son-in-law was immaterial: Graves had had enough. He wrote his final report from Dona Ana on June 8, pouring out to Manypenny all the inequities that he had seen in his brief tenure. He called the Jicarillas indigent and cowardly yet cruel and revengeful. He said that they were lazy and indolent yet praised their manufacture of crockery. He believed that the Utes were the best fighters, often using rifles while the other tribes relied on the bow and arrow. The Utes bartered skins with the New Mexicans but were unscrupulous in plundering them when necessary. Graves stated that the Navajos were the wealthiest. Although they did fight the Mexicans, they had been much more peaceful the past two years. He called the Apaches in the south the most degraded and savage people, who lived solely by plundering.[84]

Graves explained how to handle the Indians. They could not be exterminated, for "no enlightened citizen or statesman" would ever propose such an action. He believed in the current notion that the Indians were a vanishing race, destined for "final extinction" according to natural and divine laws. All a Christian government could do was to "smooth the pass-way of their final exit from the stage of human existence." Feeding them did not seem to work, yet transitioning them into farming should be continued to make their final days more palatable. If not assisted they would steal, for "[n]o animal creature, whether civilized or not, will perish for want of food when the means of subsistence is within reach." It was much too expensive to feed the Indians, so they had to grow their own food. If they did not, the United States should "cause them to know the power of the government, as well as its charity." But Graves realized that conquering them would not solve the puzzle. "What will you do with them? You will have to either take care of them or destroy them." Another problem in Christianizing and Americanizing the Indians was that contact with white society introduced "all the vicious habits of these settlements without being impressed with any of the good." The wild tribes needed to be molded into versions of the Pueblos, which would relieve the government from being forced either to feed them or to kill them. With that, the disgruntled, jaded Graves ended: "I herewith resign my office of Indian agent in New Mexico, to take effect upon the receipt of this report."

Garland was frustrated too but could not so easily walk off the job. His August report echoed much of his two previous reports, backed by news from his most conscientious and hard-working remaining agent, Michael Steck. He reported that his Gila Apaches were behaving with "strong protestations of friendship," yet there was always trouble because "Mexicans have told them that a campaign was to be made against them, and that we were coming out as spies &c." Garland also complained of Mexicans, "who do not hesitate to barter powder and lead" with the Indians for stolen property, while in contrast the Pueblos continued to "make more orderly citizens than many of the Mexican communities." Meanwhile, although some continued to steal animals for food occasionally, "the Indians within this department have exhibited no hostility towards us during the present month."[85]

Meriwether had been begging for money for a year, constantly stating that Governor Lane had left him penniless. On July 31, 1854, Congress finally appropriated $30,000 to negotiate more treaties. Meriwether was entrusted with the mediations.[86] On the last day of August Utes brought Meriwether a message from Chacón, saying that he had taken his people far west to the San Juan River to avoid the soldiers and await Meriwether's return "with the hope of procuring peace." The governor replied that Chacón could come in under a white flag but that he might as well stay away if he was not serious about stopping his "robberies and murders."[87]

Meriwether finished his annual report to the commissioner by complaining how Lane had made unenforceable treaties that left Meriwether penniless and angered the Indians. He claimed that the Indians had committed depredations resulting in property losses estimated between fifty thousand and a hundred thousand dollars. He said that the Indians began the war and forced Garland to fight them. A portion of the Jicarillas under Chacón moved near Abiquiu to farm. But when the little produce they grew was consumed and further assistance was withheld, they too began to steal. Meriwether believed that the Jicarillas had committed more depredations than any other single tribe.[88]

According to Meriwether, Mescalero country was short of game, so they had to depredate in Texas and Chihuahua. The Gila Apaches did most of their raiding in Chihuahua and Sonora. The Navajos were becoming better farmers, owned a substantial number of horses and sheep, and made blankets that "compare favorably with any other manufactured by a civilized people." They were doing well but also had a "dark side." There were "bad men among them" who "pay but little regard to the eighth commandment, which enjoins upon us not to steal." Still, the governor was optimistic that under the judicious management of agent Henry Dodge "we have little cause to complain of them during the present year."[89]

Meriwether was concerned that the Pueblos of Nambe executed some of their own people for witchcraft but hoped that the situation would be remedied as more Christian missionaries arrived to open churches and schools. His greatest concern, however, seemed to be that the Trade and Intercourse Acts "are without binding force," since the district court had decided that there is no Indian country in New Mexico Territory yet fines and punishments could only be assessed for offenses committed in Indian country. This allowed whiskey and other goods to be sold or traded without a license. How it would affect depredation claims was also an issue. Meriwether wanted to ensure that the law would be strictly enforced and that any "depredations committed by any tribe or band should be deducted from the annuity stipulated to be paid to such tribe or band, as is provided by . . . the Intercourse Act of 1834."[90]

William Messervy had turned one peace delegation away, saying that they should wait until Meriwether returned. Now that he was back, Chacón sent a messenger to tell him that "he was desirous of peace" and wanted to see him. The governor agreed and arrived in Santa Fe on September 6. Chacón said that his people never wanted war and were destitute. He admitted that some Jicarillas had been thieving but attributed it to a few bad men under José Largo. He claimed that white soldiers had attacked him and that "he would have been worse than a dog if he had not fought back." Chacón had sixty-two lodges, while Largo only had nine. Chacón said that he would capture Largo if the governor would feed his children and women. Meriwether gave him one month and directed Lafayette Head to purchase and deliver corn to Chacón's people, camped near Abiquiu. Head did so but complained that there were about one hundred lodges of people to feed and that some of the Indians "treated him in a very insolent manner, and threatened to kill him."[91]

Chacón gathered 107 lodges near Abiquiu while he searched for Largo, but the concentration of Jicarillas frightened the locals. Garland moved three companies there to keep an eye on them. Elsewhere Garland had Major Carleton make a scout down to Bosque Redondo and back, keeping a lookout for Indians said to be marauding in San Miguel County. Lieutenant Davidson sent men down to Fort Thorn on the lower Rio Grande, while others went to Las Vegas and Anton Chico to search for raiders. From Cantonment Burgwin Captain

Thompson took soldiers to Point of Rocks to intercept any raiding Indians chased out as a result of the other two movements. None of the columns discovered significant evidence of raiders. Thompson went from Point of Rocks to the Raton Mountains, down the Vermejo, and back to Cantonment Burgwin, reporting: "I could not discover recent signs of any Indians."[92]

Garland shut down his campaign for the season. His last several monthly reports reiterated that the Indians were peaceful. On October 29, 1854, Governor Meriwether wrote: "The war with the Jicarilla and Mescalero Apaches is progressing without any decided results on either side." He stated that the Navajos, Gila Apaches, and Utes were all at peace and committed no depredations, emphasizing that the Utes had not raided for a full year since he talked with them in the fall of 1853. He was pleased that Chico Velásquez had brought in a number of horses and mules stolen from Mexicans before the end of hostilities. Chico restored the animals to their owners and took forty beef cattle back to Fort Union. Meriwether gave him gifts of tobacco and other presents.[93]

It appeared that the winter would be a peaceful one, although peace never prevented people from filing depredation claims.[94] Three events, however, became the initial toppling dominos in a chain that would develop into another war. First, about twenty-five Pueblos from Taos went hunting in the Raton Mountains in late October. About November 5 Cheyennes or Arapahos discovered them, attacked, and killed twelve of them. Among the dead were several who had distinguished themselves in the spring campaign against the Jicarillas. Carson was saddened by their deaths. He asked Meriwether to keep the Plains Indians out of his agency boundaries. Meriwether, however, said that Carson was mistaken—he was sure that the Jicarillas had killed them. The Pueblos likely knew who attacked them better than Meriwether did, but this was indicative of a feud that was developing between the governor and the agent.[95]

This was preceded by an incident near Fort Defiance in early October. Despite the lack of solid evidence, it was alleged that Pvt. Nicholas Hefbiner, Company B, 3rd Infantry, had raped the wife of a Navajo. One morning while Hefbiner was out cutting hay, the husband shot him with an arrow. When Hefbiner died the next day, Captain Kendrick felt compelled to bring the murderer to justice, in spite of the memory of the war that nearly began over the attempt to arrest the murderer of Ramón Martín the previous year. Kendrick assembled the Navajo chiefs and demanded that they surrender the culprit, believing that to show weakness would undermine his authority and invite other murders. He urged Garland to make an immediate campaign against them if they did not turn the man in. But Garland, who agreed with Kendrick in theory, was reluctant to start another war. The Navajos asked if they could make remuneration with an equitable number of horses and sheep, but Kendrick wanted the guilty man. Surprisingly, the Navajos did what they had never done before: they handed over a man to the Americans for "justice." The alleged murderer, badly wounded while resisting capture, was surrendered on November 5. He was taken to Fort Defiance and identified by soldiers who had been cutting hay with Private Hefbiner. According to agent Henry Dodge, with this proof and at the "urgent request" of the Navajos, the military "had him hung until he was *dead dead dead.*"[96]

Meriwether said that the hanging of an Indian "in this summary manner without a legal trial is to be regretted." But, after all, there was no jail to hold him and an example was needed, for "it will have a decidedly good effect upon others." Garland thought the same: "It will not be without its good effect upon the neighboring tribes."[97]

Just how good an effect it had was shown in early October, when Lafayette Head brought news to Meriwether that a Mexican of Taos County had killed a Ute without provocation. Chico Velásquez and his band "were in a very excited mood" and wished to meet the governor immediately. Meriwether directed agents Kit Carson and Lorenzo Labadi to calm the Utes down. On October 20 they gathered near Abiquiu. The Muache Ute leader Velásquez and the Capote Ute leader Tamouche at once reminded Meriwether of his promise that anyone who molested their people would be brought to justice. They asked: was the governor "as good as his word?" He said that he was. He offered $100 in gold for anyone who would bring the murderer in. A Mexican constable said: "I'll have him here tomorrow morning." When Meriwether asked him how he could be so sure, the constable said that the man had boasted of the killing and even showed him the bloody blanket that the Ute wore.[98]

The next morning as Velásquez and Tamouche skeptically waited, the constable rode in with the shackled man. Meriwether questioned him. Apparently the murdered Ute had been to Taos to see agent Carson and was returning to his village when he simply stopped to visit some New Mexican herders and was promptly shot down. The governor asked why.

"I didn't know it was any harm to kill an Indian," the arrested suspect replied.

"By the time you get through my hands," Meriwether said, "you will find it is some harm to kill an Indian, when he is quiet and peaceable."

The Utes wanted Meriwether to give the man up to their justice then and there, but the governor insisted that he be taken to Santa Fe for a proper trial. If he was convicted, the Utes could come and witness the man "hung up to a tree like a dog." He was not so scrupulous when an alleged Navajo murderer was executed for killing a white man the day after being apprehended because there was no nearby jail. The double standard of white justice could not have been lost on the Utes when they learned of it, but now they reluctantly agreed to let Meriwether have the prisoner. The governor sent him to Taos County where the murder occurred, but the soldiers who were escorting him returned in a few days, "informing me that the prisoner had escaped."

Worse was yet to come out of the Abiquiu meeting. At its conclusion Meriwether presented Velásquez and Tamouche with gray cloth coats decorated with red and yellow braid and brass buttons. He said that these were the first such coats that they had ever owned and that they were very pleased with them. The gifts, however, may have been deadly. Shortly afterward Velásquez, and possibly Tamouche, contracted smallpox. It was speculated that the coats were infected, although there had been cases of smallpox appearing in some villages before this. In any event Velásquez was hit fast and hard. In Meriwether's report of November 30, he reported: "I very much regret the death of Chico Velasquez." Although he had the reputation of a "savage and a bad man," Meriwether had acquired "an influence over him" and believed that there was nothing to fear from him or his band. Even while smallpox was ravaging them, the governor said, the Utes "remain quiet and peaceable." He furnished Carson and Labadi with a vaccine and had them "vaccinate all who would come within their reach."[99]

Velásquez's death meant that Coniache became the head Muache chief. Meriwether said that he was "a mild, well-disposed Indian" but doubted that he would have the same influence over the tribe as Velásquez had; besides, he was often intoxicated. Likely watching events with keen interest was Coniache's war leader, Tierra Blanca (White Earth), whom Meriwether described as "one of the most forbidding looking beings I ever saw in all my life," with only one eye and a smallpox scarred face.[100]

Whether or not Tierra Blanca, often called Blanco, looked as fearful as Meriwether described, he soon became the new object of white fear and revulsion. Lobo Blanco was gone and Chacón had never matched the white imagination of a bloody savage. Tierra Blanca became the new top villain. The Utes were angry. Although Meriwether complimented them on their peacefulness over the past year, they were at the breaking point. Many who believed that smallpox was purposely introduced by the white people. Carson said that they thought Meriwether had caused their affliction, that "he had collected them for the purpose of injuring them."[101] That, combined with discontent over white society's justice, had them boiling. But possibly the worst affront was the continued incursions of the Mexicans and Americans into their lands, while seemingly favoring their Plains Tribe enemies.

The Muache Utes felt that they were being taken advantage of. The Treaty of 1849 allowed whites to pass through their territory but not to build settlements. The Utes were to cultivate the soil while the army built forts to protect them from their enemies. Coniache had spoken of their misgivings to agent Greiner two years earlier: the Great Father did not seem to trust them, for he did not give them powder and lead but gave their enemies plenty. No white men married Ute women, the forts built to protect them were useless, and they were forbidden to respond when Americans, Mexicans, and the Plains tribes made war on them. Not a penny's worth of the presents that they had been promised in the 1849 treaty was delivered until late in 1852. In 1851 Mexicans moved to the Conejos River and built irrigation ditches, but the Utes drove them out. Despite repeated warnings from Calhoun and Lane, settlers kept creeping in. The Utes usually just backed off, not wanting to exacerbate matters. The Mexicans promised money and gifts if they could remain but never paid. John Greiner expended much effort in trying to keep the Mexicans out of the San Luis Valley, but he was gone in 1854. Soon settlements appeared on the Conejos, Costilla, and Culebra. The white settlements east of the Sangre de Cristo near the Arkansas River, at Pueblo, Hardscrabble, and Greenhorn, were grudgingly and even less tolerated, as they used the scarce resources while cutting the Utes out of the bargain and establishing exclusive trade relations with the Cheyennes and Arapahos.

A drought hit the Utes hard. In the fall of 1853 some were reduced to peeling bark from pine and aspen trees in the San Luis Valley to feed their children. Lack of weapons thwarted their ability to hunt buffalo on the plains. For five years the Utes remained comparatively peaceful, even returning lost or stolen stock on numerous occasions, but by 1854 the pressures were building. With expanded settlements on Ute land, plowing of fields, grazing stock on sparse grass, hunger, smallpox, unlicensed traders, lack of trust, inequitable justice, fear, and increasing hate, the situation had reached the boiling point.[102]

The Utes were most irritated about the settlements along the Arkansas River, where the Americans and Mexicans continued to deplete resources while trading with the Cheyennes, Arapahos, Kiowas, and Comanches at Bent's Fort and giving them guns and ammunition in the bargain. On October 16, 1854, Charles Autobees, who had settled on the Huerfano, was traveling with four men and some Arapaho women and children with a wagonload of corn and flour to trade with the Arapahos. About five miles east of Pueblo, Coniache and a band of Utes stopped them and said that they would not harm Autobees if he would turn over the Arapahos. When Autobees refused, the Utes attacked, wounded Autobees, and stole four of his animals. Sometime that fall the Utes also killed a Mexican trader on Apache Creek near Greenhorn.[103]

These were warning signs. When the Mexican murdered a Ute and was not punished and when Utes visited Meriwether and soon after died of smallpox, it was the last straw.

6

The War of 1855

The bottomlands along the junction of Fountain Creek and the Arkansas River on the cold morning of December 25, 1854, may have been foggy. Indian riders approaching the adobe Pueblo included Tierra Blanca with one hundred Ute warriors, likely accompanied by Huero, son-in-law of Chacón, and perhaps eighty Jicarilla warriors. If they were concealed in the frosty mists, they were nevertheless seen by young Benito País, who had left the fort before dawn to fetch some milk at José Marcelino Baca's house. The boy heard a whistle and peered doggedly until he noticed Indians moving in just beyond the gravel ford on the Fountain. País rode fast to Baca's to give the alarm.

Most of the people in the outlying houses were rising for their daily chores, even though it was Christmas. Not so at the Pueblo, where there had been an all-night card game. Although some were up and about, many others slept. Other abodes were vacant. Joe Doyle, Bob Rice, and Pedro Sandoval were away on business. Dick Wootton from the Huerfano settlement noticed fresh Indian signs and warned those at Pueblo not to let any Indians inside the fort and then hurried home.

Young País reached Baca's house and told them what he had seen. Baca quickly alerted the nearby cabins. As they gathered at his house, he saw Indians coming and asked old José Barela if he thought they should greet them. "No, don't make friends with the Indians or they'll kill us!" Barela warned. Baca ordered the men to get their weapons and closed the house up tight.[1]

Blanca had already taken Baca's best white mare and confidently approached Baca and Barela, positioned on either side of the house with their rifles aimed at him.

"Amigo," Blanca said with a smile. Baca warned him that if he came any closer he would shoot. A few tense moments followed, but Blanca smiled again. He and his men slowly rode away toward the fort. When they left, Barela saddled a horse that he kept hidden and rode to warn the American settlements on the Huerfano. Half an hour after the Utes left Baca's, before eight in the morning, they heard shooting coming from the direction of the Pueblo.

Barela returned five hours later, and not until then did they feel safe enough to leave Baca's and see what had happened. They first discovered José I. Valencia's body near the ford of the Fountain. Then they saw a badly wounded Juan R. Medina stumbling toward them with his abdomen sliced open. They gave him water. He indicated that all at the fort had been killed, then he died. On the way they found the body of the Navajo Guadalupe Vigil, killed with an arrow in his back. Outside the fort were two or three dead Utes. At the gate was the mortally wounded Rumaldo Cordova, who tried to relate what had happened. A twelve-year-old boy, Félix Sandoval, later explained that a lone Indian had come to the fort asking for food but was refused admittance. When Blanca rode up, Benito Sandoval and Cordova opened the gate. Although Sandoval wanted to shoot Blanca, Cordova said: "This is my friend." As he ushered Blanca in, the chief grabbed Cordova's own gun and shot him in the mouth. Then the chaos began. One Indian grabbed Félix Sandoval and threw him on a horse. Others took Chepita Miera, Cordova's sister-in-law. After that point, no one knew what happened. Francisco Mestas, Juan Blas Martín, and Manuel Lucero's bodies lay nearby. At one point it appeared that Benito Sandoval grabbed his son, Juan. They hid in a bastion, but Utes tore through the roof and shot Benito through the top of his head then took his boy captive. The body of Joaquín Pacheco was found along the Arkansas a half-mile away. The bodies of Juan Aragón and Tanislado de Luna were never found. The bodies of five or six Utes were left unburied for the wolves.

After the Pueblo massacre the Utes went to the Wet Mountains and camped on Grape Creek, but they could not enjoy their spoils. The next morning Arapahos attacked them, killed a few, and stole their property and stock. The Utes fled, no doubt enraged at their misfortune. One of them shot an arrow into Chepita Miera's back. A month later soldiers found her scalp hanging from a tree in the Wet Mountains.

Deprived of much of what they had taken from Pueblo, the Utes returned again on December 27, killed four people, and stole more livestock, including forty of Levin Mitchell's cattle, which he claimed were worth $1,470. Men from the St. Charles settlement battled the Utes and chased them away. A few days later, Marcelino Baca, John Jurnegan, and Jonathan W. Atwood headed for Taos for help. On January 13 Baca filed a depredation claim with agent Carson. He said that the Utes had taken ten yoke of oxen, fifty-three cows, thirteen horses, and two mules, worth $4,115. Jurnegan and Atwood were his witnesses. Apparently knowing the terms of the Trade and Intercourse Act, Baca also added that at the time the Utes were "in peace and amity with the United States" and that he never attempted to recover the stolen items. Carson forwarded the claim to Governor Meriwether, who commented that the depredation was not committed in New Mexico Territory, although done by Indians of the Territory, and questioned whether Baca was "within the Indian country, and if so, had he a license to trade or a passport?" These points, and others, would be key to whether or not the claims would be approved.[2]

Garland prepared for another campaign. He made it known to Capt. Horace Brooks at Fort Massachusetts and to Major Blake at Burgwin that he wanted the mobilization to be "kept secret until the troops take the field."[3] As if Garland did not have enough concerns, on January 18 several discharged American soldiers attacked the residence of army paymaster Maj. F. A. Cunningham, beat him, and robbed him of $40,000. Soldiers were called to run the culprits down "and give them a thorough overhauling."[4]

To top it off, Mescaleros were said to have attacked the ranches of Preston Beck and Mr. Eaton near Galisteo on January 11, barely twenty miles south of Santa Fe. They killed one herder, wounded another, and stole seventy-five horses and mules.[5] Lt. Sam Sturgis, 1st Dragoons, and seventeen men, assisted by Mr. Eaton and a few civilians, set out after them. They followed a trail southeast through frigid weather for three days. On January 16 they found about nine Mescaleros, probably in the Cola del Gallo canyon in present-day northeastern Lincoln County. The Indians just left a wooded campsite and came out in the open when Sturgis opened fire, but the cold was so great and their hands so "benumbed" that "there was not a man in the party who could reload his piece." Sturgis ordered a saber charge. Corporal Nicholas Katon slashed a Mescalero, who "was literally cut in two." The dragoons reached the timber and fought about fifteen minutes, killing three and wounding four, while Katon was wounded in the arm by an arrow, trumpeter William Drown took a ball in the shoulder, and Private Rooney was mortally wounded by an arrow that went more than two inches into his head. Mr. Eaton was slightly wounded. Sturgis recovered the stolen stock and turned north to Anton Chico.[6]

A few days after Sturgis's fight, Captain Ewell battled Mescaleros in the Sacramento Mountains, a result of reports by Preston Beck and James Giddings that Mescaleros had robbed them of sheep and goats worth $4,111 (the case was not proven). Ewell took eighty-one men of the 1st Dragoons out of Los Lunas and marched east to the Pecos River then downstream to the Bonito River, where he joined Capt. Henry W. Stanton with twenty-nine dragoons and fifty infantry out of Fort Fillmore. They traveled up the Rio Hondo, cut south to the Rio Penasco, and moved upstream. On January 18 Mescaleros attacked their camp, shot arrows into it, and tried to burn them out. The next day the soldiers chased the Indians into the mountains, while the Mescaleros made hit-and-run strikes against the column. Captain Stanton took twelve men to examine an adjoining valley but rode into a trap. He took a bullet in the head, one soldier was lanced, and a third was shot. All died. The Mescaleros had held off the soldiers long enough for their families to escape, and Ewell lost their trail. On January 20 he headed for home, with horses so broken down that he walked them in.[7]

Garland, with fighting breaking out on all sides, did what he was loath to do: on January 25 he asked Meriwether to call out six companies of volunteers to serve for six months. Garland also authorized Capt. Lucien Stewart of Taos to hire a company of thirty "guides and spies" at two dollars per person per day. The general requested more regular troops because "[t]here is great uneasiness and insecurity among all the frontier settlers." He fielded more than four hundred soldiers and volunteers "with orders to carry the war into the Utah country, and force upon them the necessity of looking after their own security and that of their women and children."[8]

General Garland was going back to war. But before he could put any of his plans into operation, the Utes attacked the Pueblo area again. This time there were about 180 warriors—Utes under Tierra Blanca and Jicarillas under Guero. They arrived at the junction of the Fountain and the Arkansas on January 19, but this time no one was living there—all had been killed or captured or had fled. Baca's family had moved downstream to the settlement on the St. Charles, but even the folks there had concluded to move. Utes attacked as they headed east and killed nine Cherokee teamsters in one wagon train. The Utes then attacked the Huerfano settlers. Joe Doyle was still away on a trading trip, but his family was at Dick Wootton's, where the men fortified the place and fired away at the surprised Utes. Witnesses said that from three to seven Americans were killed.[9]

It would seem that most of the stock would have been stolen, killed, or taken away by this date, but several of the locals filed depredation reports. One of them, Tomás Suaso, was the son of Teresita Sandoval and her first husband, José Manuel Suaso. Teresita was allegedly quite a beauty and very likely not that easy to live with, for she had a number of husbands. Her third one was Alexander Barclay, who, in addition to wanting to make money by building and selling a fort to the U.S. government, was said to have moved from the Arkansas River settlements to New Mexico in order to build Teresita a big, new permanent home. Tomás, born in the early 1830s, lived somewhere in the Arkansas River settlements when the Utes attacked.[10]

I say "somewhere" because eyewitnesses in his depredation claim place him at several locations. Suaso claimed that on January 19, 1855, Utes stole thirty cows, seven American horses, one saddle horse, one Indian horse, twenty-five fanegas of corn, and one Hawken Rifle, all worth $2,110. He gathered several witnesses for validation, but they apparently did not coordinate their stories. Allen P. Tibbets, who lived on the north side of the Arkansas River near Pueblo, said he saw Utes driving off Suaso's stock. Dick Wootton said that he "resided within 100 yards of said Suaso in said years." He also saw Utes driving away Suaso's stock, but Wootton lived five miles downstream on the Huerfano and shot at the raiders from his own door. Benito Salazar was Tomás Suaso's uncle, and they lived at the Pueblo "within three hundred yards of each other." Juan Salazar said that on January 19 he was at Joe Doyle's house and saw five hundred Indians run off Suaso's cattle and horses, but the houses were miles apart. Francisco Salazar testified that Suaso, Tibbetts, and Baca all lived on the north side of the Arkansas near Pueblo. He heard about the alleged property theft but "has no personal knowledge of the stealing." José Marcelino Baca tried to help his neighbor too. Baca testified that on January 19 "he saw Indians drive off stock belonging to Tomas Suaso." On that date, however, Baca was in Taos.[11]

It seems apparent that a few of the witnesses were in collusion, although they needed to get their stories synchronized if they wanted to make an airtight case of it. The government attorneys who argued the case decades later likely never caught the internal inconsistencies. They did cut down some of the alleged losses, disallowing the fanegas of corn and the Hawken Rifle as being unproven. They initially approved the claim in 1876 for $1,460 but subsequently denied it in 1889. The reasons: on January 19, 1855, "claimant was unlawfully in the Indian country, and is, therefore, without remedy" and "the Indians alleged to have committed the said depredation were at the time . . . not in amity with the United States." The Indians, the Jicarillas and Muache Utes, "were openly and notoriously hostile from March, 1854 to July, 1854, and from December 25, 1854, to September 11, 1855."[12]

It was much harder for the government attorneys to prove witness collusion and deceit, so the broader framework of the Trade and Intercourse Acts was the ticket to a successful defense. There would be no indemnification from tribes at war, only those at peace. Peaceful tribes, however, would not be committing depredations; if they did, then they must be at war. Government attorneys may have been playing a technicality game, but it never matched the game of fabrication, falsehood, and fiction that the civilians played on the government.

Few people at the time realized the harm that false accusations played in fomenting fear, hate, and war. Judge John S. Watts became the attorney for 244 New Mexicans who sought redress from alleged depredations. In 1858 he wrote a 66-page florid, indignant missive to interior secretary Jacob Thompson, demanding justice for those who had not yet gotten money for their depredation claims.[13]

Watts's main concerns were that claims should not have had a statute of limitations, that the idea of a tribe needing to be in "amity" was fallacious, and that he saw nothing wrong in claimants testifying for one another. "I feel assured that the claims are just and honest," he wrote. Watts believed that the 244 claims collected in a report for the years 1846 to 1856 were only a small percentage of the real depredations, given that the New Mexicans were surrounded by seventy thousand "savage Indians" who all "rob and plunder with impunity." He was certain the claims were underreported, not exaggerated. Watts was convinced that Indians were not the noble creatures of the novels and poems of James Fenimore Cooper and Henry Wadsworth Longfellow; on the contrary, "as nations they are thieves and robbers, and leave behind them in their pathway desolation and death, and in nine out of ten outrages which have occurred, the Indian, and not the white man, has been the aggressor. They are given to every vice, destitute of every virtue."[14]

Like any attorney trying to prove his case, Watts selected only the supportive evidence and ignored the military reports that showed a great number of claims to be embellished or totally false and that a high percentage of conflicts were not initiated by the Indians. For him, volume of complaints and anecdotes became data. Watts protested that it was wrong for the government not to trust *ex parte* testimony, meaning testimony taken for or by claimants without the government there to cross-examine. People were, after all, basically honest, so their word "ought reasonably to be considered sufficient proof of the truth of the depredations complained of." If a man "is disinterested, and the story which he relates is a rational one," it ought to be accepted as the truth, but even if a man is interested in the outcome it should not disqualify him. If we cannot rely on eyewitnesses telling the truth, said Watts, and "substitute in their stead universal distrust and incredulity," then civil society becomes "inferior to that of savages."[15]

What Watts did not realize was that those very eyewitnesses were about as unreliable and untrustworthy as could be imagined. Numerous social and psychological studies in the late twentieth century would demolish his ideas of humans as competent, truthful, and disinterested observers.[16]

Watts wanted the government to indemnify its citizens in war or peace, regardless of amity questions. He saw the problem thus: if the Indians do no wrong there are no claims, but if they murder and rob, then the government cannot pay, for war exists. "So, if this theory be true, the act of Congress is nothing but a collection of ingenious words, so beautifully arranged as to mean nothing."[17] A more correct view may be that Congress probably had good intentions when the earliest acts were formulated. They proved nearly unenforceable, more conducive to harm than good, and the litigation that they engendered became so voluminous and entangled that there was little hope of ever sorting things out. So the government attorneys realized they would have to find ways to deny or dismiss as many claims as possible. In seeking ways to cut the Gordian knot of litigation by denying them not on individual merit but categorically through limitation statutes, amity questions, or distrusting *ex parte* testimony, the government may have been furtively operating with the knowledge that many claimants were fabricators engaged in criminal misconduct. In the long run, government suspicion and frugality ensured that justice was served—or at least that it was subverted less.[18]

A great problem thus existed in separating the wheat from the chaff. Although he contributed to the fear and furor by exaggerating Indian hostility, Governor Meriwether did second-guess his actions. He knew that Judge Watts had sent claims to Commissioner Manypenny and wanted them returned so that they would flow through the proper channels for payment, but he had reservations when he became aware of the local *partido* practice. "Hence," Meriwether told the commissioner, "in the examination of claims presented for the loss of sheep charged to have been taken by the Indians, where the pastor, shepherd or Mayor domo is the witness by whom the loss is proven, it may be well to recollect that almost invariably he is an interested party." He believed it was important that the commissioner be aware of this, "because several cases of this character have already been transmitted to your office."[19]

If Meriwether had misgivings about blaming the Indians for alleged thefts, just as the army had for years, it was mostly immaterial by this time. The Indian attack at Pueblo, even if overwhelmingly justifiable in their eye, and despite the white and Mexican exaggeration of losses, was absolutely certain to ignite a major military response.

Chasing the Utes

While some units pursued Mescaleros in the south, others readied for the northern expedition. Garland had less direct involvement in the daily activities this time, giving Col. Thomas T. Fauntleroy command of the campaign as well as of Forts Union and Massachusetts, Cantonment Burgwin, and the Northern Military District of New Mexico.[20] Fauntleroy was born in Virginia in 1796 and was a career officer, serving as a lieutenant in the War of 1812, a major during the Seminole Wars, and colonel of the 1st Dragoons starting in 1850. He replaced Cooke in command of Fort Union in September 1854. Whether Garland knew it or not, the arriving colonel was happy to be coming to New Mexico but was not particularly pleased that Garland was his boss. In November 1853 Fauntleroy was in command at Fort Leavenworth while most of his regiment was in New Mexico. Believing that he was the senior officer and best suited for the position, he wrote to secretary of war Davis requesting that he be appointed. Davis would not reply but sent the request to army headquarters, "whither it should have been originally sent." General Scott scolded him that he violated military protocol and that his "conduct deserved pointed rebuke." Beyond that, they already had "a proper person to command in New Mexico" who was selected "upon other considerations." If, however, Fauntleroy was so insistent upon joining his regiment, he should get ready, for he would be sent there the coming spring.[21]

Fauntleroy thus found himself commanding half of New Mexico, which was better than commanding one fort, but he still chafed being under an infantry colonel, even one who had been brevetted brigadier general. Fauntleroy would have at his disposal Companies D and F, 1st Dragoons, and Company D, 2nd Artillery, as well as five companies of civilian mounted volunteers in command of Lt. Col. Ceran St. Vrain: Company A, Capt. Charles Williams, and Lts. Marcelino Vigil and Matías Ortega; Company B, Capt. Francisco Gonzales, and Lts. John Mostin and Felipe Sánchez; Company D, Capt. William S. Cunningham, and Lts. Tomás Valencia and Oliver P. Hovey; Company E, Capt. Charles Deus, and Lts. Albert H. Pfeiffer and Matías Martínez; and Company F, Capt. Manuel A. Chávez, and Lts. Agapito García and Román Baca. Company C, Capt. Miguel E. Pino, and Lts. Cándido Ortiz and Ygnacio Moya, went to Major Carleton in Albuquerque to fight Mescaleros. Capt. Lucien Stewart recruited thirty "spies."[22]

Coincidentally, or because of the troop assembly at Fort Union, the entire neighborhood suddenly awoke to the possibilities. Complaints of stock thefts and murders increased. Jicarillas and Utes were supposed to be on the Canadian River, raiding at Las Vegas, Ocate Creek, near Mora, and in the San Luis Valley. They were said to have stolen 625 sheep from Julian Romero and 3,800 sheep and goats from Juan B. Valdez, Jesús M. Sánchez, and Juan Vigil. Francisco Tomás Cabeza de Baca filed a claim for $3,590, and Julián Lucero for $3,095. Juan Vigil's claim was for $5,580 for the theft of 1,200 sheep, horses and mules, but he did not file until two years later.[23] As a result of those complaints, Captain Gonzales took his newly equipped Company B out after the alleged raiders. They traveled beyond Wagon Mound and toward Point of Rocks before heading into the Raton Mountains then west to Long Canyon, where they surprised some Jicarillas eating dinner. The Indians escaped but left behind their freshly cooked horsemeat for the famished volunteers to eat. Gonzales returned to Fort Union in time to join the other companies about to pull out for Fort Massachusetts.[24]

Similar reports were coming from Abiquiu and El Rito, but agent Lorenzo Labadi found more blame with the Mexicans than with the Indians. About January 29, 1855, Apaches allegedly killed seven cattle near Abiquiu. Francisco Gallegos and about thirty men went after them. On February 13 Gallegos attacked eight lodges of Capote and Muache Utes (eleven warriors with their families), killed two men, wounded one, and took two captives, plus all of their property and animals. Labadi protested that the attacked Indians were under his charge and had never "injured or molested any white person of this Territory." Gonzales's men, however, "are very much disliked by the people for the reason that they are in the habit of ill-treating peaceable Indians and also killing any that they happen to meet with."[25]

The aggrieved Utes, including Tamouche, protested to Labadi, sending him word that they wanted to meet to get their people and property back. On February 21 a Capote Ute, Yeusache, met with the agent, affirming that the Capotes and Navajos living west of Abiquiu were all peaceful and were not assisting the Muaches in their war. In fact, Yeusache said, the army could attack all the Muaches it wanted, for neither he nor his people had any regard for them. Labadi told Meriwether that he had gone to the justice of Rio Arriba County at El Rito, who tried to redeem the Indian property, but Francisco Gallegos "refused to deliver up said property of the Indians."[26]

Strangely enough, upon receipt of Labadi's letters, Meriwether called the agent "a very credulous man" and believed that he gave too much credit "to idle reports and rumors." He did not elaborate, so it is difficult to apprehend Meriwether's intent. On the same day he wrote that he realized the locals were all "interested parties" and were prone to lie about their stock losses.[27]

Colonel Fauntleroy sent a volunteer company to Abiquiu to investigate. Capt. Charles Deus patrolled the area for several weeks, skirmishing with a band of Utes and possibly Jicarillas at Las Nutrias on March 14 and forcing them out of the area. Deus thus missed the start of Fauntleroy's campaign. The colonel left Capt. Joseph Whittlesey in charge of Fort Union and on February 20 left for Taos. The march had hardly begun when some volunteers began capturing "stray" animals that they claimed belonged to them per the governor's promises.[28]

While Fauntleroy moved north, an incident south of Albuquerque illustrated the tentative, volatile relationship that the Americans had with the New Mexicans. After Captain Ewell dragged his weary horses and men in after chasing the Mescaleros, he established a grazing camp to recruit his animals at the mouth of Comanche Canyon in the Manzano Mountains about twenty miles southeast of Los Lunas. Six dragoons were posted there on the night of February 23, when raiders—first presumed to be Mescaleros—attacked them. The assailants jumped four men inside their tent—Privates Ringgold, Culligan, Weaver, and Young—while the two others were out burning charcoal. Pulling the tent down around them, the attackers blasted the helpless soldiers until they extricated themselves and fought back. All four were hit with arrows at least four times, but they drove the attackers away. Culligan crawled to Manuel Chávez's ranch for help, Chávez sent a rider to Los Lunas, and the next morning Ewell and Lt. Isaiah Moore were at the scene. The wounded were removed, but Private Ringgold died several days later.

They found about forty or fifty cattle missing, but most surprising was the discovery that only a few of the many arrows that littered the ground had Mescalero markings, while the great majority were unmarked—something the Indians would never have done. Ewell marched east to Manzano, where the residents told the tale that Indians had just come through and killed the alcalde's son. Ewell believed that this was a sham to hide their complicity in the attack. He next went to Torreon and found the people uncooperative and suspicious. Ewell said: "When I arrived at Torreon in an instant I saw the unwillingness to say anything." He figured they were in collusion. The *Gazette*, in a flight of hyperbole, called the grazing camp fight "one of the most meritorious actions that has ever occurred in New Mexico, and the soldiers made heroes of themselves." "A more gallant defence than this has not been made under the walls of Sebastopol."[29]

While Ewell dealt with the Mexicans around Albuquerque, Fauntleroy's campaign had bogged down in Taos. Garland's February 6 order directed Fauntleroy to "hunt up and punish" Blanca and Huero for their attacks on Pueblo and not to be concerned about department boundaries. Fauntleroy was to follow them wherever they went and attack anyone shielding them. Garland said that he "does not recognize the principle, urged by peace establishment men, that we can wage war upon one part and not the whole of a Nation." The orders urged alacrity.[30]

A month later Fauntleroy was still in Taos. He said that this was because his transportation and three months of provisions for five hundred men had not arrived and his spies were not organized. In addition, he got a report that Apaches were in the mountains only eight miles from Taos and had to investigate. He wanted to disperse his companies to protect the scattered settlements, in the "hope that the apparent position of the troops will lead the Indians into the belief that nothing more active is to be done in the matter and thus lull them into a false security."[31] This was reminiscent of Governor Calhoun protesting to Colonel Sumner that he should punish the Indians, yet keep enough soldiers behind to protect the settlements, leaving too few to chase the Indians.

Fauntleroy had more worries. On March 8, 1855, discontented dragoons of Company F mutinied in Taos Plaza. The company had been thought of as an excellent unit, but the men extremely disliked Major Blake, whom they considered a harsh martinet. Company F constructed much of Fort Massachusetts but was pushed to the limit working under harsh conditions, sometimes in subzero temperatures, with poor food, no entertainment, and no time off. Blake never granted passes, but he often traipsed down to Taos for wine and song. The company had been badly used under Davidson at Cieneguilla and had barely reconstituted itself before Fauntleroy planned to take it north for more fighting. Capt. Philip Thompson took the company from Cantonment Burgwin but first stopped off at St. Vrain's distillery to get "Taos Lightning" for himself and his men. By the time they reached Taos, a number of them were intoxicated.

The men got belligerent in the plaza, but an oblivious Blake sat writing reports and let matters get out of control. A crowd gathered as fighting began. Blake ordered Thompson to arrest a sergeant, but he refused. Blake placed the man under arrest when a private rode up and told him the men were tired of being driven like slaves. Blake pulled him off his horse and struck him, and the situation degenerated. The brawl engulfed Blake, some of his officers, his men, and the townsfolk. A civilian pulled a muddy and bleeding Blake out of the mess and into a store, while the sheriff finally arrived and arrested a number of soldiers.

Blake should have left the scene, but he went outside and challenged every man in the company to a fight. One trooper raised his musketoon to shoot Blake, but Kit Carson arrived and wrestled the carbine from the man's hands. Finally, order prevailed. Thompson said that "[t]he men had no doubt been drinking" but naively stated that "no result of this nature could possibly have been anticipated."[32]

Lt. John Trevitt, 3rd Infantry, was placed in command at Cantonment Burgwin to relieve Major Blake. Blake wrote that "I was attacked in Taos by some men of F Co . . . knocked down and much bruised, so much so, that I was confined to the house for several days. My hands were so much injured that I was unable to write" or ride a horse.[33]

Fauntleroy finally pulled out of Taos on March 8, with all the soldiers except Company F, which was expected to join up later. They gathered at Fort Massachusetts "to take the field on the 15th in full campaign." With reports of Indians stealing stock in the Conejos settlement, they first moved southwest through the snowy San Luis Valley, where they picked up a trail heading northwest up the Rio Grande to the La Garita Mountains and turned north. In the vicinity of present-day Saguache, Colorado, they camped near a site that contained human bones and the detritus of an abandoned village. Some speculated that this was a camp that had been ravaged by smallpox and was one of the reasons that the Utes struck Pueblo. In the morning they turned west following Saguache Creek upstream.[34]

On March 19, about ten in the morning, they saw Indians in the valley a mile or more ahead of them, "drawn up in a line," according to Fauntleroy, "and evincing every indication to give battle." More than one hundred warriors were all mounted and in battle attire. When the distance closed to half a mile, Fauntleroy ordered the charge. The Indians "fled in the direction of the mountains for about four miles to a point most densely covered with cedar trees." Not everyone shared Fauntleroy's perspective. Captain Chávez said the Indians charged his company, all mounted, wearing war bonnets, and carrying shields and lances, "and the attack turned into a hand-to-hand conflict." Assistant Surgeon DeWitt C. Peters joined the charge. He said the Indians were in battle line but did not realize how many troops were coming until they topped a hill and came in full sight, when many of them broke and ran. Peters fell from his horse onto a prickly pear cactus, remounted, and tried to pick out the spines when his horse ran away with him. In a few moments he was behind a fleeing warrior and fired five times with his pistol but missed. Peters threw the gun away and drew close enough to punch the man with his fist. It did little damage, but Peters concluded: "This is the best way I can fight."[35]

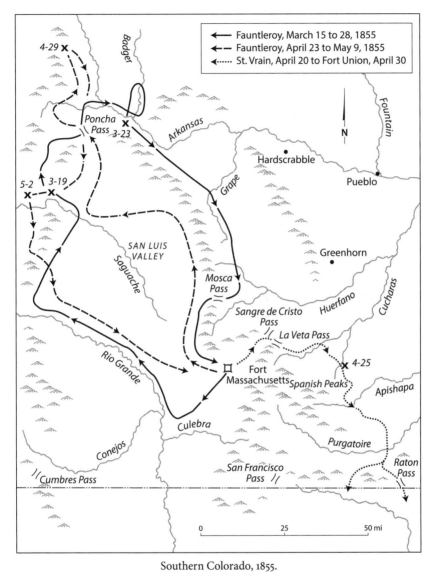

Southern Colorado, 1855.

Map by Bill Nelson. Copyright © 2017 by the University of Oklahoma Press.

The warriors put up some initial resistance. But after a chase of a few miles they stopped and made another stand, likely to buy their families time to escape. Fauntleroy said that they were overtaken at the edge of the timber "in considerable force." He ordered the men to dismount and enter the woods. "A sharp conflict ensued at this stage of the affair which continued about one hour." Tierra Blanca was said to be there, conspicuous in a bright red shirt, riding about and yelling orders. He may have commanded the Utes, while Guero led the Jicarillas. Captain Chávez said that a Jicarilla chief became too bold and charged him with his lance. The captain unerringly shot him. Before he fell, volunteer Anthony Tapía dragged him to the ground and scalped him.[36]

Sgt. Rafael Chacón of Company B wrote that the Indians "were undoubtedly waiting for us to give us battle; they offered great resistance, and we had a regular pitched battle with them." He said that they fought "with reckless valor, but in the end they had to abandon the field, leaving their dead, who were buried by order of Colonel Fauntleroy." An Indian woman that they captured later said that seven warriors were killed and a number wounded. Fauntleroy had two horses killed and two men wounded, one shot through the thigh and one through the ankle. Although it was still daylight they stopped and built campfires to warm themselves and recuperate. Sergeant Chacón said that he became ill, fainted, and fell from his horse, believing it "was because I had taken no food that day and as we went along I had kept picking up handfuls of snow and eating it to slack my thirst."[37]

On March 20 they prepared for the chase as unencumbered as possible. The wagons, cannon, and much of the food were packed up and Lt. Lloyd Beall, 2nd Artillery, with 150 men, was instructed to take them east, send the wagons to Fort Massachusetts, and cross the Sangre de Cristo to wait for the rest of the column in the Wet Mountain Valley. Fauntleroy headed north into the mountains with only seven days' rations. Picking up a trail, they twisted through the mountains with terrain so rough that the men had to lead their animals much of the way. They ended up at Poncha Pass on the evening of March 21. Fauntleroy said that they had traveled fifty or sixty miles. The pass is less than twenty-five miles in a straight line from their camp near Saguache Creek, so they must have done some very circuitous traveling, perhaps even going over Marshall Pass. Fauntleroy said that they had gone "over the highest point and most inaccessible places." Or perhaps the colonel's mileage estimates were exaggerated: marching twenty-five or thirty miles a day in "inaccessible" terrain would be nigh impossible.[38]

On the morning of March 22 they crossed Poncha Pass, which divides the Sangre de Cristo Range to the south from the Sawatch Range to the north and the Arkansas and Rio Grande watersheds. As they came out of the mountains, they saw three Indians in the distance. The soldiers chased them, killed one, and captured another. These men were Utes, but the trail that Fauntleroy was tracking had been made by Jicarillas who had left the Utes after the fight. The trail descended the Arkansas River, which Fauntleroy said they struck about eight miles from the pass, and would have been near present-day Salida. The colonel wrote: "We continued down the Arkansas about six miles to a creek which I denominated Beaver Creek at which point the Indians left the river and proceeded up the creek to a distance of about three miles north of the Arkansas, where they encamped." The troops also camped there for the night.[39]

On March 23 they followed the trail for fifteen miles. Fauntleroy does not indicate in what direction they traveled, but it was likely upstream (north) on Badger Creek. When the trail forked in three, they followed the largest for eight miles until it descended a canyon that led back to the Arkansas. From the heights they could see "a large body of Indians" at the river. Fauntleroy reached the valley and made a two-mile dash after them. The Indians hurriedly crossed the river to the south (or west) side. When the soldiers reached the river, very likely back in the vicinity of the mouth of Badger Creek, the Indians were a mile ahead of them, "ascending the mountain, at one of the most difficult and rugged points that could possibly have been selected."[40]

A two-mile mountain chase ensued. Sergeant Chacón was on a slow mule and could hardly keep up. He noticed "a lieutenant who seemed somewhat timid kept lagging behind and reining in his horse, a very spirited animal that was chafing with excitement. When I saw that he was killing time on purpose, I said to him, 'Let me have that horse to follow the enemy, you—or I will kill you.'" The lieutenant quickly swapped animals with Chacón, and he was able to join in the chase. He reported that they killed several Indians and captured several more. Fauntleroy said that only one Indian was wounded. Surgeon Peters stated that they captured about thirty horses, meat, camp utensils, and a few prisoners. One Indian woman killed one of her own children and a niece, and other women did the same in order to prevent them from being captured. They learned that the Indians that they had been chasing were Jicarillas, about thirty in number, and were led by Chacón.[41]

Stewart's spies caught a Jicarilla woman, a young boy, and eight horses. From her they learned the approximate location of one of the parties that had split off where the trail had divided into three. That evening Fauntleroy sent eighty men to find them. They crept up to the Indian camp and attacked at daybreak on March 24, but the camp had just been abandoned. Fauntleroy was running low on rations and headed for home. A march of fifteen miles took them to the lower end of the Wet Mountain Valley, where they camped. That day the spies, coursing through the surrounding countryside, discovered a small party of Jicarillas and killed one while the rest escaped. The next day they went twenty-five miles to the far upper end of the valley and camped, which Fauntleroy said was "one of the most stormy nights accompanied by snow and the most intense cold which I ever experienced." That night the Ute prisoner taken below Poncha Pass escaped. Sergeant Chacón complained that Captain Gonzales continually passed his duties on to him. That frigid night, while the captain huddled in his blankets, Chacón had to make the rounds, getting soaking wet and freezing. After Chacón finished these duties, his men had to lay him "in the midst of the sleeping soldiers to thaw me out and when my clothes were ready to be taken off they gave me other garments to don while mine were drying."[42]

On March 26 they crossed the divide to the Huerfano while the storm contin-ued. About six horses broke down each day and were shot to prevent the Indians from using them. The weather made it impossible, said Fauntleroy, "to see fifty yards before us." Sometime during the day he missed Lieutenant Beall, who was to be waiting for them with supplies; they "had to pass through snow for much of the day three and four feet deep and consequently could follow no trail." They found Beall the next day, relieved their hunger, marched west through Mosca Pass, and camped near the edge of the present Great Sand Dunes National Monument. Next day they circled around Blanca Peak and reached Fort Massachusetts.[43]

Fauntleroy was sanguine of the results of the campaign, telling Garland that they may not have killed a lot of Indians, but "it will be productive of much good." They traversed a great deal of territory and discovered many of the Indians' hiding places. He suggested "the most eligible site for a post" in that country would be in Cochetopa (Saguache) Pass. Fauntleroy ended his report with comments that led Garland to believe he was not keen to continue. He said that Company D of the Dragoons was almost totally disabled, the volunteers' horses could not ride again for twenty days, and he needed enough corn to supply two hundred animals for thirty days.[44]

Garland, expecting a quicker turnaround, wrote to headquarters that "Fauntle-roy after a hasty refit at Fort Massachusetts will again take the field in pursuit of the Utahs." Fauntleroy was doing the best he could. The tribes had split up, so he would go after the Utes and St. Vrain would chase the Jicarillas. St. Vrain took Williams, Gonzales, and Cunningham's companies, plus Stewart's spies.

They were to leave Fort Massachusetts on April 15, head east through Sangre de Cristo Pass, cross the Huerfano into Wet Mountain Valley, and travel north along its east side to the Arkansas River, up that river, and over to Poncha Pass, where Fauntleroy hoped to meet him.[45]

Fauntleroy had just written his orders when he received a disturbing letter from Garland, stating that "he expects you to immediately resume your operations against the Indians." "If you are not able to take the field yourself the General directs that you transfer your command and instructions to Lt. Col. St. Vrain who will make his reports &c. direct to these headquarters." "If the animals of your command are so much broken down as to be unable to take the field the General expects the Campaign to be made on foot."[46]

Garland's letter stung Fauntleroy. He responded: "In my infinite mortification the letter of the 6th . . . is written in a tone of deprecation generally, and I am given fully to understand that my further services in the field with the command could be easily dispensed with, and those of another quite as acceptable if not more desirable to the General." If Garland had not left him a bit of discretion, Fauntleroy said, he would gladly turn over command, as he supposed it was "the real wishes of the General." He could not fathom the sudden loss of faith in him. Nevertheless, he concluded: "I shall leave with all force *instanter*, and will endeavor Zealously to make my operations effective."[47]

Fauntleroy had to make a good show and had to do it quickly. Still, he did not leave Fort Massachusetts until about April 23, three days after St. Vrain left. With him were Company D, 1st Dragoons, apparently with its horses finally recovered; Company D, 2nd Artillery, under Capt. Horace Brooks, with most of its men acting as foot soldiers, and volunteer companies under Captains Chávez and Deus. Company D, 3rd Infantry, under Capt. Nathaniel C. Macrae, remained to garrison Fort Massachusetts. Fauntleroy followed a six-lodge Indian trail heading north along the east side of the San Luis Valley. After three days' march the tracks cut west across the head of the valley toward Saguache Pass, where they had their fight on March 19. The trail then turned north. Fauntleroy wrote that they "took up the valley to the Pancha Pass." On April 28, midway up Poncha Pass, they turned west up another canyon that comes out "about six miles west of the regular mouth of that Pass, connecting with a *Cañon* said to come from the direction of Grand River." They halted there at five after a twenty-six-mile march.[48]

When the spies found more trails converging in the direction of the Arkansas River, Fauntleroy called for a "night pursuit." It was slow going, but the moon was bright and a growing trail was evident. After another twenty-six-miles north between the Arkansas River and the Sawatch Range, they found the camp about one mile west of the trail. Fauntleroy said that it contained twenty-six lodges of Utes and was about twenty miles from Poncha Pass.[49]

About four in the morning they quietly concealed the supply train, dismounted, and crept up as close as they could. The dragoons and artillerymen, under Williams and Beall, angled off to approach the camp from the right, while the volunteers, under Chávez and Deus, did the same toward the left. Ten men were detailed to run off the Indians' horses. Their approach, said Fauntleroy, "was carried out by the officers & men with the utmost alacrity, the greatest difficulty which I had being to restrain them." The Indians in the camp, however, were not yet asleep, for they were finishing what Fauntleroy termed a scalp dance. He believed if they all had been sleeping the surprise had been greater, although they might have gotten as close as they did because the Utes were making plenty of noise. Even so, about 150 yards away, dogs barked, the Utes were aroused. "It then became necessary to make the assault."[50]

Fauntleroy said that the troops fired "on two sides of the square" and that it was "most beautiful to behold, and eclipsing almost the illumination of the camp." Peters recalled "over two hundred rifles & revolvers opened on them looking like sheets of fire coming from each soldier's mouth. This *fire* was a cross one sending missels [*sic*] of death home to many a poor red man." The Utes returned a scattered fire, but most of them broke "like chaff before the wind," according to Fauntleroy, and ran toward the thicker timber on the mountainside. It was over in twenty-five minutes. The colonel believed that they had killed forty Utes and wounded many more. They captured six children, thirty-five horses, sheep, goats, and a number of weapons. Two troopers from Company D, 2nd Artillery, were wounded, with one dying later after an amputation. Men of Company D, 1st Dragoons, searched for the Utes, but they were jumped and one dragoon was killed. Fauntleroy called the amount of "plunder & baggage" in the camp "incredible." The soldiers loaded themselves with loot yet still burned 200 buffalo robes and 150 pack saddles. They believed that Tierra Blanca was the leader because some of his personal paraphernalia was found.[51]

Fauntleroy moved south and camped at the head of the San Luis Valley on April 30, "with the expectation of proceeding to the Chowatch [Saguache] pass in which vicinity a party of Utahs are supposed to be with a considerable quantity of stock. This party I hope to chastise in like manner." Near the pass at dusk on May 1 they saw fifteen Utes about two miles away in the valley. When

Fauntleroy gave chase, the Utes ran for the mountains about two miles beyond. The troops splashed across Saguache Creek when they saw more Utes running for the mountains. The dragoons and volunteers pursued but were halted by the gathering darkness. Even so they killed two Utes and five horses and captured thirteen cattle.[52]

At daylight on May 2 they saw about fifty Indians in the upper valley, who avoided the troops and disappeared. Fauntleroy continued the pursuit and came upon scattered Utes in the timbered foothills, where sporadic firing continued for about two hours, resulting in two more dead Utes, a few wounded, and the capture of two horses, a lance, a saber, and an Indian shield. About eleven Tierra Blanca and a few warriors appeared on a high rock ledge, a point "wholly inaccessible to us," said Fauntleroy, where he "declared his name & expressed a desire for peace. Unfortunately at this moment a shot was fired at him by some men who were scattered through the hills, which effectually ended all communication at the time." Fauntleroy dismissed the effort as a ploy to buy time. In any event, he was certain that the Indians had scattered so far and wide that he would never catch them, and decided to head back to Fort Massachusetts. There, on May 9, he praised everyone for their zeal and efficiency. But, unlike Sumner, he stated that footmen were not as effective as troopers with good horses. He was proud of what he had accomplished and said that he would renew the campaign "at the earliest possible moment." One thing that bothered him was that "I have not heard from Lt. Col. St. Vrain since we parted."[53] He was not at the expected rendezvous near Poncha Pass.

Chasing the Jicarillas

Ceran St. Vrain left Fort Massachusetts on April 20, with Company F, 1st Dragoons, Volunteer Companies A and B, under Williams and Gonzales, and Stewart's spies. Kit Carson did not continue to serve as a guide. He explained that in 1854 he had guided Cooke and Carleton and others at the request of acting governor Messervy, but the superintendent ordered him to desist until called upon to make a treaty. Still, Carson felt it his duty to accompany Fauntleroy in 1855 when the regulars and volunteers were under one command. But when they separated, "I felt it my duty to remain at my agency to be ready" when the Indians sued for peace.[54]

Riding with St. Vrain and acting as his adjutant was Lt. William Craig, Company G, 3rd Infantry, who had arrived at Cantonment Burgwin in January 1855. St. Vrain had taken a liking to the young lieutenant and apparently discussed the land that he owned in the Arkansas Valley in the Vigil and St. Vrain Grant. When St. Vrain was offered the position of lieutenant colonel of volunteers, he agreed to accept only if Craig was assigned as his adjutant. When Craig saw the lands that St. Vrain owned, he agreed to resign his commission and serve as a partner in selling land parcels in return for getting one for himself.[55]

The command crossed the mountains at La Veta Pass and went down Abeyta Creek, deviating from Fauntleroy's orders to traverse Sangre de Cristo Pass and head north to the Wet Mountain Valley. Somewhere along the creek they skirmished with the Jicarillas and picked up the pace. On the Rio del Oso (Bear Creek), which flows from the northeast slope of East Spanish Peak to the Cucharas River, they discovered about sixty Jicarillas. On April 25 and 26 they chased the Indians through the mountains and forest, believing that they had killed and wounded thirteen of them. Somewhere on the high slope of the Spanish Peaks St. Vrain may have pointed out to Craig the vast sweep of land he owned, a piece of which could belong to the lieutenant if he played his cards right.

Following the Indian trail south, much as Carleton had done the year before, they had another skirmish with the Jicarillas on Trujillo Creek. While approaching the Indians, the hungry volunteers saw a herd of buffalo that they wanted to kill. But, said Chacón, "we were not allowed to fire on them for fear we might alarm the Indians." The chase continued to the area of the Chicosa Arroyo north of present Trinidad, where the Pueblo scouts were finally granted permission to shoot some deer. The volunteers mistook them for Jicarillas. Sergeant Chacón said that they "were about to charge on them, when they took refuge on the Chicosa hill; from there they displayed their signals, which were strips of white cloth two yards long, tied about their temples, and with the ends streaming down. This saved them from being attacked by us." They next caught the Jicarillas near the junction of Long Canyon and the Purgatoire, but the Indians saw them and fled into the Raton Mountains. St. Vrain charged, but caught only a few stragglers; a man of Gonzales's company killed and scalped one warrior—"a very luxuriant growth of hair," said Chacón. When they showed it to St. Vrain he became angry, believing it was a woman's scalp. "Then the soldier went back to where the dead Indian lay . . . and brought proof that the person killed was a man."[56]

While Captain Williams followed a trail to the southwest, Captain Gonzales headed southeast. In the vicinity of Dick Wootton's cabin near the head of Raton Pass, they attacked another small band of Jicarillas, killed three warriors, and captured six women and children, who indicated that it was Chacón's band they had been pursuing and that he was aiming for the junction of the Mora and

the Canadian. Gonzales crossed the mountains, angled toward Rayado, and on
Ponil Creek found another harried band of Jicarillas. Sergeant Chacón briefly
described the action: "At Ponil, after having killed several Indians, we captured
fifty squaws and their little ones. We took them to Fort Union." St. Vrain and
the various companies converged at the fort on April 30.[57]

That same day at the head of San Luis Valley Colonel Fauntleroy wrote to
Garland his concerns over St. Vrain's whereabouts and his hope to unite with
him in the vicinity. At the time, St. Vrain was 250 miles to the south, planning
to continue his own campaign. Gonzales's company rode to the Canadian River
on the prisoners' word that Chacón had fled there, but he had disappeared into
its deep canyons. Sergeant Chacón believed the Jicarillas had fled south to join
up with the Mescaleros.[58]

St. Vrain did not ride with Gonzales but instead headed back to Fort Massachusetts. Fauntleroy went to Taos to resupply, and Garland went south to
Mescalero country. Not until May 18 did Garland respond to Fauntleroy's April
10 protest of ill-treatment. Garland said that the information he received led him
to believe that "you did not again intend to take the field, but had determined to
settle yourself down at Taos and from thence to direct future operations. This
had very much the appearance of an abandonment on your part of further *active*
participation in the Campaign."[59]

Contrary to Garland's impression, Fauntleroy had made a very good showing,
better than Cooke, Sumner, Munroe, or Washington before him. Still, his men
and horses were badly depleted and only St. Vrain could continue the campaign.
Word came to Fort Massachusetts that Indians had been seen to the east on
the Huerfano and once again St. Vrain was off, this time with Williams, Deus,
and Chávez's companies and ten guides under Stewart. They left on June 2 with
twenty days' rations, crossed the range at Indian Creek Pass, and descended the
Cucharas River. An old trail led them far southeast onto the plains, where St.
Vrain said it went sixty miles to the Apishapa River near Hole in the Rock.[60] At
that point the trail turned abruptly northwest back to the mountains, which they
reached on June 5, to discover that the trail separated into several smaller ones. A
heavy rain nearly obliterated the tracks but not enough to deter Stewart's Pueblo
scouts—without them, St. Vrain said, "I would have necessarily abandoned the
pursuit."[61]

The track led south across the Purgatoire. On the afternoon of June 8 they
found that the trail again broke up. St. Vrain divided his men into four commands: one with a guard and all the packs was sent to a rendezvous on the upper

Canadian, while Williams, Deus, and Chávez chased down the separate trails, eventually to meet at the rendezvous. Williams was the only one to strike the Jicarillas; somewhere in the western Raton Mountains he charged their camp, killed six, captured seven, and took twenty-nine horses, guns, robes, and skins. A Mexican captive, dressed like the Jicarillas, "would have shared the fate of his Savage masters" had he not been recognized.

Williams joined St. Vrain and on June 10 they camped on the headwaters of the Purgatoire, a spot that St. Vrain called "a central position in this vast region unfit for the habitation of man or beast, but suitable resort only for the connecting link between the two, and a fit hiding place for his ill-gotten gain." After they had thoroughly "scoured" the countryside and found only two horses, St. Vrain called off the campaign. They all met at Maxwell's place at Rayado on June 16.

St. Vrain did not continue to Fort Union but retraced his steps back north. Near the Spanish Peaks they found a trail that led them to the Wet Mountains. On July 4, camped below Greenhorn Peak, they saw Indians approaching and set up an ambush. But when someone in Chávez's company accidentally fired his gun, the Indians disappeared into the timbered mountains. It was over. St. Vrain went up the Huerfano, crossed Mosca Pass to the San Luis Valley, and back to Fort Massachusetts. It was mid-July and the volunteers' enlistments were almost over.[62]

Contemporary opinion differed as to the effectiveness of the 1855 campaigns. Even after General Garland criticized Fauntleroy for his apparent reluctance to pursue the Utes, he gave him credit for "a triumph over these Indians seldom if ever equaled in the United States." The expedition was "conducted with skill and judgment and reflects great credit upon Col. Fauntleroy, his Officers and men." As for the volunteers, Garland was not as munificent, stating merely that "the whole period of their service was spent in active campaign" and that they matched the regulars in their enthusiasm. In contrast, Carson gave more praise to the volunteers. When Fauntleroy returned to Taos and "did not again take the field," St. Vrain took over. Carson said that if the volunteers "had continued in the service three months longer . . . there would never again have been any need of troops in this part of the country." Perhaps reflecting his intensifying quarrel with Meriwether, Carson doubted that the Indians had been sufficiently punished; nevertheless, "when they asked for peace, it was granted them." Both commanders had been very active. If the military reports are accurate, St. Vrain may have captured more Indians, but Fauntleroy killed more. His victories were more substantial, and the Utes were quick to ask for peace.[63]

"Peace Has Once More Been Restored"

As the summer solstice approached, there were intimations that peace was near. The Utes were beaten down, and the Jicarillas nearly so, but very likely no one realized that this was the beginning of an interlude of comparative harmony. Garland fretted that he would have to fight on multiple fronts, but it was not to be. After Sturgis, Ewell, and Miles had campaigned against the Apaches in the south, they too considered peace the better alternative, especially after May 1855, when Fort Stanton was established on the Rio Bonito in some of the best Mescalero land. They pled with agent Steck for help. He contacted Garland and Meriwether and said that "he had promised security to the Indians until he should get answers to his communications relative to peace." Garland reluctantly postponed further campaigning. "This step was not a little annoying, when we were prepared to strike." The Mescaleros might have peace, but with it came an influx of Mexican and American settlers and business owners, with attendant liquor sellers, prostitution, timber-cutting, overgrazing of grasses, loss of game, and tribal disintegration. Peace had a steep price.[64]

Meriwether then made a whirlwind tour of New Mexico, getting three tribes to sign virtually the same treaty. The Mimbres Apaches signed at Fort Thorn on June 9, including Chiefs Delgadito, Cuchillo Negro, and Ytan. On June 14 the Mescaleros signed, including Chiefs Barranquito, Cadete, and Josecito. Meriwether said that they were starving and "in the most destitute condition imaginable." The governor then traveled to Navajo country. Chiefs Manuelito, Segundo, and Zarcillos Largos signed a pact at Laguna Negra on June 18. All the treaties had the same articles, including the sixth, which said that annuities of the Indians should not be taken to pay the debts of individuals but as satisfaction for depredations committed by them, in such manner as the president might direct.[65] Unscrupulous individuals, under the blanket of the Trade and Intercourse Acts, could still file fraudulent claims and steal money from innocent Indians.

Even with peace treaties being made, some people sought to stir up trouble. Army headquarters in Santa Fe received word from an unknown source that Jicarillas had killed up to ten Mexicans in the mountains between Cantonment Burgwin and Mora. Captain Cunningham at Abiquiu was directed to take most of his volunteers and "punish" the marauders. The order came with a postscript: "It is best you do not communicate your movements to any of the Mexican population." Cunningham was unable to find evidence of any murders.[66]

In July Major Blake, recovered from his beating during the Taos "mutiny," got orders "to scour the mountains in the vicinity of Embudo for the Apache Indians reported to have committed depredations thereabouts." He went via Cieneguilla to Picuris Pueblo, made "careful inquiries" at various settlements, and got help from a number of Pueblos, but all their activity was for naught. Blake said that "the inhabitants about the settlements seemed to be without apprehension of danger."[67]

Civilian and government viewpoints often contrasted. Agent Carson insisted that his Utes were peaceful until "they caught the smallpox." After Fauntleroy defeated them "they have done no damage within the last two months," but he blamed the Jicarillas for some depredations.[68] Meriwether blew hot and cold. Having concluded three peace treaties, he naturally said that the Gilas, Mescaleros, and Navajos were peaceful. The Capote Utes had gone to the San Juan River to get away from the trouble, and the Muaches would hopefully sign a treaty. Agent Labadi wrote from Abiquiu that "no depredations have been committed" by any Indians near his agency and that the Capotes and others "are friendly disposed." Like Carson, Meriwether blamed the Jicarillas, saying that they had recently killed fifteen (unnamed) people, while "in no instance have our troops been able to overtake these marauding parties": "the truth is that the military force stationed here is inadequate to the protection of the Territory."[69]

In reality the military could not find marauders because the marauders were mostly *humo y niebla*. The army was the "usual suspect" in the inadequate protection blame-game, while trumping up charges against the Indians had been the standard tactic used by governors and citizens ever since General Kearny rode to town in 1846. If the military were skeptical, the locals would create real problems. When Utes visited Abiquiu to talk to agent Labadi, a volunteer company captured them and carried them to Santa Fe, where Garland "immediately ordered them to be released." Meriwether hoped to meet with them for peace talks and knew that it was essential "to prevent further molestation of these friendly Indians."[70]

The talk of keeping the Indians friendly was not always in line with the walk. Carson wrote of six Utes captured by Fauntleroy: one was "in the possession" of volunteer Captain Chávez; one was with a Lieutenant Chávez; one was held by Capt. Horace Brooks; "one was sold to a Mexican in Embudo, or Rio Arriba"; and two were still being held at Fort Union. Of several Jicarilla women detained at Fort Union, one died of dysentery.[71] The United States, despite its talk of freedom and protection, was still engaged in the old "captives and cousins" system that had operated in New Mexico for centuries, taking Indian prisoners and buying and selling them, a practice that continued even after the Civil War had supposedly put an end to slavery.[72]

Just when the situation with the New Mexico Indians seemed to be improving, the locals east of the Sangre de Cristo began their usual complaints. Lucien Maxwell said that Comanches had raided his ranch in mid-July, killed more than two hundred sheep, and broke into his house, but he still traded with them. A pragmatist, Maxwell did not believe that the Comanches were hostile and said that, after all, they were only doing "what war parties usually do." Still, Major Blake hurried to Rayado to halt the depredating Indians who were long gone. Carson, who said he would not join any more army expeditions, went with Blake nevertheless. Seeming to have a more belligerent attitude than usual, Carson reported: "I would respectfully suggest that if war be declared against the Comanches, it will be necessary to bring into the field a very large force, [because] they are one of the most powerful tribes on the continent."[73]

The army certainly did not want war with the Comanches. Three tribes had signed treaties, and two more were about to. At the end of July Garland wrote that he was "highly gratified" to report that conditions in his department were "very much improved." The Navajos were peaceful and the Mescaleros had moved to the country assigned by the treaty and had not committed any depredations. The Muaches talked to agent Labadi and asked for peace, and the Jicarillas, who "have suffered greatly," were scattered, reduced in number, and suing for peace. "The campaign is drawing to a close," Garland wrote.[74]

In his monthly report Meriwether expressed similar sentiments. The Capotes were ready to sign a treaty and indicated that the Muaches "were very desirous of peace but were afraid to come in and ask for it, since Blanco was fired on by a volunteer when he was talking to Colonel Fauntleroy." Even so, since then "I have heard of no depredation having been committed by the Muache." The Mescaleros, Mimbres, Gilas, and Navajos remained quiet.[75]

On August 8, 1855, Governor Meriwether and agent Labadi, with an army escort, met the Capote Utes at Abiquiu, signed a peace treaty designating the territory they were to reside in and the payments they would receive in return for their promise to make restitution for past injuries. The ubiquitous clause, this time article 7, stipulated that the Capotes would lose their annuities to pay for depredations proven against them. The agreement was signed by Tamouche, Yeusache, Joaquín, and eight others.[76]

By this time the feud between Carson and Meriwether was getting worse. The governor wrote that nearly everything Carson said in his latest report about depredations, men being killed, and mules stolen was in error. He refused to pay for John Mostin's services to Carson as an interpreter, because Mostin "can neither speak the Indian or Spanish languages as well as Mr. Carson himself."[77]

Utes and Jicarillas visited agent Labadi in August, telling him that they were suffering because of the war and "their people were dying from famine." Labadi took some of them to Santa Fe, where the governor agreed to meet with them the next month.[78] They finally signed their treaties at Abiquiu on September 11 and 12, but the proceedings were not without incident. Carson left his agency on September 8 and stopped at Embudo to obtain the Ute captive being held by Mexicans, but he had been sold. Meriwether brought Indian prisoners with him, some of whom had been in the guardhouse for nearly a year. Carson arrived with Tierra Blanca, disliked by Meriwether as "a shrewd, cunning rascal."[79]

Meriwether butted heads with Carson, grousing that he supplied one hundred sheep to feed the assemblage. He said that he had told Carson not to give the Indians more than ten or fifteen sheep each morning and evening, but instead he "had delivered all the sheep." Meriwether lectured Carson and complained that Carson grew indignant, got on his "highhorse," and protested that he was the agent and could distribute the sheep however he saw fit.

They sorted out and swapped the prisoners held by both sides, but the proceedings were disrupted when people ran in crying that Navajos were attacking. Meriwether said that he stood his ground and told everyone that he was in charge and no one would be molested. Carson, he said, warned: "If you don't get under the bank of the river, these Indians will kill you." Meriwether said he was not afraid and that it was Carson who "lay under the bank of the river."

Captain Ewell investigated the "attack" and found it to be a false alarm. When Tierra Blanca asked for more sheep, Meriwether said that he had no more. Carson allegedly said that if he were superintendent "these Indians should not go off hungry." The governor retorted that if Carson had been superintendent maybe "you might not have hidden under the bank of the river as you did." Hot words were exchanged, and Meriwether suspended Carson as Indian agent, whereupon Carson supposedly became so belligerent that Meriwether had Ewell arrest him.[80]

Charged with disobedience, insubordination, and cowardice, Carson supposedly got out of the mess by writing a letter of apology, which the governor magnanimously accepted, although not without scornful comment that Kit never could write a letter himself "but could only write his name at the bottom." Whether this happened the way Meriwether told it is unknown. Carson wrote about none of it in his autobiography, merely stating: "I cannot see how the

Superintendent can expect any of the Indians to depart satisfied after he has called them to see him from a distance of two or three hundred miles . . . without anything to eat, except what they have brought with them." Some historians dismiss Meriwether's remembrances and allegations as a flight into fancy.[81]

As the superintendent and the agent battled, the *Gazette* expressed surprising optimism. "Order reigns," the paper trumpeted. "It has been a long time since our Territory enjoyed such a season of peace as we have experienced for the last three months. Indian depredations seem to have ceased entirely." It praised the treaties and was certain that the upcoming ones would be equally as effective. The course pursued by the civil and military authorities was "worthy of com- mendation," as was the "gallant conduct of our regulars and volunteers," who were "entitled to great praise."[82]

While the newspaper and the governor boasted of the new peace accords, Carson tried to rain on their parade. His opposing opinion in the *Gazette* stated that there was no peace: seventeen persons (unnamed) had been killed and five hundred animals had been driven off. As usual he did not blame it on his Utes but on the Jicarillas and Comanches. The *Gazette*, giving Carson his due, said that it might mistakenly have said that no depredations had occurred in the last three months, when it really meant the last three weeks. In any case the newspaper concluded—somewhat unexpectedly given its history of crying wolf—that people must realize that many of the depredations Carson cited "may have turned out to be merely rumour, which is often the case."[83]

Meriwether was pleased with his accomplishments, but Carson contradicted him, saying that Indians who still committed depredations were "those who have lost their families during the war. They consider they have nothing further to live for than revenge for the death of those of their families that were killed by the whites; they have become desperate; when they will ask for peace I cannot say."[84]

Thus a continuous battle raged between people with different philosophies as to how to deal with the Indians, between the uneducated frontierspeople and the bureaucrats, and among people in positions of authority all engaged in a power struggle. When Meriwether refused to pay for Carson's use of a clerk, even though he knew he could not write, it demonstrated appalling pettiness and spite and showed what even a territorial governor would do if he thought it would accrue to his own advantage.

The treaty signing was almost a sideshow. On September 11 the Muache leaders Coniache, Tierra Blanca, Benito, and twelve others placed their marks, and the next day the Jicarillas Guero, José Chávez, Pantaleón, and ten others did the same.

The agreements with the Capotes, Muaches, and Jicarillas were virtually identical except for the territorial boundaries assigned to them. On September 30 Garland reported that "the Indians during the past month have been unusually quiet."[85]

"I can now have the pleasure of informing you that peace has once more been restored to this territory," Meriwether reported. He was proud that within the previous few months he had concluded six peace treaties. He estimated that the Muache, Mescalero, and Jicarilla tribes had only 250, 150, and 60 warriors, respectively. Except for the occasional theft, he expected no more trouble. Meriwether saw more potential problems with the Pueblos, but typically considered them problems not of their making. The New Mexico legislative assembly passed a law that constituted several Pueblos into corporate and political bodies, with power to sue and be sued. Meriwether believed that the Indians would not know what to do with this power and instead it would be "interested persons [who] stir up litigation between the different pueblos, and between the Mexican population and the pueblos." There were already more than twenty lawsuits pending, and very soon "the lawyers engaged and the officers of the courts will have claims for fees sufficient to cover all" that the pueblos were worth.[86]

In addition, Meriwether saw a need to amend the Trade and Intercourse Act. Although he realized that some claims were fraudulent, he believed that many of them would be paid. Because the claimants "are in many instances poor," they could not wait too long for their money. It was impossible for the Indians to make restitution, so he believed that the required step to ask the Indians for payment should be eliminated. He wanted to "dispense with demands for satisfaction of claims arising previous to the conclusions of the late treaties."

The governor saw flaws in the system. Instead of understanding that fraud was the main problem, however, he wanted to streamline the process of removing money from the Indians' pockets directly into the hands of his constituents.

Commissioner Manypenny's report for 1855 reiterated what he and others had been saying for years: whites had intruded in Indian country and destroyed their food resources to such an extent "as to compel them to plunder or steal from our citizens or starve." This was the main cause of depredations. In addition, whenever the annuities were due for distribution, "a miserable class of men who deal in spirituous liquors, games, and other vices . . . carry off large amounts of the funds of the Indians, obtained by the most shameful, dishonorable, and unlawful means." Manypenny echoed Meriwether in seeking ways to cut corruption, one of them being to eliminate the ability of lawyers to litigate for the Pueblos, which would require that "Congress repeal this act of the territorial legislature."[87]

American and Mexican citizens and settlers, by destroying the Indians' economic system, were the root cause of depredations—they cheated the Indians, sold them whiskey, and stole their annuities. Congress needed to repeal laws that enabled litigious, avaricious white people from preying upon the Indians. The Trade and Intercourse Acts were a chief cause of fraud and war—not intrinsically, but because they were exploited by fallible human beings who easily rationalized their greed. If some perspicacious folks realized that, few made mention of it.

One more depredation incident is worth mentioning, which may encapsulate the myriad cases that came before and those that would follow. In late October Lieutenant Colonel Miles, only a week after praising the Mescaleros for their good behavior, got news that they had allegedly driven off eighteen mules from Frank Fletcher's ranch between Las Cruces and Dona Ana. Miles asked the Mescaleros to find and return the stock. Meriwether had taken a leave of absence in early fall to go back east. W. W. H. Davis, as acting governor, demanded that agent Steck tell the Indians the animals must be returned or the soldiers would destroy them.

Palanquito rounded up some mules and returned them, but Miles was dubious. He did not believe that Palanquito even knew of any theft. Because the Mescaleros had been peaceful, Miles believed that the theft contention was simply a ruse by Fletcher to stir up trouble and gain compensation. Miles wrote to Steck: "I have so little confidence in Fletcher, that I must have the evidence of someone besides himself to believe he ever lost any mules at all—this is my private opinion, which I would thank you to keep to yourself." Miles added that the people of Las Cruces and Mesilla had been treating the Indians "most shamefully and I doubt not Fletcher was [involved in] any outrages committed against them." The allegation details did not make sense. "From the direction of the trail and the place found, I believe the [Mexicans] to be guilty. I do not myself believe the Mescaleros stole the mules, or had knowledge of the theft until I informed them. The chiefs deserve credit for the zeal displayed in recapturing them and [this] shows most conclusively their desire to keep unbroken the treaty." The next month the *Gazette* commented on the robbery: "It is now thought the depredation was the work of the thieves who hang around Manzano," some of the same suspect Mexicans that Ewell had confronted the previous February.[88]

Army officers had realized almost from the start that civilians had been falsifying claims against the Indians, but Miles added a novel insight: although Indians had been returning "stolen" stock for years, many of them might never have been stolen at all. The Indians may have believed that it was a better idea just to give up some of their own animals to placate the Americans and Mexicans, rather than protest and have the army come down hard on them.[89]

Regardless of the occasional thefts—by Indians, Americans, or Mexicans—the prospects for peace seemed favorable. In his monthly report for October Garland wrote: "The Lieutenant General commanding the Army [Winfield Scott] will be gratified to know that not a circumstance has occurred within the month, indicating a hostile disposition on the part of the Indians of New Mexico, not even a theft has been committed."[90]

A robbery was committed only a week later, but the circumstances exemplify much of what had been going on for the past nine years. Citizens complained to Lt. Isaiah Moore, 1st Dragoons, at Los Lunas, that Gila Apaches had stolen stock near Socorro. Why had it happened? Moore said that three weeks earlier about twenty-five Mexicans "entered Apache country to steal animals; though unsuccessful, losing two men killed and several wounded, the Indians are now retaliating." And so it went, yet Garland was optimistic. In his November report he mentioned the Indian retaliation but still wrote: "Our Indian relations, I am happy to say are perfectly satisfactory in this department."[91]

The possibility of peace and harmony with the Indians seemed more likely than it had been in years, but naturally it was not to be. The seeds of discontent germinated within days of the public becoming aware of details of the six recent treaties. What were the authorities thinking when they gave away so much good land to the Indians? The treaty with the Mimbres gave them territory that included the old Santa Rita copper mines. What if silver or gold was also discovered in that area? Also, Meriwether allowed the distribution of Mescalero annuities and rations at Dona Ana. Miles moaned to Steck that this was "a great mistake" because the Mescaleros now believed that Dona Ana was part of their treaty land. The *Gazette* complained that the Indians should have been given lands somewhere completely off the map. They had to live somewhere, certainly, but not in my backyard. Diego Archuleta, who became Ute agent in 1857, bawled that "the treaties negotiated by . . . Meriwether were in direct violation of the rights of individuals, because the selection of reservations were not only upon private grants, but also so proximate to the settlements" that they were a great injustice to the people.[92]

While the treaties went to the Senate for consideration, other parties sought to block them. William Pelham, the surveyor general for New Mexico Territory, wrote to Michael Steck inquiring about the nature of the land to be transferred to the tribes. On October 4 Steck replied that one section of nine square leagues around the Santa Rita copper mines was one of "the best established grants in the Territory." In addition, southwest of that grant were abandoned gold mines, plus reserves of iron, silver, and lead. Steck told Pelham that "a better selection might have been made." It was the "humane course" to "locate and civilize" the Indians, so Meriwether's first priority should have been to remove them as far from the settlements and private grants as possible. Steck suggested moving the Mimbres farther west on the Gila River, while the Mescalero needed to be moved because they had been given good lands east of the Rio Grande that were too close to settlements and communication routes. If they remained, "they will retard the development of the rich mineral resources of the Organ Mountains, and the agricultural and grazing resources" of the White Mountains and Pecos. Steck said that the Mescaleros also should be sent west, to "open for settlement the finest and most desirable portion of New Mexico."[93]

Armed with this information, Pelham wrote to Thomas A. Hendricks, commissioner of the General Land Office, that the land being ceded to the Indians contained gold, silver, copper, lead, and iron. In view of this, the treaties being considered were "a matter of primary importance to the Government, both politically and pecuniarily. Should this treaty be ratified the interests of the Territory will be seriously injured by depriving its inhabitants from working the mines located within the limits proposed to be established." Pelham said that it was his duty "to inform you of the facts reported to me, in order that you may protest against the ratification of the above mentioned treaty." In turn, Hendricks notified secretary of the interior Robert McClelland, reiterating what had been said in the previous letters, but without further recommendation other than to make him aware of the situation so that he could take necessary and proper action.[94]

Inevitably, the U.S. Senate knew where America's interests lay. That mysterious force of Manifest Destiny seemed to have a mind and will of its own, assuring that America got the best harbors on the Pacific as well as all the good rivers, valleys, and routes that were needed for roads and rails to connect the east and west coasts. It got the best farmlands, grazing lands, mineral lands, rivers, and water rights. Manifest Destiny, depicted in paintings as an angelic woman in a diaphanous white gown floating serenely, yet watchfully, over the immigrants heading west, was quite a bitch in reality. Anyone not under her wing and not part of the American vision was going to be trampled. Those outside the fold were manifestly destined to be nailed. On March 13, 1857, the Senate rejected all of Meriwether's treaties.

Not knowing what was to happen, the affected tribes waited patiently for the most part, hoping to live unmolested on their promised reserves, receiving annuities and food and living in peace. Perhaps those who were not already engaged in the practice might even learn farming or stock-raising. But they had to be fed before they became self-sufficient. That was the main understanding of the civilian and military authorities from day one: people will steal before they will starve. So the Indians waited, but few promises were kept, they were still hungry, and the treaties that they signed were tossed in the trash.

James L. Collins was editor of the *Gazette* in January 1856 when he printed the congratulatory resolutions passed by the Territorial Assembly, complimenting Colonel Fauntleroy and General Garland for their fine work in subduing the Indians. Fauntleroy in particular was singled out for "his gallantry, brave deportment and soldierly daring while traversing the snow clad heights, and breasting with unshrinking courage the wintry storms and tempests of the north" to overtake the "savage and inhuman hordes," and to defeat them and save our "beloved Territory."[95]

So the war was over and all was well . . . but wait. The Americans would find it more difficult to obtain land and make money without staging incidents and promoting the fear necessary to cook up a war. Be careful what you wish for. Peace was not going to be as lucrative. Before you knew it, the army might even start pulling out the troops, closing the forts, and cutting contracts again. In the fall of 1855 the *Gazette* proclaimed that it would "much regret to see an Indian war again break out, when the prospect for peace is so flattering."[96] A few months later, after congratulating the army for a job well done, the *Gazette* was moaning about depredations and the need for the troops to remain.

By March 1856 the *Gazette*'s calls for more chastisement of the Indians led an unnamed correspondent to write a long missive defending government policy. The author may have been William Davis, one-time editor and now acting governor while Meriwether was back East promoting ratification of his treaties. The writer argued that the situation had improved, so "[l]et us give the policy a fair trial." The Indians had not broken their promises; to the contrary, they had been very faithful and "have not committed a single depredation." The few alleged thefts might have been committed by Mexicans—if the tribes were guilty it was because they were starving. Any robberies that might have occurred were likely committed by the Gila and Mogollon Apaches farther west. It was also false to claim that no plans had been made to feed or supply the Indians or give them equipment with which to farm. The treaties provided for all those contingencies, but they would not be effective until ratified by the Senate. The correspondent concluded that "if you do not like the Indian policy . . . it is your duty to suggest a better one, and until you do this, the government will not be likely to change course in this particular."[97]

Editor Collins countered, stating that Meriwether never had an Indian policy but hastily concocted so-called treaties "wholly at variance with the interests of New Mexico and her people, that could have nothing for its object but to create an excuse for his Excellency's visit to Washington." Collins said that the treaties should never have "inconvenienced" the citizens by locating "a set of marauding savages within their vicinity." Collins pointed out that if California and Texas had removed the Indians from their states, New Mexico could have done the same. He objected to giving away lands owned in private grants, letting the Indians stay too close to white settlements (believing that Apaches to the west were the only ones committing robberies), and to supplying nonessentials when food was the priority. "In short sir," Collins wrote, "if the Governor would buy more corn and fewer calico shirts for the Indians, they would be better accommodated and more likely to quit robbing." The contention that they were behaving themselves "is simply ridiculous."[98]

The *Gazette* also printed a resolution adopted by the Territorial Legislative Assembly, which was in effect a laundry list of alleged depredations said to have occurred over the past several months. It stated that Meriwether's celebration of peace was wrong, because Mescaleros were killing and stealing in the south and other tribes had stolen stock in San Pedro, Isleta, Chilili, Los Lunas, Socorro, and Sabinal. The counties of Bernalillo and Dona Ana were purportedly under siege. How did the Assembly verify all these charges? Simply "for the reason that they have been received from such reliable sources, they should be given undoubted faith and credit and from which we infer beyond all kind of doubt, that the Territory is at this time in a state of war with these Indians." Proof by the word of duplicitous business owners and yeoman farmers was about as dubious as you could get, but a copy of the resolution insisting that action be taken against the Indians "who so frequently and barbarously destroy the lives and property of the inhabitants of this Territory" was sent to President Pierce.[99]

As in so many instances, at a time when civilians swore that Indians had denuded the country of its livestock there were significant sheep drives to California, even though the price of mutton was falling. In 1855 and 1856 J. Francisco Chávez drove 18,000 head and James Quinn drove 15,000 head. In November 1855 Rafael Luna and Anastacio García of Bernalillo County reported that Indians had

stolen 4,000 of their sheep. In 1856 the Luna and Armijo families combined to
herd 19,000 sheep to California. In 1857 Sidney Hubbell and Joaquín Perea made
a successful drive, leading to an even larger one the next year, when the Hubbell,
Perea, and Jaramillo families drove an incredible 100,000 sheep to California.
Almost all of these sheep came from the Rio Abajo, the area that the Territorial
Assembly contended had been devastated by Indian raids.[100]

What else was to be expected? Most of the tribes had been subdued or placated
and there was comparative peace, but that would never be allowed to stand. Better
to accept the word of "honorable" people that the Indians continued to despoil the
land rather than chance losing the army, the posts, the contracts, and the money
that they brought in. Regardless of their protestations, a significant number of
citizens did not want peace, which was not as lucrative as war. Those in power
continued to use fear and threats of devastation and death to hold that power.

Despite the citizens' anger toward Governor Meriwether, mainly because he
did not give them a big enough cut of the pie and peace might bring dangers to the
economy and political situation, New Mexico Territory did experience a time of
comparative tranquillity in 1856. It was a remarkable year in one respect: virtually
no depredation claims were filed against the New Mexico tribes. Certainly there
were still some of the usual complaints and allegations of theft, but for some
reason the civilians literally ceased filing formal claims that year. Claims had
been at a high in 1847, when the Americans arrived in force; they had declined
for three years until Sumner cut civilian contracts and removed the troops from
the towns in 1851—with a corresponding new high in claims. They declined
steadily again after that and by 1856 had all but disappeared.[101]

Although 1856 was a more peaceful year than any in the previous decade,
some people still felt the need to broker fear and keep the pot boiling. James L.
Collins, who succeeded Meriwether as Indian superintendent in 1857, wrote to
the commissioner of Indian Affairs, Charles E. Mix, that 1856 had more murders
and robberies than in any previous year—an outlandish declaration.[102]

The Jicarillas and Moache Utes had enough fighting after Garland's 1855
campaigns. It would be incorrect to say that they had been beaten down so
completely that they gave up their warlike ways. More accurately, they had been
beaten down so completely that the Americans gave up *their* warlike ways—there
was little left to steal. The idea that the Indians all thrived on war and plunder was
often more a white fantasy than a reality—a tool to foment fear, make money, and
obtain and hold power. When the whites acquired most of the land they wanted
from the Indians, they had less occasion to attack them and file claims against

them. American and Mexican civilians increasingly molested different tribes, generally shifting their complaints against the Jicarillas and Utes to the Apache tribes farther to the south and west. The tentative peace in New Mexico held until November 1856, when Mogollon Apaches captured and killed agent Henry Dodge, leading to a military campaign against them in the spring of 1857, led by Col. Benjamin L. E. Bonneville, 3rd Infantry, who was in temporary command of the Department of New Mexico during Garland's absence.

For the most part, however, the wars with the Jicarillas and Moache Utes were over.

The Civilians, the Army, and Frontier Security

Are there any lessons to be learned from studying the New Mexico frontier during the years 1846 to 1855? A major premise expressed in the introduction was that the Trade and Intercourse Acts, passed to facilitate peaceful resolution to conflicts between the whites and Indians, were a dismal failure. The acts that sanctioned a depredation claim system were a windfall for dishonest people. Swindling the government by accusing Indians of robbery and murder, and profiting from it, was a key cause of the Indian wars in New Mexico Territory and may very well be established as a key cause of most of the Indian wars of the nineteenth century. A quotation attributed to Ben Franklin is apt: "There is no kind of dishonesty into which otherwise good people more easily and frequently fall than that of defrauding the government."[103]

Thousands defrauded the system, which does not say much for the character of our businesspeople and yeoman farmers, who proved to be less the salt of the earth than those who salted the earth. Making claims for nonexistent losses was a comparatively risk-free way to get government money. A rung above the dishonest civilians were the local government authorities. Their overheated response to events often fostered an environment of fear that only made matters worse. Sometimes the authorities were duped and did not realize how they escalated the situation, and sometimes they were willing participants in the chicanery.

New Mexicans strove for security, but their solutions may have produced insecurity. On one level the citizens exploited a system that allowed them to lie. If caught, they could claim plausible deniability. On the next level the authorities were architects of a system that facilitated fraud or could be perpetrators themselves. This stemmed from their inability to distinguish perceived risks from actual risks involved in building a system or process, be it political, commercial, social, or security-related. The civil and military authorities were tasked with keeping New Mexico safe, but how they perceived the threats made all the difference. Their security system generated unintended consequences. New Mexicans used the Indian as the outside bogeyman, but in many systems *the insiders are the most dangerous.* Authority is loath to admit it, because it then becomes a management failure. The Trade and Intercourse Acts were commercial and security systems that failed.[104]

Authority loves fear. Fear is the barrier between ignorance and understanding. When you live in fear, authority will make the decisions, for power tends to give advantage to those who control it more than to those whom it is supposed to protect. Exaggerate the threat of outside attackers, make the people afraid enough, and you can get more "protection" in the form of soldiers, equipment, funds, contracts—whatever is necessary to give the people a greater sense of security. But remember that security measures are often contrived and ephemeral, with decisions made based on perceptions instead of reality and often dictated by the self-interest of those in power. The people of New Mexico lived in fear because it was in the best interests of the authorities and the media to perpetuate it.[105]

Authority needs villains. In the event of some villains' demise, others must take their place. When Lieutenant Bell's soldiers killed Lobo Blanco in 1854, Garland, Davis, and others soon replaced him with Fleche Rayada, Chico Velásquez, and Chacón. This need for villains coincides with centuries-long fears of witches, Indians, blacks, Mexicans, Catholics, Chinese, immigrants, Muslims—the "Others"—and remains a dark feature of American history. Some of America's first villains were white witches. After the "Enlightenment" made witch persecution somewhat gauche, the Indians became the new red devils. Fearing Indians, "the vilest race of beings that ever infested the earth," according to British general Jeffrey Amherst, a vile solution to their existence was needed. One of Amherst's officers subsequently recorded: "We gave them two blankets and a handkerchief out of the smallpox hospital. I hope it will have the desired effect." Somehow smallpox was also passed to the Utes, which was a factor in their attack on Pueblo. White people may not have plotted to infect them, but the psychological motivations one century after Amherst had not changed. We do what we fear in others; we become who we fear; and in the process we take action to disregard rights in the name of preserving those rights.[106]

It is easy to succumb to our anxieties and overestimate outside threats. The seemingly peculiar circumstance on the New Mexico frontier was that, while the civilians and the civilian authorities were crying wolf, spreading tales of robbery and murder, and demanding more soldiers for protection, the army was applying the brakes. New Mexico's department commanders (Washington, Munroe, and Sumner) all acted as dampers to the hot-blooded civilians who wailed jeremiads about their imminent destruction by the Mexicans and Indians, while Governors Calhoun and Lane groaned about a lack of military action. Only about six battles with the Jicarillas and Utes occurred during the six years when Washington, Munroe, and Sumner had stints as military and civil governors; when Garland took over, there were twenty fights within two years. The civilians were overjoyed. Many army officers saw through the poorly veiled protestations and demands for more troops as little more than avenues for personal gain. Disliking New Mexico and its people, and frustrated and enraged by the chicanery, Sumner was ready to abandon the territory to the Mexicans and Indians.

The military was faced with nearly impossible tasks. Per the Trade and Intercourse Acts, it was a constabulary force to protect the Indians as well as the whites. The army quickly realized that often it was not the Indians but the white frontierspeople who were the major adversaries. The army often had to impose itself between rabid civilians and the Indian population. Unfortunately, if officers harmed civilians while protecting Indians, it would have ended their careers and sparked civil and criminal prosecutions, where they would certainly be convicted in any frontier court. It is true that many officers held a condescending attitude toward frontier civilians that often bordered on disgust—a sentiment frequently mirrored by the civilians. Many officers battled their consciences before battling Indians. Col. Ethan A. Hitchcock, 2nd Infantry, wrote: "It is a hard case for troops to know the whites are in the wrong, and yet be compelled to *punish* the Indians if they attempt to defend themselves."[107]

The situation changed when Garland replaced Sumner and Meriwether replaced Lane. Initially Garland was not all that sympathetic to civilian complaints, perceiving some of them as self-serving. When the Utes attacked Pueblo, however, he bonded with the civilians. The civilians firmly believed that they had an army commander who wanted to kill Indians as much as they did. With the military and the civilians on the same page, the war was prosecuted to the bitter end. The Utes and Jicarillas were hounded and killed until they begged for peace, the Mescaleros were beaten in a few fights, and a fort was built in their homeland, forcing them to sue for peace. A combination of troop maneuvers, threats, and an olive branch held out to the Navajos and Apaches farther west had temporarily dampened their enthusiasm for fighting.

One point to consider in the course of civilian and military cooperation is how well the branches worked with each other. Governors Calhoun and Lane were at loggerheads with commanders Washington, Munroe, and Sumner more often than not. Meriwether and Garland found more common ground in wanting to chastise or even annihilate the Indians. When the civil government and the military had little in common and the military exercised skepticism and restraint, there was less warfare. Once the two branches shared similar attitudes and goals, war was all but assured. In other words, it might serve the country well if the civilians and military are at odds—just as the Constitution has provided checks and balances for the executive, legislative, and judicial branches of government. Too much unity of mind and body does not necessarily translate into peace.

Some vexing elements remain. It appears that fewer civilians and Indians were killed when there were fewer soldiers in the mix. When troop strength increased, more people died. It may seem counterintuitive—after all, the army (or police force) is supposed to offer protection and safety. Then again, fewer adversaries will fight and die if they are not placed in close proximity. Many of the robberies and murders were contrived: needlessly bringing flame and gunpowder together would only make an explosion more likely. Throwing more people with guns into harm's way became a self-fulfilling prophesy. The surge is self-defeating. More soldiers equals more fighting.

Increased troop strength was also linked with more depredation claims. The civilians seemed to be testing the army, making allegations, having soldiers chase marauders who may or may not have existed, but all the while hoping that the soldiers would run into Indians and start a fight. That would then become an "I told you so" and justify the army's presence—another self-fulfilling prophecy. Thus the army may have had a destabilizing influence on the frontier as often as it had a pacifying effect. Like reagents in a test tube, public greed (augmented by fraud) plus fabricated fear plus military force (augmented by political authority) coalesced to form an unstable amalgam, nearly guaranteed to ignite with the slightest mishandling. Self-interest × (fraud) + fear + force × (authority) = war. If the army was sometimes a destabilizing force, it was not through its own volition: the people manipulated the army for their own enrichment, which often resulted in war.

The great majority of people moving west might have believed that it was their manifest destiny to spread across the continent, tame the wilderness, and turn the deserts green, but the altruistic coin had a selfish flip side. The profit motive was always present; if others had to be hurt to gain an advantage, so be it. The army was often caught in the middle. It was there to keep the peace or fight if necessary. In New Mexico Territory, however, the record is replete with army officers who questioned civilian allegations of Indian theft and murder—discovering that the revered commoners of Jeffersonian and Jacksonian America were often a passel of swindlers.

Concentrating on the clashes with the Jicarillas and Utes, in at least fifty-two instances the army investigated reports of raiding and found them to be without merit. In an additional ten instances the civilian governors assessed the rumors of Indian raiding and judged them false. There were also twenty-three civilian inquiries into reports of Indian/Mexican rebellions that proved to be false.

But 43 reports of depredations proved to be true, although 6 of those were committed by American soldiers and 14 by Mexican and/or American outlaws and criminals. Thus 85 out of 108 reports of Indian raids were bogus to a lesser or greater extent—about 79 percent. Of the 325 depredation claims listed, unfortunately the great majority were unadjudicated at the time the listings were printed. Of the 79 decided, 50 were denied and 29 approved—a 63 percent denial rate. This ratio, however, does not provide a true picture of which claims actually had merit. Many were categorically denied through limitation statutes, tribal amity disqualifications, or illegal residence prohibitions. Certainly otherwise legitimate claims were denied on those grounds. But some exaggerated or fabricated claims undoubtedly were approved and paid, because the claimant could afford a good lawyer. The approval/denial ratio of the claims that went to court was not as reliable an indication of legitimacy as were the on-the-ground investigations, which showed that about three-quarters of the allegations of Indian raids were deceitful. The numbers examined here are incomplete, and perhaps they would show different percentages on other frontiers, but I consider the evidence substantial enough to venture a very conservative estimate that at least half of the depredation claims were completely fabricated and that the great majority of the remaining half were inflated.

Powerbrokers and the media, using smoke, fog, and mirrors, manufactured and manipulated society's fear of outsiders, concealing the reality that most of our problems originated from within, augmented by our own bigotry and greed. False accusations caused much of the Jicarilla-Ute conflict. Americans manipulated the Trade and Intercourse Acts for their own gain and, by their avaricious conduct, precipitated the warfare that would expedite their conquest over the Indian tribes.

Appendix A

Chronology of Depredation Claims

Entries contain claimant's name, claim number if known, date of alleged incident, location if known, tribe named as perpetrator, dollar amount of claimed losses, type of losses if known, date claim was filed if known, and other pertinent information.

1846

Brent, Robert T. and Preston Beck. #6514. 9-12-1846. Navajo, $8,775 (135 livestock). Filed 11-29-1851. Beck had coffee contract in 1853.

Sandoval, Josepha. 9-30-1846. Navajo, $535.

Luna, Ramón. 11-1846. Navajo, $425. Luna was a prefect in Sabinal.

1847

Gonzales, Santiago. #3390. Several claims 1847 through 1852. Navajo, $2,065.

Gutares, Juan Pablo. 1-18-1847. Navajo, $600.

Gonzales, Juan Albino. #10334. 1-25-1847. Navajo, $500.

Gonzales, José María. 2-7-1847. Navajo, $199.

Luna, Raphael. 2-12-1847. Navajo, $3,450.

Silva, Mariano. #3071. 2-14-1847. Navajo, $150.

Jaramillo, Vincente. #2929. 2-15-1847. Navajo, $795.

Gonzales, Ylaria. 2-15-1847. Navajo, $2,050.

Baca, Antonio. 3-5-1847. Navajo, $360.

Baca, Ama María. 3-8-1847. Navajo, $1,695.

Vigil, Manuel. #5635. 3-15-1847. Navajo, $225.

Lucero, Julián. 3-15-1847. #10215. Navajo, $1,575.

Gonzales, Sabino. 3-15-1847. Navajo, $710.

Gonzales, Bárbara. 3-15-1847. Navajo, $175.

Gonzales, Juan Domingo. 3-15-1847. Navajo, $950.

DeBarcelo, Dolores Griego. 4-16-1847. Navajo, $270.

Sánchez, Rafael. #9941. 5-5-1847. Navajo, $800.

Sánchez, Juan Gómez. #8471. 5-5-1847. Navajo, $2,830 (900 sheep).

Contreras, Juan Andrés. #3628, #10221, #10222. 5-5-1847. Apache, $4,610 (2,130 sheep). Matías Contreras, administrator.

Baca, Jesús María. #2099. 5-8-1847. Apache, $680. Various property lost. Not proven.

Candelaria, José Francisco. #2153, #3656. 6-1847. Ceboletta. Navajo, $40 (mare and mule). Filed 3-26-1853. Not proven, no treaty.

Chaves, Rafael. #4097. 6-1847. Navajo, $2,728.

Sandoval, Antonio. #3814, #3815, #3816. 6-4-1847. Navajo, $38,435 (15,000 sheep).

Biggs, Thomas. 6-20-1847. Navajo, $7,150.

Montoya, Tomás. #4101. 6-1847. Navajo, $50.

Chávez, Jesús M. #1754. 7-29-1847. Navajo, $390.

Pino, Vincente. #2648. 8-47 Navajo, $240.

Lucero, Julián. #10216. 8-15-1847. Navajo, $168. Sévero Vigil, administrator.

Gonzales, Juan Albino. #3203. 8-15-1847. Navajo.

Gonzales, Sabino. 9-10-1847. Navajo.

Gonzales, Juan Domingo. #10030. 9-12-1847. Navajo.

Sandoval, Antonio. #3823. 9-15-1847. Navajo, $3,625. Filed 10-7-1853.

Savade, Lorenzo. 9-26-1847. Navajo, $660.

Chaves, Antonio José. 9-29-1847. #3999, Apache. #4324, Navajo, $2,900.

Trujillo, Manuel. #8161. 9-29-1847. Navajo, $480.

Chávez, Maria Francisco. #2150. 10-5-47 and 3-8-1848. Valencia County and Bernalillo County. Navajo, $1,590 (livestock, cooking utensils). Filed 12-20-1854. Not proven.

Gonzales, José María. #7012. 10-6-1847. Navajo.

Luna, Juan. 10-25-1847. Navajo, $600.

Luna, Ramón. 10-25-1847. Navajo, $250. Mentioned in *Santa Fe Republican*.

Luna, Antonio José. 10-25-1847. #2484, #2485, #2486, #2487. Navajo, $5,040.

Valencia, Bernardo. 10-25-1847. #1519, Apache. #3829, Navajo, $640.

Romero, José Jesús. #3640. 10-26-1847. Navajo, $190.

Coponlara, John Joseph. 11-1847. Apache, $6,510. Letter from Governor Meriwether 8-30-54, said a Joseph Caponlade filed an Apache claim for $10,510.

Apodaca, Salvador. #2037. 11-10-1847. Navajo $3,450.

Armijo, Pedro. 11-11-1847. #2395, #2396, #2397, #2398. Navajo, $3,585.

Gallegos, José Antonio. 12-19-1847. #4522, #10229. Navajo, $400.

Pino, Vincente. #2832. 12-19-1847. Navajo, $4,088.

Sones, Pedro. 12-24-1847. Navajo, $660. Filed 6-10-1854.

1848

Sones, Pedro. 1-6-1848. Navajo, $675. Filed 6-10-1854.

Gallegos, José Dolores. 1-1848. Navajo, $165.

Luna, Juan. 1-26-1848. Navajo, $425.

Abeita, Sylvester. 2-1848. #10234, #10235, #10236. Navajo, $5,000.

Luna, Antonio José. 2-12-1848. #2488, #2489. Navajo, $700.

Montoya, José Antonio. 2-14-1848. #3169, #3206. Navajo, $8,855.

Chavis, María Francisco. 3-8-1848. Navajo, $1,590.

Lavade, Lorenzo. 3-14-1848. Navajo, $350.

Campos, Pedro. 3-15-1848. Navajo, $200.

Campos, Domingo. 3-15-1848. Navajo, $620.

Armijo, Juan Antonio. 3-15-1848. Navajo, $700.

Sones, Pedro. 3-18-1848. Navajo, $600.

Abeita, Jesús. #2812. 3-18-1848. Navajo, $795.

Luján, José de Jesús. #2283. 3-25-1848. Las Vegas, San Miguel County. Navajo, $8,200 (3,850 sheep, mares, mules, gun). Approved for $4,240.

Padilla, José Mariano. #3442. 4-10-1848. Navajo, $260.

Sones, Pedro. 4-15-1848. Navajo, $200.

Montoya, Tomás. #4101. 6-1848. Navajo.

Gallegos, José Dolores. 6-1848. Navajo.

Maxwell, Lucien and James H. Quinn. #2354, #3647, #3897, #3810. 6-12-1848. Taos County. Jicarilla, $7,200 (mules, horses). Filed 3-10-1854. Not proven.

Rohmann, A. B. #9731. 7-1848. Mescalero, $2,625. Filed 12-29-1856.

Chavis, Antonio Teroza. 8-1-1848. Navajo, $625.

Pino, José María. #9278. 8-10-1848. Navajo, $1,375.

Padilla, José Mariano. #5495. 9-13-1848. Navajo, $1,450.

Armijo, Pedro. #4521. 10-7-1848. Navajo, $940.

Luna, Antonio José. 10-12-1848. #2162. Apache.

Armijo, Juan Antonio. 10-15-1848. Navajo, $120.

Armijo, Pedro. 10-16-1848. Navajo, $3,950.

Sandoval, Antonio. #3651. 12-15-1848. Navajo, $2,800. Filed 10-17-1853.

Lema, Raphael. 12-24-1848. Navajo, $500. Filed 8-23-1854.

Armijo, José. #7750. 12-24-1848. Navajo, $905. Filed 8-23-1854.

Trujillo, Manuel Antonio. #8461. 12-24-1848. Navajo, $2,100. Estate of. Filed 8-23-1854.

Silva, Mariano. #3071. 12-24-1848. Navajo, $1,750. Filed 8-23-1854.

Abeita, Sylvester. #2061. 12-24-1848. Navajo, $2,100 (105 cattle). Not proven.

Contreras, Juan Andrés. #10221, #10222. 12-27-1848. Mescalero, $1,250. Filed 8-23-1854.

1849

Pino, José de Jesús. 1-15-1849. Navajo, $2,084.

Baca, Pedro. #2097. 2-1-1849. Navajo, $1772 (cattle, mules). Not proven.

Ruis, Enacio. #2415. 2-15-1849. Apache. $501 (horses). Not proven.

Romero, Manuel Antonio. #1942. 2-15-1849. Apache, $80.

Luján, José de Jesús. #2601. 3-1849. Navajo, $7,682.

Candelario, Ésteban. 3-26-1849. Navajo, $1,380.

Luna, Antonio José. #2163. 3-28-1849. Navajo, $285.

Gonzales, Antonio José. 4-1849. Navajo, $25.

Lucero, Pablo. #6090. 4-1849. Navajo, $160.

Lucero, Juan José. #8157. 4-9-1849. Navajo, $175.

Martínez, José Benito. #5994. 6-12-1849. Jicarilla, $1,735. Filed 7-16-1855.

Lucero, Julián. #10217. 7-7-1849. Apache, $720.

Sandoval, Antonio. 7-10-1849. Navajo, $2,500. Filed 10-7-1853.

Luna, Juan. 8-15-1849. Navajo, $4,500.

Pino, Vincente. #2834. 9-10-1849. Jicarilla, $2,790.

Luna, Rafael. 9-20-1849. Navajo.

Robert T. Brent & Preston Breck. #2114, #2593. 9-1849. Santa Fe. Navajo, $8,710 (134 horses, mules). Not proven.

Luna, Rafael. #2305. 10-27-1849. Valencia County. Navajo, $700 (sheep, cows). Not proven.

Gonzales, José María. #7012. 12-10-1849. Apache, $108.

Ortiz, Antonio Matías. #2307, #2308, #2309, #2310, #2311, #2312, #2313, #2314. 12-14-1849. Mescalero, $15,675.

1850

Candelaria, Ésteban. 1-3-1850. Navajo, $5,050.

Olona, Manuel. #2379. 1-22-1850. Valencia County. Apache, $450 (7 mules, 1 horse). Not proven.

Romero, José Dolores. #9729. 2-1850. Jicarilla, $1,300.

García, Román. #9865. 4-1850. Jicarilla, $7,659 (3,807 sheep).

Ulibarri, Santiago. #9749. 4-1850. Jicarilla, $3,429 (1,662 sheep).

Gonzales, Reges. #4014. 5-18-1850. Navajo, $11,055.

Montoya, José Antonio. #3392. 5-18-1850. Navajo.

Chavis, José Antonio. #4317, #5438. 6-23-50 and 6-24-1850. Navajo, $17,440 (6,700 sheep).

Quinn, James H. & Lucien Maxwell. #1317. 6-26-1850. Ute, $5,175 (175 cattle, 10 horses, mules). Filed 10-30-1852. No treaty annuities, no payment. Had army contract for beef at Rayado 1849.

Abrew, (Abreu) Manuel. #3807. 6-26-1850. Rayado. Ute. Perpetrators were Jicarilla. No payment.

Guteris, Ramón. 6-1850. Navajo, $899.

Connelly, Henry. #2146, #2147, #2148, #2149, #2150. 7-1850. Jicarilla, $6,800 (65 of his mules and 20 of William C. Skinner). Filed 2-27-1854. Had 3 corn contracts.

Lacome, Auguste & Bros. #1653, #2284. 7-23-1850. Taos County. Ute, $692 (dry goods, tobacco, etc.). Filed 12-5-1850. Approved per Treaty of 12-30-4189.

Connelly, Henry. #2662, #2663, #2664. Raids from 1846 to 1850. Navajo, $23,866 (15,911 sheep).

Sandoval, Antonio. #3945. 9-7-1850. Navajo, $9,344 (3,700 sheep).

Pino, Vincente. 9-13-1850. Navajo.

Gonzales, María Gertrudes. #2237. 9-25-1850. Navajo, $135 (oxen and cart). Not proven.

Sandoval, Antonio. #2430. 12-10-1850. Bernalillo County. Navajo, $6,500 (sheep). Filed 10-7-1853. Not proven.

Luzero, Pedro. 1850 to 1852. Apache, $1,720.

1851

Guteris (Gutirres), Ramón. 1-1851. Navajo.

Lucero, Juan José. #3391. 1-14-1851. Navajo.

Tenorio, José. #3635. 1-14-1851. Navajo, $600.

Martín, José. #3416. 1-14-1851. Navajo, $130.

Montoya, José Antonio. #10731. 1-14-1851. Navajo.

Sandoval, Josepha. 1-14-1851. Navajo.

Gallegos, María Mesta. 1-14-1851. Navajo, $481.

Chavis, José Antonio. #2145. 1-31-1851. Bernalillo County. Apache, $1,000 (40 cows). Filed 10-7-1853. Not proven.

Biggs, Thomas. 2-12-1851. Apache, $200.

Pino, Vincente. 2-16-1851. Navajo.

Medina, José María. #5385. 2-1851. Navajo, $50. Mariano Gonzales, administrator.

Baca, Domingo. #2109. 2-25-1851. Navajo, $300 (2 mules). Francisco Tomás Cabeza de Baca, administrator. Not proven.

Baca, Domingo. #4884. 3-25-1851. Navajo, $300. Francisco Tomás Cabeza de Baca, administrator.

Lucero, Nazario. 3-26-1851. Gila, $180. Filed 8-23-1854.

Sandoval, José Andrés. #2514. 3-1851. Navajo, $220. Filed 2-1852.

Chavis, Bernardo. #2138. 3-26-1851. Apache, $540 (mules, horses). Not proven.

Pino, Vincente. 4-1851. Jicarilla.

Luna, Antonio José. 4-3-1851. Navajo, $1,600.

Luna, Rafael. 4-3-1851. Navajo.

Ruivali, José. #9121. 6-26-1851. Navajo, $470.

Martín, José Benito. #2333. 7-8-1851. Apache, $1,110 (mules, horses). Not proven.

Gomes, Manuel Gregoria. 7-10-1851. Jicarilla, $4,635 (25 mules, 57 mares, 14 horses, 22 cattle). Filed 7-28-1855.

Aragón, Ésteban. #2059. 7-25-1851. Santa Ana County. Navajo, #3,370 (horses, mules). Filed 6-5-1854. Approved for $3,160. Treaty of 9-9-1849.

Montoya, José Ignacio. #10731. 7-25-1851. Jicarilla, $1,350. Filed 6-4-1854.

Lucero, Antonia Serafín. #2315. 7-28-1851. Santa Ana County. Navajo, $1,850 (horses, mules). Filed 6-4-1854. Approved for $940. Treaty of 9-9-1849.

Lucero, Jesús, et al. #2316. 8-1851. San Miguel County. Apache, $3,400 (cattle, horses, mules). Not proven. Letter from Isidor Samson says the raiders were Comanche and only cattle were killed, late June 1851.

Rumley, Charles S. 8-1851. Navajo, $4,788.

Salas, Francisco. #3205. 8-15-1851. Jicarilla, $626. Filed 6-17-1854.

Gallegos, Querino. #1386. 8-15-1851. Mescalero. $3,870 (horses, cattle). Filed 8-8-1874. Approved for $2380.

Apodaca, Raphael. #2076. 8-19-1851. Bernalillo County. Navajo, $800 (horses, mules). Filed 10-7-1853. Not proven.

Luzero, Jesús; José Felipe Madril; Rafael Aragone; Juan Baptista Durán; José Antonio Flores; Julián Baca. 8-1851. Jicarilla, $3,400.

Gullegos, José Dolores. 9-1851. Navajo.

Armijo, Pedro. #2969. 9-8-1851. Bernalillo County. Navajo, $150 (horses, mules). Filed 12-20-1854. Not proven.

Chavis, Ramón. #2141. 9-8-1851. Navajo, $240 (horses, mules). Not proven.

Gruale, Tomás. 9-8-1851. Navajo, $508. Filed 8-25-1854.

Armijo, Pedro. 9-8-1851. Navajo, $150.

Martín, Juan Ignacio. 9-12-1851. Jicarilla, $780.

Montoya, Estanislao. #1593. 9-12-1851. Apache, $2,350. Filed 8-23-1854.

Casados, Miguel. #1428. 9-15-1851. San Miguel County. Navajo, $595 (horses, mules). Filed 8-17-1874. Approved for $405 but barred. Treaty of 9-9-1849.

Gonzales, Cristino. #1391. 9-15-1851. Manuelito, San Miguel County. Navajo, $1,790 (oxen, cows). Filed 8-8-1874. Approved.

Baca, José Albino. #2104. 10-16-1851. Santa Fe. Navajo, $4,275 (57 mules). Filed 7-22-1854. Not proven.

Luna, Antonio José. 11-21-1851. Apache, $3,893 (1,533 sheep). Filed 8-23-1854.

Baca, José Albino. 11-22-1851. Navajo, $5,200. Filed 12-5-1851.

Trujillo, Henríques. 11-26-1851. Apache, $183. Filed 8-23-1854.

Chavis, Antonio José. #2818. 12-6-1851. Apache, $750. Filed 8-23-1854.

Lenna, (Luna?) Antonio José. 12-18-1851. Apache, $3,189 (1,532 sheep). Filed 8-23-1854.

Lenna, Antonio José. 12-19-1851. Apache, $125. Filed 8-23-1854.

Lenna, Ramón. 12-19-1851. Apache, $450. Filed 8-23-1854.

Gallegos, José Antonio. #10427. 12-21-1851. Apache, $100. Filed 8-23-1854.

Trujillo, Manuel. 12-21-1851. Apache, $486. Filed 8-23-1854.

Sánchez, Dubirjeu. #2434. 12-21-1851. San Miguel County. Apache, $75 (oxen). Filed 8-23-1854. Approved.

Chavis, Pedro. #2139. 12-21-1851. Apache, $103 (oxen). Filed 8-23-1854. Not proven.

Montanio, Lorenzo. #2346. 12-29-1851. Bernalillo County. Navajo, $420 (horses, oxen, mules). Filed 12-20-1854. Approved. Treaty of 9-29-1849.

Páez, Antonio A. #8355. 12-1851. Kiowa $550. Filed 10-7-1854.

Sandoval, Josefa. #2431. 1851. Bernalillo County. Apache, $535 (cows, oxen, horse). Not proven.

1852

Steck, Michael. 1-1-1852. Apache, $1,380. Filed 1-5-1855.

Armijo, Manuel R. #2072. 1-15-1852 and 2-1852. Apache, $7,875 (85 mules, 60 oxen). Filed 12-27-1852. Not proven.

Constante, Antonio. #2162. 1-28-1852. Dona Ana County. Apache, $7,418 (merchandise). Filed 6-1-1854. He first claimed $5000 then changed the amount. Letter to Governor Meriwether 8-30-1854. Not proven.

Stevenson, Hugh. 2-7-1852. Apache, $780. Filed 8-3-1853.

Richardson, Israel B. US Army. #2401. 2-7-1852, 9-8-1852, 11-1-1852. Apache, $400 (horses, etc.). Filed 10-1-58. $60 approved but barred. Treaty of 7-1-1852.

Armijo, Manuel & Rafael. 2-9-1852. Apache. Rafael Armijo was Albuquerque merchant.

Olona, Manuel. #4882. 2-15-1852. Apache, $150. Filed 8-23-1854.

Romero, Hoban (Haban?). 2-15-1852. Cheyenne, $450.

Jaramillo, Vincente. #2929. 2-15-1852. Navajo, $800.

Lucero, Juan José. 2-1852. Navajo.

Romero, Haban (Hoban?). #2407. 2-1852. Taos County. Navajo, $450 (horses, mules). Not proven.

Romero, Manuel. #2408. 3-25-1852. Santa Fe County. Navajo, $525 (horses). Filed 6-23-1854. Not proven.

Baca, F. Tomás Cabeza de. #2164. 3-1852. Navajo, $2,695. Had army hay contract.

Montoya, Joaquín. #1460. 4-10-1852. San Miguel County. Navajo, $450 (oxen, cows, etc.). Filed 12-9-1874. Wrote letter to S. M. Baird of theft on 5-6-1852. Not proven.

Gonzales, Rufino. #1448. 4-25-1852. San Miguel County. Cheyenne, $825 (cows, horses, asses). Filed 12-9-1874. Approved for $605.

Gallegos, Nazario. #1439. 6-1-1852. Indians, $1,050 (460 sheep, mule, horses). Filed 8-17-1874. Approved. Treaty of 9-9-1849.

Lafoll, José Dolores. 6-12-1852. Jicarilla, $1,350. Filed 9-26-1854.

García, Ésteban. #2030. 6-16-1852. Jicarilla, $260. Filed 2-13-1855.

García, Juanita. #1436. 6-17-1852. Navajo, $725 (horses, mules). Not proven.

Aragón, Régis. #2063. 6-1852. San Miguel County. Apache, $190 (horses, cattle, mules). Filed 10-7-1854. Approved for $110.

Sánchez, Antonio María. #3324. 7-8-1852. Apache, $130.

Baca, Pablo. #2103. 7-1852. San Miguel County. Jicarillas, $2,275 (various property). Filed 1-25-1855. Not proven.

Telles, José. Summer of 1852. Apache, $35. Filed 6-27-1855.

Aragón, Régis. #2960. 7-1852. Comanche, $450. Filed 10-7-1854.

Sánchez, Antonio M. #2435. 7-8-1852. Lucero, San Miguel County. Apache, $130 (horses, mules). Filed 2-13-1855. Not proven.

Hoppin & Hubbell. #2543. 8-12-1852. Gila, $3,500 (mules, horses). Filed 9-20-1852. Not proven.

Gomes, Manuel Gregoria. 8-24-1852. Jicarilla.

García, Ésteban. #2030. 8-25-1852. Jicarilla. Filed 2-13-1855.

Aragón, Régis. 9-1852. Apache. Filed 10-7-1854.

Gullegos, María Mesta. #3981. 9-20-1852. Navajo.

Morris, Gouverneur. U.S. Army. #2343. 9-22-1852, 9-29-1852, 10-4-1852. Apache, $175 (2 mules, 1 cow). Filed 4-5-1853. Not proven.

Montoya, Vincente. #2349. 9-30-1852. Bernalillo County. Navajo, $115 (1 mare, 3 oxen). Filed 12-20-1854. Not proven.

Francisco, John M. 10-14-1852. Ute, $199. Filed 11-21-1853. Had two fodder contracts. Sutler at Ft. Massachusetts.

Steck, Michael. #2438. 11-1-1852. Lucero. Apache, $1,440 (various property). Not proven.

Aragón, José Francisco. #2060. 11-1852. Bernalillo County. Navajo, $100 (horses). Filed 3-1855. Approved for $70. Treaty of 9-24-1850.

Abeita, Juan. #2064. 11-1852. Socorro County. Mescalero, $104 (goats). Filed 8-23-1854. Not proven.

Vigil, Gabriel. 11-27-1852. Jicarilla, $700. Filed 7-28-1855.

Aguerre, Pedro. #2077. 12-1-1852. Dona Ana County. Apache, $640 (16 oxen). Filed 12-29-1854. Not proven.

Baca, Louis. #1655. 12-10-1852. Apache, $950. Filed 8-29-1854.

Olona, Manuel. #2380. 12-15-1852. Valencia County. Apache, $450 (mules). Filed 12-20-1854. Not proven.

Vigil, Manuel. #7298. 12-25-1852. Apache, $405. Filed 8-23-1854.

Chavis, Manuel. #1462. 1852. Apache, $430. Filed 6-27-1855.

Carrera, Juan José. 1852. Apache, $50. Filed 6-27-1855.

Perea, Francisco. #2386. 1852. Dona Ana County. Apache, $100 (oxen). Filed 6-27-1855. Not proven.

Rodereques, José María. 1852. Apache, $210. Filed 6-27-1855.

García, José. #5855. 1852. Apache, $70. Filed 6-27-1855.

Maléndez, Pablo. 1852. Apache, $60. Filed 6-27-1855.

Valdez, Juan Benito. 1852 to 1855. Ute, $4,503. Filed 9-26-1855.

1853

Telles, José. 1853. Apache, $55. Filed 6-27-1855.

Gonzales, Yalario. #6029. 1-1853. Apache, $150. Filed 6-10-1854.

Chaves, José Loretto. 1-20-1853. Cheyenne, $310.

Apodaca, José. #2075. 1-29-1853. Socorro County. Apache, $300 (mules, horses). Filed 8-23-1854. Approved for $150. Treaty of 7-1-1852.

García, Antonio José. #3421. 2-7-1853. Gila, $200.

Conner, William J. 2-15-1853. Socorro. Apache, $110 (cow, ox, two heifers). Filed 8-23-1854.

López, Juan N. 2-15-1853. Gila, $70. Filed 8-23-1854.

Lucero, Gabriel. 2-15-1853. Apache, $200. Filed 7-28-1855.

Lenna, Lorenzo and José María Padilla. #5495. 2-15-1853. Apache, $125. Filed 8-23-1854.

Montoya, Antonio. #8474. 2-15-1853. Gila, $250. Filed 8-23-1854.

Baca, Pedro. #2096. 2-18-1853. Socorro County. Apache $180 (oxen). Filed 8-23-1854. Not proven.

Montolla, Juan. #2347. 2-20-1853. Socorro County. Apache, $400 (horses, oxen). Filed 8-14-1854. Not proven.

Gallegos, Francisco. #1458. 3-1853. San Miguel County. Navajo, $1,000 (horses). Filed 12-1874. Approved for $765. Treaty of 9-9-1849. Lorenzo Labadi letter 2-18-55, accuses Francisco Gallegos of stealing Ute property at Abiquiu. He refuses to return stolen property.

Baca, F. T. Cabeza de. #2107. 3-23-1853. Santa Ana County. Navajo, $2,695 (goats, sheep). Approved for $1,230. Treaty of 9-9-1849.

Baca, Lewis. 3-2-1853. Apache.

Cordova, Juan B. 3-15-1853. Apache, $150. Filed 8-23-1854.

García, Inés. 4-25-1853. Mescalero, $500. Filed 7-1-1854.

Chavis, Manuel. 5-5-1853. Jicarilla, $600 (4 horses, 3 mules). Filed 5-19-1853. No evidence.

Devine, Joseph H. #2184. 5-13-1853. Apache. $5,000 (mules, horses). Approved for $3,500. Treaty 7-1-1852.

Gonzales, José. 5-20-1853. Jicarillas, $65 (2 horses). Filed 6-13-1853. No evidence.

Masse, Juan Rafael. #2582. 5-30-1853. Los Lunas. Apache, $1,450 (horses, mules). Not proven.

Mares, Juan de Jesús. #2345. 6-13-1853. Taos County. Jicarilla, $2,530 (cattle, horses, property). Filed 9-26-1855. Approved for $900. Treaty of 7-1-1852.

Baca, Diego. #3474. 7-19-1853. Apache, $450 (2 horses, 3 mules). Witnesses contradict claimant's statements.

Peters, John. 7-20-1853. Jicarilla, $130 (horse, mule). Filed 7-30-1853. "No evidence to substantiate the statements of the claimant."

Valle, Alexander. 7-22-1853. Jicarilla, $415 (5 horses). Filed 7-28-1853. No evidence.

Sera, José A. #2461. 7-22-1853. Santa Fe. Jicarilla, $200 (horses). Not proven.

Luna, José Antonio. 7-22-1853. Jicarilla, $170 (6 horses). Filed 7-28-1853. No evidence.

Rhine, Samuel & Brothers. #4226. 8-3-1853. Apache, $10,058. Filed 12-15-1853. Michael Steck arrests some chiefs who acknowledge the theft.

Ivers, William. #2264. 8-11-1853. Apache, $1,804 (mules, horses, goods). Not proven.

García, Inés. 9-27-1853. Mescalero. Filed 7-1-1854.

Olona, Manuel. #4883. 11-1853. Valencia County. Apache, $150. Filed 12-20-1854.

Cordova, Juan B. 11-1853. Apache. Filed 8-23-1854.

Chavis, María Josepha. 11-5-1853. Gila, $825. Filed 8-23-1854.

Luna, Francisco. #2297. 11-6-1853. Socorro County. Gila, $130 (horses). Filed 8-23-1854. Not proven.

Noel, Gustavus A. J. 11-15-1853. Navajo, $660. Filed 8-17-1854.

Abreu, Francisco P. #2066. 11-16-1853. Socorro County. Apache, $210 (horses, mules, oxen). Filed 6-10-1854. Not proven.

Tenorio, José. #2476. 12-24-1853. Bernalillo County. Navajo, $100 (horse). Not proven. Filed 8-25-1854.

Montoya, José Antonio. #2530. 12-24-1853. Bernalillo County. Navajo, $300 (mules). Filed 12-20-1854.

McGowan, Timothy. #2344. 12-1853. Apache, $10,755 (corn, fodder, tobacco, etc.). Filed 5-16-1855. No evidence. Governor Meriwether contradicts the claim.

Naranjo, Francisco. #1437. 1853. San Miguel County. Navajo, $145 (mare and jack). Approved for $120 but barred.

1854

Miera, Ignacio. #4319. 1-15-1854. Navajo, $910. Filed 6-4-1854.

Sánchez, Jesús María. #2436. 2-2-1854. Taos County. Ute, $180 (property, 6 mares). Filed 10-21-1854. Not proven.

Padilla, Félix. 2-15-1854. Cheyenne, $973. Filed 9-26-1855.

Gurule, Petra. 3-10-1854. Mescalero. $2,775. Filed 6-1-1854.

Miera, Ignacio. #2339. 3-10-1854. Mescalero, $406 (sheep, horses). Filed 6-4-1854. Approved for $300. Treaty of 7-1-1852.

Vigil, Manuel. 3-15-1854. #10213, #10214. Apache, $840.

Gruale, Tomás. 3-19-1854. Navajo. Filed 8-25-1854.

García, Inés. 4-18-1854. Mescalero. Filed 7-1-1854.

Moore, William H. & Burton L. Rees. #10036, #10673. 5-9-1854. Mescalero, $2,860. Filed 8-24-1854. Had 9 corn contracts.

Trujillo, Pablo. #2481. 5-15-1854. Guadalupita, Mora County. Jicarilla, $470 (horses). Filed 3-7-1860. $375 approved but barred. Treaty of 7-1-1852.

Chavis, Manuel. #10754. 5-10-1854. Mescalero, $740. Filed 6-15-1854.

García, Vicente. #1876. 6-29-1854. Santa Fe County. Kaw, $170 (mules). Filed 8-17-1854. First approved for $100 under Treaty of 3-17-54, then denied because no proof of Kaw established.

Sandoval, Anastacio. #1877. 6-29-1854. Santa Fe County. Kaw, $640 (mules, horses). Filed 8-17-1854. First approved, but later denied because no proof of Kaw established.

Frisarra (Ylisario), Mariano. 7-2-1854. Mescalero, $7,640. Filed 8-17-1854. (*Santa Fe Weekly Gazette*, July 15, 1854, near Anton Chico, 4,000 sheep.)

Baca, Diego. #3974. 7-10-1854. Apache. Witnesses contradict claimant.

Martín, Juan Ignacio. 7-15-1854. Jicarilla.

Baca, F. Tomás Cabeza de. #2108. 8-1-1854. Apache, $2,330 (horses, mules). Not proven.

Baca, Francisco Tomás Cabeza de. #1464, #1465, #1466. 8-21-1854. Jicarilla, $2,465. Filed 2-7-1855.

Borrego, Juan Antonio. #2112. 8-25-1854. Rio Arriba County. Jicarillas, $720 (mules, horses, ox). Filed 12-28-1854. Approved for $315. Treaty of 7-1-1852.

Ortiz, Caspar. #2377. 9-27-1854. Apache, $825 (property). Filed 10-9-1854. Not proven.

Trujillo, José Anastacio. #2483. 10-15-1854. Mora County. Jicarilla, $370 (horses). Approved for $300. Treaty of 7-1-1852.

Valdez, Juan D. #2500. 10-27-1854. Apache, $131 (mules, blankets, etc.). Not proven.

López, Francisco. #2287. 11-19-1854. San Miguel County. Jicarilla, $470 (oxen, cows). Filed 2-10-1855. Approved for $225. Treaty of 7-1-1852.

García, Félix. #6076. 11-29-1854. Jicarilla, $2,225. Filed 12-30-1854.

Giddings, James M. & Preston Beck. #1316. 12-6-1854. Mescalero, $4,111 (sheep, goats). Filed 12-28-1854. Not proven.

Aguirre, Pedro. #2078. 12-6-1854. Dona Ana County. Mescalero, $2,120 (mules, horses). Filed 12-29-1854. Not proven.

Majors & Russell. #2357. 12-9-1854. Fort Union. Jicarilla, $9,960 (249 cattle). Filed 1-26-1855. Not proven.

Kronig, William. #498. 12-24-1854. Pueblo, Colo. Ute, $1,080.

Baca, José Marcelino. #2101. 12-25-1854. Pueblo, Colo. Ute, $3,925 (oxen, cow, horses). Filed 1-18-1855.

Mitchell, Levin. 12-27-1854. Ute, $1,470. (40 cattle). Filed 4-30-1855.

Sánchez, Jesús María. 1854–1855. Conejos, Colo. Ute, $3,305. Meriwether says there was no settlement at Conejos in 1854 for anything to be stolen.

Armijo, Rafael & Co. #2090. 1854. Santa Fe. Apache, $3,570 (mules, etc.). Not proven.

Rodereques, José María. #4529. 1854. Apache.

García, José. 1854. Apache.

1855

Kronig, William. #499. 1-19-1855. Pueblo, Colo. Ute.

Suaso, Tomás. #2560. 1-19-1855. Pueblo, Colo. Ute, $2,110. Investigation trimmed the claim to $1,390, but denied case for claimant being unlawfully in Indian country and tribes not in amity.

Baca, José M. #2102. 1-19-55, Pueblo, Colo. Ute, $1,053 (corn, farming equipment). Not proven.

Baca, F. T. Cabeza de. 1-30-1855. Ute, Apache, $3,590. Filed 10-7-1872.

Lucero, Julián. #10218. 2-6-1855. Jicarilla, Ute, $3,095. Filed 9-26-1855.

Vigil, Juan de Jesús. #2502. 2-6-55 and 2-8-1855. Taos County. Ute, Jicarilla, $5,580 (1,200 sheep, horses, mules). Filed 3-7-1856. Approved for $2,530. Treaty of December 30, 1849.

Duvall, Alexander. #2185. 2-15-1855. Santa Fe. Gila, $60 (mule). Filed 9-1-1855. Approved. Treaty of 7-1-1852. Had army beef contract.

Lucero, Julián. 2-24-1855. Jicarilla, Ute. Filed 9-26-1855.

Martínez, Vincente. 2-28-1855. Ute, Jicarilla, $491.

Maxwell, Lucien B. #1254. 3-2-1855. Taos County. Arapaho, $10,400 (2,100 sheep). Filed 4-1856. Approved for $4,200. Treaty of 7-27-1853.

Orgín, Juan Manuel. #2378. 3-16-1855. Ute, $1,568 (horses, sheep, etc.). Filed 9-26-1855. Not proven.

Martínez, José Benito. #8474. 4-1855. Jicarilla, $1,450. Filed 9-26-1855.

Fernández, José Delores. #2211. 5-17-1855. Taos County. Jicarilla, $220 (7 cows, 3 bulls). Filed 11-2-1855. Not proven.

Mares, Juan de Jesús. #2591. 6-15-1855. Jicarilla.

Laury, Rev. John. 6-26-1855. Jicarilla, $615. Filed 9-27-1855.

Lucero, Julián. 9-15-1855. Jicarilla, Ute. Filed 9-26-1855.

Remaris (Ramírez), Serafín. #283. September 1855. Bernalillo County. Mescalero, $1,275 (horses, mules). Approved for $680. Treaty of 7-27-1853.

Larragoite, Benito. #2317. 11-25-1855. Jicarilla, $350 (mules, oxen). Not proven.

A Note about Case Numbers and Names

Some of the congressional documents did not include case numbers. To try to find them I consulted the NARA Depredation index, which gives names and case numbers but no incident dates. When one person filed several cases I tried to match the lowest case number, generally meaning that it was filed earlier, with the earliest incident date, assuming that would be the logical sequence. Of course, people could have made several filings then filed later on an earlier incident that they "forgot" about. Another problem comes with name spellings, which often differed by a letter or two, such as Chavis and Chávez, or Gullego and Gallegos, Montoya and Montolla. Some of these may have been the same people, with scribes spelling the names differently.

Appendix B

Statehood and Territorial Proponents,
with Depredation Claims and Army Contracts

DC means Depredation Claim.
AC means Army Contract.

Statehood Proponents

Álvarez, Manuel
Angney, William Z.
Baird, Spruce M.
Cabeza de Baca, F. Tomás (DC)
Castillo, Florentino
Cordova, Raymundo
Cunningham, Francis A.
Gallegos, José Manuel
Gallegos, José Pablo
Gold, George
Gonzales, Dionicio
Gonzales, Hilario (Ylario?) (DC)
Jaramillo, Gerónimo
Leyva, Fr. José Francisco
Martínez, Pascual
Martínez, Vincente (DC)
Mascarena, Miguel
Messervy, William S.

Naugle, Joseph
Ortiz, J. F.
Otero, Francisco
Parea, José
Pillans, Palmer J.
Pino, Facundo
Quintana, Miguel
Robinson, James D.
Romero, Miguel
Salasar, Diego
Sandoval, José Andrés (DC)
Torres, Juan
Valdez, Seledonio
Vigil, Esquipila
Vigil, José Ramón (DC)
Weightman, Richard
Wheaton, Theodore

Territory Proponents

Archuleta, Diego
Armijo, Rafael (DC)
Armijo, Santiago
Ashurst, M.
Baca, Juan Cruz
Baca, Manuel Antonio
Baca y Pino, Juan Antonio
Beaubien, Charles
Brent, Robert (DC)
Calhoun, James C.
Collins, James L.
Connelly, Henry (DC)
Duvall, Alexander (DC, AC),
    army contract for beef in 1851
Francisco, John M. (DC, AC)
Giddings, James M. (DC)
Houghton, Joab
Hubbell, James S. (DC)
Johnson, Thomas S. J.
Kelly, John
Lucero, Salvador
Luna, Ramón (DC)
Martínez, Padre Antonio José
Maxwell, Lucien (DC, AC),
    army contract for beef
McCutcheon, Thomas R.

McGrorty, William
Montoya, Miguel (DC)
Ortiz, Cándido
Ortiz, Tomás (AC), army contract for hay
Otero, Antonio José (DC)
Otero, Manuel Antonio
Perea, Pedro José
Quinn, James H. Quinn (AC), army
    contract for beef in 1849
Ramírez, Serafino
Reynolds, A. W.
Sánchez, Juan José (DC)
Sandoval, Antonio (DC)
Sarracino, Francisco
Skinner, William Curtis
Smith, Hugh N.
St. Vrain, Ceran (AC)
Tenorio, Julián
Tuley, Murray F.
Tullis, John R.
Turley, Jess
Vaughn, E. J.
Vigil, Donaciano (DC)
Whitlock, Dr. John M. (AC),
    army contract for beef in 1858
Yrisarri, Mariano

Appendix C

Depredation Claims, Tribes, and Treaties

Year	Navaho	Apache*	Mescalero	Jicarilla	Ute	Other	Total Indians**
1846	3 UT	0	0	0	0	0	3
1847	45	5	0	0	0	0	50
1848	30 UT	1	2	1	0	0	34
1849	13 T	4	1	2	0 T	0	20
1850	10	2	0	4	3	0	19
1851	29	18 UT	1	6 UT	0	1	55
1852	10	25 T	1	6	2	2	46
1853	6	24 UT	2	7	0	1	40
1854	2	8	8	8	5	3	34
1855	0 UT	2 UT	1 UT	10 UT	10 UT	1	24***
Total	**148**	**89**	**16**	**44**	**20**	**8**	**325**

T = ratified treaty

UT = unratified treaty

  * Including Apaches, Gilas, Coyoteros, Mogollons, Mimbres, and other Apaches.

** Including Comanches, Cheyennes, Arapahos, Kiowas, Kaws, and others.

*** 6 of these 24 are Ute-Jicarilla combined.

Appendix D

Depredation Claims and Troop Strength

Year	Number of Claims	Troop Strength
1846	3	
1847	50	about 3,300
1848	34	3,157 for half a year, then 960
1849	20	885 (16 companies)
1850	19	800
1851	55	1,459 (21 companies)
1852	46	1,569 (21 companies)
1853	40	1,351 (21 companies)
1854	34	1,386 (23 companies)
1855	24	1,743 (24 companies)
Subtotal	**325**	
1856	0	
1857	7	
1858	0	
1859	3	
Total	**335**	

Appendix E

Presiding Officials, 1846–1855

Governor

September 1846	Charles Bent
January 1847	Donaciano Vigil
June 1850	Henry Connelly (prevented from assuming power by John Munroe)
March 3, 1851	James S. Calhoun
September 13, 1852	William Carr Lane
August 8, 1853	David Meriwether

Department Commander

Military Department No. 9

November 3, 1846	Brig. Gen. Stephen W. Kearny
June 11, 1847	Col. Sterling Price
August 29, 1847	Lt. Col. Alton R. Easton
December 11, 1847	Brig. Gen. Sterling Price
August 27, 1848	Maj. Benjamin L. Beall
October 11, 1848	Bvt. Lt. Col. John M. Washington
December 26, 1848	Bvt. Maj. Gen. William J. Worth
May 1849	Bvt. Lt. Col. John M. Washington
October 23, 1849	Bvt. Col. John Munroe
July 19, 1851	Bvt. Col. Edwin V. Sumner
July 1, 1853	Lt. Col. Dixon S. Miles
July 20, 1853	Bvt. Brig. Gen. John Garland

Department of New Mexico, October 31, 1853

October 11, 1856	Col. Benjamin L. E. Bonneville

Commissioner of Indian Affairs

1845–1848	William Medill
1849–1850	Orlando Brown
1850–1853	Luke Lea
1853–1857	George W. Manypenny

Secretary of the Interior

1849–1850	Thomas Ewing
1850	Thomas M. T. McKennan
1850–1853	Alexander H. H. Stuart
1853–1857	Robert McClelland

Secretary of War

1845–1849	William L. Marcy
1849–1850	George W. Crawford
1850–1853	Charles M. Conrad
1853–1857	Jefferson Davis

President

1845–1849	James K. Polk (Democrat)
1849–1850	Zachary Taylor (Whig)
1850–1853	Millard Fillmore (Whig)
1853–1857	Franklin Pierce (Democrat)

Notes

Abbreviations

AFUC   Letters Received, Department of New Mexico. Arrott Fort Union Collection, Thomas Donnelly Library, New Mexico Highlands University, Las Vegas, New Mexico.

AGO   Letters Received by the Office of the Adjutant General, Main Series, 1822 to 1860. National Archives and Records Administration (NARA), Record Group (RG) 94.

NALS   Letters Sent, 9th Military Department, Department of New Mexico, October 1849 to August 1856. National Archives and Records Administration (NARA), Record Group (RG) 393, M1072, M1102, M1120.

OCJC   Annie Heloise Abel, ed., *The Official Correspondence of James S. Calhoun While Indian Agent at Santa Fe and Superintendent of Indian Affairs in New Mexico* (Washington, D.C.: Government Printing Office, 1915).

OIA   Letters Received, New Mexico Superintendency. Office of Indian Affairs, M234, Rolls 546, 547.

SFR   Gary D. Lenderman, ed., *The Santa Fe Republican: New Mexico Territory's First Newspaper 1847–1849* (San Bernardino: CreateSpace, 2011).

SFWG   *Santa Fe Weekly Gazette.*

TSDC   Thomas Suaso Depredation Claim, #2560. National Archives and Records Administration (NARA), Record Group (RG) 123.

Introduction

1. Francis Paul Prucha, ed., *Documents of United States Indian Policy* (Lincoln: University of Nebraska Press, 1990), 7.

2. Ibid., 10.

3. Ibid., 12; Henry Knox to President of the United States, June 15, 1789, *American State*

Papers: Indian Affairs, 13 (quotations).

4. Larry C. Skogen, *Indian Depredation Claims, 1796–1920* (Norman: University of Oklahoma Press, 1996), 24; Prucha, *Documents of United States Indian Policy*, 14–16; Lester S. Jayson, *Handling Federal Tort Claims* (New York: M. Baender, 1964–), 1:1-8, 2-18 (quotations).

5. "An Act to Regulate Trade and Intercourse with the Indian Tribes and to Preserve Peace on the Frontiers," http://avalon.law.yale.edu/18th_century/na030.asp.

6. Skogen, *Indian Depredation Claims*, 25.

7. "An Act to Regulate Trade and Intercourse."

8. *Annals of the Congress of the United States 1789–1824*, Fourth Congress, First Session, vol. 5, December 7, 1795, to June 1, 1796 (Washington, D.C.: Gales and Seaton, 1834–1856), 894–905 (following quotations from the congressional debate also from this source).

9. Skogen, *Indian Depredation Claims*, 25–26.

10. Ibid., p. 66.

11. Prucha, *Documents of United States Indian Policy*, 66–67.

Chapter 1

1. Henry B. Judd to John H. Dickerson, August 16, 1849, in *Message from the President of the United States to the Two Houses of Congress*, January 31, 1850, Exec. Doc. No. 24, 1st Session, 31st Congress (following Judd quotations also from this source); Leo E. Oliva, *Fort Union and the Frontier Army in the Southwest*, Southwest Cultural Resources Center Professional Papers No. 41 (Santa Fe: National Park Service, 1993), 22–23; Veronica E. Velarde Tiller, *The Jicarilla Apache Tribe: A History* (Albuquerque: BowArrow Publishing Company, 2000), 34.

2. Gary D. Lenderman, ed., *The Santa Fe Republican: New Mexico Territory's First Newspaper 1847–1849* (San Bernardino: CreateSpace, 2011), 148 (hereinafter cited as *SFR*).

3. Louise Barry, *The Beginning of the West: Annals of the Kansas Gateway to the American West, 1540–1854* (Topeka: Kansas State Historical Society, 1972), 884–85; David Dary, *The Santa Fe Trail: Its History, Legends, and Lore* (New York: Alfred A. Knopf, 2000), 218.

4. The attack is generally said to have occurred near Point of Rocks, which is in the southeast corner of present-day Colfax County, New Mexico, about twelve miles northeast of Abbott. It is also said to have happened at Rock Springs, ten miles "beyond" Point of Rocks and eighty miles from Rayado, but Rayado is only about fifty miles from Point of Rocks. See Edwin L. Sabin, *Kit Carson Days, 1809–1868*, vol. 2, *Adventures in the Path of Empire* (Lincoln: University of Nebraska Press, 1995), 619–20.

5. W. W. H. Davis, *El Gringo: New Mexico and Her People* (Lincoln: University of Nebraska Press, 1982), 45.

6. Annie Heloise Abel, ed., *The Official Correspondence of James S. Calhoun While Indian Agent at Santa Fe and Superintendent of Indian Affairs in New Mexico* (Washington, D.C.: Government Printing Office, 1915), 63–65 (hereinafter cited as *OCJC*; following Calhoun quotations also from this source); Barry, *Beginning of the West*, 885; Sabin,

Kit Carson Days, 618–19. The story of Ann and Virginia White is told in Gregory Michno and Susan Michno, *A Fate Worse Than Death: Indian Captivities in the West* (Caldwell, Idaho: Caxton Press, 2007), 99–103.

7. William A. Keleher, *Turmoil in New Mexico, 1846–1868* (Santa Fe: Rydal Press, 1952), 7.

8. William S. Kiser, *Dragoons in Apacheland: Conquest and Resistance in Southern New Mexico, 1846–1861* (Norman: University of Oklahoma Press, 2012), 14.

9. Keleher, *Turmoil in New Mexico*, 15–16.

10. Kiser, *Dragoons in Apacheland*, 16–17.

11. William E. Unrau, *Indians, Alcohol, and the Roads to Taos and Santa Fe* (Lawrence: University Press of Kansas, 2013), 3, 62, 66; Prucha, *Documents of United States Indian Policy*, 21, 35, 67.

12. Unrau, *Indians, Alcohol, and the Roads*, 28, 46, 53, 112; George P. Hammond, *Alexander Barclay, Mountain Man* (Denver, Colo.: Fred A. Rosenstock Old West Publishing Company, 1976), 25, 46 (quotations).

13. Fitzpatrick to Alfred Cumming, November 19, 1853, *Annual Report of the Commissioner of Indian Affairs 1853*, 129.

14. John S. D. Eisenhower, *So Far from God: The U.S. War with Mexico, 1846–1848* (New York: Anchor Books, 1989), 206–7.

15. Josiah Gregg, *Commerce of the Prairies: Life on the Great Plains in the 1830's and 1840's* (Santa Barbara: Narrative Press, 2001), 9–14, 23; Barry, *Beginning of the West*, 580.

16. Barry, *Beginning of the West*, 577, 582, 587, 588.

17. Robert W. Frazer, *Forts and Supplies: The Role of the Army in the Economy of the Southwest, 1846–1861* (Albuquerque: University of New Mexico Press, 1983), ix.

18. George F. Ruxton, *Adventures in New Mexico and the Rocky Mountains* (London: John Murray, 1847), cited in Joseph G. Dawson III, *Doniphan's Epic March: The 1st Missouri Volunteers in the Mexican War* (Lawrence: University Press of Kansas, 1999), 93 (first quotation); Chris Emmett, *Fort Union and the Winning of the Southwest* (Norman: University of Oklahoma Press, 1965), 53 (second and third quotations).

19. Eisenhower, *So Far from God*, 233–34; Frank McNitt, *Navajo Wars: Military Campaigns, Slave Raids, and Reprisals* (Albuquerque: University of New Mexico Press, 1972), 100–101 (quotation).

20. McNitt, *Navajo Wars*, 121–22; Dawson, *Doniphan's Epic March*, 105.

21. McNitt, *Navajo Wars*, 98, 122–23 (quotation).

22. Eisenhower, *So Far from God*, 235–40; Michael McNierney, ed., *Taos 1847: The Revolt in Contemporary Accounts* (Boulder, Colo.: Johnson Publishing Company, 1980), 38–39, 84–85.

23. Tiller, *Jicarilla Apache Tribe*, 4–5, 9, 13, 27, 29; Pekka Hämäläinen, *The Comanche Empire* (New Haven, Conn.: Yale University Press, 2008), 33, 35, 40.

24. Tiller, *Jicarilla Apache Tribe*, 13, 28; *The Jicarilla Apache Tribe of the Jicarilla Apache Reservation, New Mexico, Petitioner, v. The United States of America, Defendant*, Docket No. 22-A, November 9, 1966, 351–63 (quotation on 363), http://digital.library .okstate.edu/icc/v17/iccv17p338.pdf.

25. David M. Johnson et al., *Final Report on the Battle of Cieneguilla: A Jicarilla Apache Victory over the U.S. Dragoons, March 30, 1854* (Albuquerque, N.Mex.: U.S. Department of Agriculture, Forest Service, Southwestern Region, 2009), 8.
26. Tiller, *Jicarilla Apache Tribe*, 32.
27. Ibid., 12, 14, 21, 24–25, 27.
28. Ibid., 19.
29. *Jicarilla Apache Tribe v. The United States of America,* 345; Tiller, *Jicarilla Apache Tribe*, 10.
30. The Cheyennes and Jicarillas were enemies, so the contention that these two tribes were raiding together is very unlikely. The Mora River flows into the Canadian River about sixty miles east of Las Vegas. The Canadian River was often called the Red River, because the Spanish, Mexicans, and some of the Indians called it the Rio Colorado (Red River), which has confused readers and historians alike. To make matters worse the Red River that serves as the Oklahoma-Texas boundary has several branches that begin in west Texas just south of the Canadian River, and there is an actual Red River flowing west from the Sangre de Cristo into the Rio Grande in Taos County.
31. Benjamin B. Edmonson to Sterling Price, June 14, 1847, in *Message of the President of the United States to the Two Houses of Congress,* December 7, 1847, Exec. Doc. No. 1, 1st Session, 30th Congress (Washington, D.C.: Wendell and Van Benthuysen, 1847), 535–37, in Arrott Fort Union Collection (hereinafter cited as AFUC, generally consisting of letters received, 9th Military Department/Department of New Mexico), Thomas Donnelly Library, New Mexico Highlands University, vol. 47, 42–44 (following Edmonson quotations also from this source).
32. Las Valles (the valleys), with varied spellings, is mentioned in numerous reports. It was variously said to be ten or fifteen miles south of Las Vegas. There was confusion because there were two Las Valles. Las Valles de San Augustin, also known as Lourdes, was ten miles south. When it was abandoned in the 1870s, the inhabitants moved about forty-five miles east near the Canadian River to found the village of Trementina, which is now a ghost town. Fifteen miles below Las Vegas was Las Valles de San Antonio, later known as La Liendre (a string of nits), now also a ghost town. Sterling Price to AAG of the Army, July 20, 1847, in *Message of the President of the United States,* December 7, 1847, 534–35.
33. Ibid.
34. A. T. Andreas, *History of Cook County, Illinois, from the Earliest Period to the Present* (Chicago: A. T. Andreas, Publisher, 1884), 215. This regiment is sometimes designated the 5th Illinois.
35. *SFR,* September 10, 1847, September 17, 1847 (quotations).
36. *SFR,* September 17, 1847.
37. Andreas, *History of Cook County,* 217 (first quotation); *SFR,* October 16, 1847, October 30, 1847 (second through fourth quotations), October 9, 1847 (fifth quotation). Rio Abajo means "downriver" and generally refers to the area between Albuquerque and Socorro. Rio Arriba means "upriver" and generally refers to the area north of Santa Fe.

38. *SFR*, October 9, 1847; U.S. Senate, *Exec. Doc. No. 55*, 1st Session, 35th Congress, 1857–58 (Washington, D.C.: William Harris, 1858).

39. Over the years Contreras made five claims, filed by his administrator, Matías Contreras, while Sandoval filed six claims (see appendix A for a list of claims). I have not located all the claims by any means. An index of Indian Depredation Cases in the National Archives in Washington, D.C., listing claims in Record Groups 75 and 123, shows 7,700 claims, while a supplementary index lists additional claims numbered from 7,701 to 10,841. The breakdown of claims by tribes in the first index alone shows 1,113 claims made against the various Apache tribes, 726 against the Navajos, 334 against the Utes, 54 against the Apaches and Navajos together, and a few score against these tribes in conjunction with several other tribes. The great majority of these claims came after the Civil War, when Americans began saturating the frontiers. During the pre–Civil War years in New Mexico, the Americans and the New Mexicans were just testing the depredation claim waters. Many of the claims that I have found are in "Claims for Indian Depredations in New Mexico" (letter from the secretary of the interior), in U.S. House of Representatives, *Exec. Doc. No. 123*, 1st Session, 35th Congress, 1857–58 (Washington, D.C.: Government Printing Office, 1858), 1–62; U.S. Senate, *Exec. Doc. No. 55*, 1st Session, 35th Congress, 1857–58 (Washington, D.C.: William Harris, 1858); U.S. House of Representatives, *Exec. Doc. No. 182*, 2nd Session, 48th Congress, 1884–85 (Washington, D.C.: Government Printing Office, 1885); U.S. House of Representatives, *Exec. Doc. No. 125*, 1st Session, 49th Congress, 1885–86 (Washington, D.C.: Government Printing Office, 1886); U.S. House of Representatives, *Exec. Doc. No. 77*, 2nd Session, 49th Congress, 1886–87 (Washington, D.C.: Government Printing Office, 1887); U.S. House of Representatives, *Exec. Doc. No. 34*, 1st Session, 50th Congress, 1887–89 (Washington, D.C.: Government Printing Office, 1889).

40. *SFR*, November 13, 1847.

41. *SFR*, November 27, 1847.

42. *SFR.*, December 25, 1847.

43. *SFR*, January 1, 1848, January 8, 1848 (quotation).

44. *SFR*, January 22, 1848 (first quotation), March 18, 1848 (following quotations also from this source).

45. U.S. House of Representatives, *Exec. Doc. No. 182*, 2nd Session, 48th Congress, 1884–85. See also appendix A for depredations in 1848.

46. *SFR*, April 2, 1848.

47. McNitt, *Navajo Wars*, 128; *SFR*, April 2, 1848 (quotations).

48. McNitt, *Navajo Wars*, 128–31; Deloria and DeMallie, *Documents of American Indian Diplomacy*, 1264–65.

49. Richard Griswold Del Castillo, *The Treaty of Guadalupe Hidalgo: A Legacy of Conflict* (Norman: University of Oklahoma Press, 1990), 34, 36, 43, 47–49.

50. Ibid., 49–50, 190–91.

51. The behavior of the U.S. volunteers in New Mexico was often offensive, but their behavior in Mexico could be outrageous. If the reminiscences of Samuel E. Chamberlain, a

private in the 1st Dragoons, are even partially accurate, army treatment of Mexicans was horrendous. Soldiers robbed, raped, and killed civilians on numerous occasions. In one instance in a cave near Saltillo that Chamberlain called "the slaughter pen," the soldiers killed and scalped more than twenty men, women, and children. In Chamberlain's estimation the worst of the volunteers were from Kentucky and Arkansas. Volunteers raped and killed many, including a notorious incident at Agua Nueva on Christmas Day. They ill-treated the "greasers" as they would their "Negroes" back home. The men were very often drunk and uncontrollable. Chamberlain said that "the conflict was no longer war but murder, and a disgrace to any nation calling itself Christian." Samuel E. Chamberlain, *My Confession: The Recollections of a Rogue* (New York: Harper and Brothers, 1956), 87–88, 90, 139, 177.

52. Gregory Michno, *The Settlers' War: The Struggle for the Texas Frontier in the 1860s* (Caldwell, Idaho: Caxton Press, 2011), 399–401.
53. See appendix D.
54. *SFR*, June 27, 1848.
55. *SFR* June 17, 1848, June 27, 1848.

Chapter 2

1. Ralph Adam Smith, *Borderlander: The Life of James Kirker, 1793–1852* (Norman: University of Oklahoma Press, 1999), 90–92.
2. Brian DeLay, *War of a Thousand Deserts: Indian Raids and the U.S.–Mexican War* (New Haven, Conn.: Yale University Press, 2008), 265, 398n21.
3. Janet Lecompte, "The Manco Burro Pass Massacre," *New Mexico Historical Review* 41, no. 4 (October 1966): 307–8.
4. *SFR*, June 17, 1848 (following Maxwell quotations also from this source); Janet Lecompte, *Pueblo, Hardscrabble, Greenhorn: Society on the High Plains, 1832–1856* (Norman: University of Oklahoma Press, 1978), 208–9, 315n4; Lucian Maxwell, Claim 2354, in U.S. House of Representatives, *Exec. Doc. No. 125*, 1st Session, 49th Congress 1885–86. Indian agent John Greiner had a different story. Writing in 1851, he claimed that Maxwell had only lost twenty horses and mules in the first incidents but lost the majority in the Manco Burro attack on June 19 (Lecompte, "Manco Burro Pass Massacre," 317n16).
5. Lecompte, "Manco Burro Pass Massacre," 310–11; Smith, *Borderlander*, 196.
6. Lecompte, "Manco Burro Pass Massacre," 310–13 (quotation on 311); Smith, *Borderlander*, 196; Barry, *Beginning of the West*, 756–57.
7. Lecompte, "Manco Burro Pass Massacre," 312.
8. Ibid., 312–14; *SFR*, June 27, 1848.
9. Smith, *Borderlander*, 196–97; *SFR*, August 1, 1848 (quotations); William H. Roberts, *Mexican War Veterans: A Complete Roster* (Washington, D.C.: Bretano's, A. S. Witherbee and Co., Proprietors, 1887), 63.
10. *SFR*, August 9, 1848.
11. McNitt, *Navajo Wars*, 127; *SFR*, August 23, 1848 (quotation).

12. McNitt, *Navajo Wars*, 133; *SFR*, September 12, 1848 (first and second quotations), November 2, 1848 (third quotation), November 15, 1848 (fourth quotation), November 25, 1848 (fifth quotation).

13. Robert W. Larson, *New Mexico's Quest for Statehood, 1846–1912* (Albuquerque: University of New Mexico Press, 1969), 13–15. A number of these men would later file Indian depredation claims.

14. The Northwest Ordinance of 1787, for instance, prohibited the establishment of slavery, but it never abolished it and allowed nonslave owners to exclude blacks from the Northwest Territory. In various states from the Northwest Territory entering the Union, whites banned blacks from voting and from testifying in court, excluded free blacks from militia service, or completely banned them from the state. Some "free" states in the old Northwest were more restrictive than some of the "slave" states in the South. Eugene H. Berwanger, *The Frontier against Slavery: Western Anti-Negro Prejudice and the Slavery Extension Controversy* (Urbana: University of Illinois Press, 1967), 7, 20–23.

15. Larson, *New Mexico's Quest for Statehood*, 15–16.

16. Marcy to Washington, October 13, 1848, U.S. House of Representatives, *Exec. Doc. No. 17*, 1st Session, 31st Congress, 1849, 263, cited in McNitt, *Navajo Wars*, 133.

17. Peter R. Decker, *"The Utes Must Go!": American Expansion and the Removal of a People* (Golden, Colo.: Fulcrum Publishing, 2004), 8–12.

18. Virginia McConnell Simmons, *The Ute Indians of Utah, Colorado, and New Mexico* (Boulder: University Press of Colorado, 2000), 61, 64.

19. Allan Nevins, *Fremont: Pathmarker of the West* (New York: Longmans, Green and Co., 1955). 344.

20. Ibid., 350; Alpheus H. Favour, *Old Bill Williams, Mountain Man* (Norman: University of Oklahoma Press, 1962), 178–79 (quotation).

21. Favour, *Old Bill Williams*, 180.

22. Ibid., 185–93 (quotation on 185); Nevins, *Fremont*, 355–68.

23. Favour, *Old Bill Williams*, 203–4.

24. John H. Dickerson to Benjamin L. Beall, December 10, 1848, National Archives and Records Administration, Letters Sent, 9th Military Department, Department of New Mexico, October 1849 to August 1856. Record Group 393, M1102 (hereinafter cited as NALS).

25. Dickerson to Beall, December 10, 1848, NALS, M1102.

26. Dickerson to Beall, January 27, 1849, NALS, M1102 (first and second quotations); Beall to Dickerson, January 29, 1849, NALS, M1102; Lancaster Lupton to Beall, February 20, 1849, NALS, M1102 (third and fourth quotations).

27. Thomas Fitzpatrick to Benjamin Beall, February 24, 1849, NALS, M1102 (quotations); Major Beall, "Minutes of the Proceedings," February 26, 1849, NALS, M1102.

28. Beall to Whittlesey, March 9, 1849, NALS, M1102 (quotations); Beall to Dickerson, March 11, 1849, NALS, M1102.

29. Whittlesey to Beall, March 15, 1849, NALS, M1102 (following Whittlesey quotations also from this source); Beall to Dickerson, March 15, 1849, NALS, M1102; Favour, *Old Bill Williams*, 205.

30. Favour, *Old Bill Williams*, 206–7.
31. Henry B. Judd to Dickerson, March 25, 1849, NALS, M1102; Beall to Dickerson, March 26, 1849, NALS, M1102; H. B. Judd, April 3, 1849, NALS, M1102 (quotation); Judd to Dickerson, April 4, 1849, NALS, M1102; J. M. Washington to Roger Jones, March 29, 1849, AFUC, vol. 47, 57.
32. Dickerson to Beall, April 5, 1849, NALS, M1102 (quotations); John Chapman to Judd, April 10, 1849, NALS, M1102.
33. Judd to Lt. John Adams, April 28, 1849, NALS, M1102; Beall to Dickerson, May 1, 1849, NALS, M1102; James S. Calhoun to Orlando Brown, November 15, 1849, *OCJC*, 77.
34. *SFR*, April 29, 1849 (following *Republican* quotations also from this source).
35. *Message from the President of the United States*, December 24, 1849; Kiser, *Dragoons in Apacheland*, 60–61.
36. Washington to Jones, May 25, 1849, Letters Received by the Office of the Adjutant General (hereinafter cited as AGO), Main Series 1822–60, NARA, RG 94, Publication M567, roll 0432.
37. Medill to Calhoun, April 7, 1849, *OCJC*, xi–xiii, 3–4 (quotation); William W. Winn, *Triumph of the Ecunnau-Nuxulgee: Land Speculators, George M. Troup, State Rights, and the Removal of the Creek Indians from Georgia and Alabama, 1825–38* (Macon, Ga.: Mercer University Press, 2015), 321–23.
38. Calhoun to Medill, July 29, 1849, *OCJC*, 19–20.
39. Judd to Dickerson, May 3, 1849, AFUC, vol. 51, 254 (quotations); Dickerson to Judd, May 7, 1849, AFUC, vol. 51, 257.
40. Lt. John Adams to Sgt. James Batty, May 19, 1849, NALS, M1102.
41. Batty to Adams, May 22, 1849, NALS, M1102 (first, second, and third quotations); Beall to Washington, May 22, 1849, NALS, M1102 (fourth and fifth quotations).
42. Washington to Jones, May 25, 1849, *in Message from the President of the United States to the Two Houses of Congress,* January 31, 1850, Exec. Doc. No. 24, 1st Session, 31st Congress, 15; AGO, RG 94, M567, R0420.
43. Grant Foreman, *Marcy and the Gold Seekers: The Journal of Captain R. B. Marcy, with an Account of the Gold Rush over the Southern Route* (Norman: University of Oklahoma Press, 1939), xi, 29, 30, 38, 40 (quotation), 149, 152, 236.
44. Ibid., 237–38.
45. Judd to Dickerson, May 26, 1849, AFUC, vol. 51, 260 (quotation); Charles L. Kenner, *The Comanchero Frontier: A History of New Mexican–Plains Indian Relations* (Norman: University of Oklahoma Press, 1969), 85.
46. Judd to Dickerson, May 28, 1849, AFUC, vol. 51, 261 (first quotation); Judd to Dickerson, June 11, 1849, AFUC, vol. 51, 264 (second and third quotations); Judd to Dickerson, June 13, 1849, AFUC, vol. 51, 265 (fourth quotation).
47. Dickerson to Beall, June 11, 1849, NALS, M1102 (first quotation); Dickerson to Beall, June 15, 1849, NALS, M1102; Whittlesey to Dickerson, June 18, 1849, NALS, M1102; Judd to Dickerson, June 20, 1849, AFUC, vol. 51, 267 (second and third quotations).

48. Judd to Dickerson, June 20, 1849, AFUC, vol. 51, 267; Whittlesey to Dickerson, June 18, 1849, NALS, M1102 (quotations). About this time, José Benito Martínez claimed that Jicarillas had stolen $1,735 worth of his stock. He claimed the incident occurred on June 12, 1849, but did not file for compensation until July 16, 1855.

49. Judd to Dickerson, June 20, 1849, AFUC, vol. 51, 267–68.

50. Foreman, *Marcy and the Gold Seekers*, 243–44.

51. Ibid., 245, 248, 265.

52. Ibid., 266–70, 275; Hammond, *Alexander Barclay*, 93 (quotations).

53. Foreman, *Marcy and the Gold Seekers*, 276, 279, 290.

54. Beall to Dickerson, July 26, 1849, NALS, M1102.

55. There are similarities between the situation of Washington and that of Colorado governor John Evans and Col. John M. Chivington in 1864. Evans had been calling for more troops for protection and may have felt that he had to use them to kill Indians before their enlistment expired; the result was the infamous Sand Creek affair of November 29, 1864.

56. McNitt, *Navajo Wars*, 136–38, 145, 153; Emmett, *Fort Union and the Winning of the Southwest*, 78 (first quotation); Charles J. Kappler, ed., *Indian Treaties, 1778–1883* (Mattituck, N.Y.: Amereon House, 1972), 583–84 (second quotation).

57. The percentages of claims against Navajos were 91 percent in 1847; 91 percent in 1848; 67 percent in 1849; 57 percent in 1850; 1851, 52 percent in 1851; 24 percent in 1852; 14 percent in 1853; 6 percent in 1854; and 0 percent in 1855.

58. Whittlesey to Beall, July 13, 1849, NALS, M1102.

59. Dickerson to Judd, July 15, 1849, AFUC, vol. 51, 270; Judd to Dickerson, August 16, 1849, *Message from the President of the United States*, January 31, 1850.

60. Judd to Dickerson, September 16, 1849, *Message from the President of the United States*, January 31, 1850, 32–33.

61. Ibid. (quotations); Judd to Dickerson, September 28, 1849, AFUC, vol. 51, 277; Oliva, *Fort Union*, 23. Papin and Herman Grolman, both Las Vegas merchants, were appointed post sutlers at this time. Judd, September 14, 1849, AGO, RG 94, J134, R0408.

62. Washington to Jones, September 23, 1948, AGO, RG 94, M567, R0421.

63. Judd to Dickerson, September 29, 1849, AFUC, vol. 50, 22; Dickerson to Judd, September 26, 1849, AFUC, vol. 51, 276 (quotation).

64. Calhoun to Medill, October 5, 1849, *OCJC*, 42 (first and second quotations); Calhoun to Medill, October 15, 1849, *OCJC*, 52 (third quotation), 49–50 (fourth quotation); Calhoun to Medill, October 13, 1849, *OCJC*, 46 (fifth quotation).

65. Calhoun to Medill, October 27, 1849, *OCJC*, 61–62.

66. Washington to Jones, October 23, 1849, AGO, RG 94, M567, R0421 (quotations); Munroe to Freeman, October 30, 1849, AGO, RG 94, M567, R0412; Emmett, *Fort Union and the Winning of the Southwest*, 78.

67. Larson, *New Mexico's Quest for Statehood*, 20–21; Calhoun to Medill, October 29 and October 30, 1849 (quotation), OCJC, 63–66; Calhoun to Orlando Brown, November 2, 1849, *OCJC*, 68. Orlando Brown had replaced William Medill as commissioner back

on June 30, 1849, but the slow mails meant that Calhoun did not know about it until November. Medill had been trying to reform the agency and restrict traders' influence in distribution of annuities, but his reforms were ended when Zachary Taylor was elected president and Indian Affairs were placed in the Department of the Interior under the new secretary, Thomas Ewing. See Robert M. Kvasnicka and Herman J. Viola, eds., *The Commissioners of Indian Affairs, 1824–1977* (Lincoln: University of Nebraska Press, 1979), 36–37.

68. Lafayette McLaws to Grier, October 29, 1849, NALS, M1102 (first quotation); Grier to McLaws, November 1, 1849, NALS, M1102; Grier to Adams, November 30, 1849, AGO, RG 94, M567, R0431 (second quotation); Thelma S. Guild and Harvey L. Carter, *Kit Carson: A Pattern for Heroes* (Lincoln: University of Nebraska Press, 1984), 186; Milo Milton Quaife, ed., *Kit Carson's Autobiography* (Lincoln: University of Nebraska Press, 1966), 132.

69. Grier to Adams, November 30, 1849, AGO, RG 94, M567, R0431; Guild and Carter, *Kit Carson*, 186; Quaife, *Kit Carson's Autobiography*, 132 (quotation).

70. Tucumcari Mountain, elevation 4,956 feet, just south of the present town of the same name, is actually located about fifteen miles south of the Canadian River, not to the north, as Grier wrote. The Indian camp was on the Canadian River, likely near where Fort Bascom was later built. Grier to Adams, November 30, 1849, AGO, RG 94, M567, R0431 (quotations); Guild and Carter, *Kit Carson*, 186; Quaife, *Kit Carson's Autobiography*, 133.

71. Grier to Adams, November 30, 1849, AGO, RG 94, M567, R0431 (first quotation); Quaife, *Kit Carson's Autobiography*, 133–35 (second and third quotations); Sabin, *Kit Carson Days*, 620–21 (fourth quotation); Guild and Carter, *Kit Carson*, 186–87 (fifth quotation).

72. Guild and Carter, *Kit Carson*, 186 (first quotation); Quaife, *Kit Carson's Autobiography*, 135 (second quotation).

73. Grier to Adams, November 30, 1849, AGO, RG 94, M567, R0431 (first quotation); Quaife, *Kit Carson's Autobiography*, 136 (second quotation); Guild and Carter, *Kit Carson*, 187; Hammond, *Alexander Barclay*, 179 (third and fourth quotations); Grier to McLaws, December 3, 1849, NALS, M1102 (fifth quotation).

74. James A. Bennett, Clinton E. Brooks, and Frank D. Reeve, eds., *Forts and Forays: A Dragoon in New Mexico, 1850–1856* (Albuquerque: University of New Mexico Press, 1996), xviii–xix; Calhoun to Brown, March 15, 1850, OCJC, 160–61.

75. Bennett et al., *Forts and Forays*, xviii; Sabin, *Kit Carson Days*, 619, 621–22; Oliva, *Fort Union*, 24n77; Tiller, *Jicarilla Apache Tribe*, 35.

76. SFR, November 28, 1849.

77. Judd to McLaws, December 1, 1849, AFUC, vol. 51, 282 (first quotation); Judd to McLaws, December 14, 1849, AFUC, vol. 51, 283 (second quotation).

78. Calhoun to Brown, January 1, 1850, OCJC, 96–97 (first quotation); Kappler, *Indian Treaties*, 585–87 (second quotation on 586).

79. Calhoun to Brown, January 17, 1850, OCJC, 99; Calhoun to Brown, January 31, 1850, OCJC, 125–26 (quotations); Cyrus Choice to Calhoun, February 6, 1850, OCJC, 143–44.

Not about to let the opportunity slip, locals exaggerated the theft of García's stock until twenty-four people claimed that the Utes had stolen 2,427 sheep, 518 goats, 71 cattle, 4 mules, and 3 horses.

80. Mariano Valdez to Prefect of the County of Taos, January 26, 1850, NALS, M1102 (first quotation); Beall to McLaws, January 27, 1850, NALS, M1102 (second, third, and fourth quotations).

81. Beall to McLaws, March 13, 1850, NALS, M1102.

82. Calhoun to Lacome, February 26, 1850, *OCJC*, 168–69; Lacome to Calhoun, March 16, 1850, *OCJC*, 170–71.

83. Calhoun to Brown, March 31, 1850; *OCJC*, 181–83.

84. Calhoun to Brown, February 27, 1850, *OCJC*, 157–59.

85. Munroe to Mackall, March 1, 1850, Secretary of War to Munroe, undated (first quotation), Munroe to Freeman, March 15, 1850 (second quotation), AGO, RG 94, M567, R0431.

86. Van Horne to McLaws, February 2, 1850, AGO, RG 94, M567, R0431.

87. Holbrook to Grier, April 7, 1850, NALS, M1102.

88. Quaife, *Kit Carson's Autobiography*, 136–37; Grier to McLaws, April 12, 1850, NALS, M1102 (quotations); McLaws to Grier, May 21, 1850, NALS, M1072. Sergeant Holbrook was later killed at the Battle of Cieneguilla, March 30, 1854.

89. Barry, *Beginning of the West*, 890, 916. There may have been one more; some reports say that ten bodies were found, others say eleven.

90. Alexander to McLaws, May 24, 1850, 197; Burnside to Ward, May 23, 1850 (quotations), 198, OCJC.

91. Burnside to J. N. Ward, May 23, 1850, *OCJC*, 198–99.

92. Munroe to R. Jones, May 24, 1850, in Thomas Suaso Depredation Claim, #2560, RG 123, NARA (hereinafter cited as TSDC).

93. Burnside to Plympton, June 12, 1850, *OCJC*, 199–200 (following Burnside quotation also from this source).

Chapter 3

1. Grier letter, June 18, 1850, NALS, M1102.

2. Larson, *New Mexico's Quest for Statehood*, 23–24.

3. Calhoun to Brown, June 19, 1850, *OCJC*, 213.

4. See appendix B for additional names. Some of these men changed allegiances.

5. George Archibald McCall, *New Mexico in 1850: A Military View* (Norman: University of Oklahoma Press, 1968), 40–41.

6. Ibid., 66–68.

7. Larson, *New Mexico's Quest for Statehood*, 28–31; Ralph Emerson Twitchell, *The History of the Occupation of the Territory of New Mexico from 1846 to 1851* (Denver: Smith-Brooks Company, 1909), 381, 385.

8. Larson, *New Mexico's Quest for Statehood*, 33–36.

9. Twitchell, *History of the Occupation*, 162, 164, 167–75.

10. Ibid., 177–79.

11. Larson, *New Mexico's Quest for Statehood*, 36–37.

12. Calhoun to Brown, July 15, 1850, *OCJC*, 217 (first quotation); Larson, *New Mexico's Quest for Statehood*, 39 (second quotation).

13. Twitchell, *History of the Occupation*, 193–94 (first, second, and third quotations); Scott, August 27, 1850, AGO, RG 94, M567, R0432 (fourth quotation).

14. Larson, *New Mexico's Quest for Statehood*, 56–59 (quotations); Conrad to Munroe, September 10, 1850, *OCJC*, 220–21.

15. Twitchell, *History of the Occupation*, 197–98.

16. Grier to McLaws, May 26, 1850; Grier to McLaws, June 1, 1850; Grier to McLaws, June 6, 1850; Whittlesey to Grier, June 17, 1850, all in NALS, M1102.

17. Whittlesey to McLaws, June 10, 1850 (quotations); Grier letter, June 18, 1850, both in NALS, M1102.

18. Calhoun to Brown, June 12, 1850, *OCJC*, 208–9 (first and second quotations); Brown to Hugh Smith, February 27, 1850, *OCJC*, 224; Whitlock to Judge, June 21, 1850, NALS, M1102 (third and fourth quotations).

19. Kendrick to McLaws, June 22, 1850, AFUC, vol. 50, 38 (first and second quotations); Alexander to McLaws, June 22, 1850, AFUC, vol. 51, 305; Adams to Las Vegas, June 24, 1850, AFUC, vol. 51, 307 (third and fourth quotations).

20. Grier to McLaws, June 26, 1850, AFUC, vol. 54, 8 (quotation); Grier to McLaws, June 26, 1850, NALS, M1102.

21. Frazer, *Forts and Supplies*, 51.

22. "Manuel Abrew [*sic*] et al. v. the United States and Utah and Apache Indians," in *Court Cases Decided in the Court of Claims of the United States at the Term of 1901–1902*, vol. 37 (Washington, D.C.: Government Printing Office, 1902), 511–12. Also see appendix A.

23. Whittlesey to McLaws, June 27, 1850, AFUC, vol. 54, 9.

24. Calhoun to Brown, July 30, 1850, *OCJC*, 229 (first quotation); Calhoun to Brown, July 15, 1850, *OCJC*, 217 (second and third quotations).

25. McLaws to Grier, June 28, 1850, NALS, M1072.

26. Calhoun to Brown, July 30, 1850, *OCJC*, 229–31.

27. Ibid., 230–31.

28. Grier to McLaws, July 23, 1850, NALS, M1102 (first quotation); Grier to McLaws, July 31, 1850, TSDC (second, third, and fourth quotations).

29. Grier to McLaws, July 31, 1850, TSDC.

30. Grier to McLaws, July 31, 1850, NALS, M1102.

31. Whether or not Grier attacked the actual band that had hit Rayado, he recovered 80 cattle. Maxwell filed a claim for 175 cattle.

32. Alexander to McLaws, August 5, 1850, AFUC, vol. 51, 312 (first and third quotations; Grier to McLaws, August 7, 1850, NALS, M1102 (second quotation).

33. Calhoun to Brown, August 12, 1850, *OCJC*, 250–52.

34. Calhoun to Brown, August 25, 1850, *OCJC*, 254; Calhoun to Brown, September 30, 1850, *OCJC*, 259; Calhoun to Brown, October 12, 1850, *OCJC*, 262 (quotation).

35. Calhoun to Brown, October 12, 1850, *OCJC*, 262–63.

36. T. L. Brent to T. S. Jesup, October 9, 1850, AFUC, vol. 47, 204.
37. Sarracino to Calhoun, January 29, 1851, *OCJC*, 283–84 (see also appendix A).
38. Ibid.
39. Pino to Luna, January 20, 1851, AFUC, vol. 1, 2.
40. Skinner to Howe, January 23, 1851, TSDC (see also appendix A).
41. Munroe to Jones, January 27, 1851, AFUC, vol. 1, 3.
42. Hubbell to Pleasanton, March 27, 1851, TSDC.
43. Pleasanton to Adjutant J. W. Allen, March 28, 1851, in U.S. Senate, *Exec. Doc. No. 1*, 1st Session, 32nd Congress, 132–33.
44. Ibid.
45. Oliva, *Fort Union*, 36.
46. Gordon to Munroe, March 21, 1851, NALS, M1102.
47. Watrous to Alexander, undated letter, TSDC.
48. Alexander to Adams, March 5, 1851, Adams to Alexander, March 8, 1851, TSDC (following Adams quotations also from this source).
49. Grolman to Secretary of Territory, March 11, 1851, AFUC, vol. 51, 319.
50. McLaws to Alexander, March 14, 1851, AFUC, vol. 51, 322.
51. Cumming to Calhoun, March 15, 1851, *OCJC*, 298.
52. McLaws to Alexander, March 16, 1851, Alexander to Chapman, March 17, 1851 (first quotation), Chapman to Alexander, March 18, 1851 (second quotation), TSDC.
53. Chapman to Alexander, March 18, 1851, TSDC (first quotation); Alexander to McLaws, March 19, 1851, TSDC (second quotation).
54. Calhoun to Lea, March 22, 1851, Calhoun to the People of New Mexico, March 18, 1851, *OCJC*, 299–302.
55. McLaws to Howe, March 11, 1851, AFUC, vol. 1, 17; Smith to J. N. G. Whistler, March 24, 1851 (first, second, and third quotations), D. T. Chandler to McLaws, March 24, 1851 (fourth quotation), TSDC.
56. Kendrick to McLaws, March 25, 1851, in U.S. Senate, *Exec. Doc. No. 1*, 1st Session, 32nd Congress, 134–36.
57. Ibid.
58. J. W. Allen, Orders No. 19, March 18, 1851, Holliday to Howe, March 28, 1851, in U.S. Senate, *Exec. Doc. No. 1*, 1st Session, 32nd Congress, 132–34.
59. Munroe to Jones, March 30, 1851, in U.S. Senate, *Exec. Doc. No. 1*, 1st Session, 32nd Congress, 126–27.
60. Deloria and DeMallie, *Documents of American Indian Diplomacy*, 1275–76.
61. John O. Baxter, *Las Carneradas: Sheep Trade in New Mexico, 1700–1860* (Albuquerque: University of New Mexico Press, 1987), 2, 9, 10, 13, 17, 21 (quotation), 23–24.
62. Ibid., 28–30.
63. Ibid., 42, 51, 52, 59, 61, 64, 103, 104, 107, 109.
64. James F. Brooks, *Captives and Cousins: Slavery, Kinship, and Community in the Southwest Borderlands* (Chapel Hill: University of North Carolina Press, 2002), 6, 30–31, 198, 201, 258, 291–92; Kenner, *Comanchero Frontier*, 96–97.

65. DeLay, *War of a Thousand Deserts*, 40, 60, 80, 84, 88; Eliot West, *The Contested Plains Indians, Goldseekers, and the Rush to Colorado* (Lawrence: University Press of Kansas, 1998), 77, 80, 192.

66. DeLay, *War of a Thousand Deserts*, 109; Hämäläinen, *Comanche Empire*, 211.

67. Calhoun to Medill, October 1, 1849, 32 (first quotation), Calhoun to Brown, February 27, 1850, 158 (second quotation), Calhoun to Brown, February 3, 1850, 142 (third quotation), *OCJC*.

68. Davis, *El Gringo*, 203–4.

69. McCall, *New Mexico in 1850*, 88–89, 178–79.

70. Members of the Legislature to Calhoun, July 9, 1851, *OCJC*, 386–87.

71. Calhoun to Lea, February 2, 1851, *OCJC*, 289.

72. Brooks, *Captives and Cousins*, 378–81.

73. John Russell Bartlett, *Personal Narrative of Exploration and Incidents in Texas, New Mexico, California, Sonora, and Chihuahua Connected with the United States and Mexican Boundary Commission during the Years 1850, {'}51, {'}52, and {'}53* (New York: D. Appleton and Company, 1854), 386.

74. Brent to Jesup, October 9, 1850, AFUC, vol. 47, 204.

75. Baxter, *Las Carneradas*, 113–14.

76. Ibid., 111 (quotation), 115.

77. Ibid., 119–27; Lane to Manypenny, May 26, 1853, Office of Indian Affairs, Letters Received, New Mexico Superintendency, M234, rolls 546, 547 (quotations) (hereinafter cited as OIA).

78. Baxter, *Las Carneradas*, 140, 143.

79. Chapman to Alexander, March 31, 1851, TSDC.

80. Chapman to McLaws, April 15, 1851 (first and second quotations), McLaws to Chapman, April 18, 1851, TSDC (third quotation).

81. Chapman to J. N. Ward, April 21, 1851, TSDC.

82. J. B. Doyle to Alexander, April 20, 1851, Grolman to Alexander, April 21, 1851 (quotations), TSDC; Ewell to McLaws, May 1, 1851, AFUC, vol. 54, 37.

83. McLaws to Alexander, April 25, 1851 (first quotation), Ward to Alexander, May 1, 1851 (second, third, and fourth quotations), Chapman to Alexander, May 4, 1851, TSDC.

84. Chapman to Alexander, May 4, 1851, TSDC.

85. Calhoun to Munroe, May 7, 1851, *OCJC*, 350.

86. Munroe to Jones, May 31, 1851, *OCJC*, 329 (quotation); McLaws to Alexander, May 8, 1851, TSDC.

87. Whittlesey to McLaws, May 24, 1851, AGO, RG 94, M567, R0450.

88. Ewell to Alexander, May 26, 1851, TSDC.

89. McLaws to Chapman, May 30, 1851, McLaws to Alexander, May 30, 1851 (first and third quotations, 343), McLaws to Pleasanton, May 30, 1851, Calhoun to Lea, June 1, 1851 (second quotation, 355), Munroe to Jones, June 29, 1851, *OCJC*, 342–46, 355.

90. Chapman to Alexander, June 4, 1851, AGO, RG 94, M567, R0450.

91. Ibid.

92. Chapman to Alexander, June 8, 1851, AGO, RG 94, M567, R0450.

93. Beaubien to Calhoun, June 11, 1851, NALS, M1072.
94. Calhoun to Monroe, June 14, 1851, *OCJC*, 361; Kendrick to Munroe, June 22, 1851, NALS, M1102 (quotations); McLaws to Gordon, June 24, 1851, NALS, M1072.
95. Munroe to Jones, July 13, 1851, AFUC, vol. 1, 93–94; Samson to Alexander, June 28, 1851, Samson to Chapman, June 28, 1851 (first quotation), Samson to Munroe, June 30, 1851 (second quotation), AGO, RG 94, M567, R0450.
96. Adams to Ward, July 1, 1851, AGO, RG 94, M567, R0450. Lucero later filed a depredation claim, stating that the incident happened in August 1851, that he lost $3,400 worth of cattle, horses, and mules, and that the raiders were Apaches. Adams's investigation may be a reason why Lucero changed the date of the supposed raid and the name of the tribe. See appendix A.
97. Munroe to Jones, July 13, 1851, AFUC, vol. 1, 93–94.
98. Adams to Ward, July 4, 1851 (quotations), Adams to McLaws, July 6, 1851, AGO, RG 94, M567, R0450.
99. Adams to McLaws, July 6, 1851, AGO, RG 94, M567, R0450.
100. Munroe to Jones, July 13, 1851, AFUC, vol. 1, 94–95; Alexander to McLaws, July 5, 1851 (first quotation), AGO, RG 94, M567, R0450; Munroe to Jones, June 30, 1851 (second, third, and fourth quotations), Calhoun to Lea, June 30, 1851, *OCJC*, 358–59, 369. Calhoun said that he bought the captive boy from Eagle Feathers.
101. Calhoun to Lea, June 30, 1851, 369 (first quotation), Calhoun to Webster, June 30, 1851, 363–64 (second through fifth quotations), *OCJC*.
102. House of Representatives to Fillmore, June 30, 1851, *OCJC*, 367.
103. Calhoun to Lea, June 30, 1851, *OCJC*, 369, 371–75 (see also appendix A).
104. Calhoun to Lea, June 30, 1851, *OCJC*, 365.
105. Current fraud statistics are astonishing. In 2010 alone, fraud bureaus received more than 132,000 case referrals. See "Fraud Statistics," http://www.insurancefraud.org/statistics.htm; "How Many U. S. Citizens Cheat on Their Taxes? http://www.answers.com/Q/How_many_US_citizens_cheat_on_their_taxes; "Insurance Fraud," http://criminal.findlaw.com/criminal-charges/insurance-fraud.html.
106. Hammond, *Alexander Barclay*, 168.

Chapter 4

1. Jones to Sumner, March 29, 1851, NALS, M1102.
2. *Annual Report of the Secretary of War,* November 29, 1851, in Oliva, *Fort Union*, 47.
3. Frazer, *Forts and Supplies*, 61–62.
4. Sumner to Calhoun, July 20, 1851, *OCJC*, 381.
5. Conrad to Sumner, April 1, 1851, *OCJC*, 383.
6. Frazer, *Forts and Supplies*, 50; Nesbitt and Parker to Calhoun, Calhoun to Lea, July 25, 1851 (quotations), *OCJC*, 381, 388–89.
7. Calhoun to Lea, July 29, 1851, *OCJC*, 391. One new arrival, John S. Watts, was not just another attorney but an associate judge of the Territorial Supreme Court. Watts later wrote a plea for government payment for 244 depredation filers. John S. Watts, *Indian Depredations in New Mexico* (Washington, D.C.: Gideon, 1858).

8. Calhoun to Sumner, August 4, 1851, Sumner to Calhoun, August 8, 1851, *OCJC*, 396–98 (quotations).

9. McNitt, *Navajo Wars*, 194–99; Sumner to Jones, October 24, 1851, *OCJC*, 416–19 (quotations).

10. Sumner to Jones, October 31, 1851, AGO, RG 94, M567, R0454.

11. Scott, December 26, 1851, AGO, RG 94, M567, R0454. Sumner's experience with horses was similar to that of Captain Ewell in a winter expedition in 1855, when the terrain and weather broke them down so badly that the infantry outmarched them.

12. Sumner to Jones, October 24, 1851, *OCJC*, 417–18 (following Sumner quotation also from this source).

13. Robert M. Utley, ed., "Captain John Pope's Plan of 1853 for the Frontier Defense of New Mexico," *Arizona and the West: A Quarterly Journal of History* 5, no. 2 (Summer 1963): 161.

14. Hammond, *Alexander Barclay*, 85–86.

15. Oliva, *Fort Union*, 58–59; McCall, *New Mexico in 1850*, 144; Hammond, *Alexander Barclay*, 97 (quotation).

16. Oliva, *Fort Union*, 60 (first quotation); Calhoun to Lea, August 31, 1851, 414 (second quotation), Woolley, Wingfield, and Greiner to Lea, August 29, 1851, 422 (third and fourth quotations), *OCJC*.

17. Calhoun to Webster, September 15, 1851, 425 (first quotation), Calhoun to Wingfield, September 17, 1851, 427 (second quotation), Wheaton to Calhoun, September 20, 1851, 427 (third quotation), Calhoun to Lea, October 1, 1851 (fourth, fifth, and sixth quotations), 433, Calhoun to Webster, October 29, 1851, 441 (seventh quotation), Calhoun to Lea, October 29, 1851, 442 (eighth quotation), *OCJC*.

18. Greiner to Calhoun, October 20, 1851, *OCJC*, 438.

19. Frazer, *Forts and Supplies*, 48.

20. Ibid., 4, 6, 8, 30 (quotation), 49; McCall, *New Mexico in 1850*, 40.

21. Frazer, *Forts and Supplies*, 43–44; Ronald K. Wetherington, *Ceran St. Vrain: American Frontier Entrepreneur* (Santa Fe: Sunstone Press, 2012), 38, 42.

22. Frazer, *Forts and Supplies*, 49–50.

23. Ibid., 51–53; Wetherington, *Ceran St. Vrain*, 55–56.

24. Frazer, *Forts and Supplies*, 57–58, 62, 70 (quotations); Emmett, *Fort Union*, 109; Hammond, *Alexander Barclay*, 113–14. The idea of using soldiers as farmers went through several phases. Years before, Inspector General Col. George Croghan had been opposed to making troops into "awkward ploughmen," who only lost respect in the eyes of the Indians. Croghan asked: why they grew hay and corn? To feed the cattle. Why did they have cattle? To eat the hay and corn. Francis Paul Prucha, ed., *Army Life on the Western Frontier: Selections from the Official Reports Made between 1826 and 1845 by Colonel George Croghan* (Norman: University of Oklahoma Press, 1958), 6–7 (quotation above).

25. Sumner to Swords, October 22, 1851, NALS, M1072.

26. Frazer, *Forts and Supplies*, 80.

27. Ibid., 71–72.

28. St. Vrain to Sumner, October 14, 1851, NALS, M1102.

29. Bowen letters, AFUC, cited in Emmett, *Fort Union*, 114.

30. Barry, *Beginning of the West*, 1051.

31. Bowen letters, AFUC, cited in Emmett, *Fort Union*, 114–15.

32. Beck to Calhoun, November 9, 1851 (quotation), J. C. McFerran to W. R. Shoemaker, November 10, 1851, *OCJC*, 445–46.

33. Munroe to Jones, October 10, 1851, AGO, RG 94, M567, R0450.

34. Sumner to Calhoun, November 10, 1851, *OCJC*, 449–50.

35. Calhoun to Sumner, November 10, 1851, *OCJC*, 447–48.

36. Sumner to Calhoun, November 10, 1851 (quotation), Calhoun to Sumner, November 10, 1851, *OCJC*, 450–51.

37. Sumner to Calhoun, November 10, 1851, *OCJC*, 452.

38. Several letters were written and sent by Calhoun and Sumner on November 10 and 11, 1851, *OCJC*, 453–56; also Beck to Calhoun, November 11, 1851, *OCJC*, 453.

39. Sumner to Calhoun, November 13, 1851, *OCJC*, 457 (first quotation); Sumner to Jones, November 20, 1851, *OCJC*, 445 (second and third quotations).

40. *Message from the President of the United States*, 1851, Exec. Doc. No. 1, 1st Session, 32nd Congress, 18–19.

41. Francisco Gómez Palacio, *Claims of Mexican Citizens against the United States for Indian Depredations, Being the Opinion of the Mexican Commissioner in the Joint Claims Commission, under the Convention of July 4, 1868, between Mexico and the United States* (Washington, D.C.: Judd and Detweiler, 1871), 38, 42, 44, 59 (quotations), 74, 76, 92.

42. *Report of the Secretary of War*, November 29, 1851, U.S. Congress, Exec. Doc. No. 1, 1st Session, 32nd Congress (Washington, D.C.: A. Boyd Hamilton, 1851), 105–13 (following Conrad quotations also from this source).

43. *Report of the Quartermaster General*, November 22, 1851, U.S. Congress, Exec. Doc. No. 2, 1st Session, 32nd Congress (Washington, D.C.: A. Boyd Hamilton, 1851), 224–26.

44. Sumner to Jones, January 1, 1852, *OCJC*, 434.

45. *Santa Fe Weekly Gazette*, February 19, 1853, 3 (hereinafter cited as *SFWG*).

46. McNitt, *Navajo Wars*, 205–7; Sumner to Jones, January 1, 1852, *OCJC*, 434 (quotations).

47. Calhoun to Lea, January 30, 1852, 471 (first quotation), Greiner to Calhoun, January 29, 1852, *OCJC*, 467–69 (second quotation).

48. Greiner to Calhoun, January 29, 1852, *OCJC*, 468. Author James Brooks wrote that in New Mexico the Indians and Mexicans both learned that survival often depended on an exchange of material and human resources, with captives often being integrated into families and in effect becoming cousins. Americans could not abide by that association and broke it apart. Brooks also found that Indians did not take anywhere near as many captives from New Mexicans as the New Mexicans took from them. Brooks, *Captives and Cousins*, 30–31, 353–54, and passim.

49. Greiner to Calhoun, January 29, 1852, *OCJC*, 467–69.

50. Wingfield to Lea, February 6, 1852, *OCJC*, 471.

51. Sumner to Jones, January 27, 1852, AGO, RG 94, M567, R0471.

52. Emmett, *Fort Union*, 123–24 (first quotation on 123); Sumner to Jones, February 3, 1852, AGO, RG 94, M567, R0471 (second and fourth quotations); Howe to McFerran, January 25, 1852, *OCJC*, 476 (third quotation).

53. Citizens of Socorro to Calhoun, February 11, 1852, 480–81 (first quotation), Calhoun to Sumner, February 11, 1852, Calhoun to Overman, February 25, 1852, 483 (second quotation), Calhoun to Webster, February 29, 1852, 485 (third quotation), Calhoun to Lea, February 29, 1852, 487 (fourth quotation), *OCJC*.

54. Calhoun to Lea, February 29, 1852, *OCJC*, 487; "Claims for Indian Depredations in New Mexico," 46 (quotation); Meriwether to Manypenny, August 30, 1854, OIA.

55. "Claims for Indian Depredations in New Mexico," 51; Calhoun to Lea, February 29, 1852, *OCJC*, 487. Richardson, as a major general of volunteers, was mortally wounded at the Civil War Battle of Antietam, on September 17, 1862.

56. Robertson to Graham, March 20, 1852, AGO, RG 94, M567, R0471.

57. Sumner to Calhoun, March 21, 1852 (first quotation on 492), Calhoun to Sumner, March 27, 1852, Calhoun to Sumner, March 28, 1852, Brooks to Whiting, March 28, 1852, Sumner to Calhoun, March 30, 1852, Calhoun to Webster, March 31, 1852 (second quotation on 510), *OCJC*, 492–93, 507, 509–10.

58. Sumner to Conrad, March 27, 1852, AFUC, vol. 1, 208.

59. Sumner to Morris, April 1, 1852 (first quotation), Calhoun to Sumner, April 7, 1852 (second and third quotations), *OCJC*, 517–18. Major Morris also filed a depredation claim, saying he had lost two mules and a cow to the Apaches. It was not proven.

60. Greiner, March 31, 1852, in John Ward, "Indian Affairs in New Mexico under the Administration of William Carr Lane from the Journal of John Ward," *New Mexico Historical Review* 16, no. 2 (April 1941), 211–12 (first, second, and third quotations); John Greiner, "Private Letters," in Oliva, *Fort Union*, 87 (fourth quotation).

61. Greiner to Sumner, April 4, 1852, Greiner to Baird, April 7, 1852, *OCJC*, 519–20.

62. Sumner to Calhoun, April 8, 1852, *OCJC*, 521.

63. Sumner to Jones, April 9, 1852, AGO, RG 94, M567, R0471.

64. Calhoun to Lea, April 6, 1852, 515 (first quotation), Calhoun to Sumner, April 12, 1852, 524 (second quotation), Calhoun to Sumner, April 18, 1852, Sumner to Jones, April 22, 1852, 525 (third quotation), Calhoun and Sumner to the Public, April 21, 1852, 528 (fourth quotation), *OCJC*.

65. Greiner to Lea, April 30, 1852, *OCJC*, 529–31.

66. Carleton to Sumner, April 27, 1852, 240 (first quotation), Carleton to Sumner, May 1, 1852, 244, Sumner to Carleton, May 10, 1852, 254 (second quotation), AFUC, vol. 1.

67. Calvin Horn, *New Mexico's Troubled Years The Story of the Early Territorial Governors* (Albuquerque: Horn and Wallace, 1963), 32–33; Barry, *Beginning of the West*, 1107 (quotation).

68. Greiner to Lea, June 30, 1852, *OCJC*, 540.

69. U.S. Senate *Senate Doc. No. 1*, 2nd Session, 32nd Congress, 24–27, in Keleher, *Turmoil in New Mexico*, 61–65.

70. Annie Heloise Abel, ed., "The Journal of John Greiner," *Old Santa Fe: A Magazine of History, Archaeology, Genealogy and Biography* 3, no. 11 (July 1916): 190–92, 193–95 (following Greiner quotations also from this source: 201, 207, 212, 214, 216, 220).

71. Greiner to Lea, August 31, 1852, OIA.

72. Abel, "Journal of John Greiner," 240, 241, 243.

73. Horn, *New Mexico's Troubled Years*, 37–39.

74. Ibid., 40–41; Sumner to Lane, September 27, 1852, AGO, RG 94, M567, R0472 (quotations).

75. Horn, *New Mexico's Troubled Years*, 40–41; Ralph Emerson Twitchell, "Historical Sketch of Governor William Carr Lane," *Historical Society of New Mexico* 4 (November 1, 1917): 10–11 (quotations).

76. Ralph P. Bieber, ed., "Letters of William Carr Lane," *New Mexico Historical Review* 3, no. 2 (April 1928): 185–86 (first, second, and third quotations); Horn, *New Mexico's Troubled Years*, 39 (fourth quotation).

77. Horn, *New Mexico's Troubled Years*, 43–44.

78. Ibid., 42; Twitchell, "Historical Sketch," 11.

79. Ward, "Indian Affairs in New Mexico," 213–16, 219.

80. Greiner to Lane, December 31, 1852, OIA (following quotations from his discussion with Chief Coniache also from this source).

81. Lecompte, *Pueblo, Hardscrabble, Greenhorn*, 240; Ward, "Indian Affairs in New Mexico," 225–26 (quotations).

82. Twitchell, "Historical Sketch," 12–16.

83. Ibid. Lane was not so sanguine when speaking of Sumner. He wrote to Gen. Winfield Scott that his "conduct deserves reprehension" and hoped "the folly, disloyalty & tyranny of Col. Sumner, shall be rebutted." Lane to Scott, December 29, 1852, AGO, RG 94, M567, R0473.

84. *SFWG*, February 19, 1853, 3.

85. Bowen letters, cited in Emmett, *Fort Union*, 141.

86. Ibid., 142–43 (first to fourth quotations) Carleton to Bowen, December 11, 1852, AFUC, vol. 1, 305 (fifth quotation); Hammond, *Alexander Barclay*, 100–101 (sixth quotation).

87. Carleton to Bowen, December 11, 1852, AFUC, vol. 1, 306.

88. Robert W. Frazer, *Forts of the West: Military Forts and Presidios and Posts Commonly Called Forts West of the Mississippi River* (Norman: University of Oklahoma Press, 1965), 96; Ransom to Sumner, August 25, 1852, NALS, M1102 (quotation).

89. Ransom to Sumner, January 21, 1853, NALS, M1102.

90. Bowen letters, cited in Emmett, *Fort Union*, 151–52.

91. Emmett, *Fort Union*, 142.

92. Sumner to Cooper, January 24, 1853, AGO, RG 94, M567, R0488.

93. Twitchell, "Historical Sketch," 17; Ward, "Indian Affairs in New Mexico," 207–8.

94. Horn, *New Mexico's Troubled Years*, 46–47.

95. William B. Carson, ed., "William Carr Lane, Diary," *New Mexico Historical Review* 39 (July 1964): 195.

96. Averam B. Bender, *The March of Empire: Frontier Defense in the Southwest, 1848–1860* (New York: Greenwood Press, 1968), 156.

97. Steele to Howe, February 1, 1853, Howe to Sumner, February 3, 1853, Sumner to Howe, February 12, 1853, AGO, RG 94, M567, R0488 (quotations).

98. *SFWG*, February 19, 1853, 3.

99. Ibid.

100. Lane to Vigil, May 9, 1853, OIA (first quotation); McNitt, *Navajo Wars*, 218–22 (second quotation on 222).

101. McNitt, *Navajo Wars*, 223; Samuel D. Sturgis to Ransom, May 24, 1853 (first quotation), Sturgis to Ransom, June 7, 1853, NALS, M1072 (second quotation).

102. Ward, "Indian Affairs in New Mexico," 344.

103. Sumner, Orders No. 23, June 6, 1853, AFUC, vol. 2, 17.

104. McNitt, *Navajo Wars*, 225, 227; Sumner to Cooper, December 19, 1852, AGO, RG 94, M567, R0488.

105. Steck to Lane, May 20, 1853, OIA.

106. Wingfield to Lane, May 3, 1853, OIA.

107. Wingfield to Lane, May 15, 1853, OIA.

108. Wingfield to Lane, May 18, 1853, OIA.

109. Bowen letters, cited in Emmett, *Fort Union*, 154.

110. Carson, "William Carr Lane, Diary," 198 (first quotation); Bieber, "Letters of William Carr Lane," 196 (second quotation).

111. *SFWG*, August 13, 1853.

112. David Meriwether, *My Life in the Mountains and on the Plains* (Norman: University of Oklahoma Press, 1965), 141.

113. Ibid., 141–43, 146–47; Oliva, *Fort Union*, 100. With Gunnison's party was Richard H. Kern, who had survived Frémont's winter expedition of 1849, but whose luck would run out four months later in Utah. He was killed by Indians with Gunnison and eight others.

114. Meriwether, *My Life in the Mountains*, 157–58 (first quotation on 157), 163 (second quotation).

115. Meriwether, *My Life in the Mountains*, 164–65; Meriwether to Manypenny, August 10, 1853, OIA.

116. Meriwether, *My Life in the Mountains*, 164–65 (first quotation); Lane to Meriwether, August 15, 1853, OIA (second quotation).

117. *SFWG*, February 19, 1853.

118. Ward, "Indian Affairs in New Mexico," 328, 332, 335, 339, 341, 346, 348, 351.

119. Carson, "William Carr Lane, Diary," 216 (first quotation); Garland to Thomas, October 29, 1853, NALS, M1072 (second quotation); Miles to Ransom, July 4, 1853, NALS, M1072 (third quotation).

120. Meriwether to Manypenny, August 31, 1853, in *Annual Report of the Commissioner of Indian Affairs, 1853* (Washington, D.C.: Robert Armstrong, Printer, 1853), 189–93.

121. Ibid.

122. Graves to Manypenny, August 31, 1853, *Annual Report, 1853*, 194–201.

123. Meriwether, *My Life in the Mountains*, 167–68.

124. Garland to Thomas, October 29, 1853, AGO, RG 94, M567, R0482.

125. Graves to Meriwether, August 20, 1853 (first, second, and third quotations), Graves to Meriwether, August 22, 1853 (fourth quotation), Meriwether to Garland, August 28, 1853 (fifth quotation), NALS, M1102.

126. Emmett, *Fort Union*, 162; Carleton to Blake, August 12, 1853, in Oliva, *Fort Union*, 122 (quotation).

127. Nichols to Blake and Ransom, September 3, 1853, NALS, M1072.

128. Macrae to Nichols, September 17, 1853 (quotation on 47), Macrae to Nichols, September 18, 1853, Macrae to Nichols, October 1, 1853, AFUC, vol. 2, 47, 48, 51; Ransom to Macrae, October 12, 1853, NALS, M1102.

129. Hunter, "Capture of Mrs. Wilson," 22–23 (first quotation); Meriwether, *My Life in the Mountains*, 174; Meriwether to Manypenny, December 13, 1853, OIA (second quotation). For the story of Jane Wilson's captivity, see Michno and Michno, *A Fate Worse Than Death*, 109–14.

130. Garland to Cooper, October 28, 1853, AFUC, vol. 2, 58.

131. Frazer, *Forts and Supplies*, 71, 77, 89–90; Garland to Cooper, November 27, 1853, AGO, RG 94, M567, R0482 (first and second quotations); Garland to Cooper, July 30, 1854, AGO, RG 94, M567, R0498 (third quotation).

132. Meriwether to Manypenny, November 28, 1853, OIA.

133. Meriwether to Manypenny, November 24, 1853, OIA; Graves to Manypenny, November 29, 1853, OIA.

134. Backus to Nichols, November 10, 1853, AGO, RG 94, M567, R0482 (quotations); Meriwether to Manypenny, December 21, 1853, OIA.

135. Graves to Manypenny, November 29, 1853, OIA.

136. Meriwether to Manypenny, December 29, 1853, OIA.

137. *SFWG*, December 31, 1853.

138. Carson, "William Carr Lane, Diary," 197 (first quotation); Lane to Manypenny, January 5, 1854, OIA (second quotation).

Chapter 5

1. José Rivera statement, January 7, 1854, OIA.

2. López to Meriwether, January 8, 1854, OIA.

3. Garland to Meriwether, January 18, 1854, AFUC, vol. 2, 87.

4. Nichols to Cooke, January 18, 1854, AFUC, vol. 2, 88.

5. Cooke to Nichols, January 26, 1854, 91 (quotations), Cooke to Nichols, January 29, 1854, 84, AFUC, vol. 2.

6. Cooke to Nichols, January 29, 1854, AFUC, vol. 2, 94.

7. Meriwether to Manypenny, January 29, 1854, OIA.

8. Cooke to Nichols, February 20, 1854, AFUC, vol. 2, 98 (first quotation); Cooke to Bell, February 13, 1854, TSDC (second, third, and fourth quotations).

9. Cooke to Bell, March 1, 1854, AGO, RG 94, M567, R0497.

10. Bell to Cooke, March 7, 1854, AGO, RG 94, M567, R0497. The following story and Bell quotations are also from this report.

11. It is not known how Lobo Blanco was identified or if he was killed there. Certainly he was the most notorious Jicarilla chief, and minor fame would accrue to the man who claimed to be his killer. Lobo was said to have been the perpetrator of the massacre of the White party and the mail party at Wagon Mound. However, with the death of the main villain, the Americans and New Mexicans needed another bogeyman to

replace him. After this fight Lobo was increasingly forgotten as the main perpetrator of those massacres, and other chiefs, who were still alive and could be the new focus of fear and hatred, took Lobo's place.

12. The four wounded men were Edward Golden, Adam Slonski, William Walker, and John Steel.

13. Cooke to Nichols, March 8, 1854, AGO, RG 94, M567, R0497.

14. *SFWG*, March 25, 1854.

15. Meriwether, *My Life in the Mountains*, 174–75; Meriwether to Manypenny, March 17, 1854, OIA (quotations).

16. Cooke to Bell, March 9, 1854, Cooke to Blake, March 11, 1854, AFUC, vol. 2, 103, 104 (quotation).

17. Johnston to Blake, March 13, 1854, Blake to Nichols, March 14, 1854, NALS, M1120.

18. Nichols to Cooke, March 12, 1854, AFUC, vol 2., 105 (first quotation); Blake to Nichols, March 14, 1854, NALS, M1120 (second quotation); Cooke to Nichols, March 14, 1854, AFUC, vol. 2, 106–7 (third quotation).

19. Cooke to Nichols, March 14, 1854, AFUC, vol. 2, 106–7.

20. Cooke to Blake, March 19, 1854, in Johnson et al., *Final Report on the Battle of Cieneguilla*, 94.

21. Blake to Nichols, March 20, 1854, Blake to Nichols, March 22, 1854, NALS, M1120 (quotation).

22. Homer K. Davidson, *Black Jack Davidson, a Cavalry Commander on the Western Frontier: The Life of General John W. Davidson* (Glendale, Calif.: Arthur H. Clark Company, 1974), 21, 23, 168.

23. Cooke to Sturgis, March 22, 1854, Cooke to Bell, March 23, 1854 (quotation), AFUC, vol. 2, 111, 112.

24. Davidson to Blake, March 25, 1854, NALS, M1120.

25. Bell to Lt. Robert Williams, December 27, 1854, in Johnson et al., *Final Report on the Battle of Cieneguilla*, 111.

26. Bennett et al., *Forts and Forays*, 53 (first quotation); Davidson to Blake, March 25, 1854, NALS, M1120 (second and third quotations). Bronson's real name was James A. Bennett, and he was later a witness at the court of inquiry concerning the fight at Cieneguilla.

27. Tom Dunlay, *Kit Carson and the Indians* (Lincoln: University of Nebraska Press, 2000), 148, 162 (quotations).

28. Carson to Messervy, March 27, 1854, OIA.

29. Messervy to Carson, March 29, 1854, OIA.

30. Cooke to Blake, March 28, 1854, in Johnson et al., *Final Report on the Battle of Cieneguilla*, 99 (first quotation); Blake to Cooke, March 30, 1854, NALS, M1120 (second and third quotations); Blake to Nichols, March 30, 1854, AGO, RG 94, M567, R0497.

31. Davidson to Blake, April 1, 1854, NALS, M1120 (following Davidson quotations also from this source).

32. Bell to Williams, December 27, 1854, in Johnson et al., *Final Report on the Battle of Cieneguilla*, 112, 113 (following Bell quotations also from this source).

33. Bennett et al., *Forts and Forays*, 53–54.

34. Will Gorenfeld, "The Historical Record," in *Battles and Massacres on the Southwestern Frontier: Historical and Archaeological Perspectives*, edited by Ronald K. Wetherington and Frances Levine (Norman: University of Oklahoma Press, 2014), 16; Davidson to Nichols, October 22, 1853, NALS, M1102 (quotation).
35. Gorenfeld, "The Historical Record," 18–19; Bronson and Strowbridge testimony in Davidson Court of Inquiry, in Johnson et al., *Final Report on the Battle of Cieneguilla*, 150 (first quotation), 156 (second quotation); Davidson to Blake, April 1, 1854, NALS, M1120 (third quotation).
36. Bronson testimony in Johnson et al., *Final Report on the Battle of Cieneguilla*, 150.
37. Johnson et al., *Final Report on the Battle of Cieneguilla*, 52, 61, 150; Gorenfeld, "The Historical Record," 20–21; Bennett et al., *Forts and Forays*, 54 (quotation).
38. Pvt. Peter Weldon testimony in Davidson Court of Inquiry, in Johnson et al., *Final Report on the Battle of Cieneguilla*, 166.
39. Strowbridge testimony in Davidson Court of Inquiry, in Johnson et al., *Final Report on the Battle of Cieneguilla*, 157 (first quotation); Gorenfeld, "The Historical Record," 23 (second quotation).
40. Gorenfeld, "The Historical Record," 24–25.
41. Francisco testimony in Davidson Court of Inquiry, in Johnson et al., *Final Report on the Battle of Cieneguilla*, 135–39.
42. Johnson et al., *Final Report on the Battle of Cieneguilla*, 66–67, 71; Gorenfeld, "The Historical Record," 39n81.
43. Garland to Thomas, April 1, 1854, TSDC. When Lieutenant Bell's critical letter came to light, the army had to do some damage control. The court of inquiry in March 1856 was mostly a whitewash. David Bell was then under the command of Col. Edwin Sumner at Fort Leavenworth. But Sumner refused to allow him to attend the inquiry, so Davidson conducted his defense without his accuser present. The army witnesses were all friendly and seemed to have been coached to give the same account of a heroic Davidson attacked by an overwhelming force of Indians, fighting desperately for several hours, until dwindling ammunition and mounting casualties forced him into a controlled withdrawal. The court concluded that Davidson could not have avoided the battle; exhibited great skill in fighting a greatly superior force of Indians; showed prudence, coolness, and courage under pressure; and made great exertions to bring out his wounded. His report of the affair was worthy of "a modest, and gallant gentleman." Bell's remarks were no more than "malicious criticism." Fine surveys of the battle, the archaeology, and the court of inquiry are David M. Johnson, "The Archaeological Record," in *Battles and Massacres on the Southwestern Frontier Historical and Archaeological Perspectives*, edited by Ronald K. Wetherington and Frances Levine (Norman: University of Oklahoma Press, 2014); Will Gorenfeld, "The Historical Record," in *Battles and Massacres on the Southwestern Frontier: Historical and Archaeological Perspectives*, edited by Ronald K. Wetherington and Frances Levine (Norman: University of Oklahoma Press, 2014); John Garland, March 26, 1856, in Johnson et al., *Final Report on the Battle of Cieneguilla*, 176–77.

44. Nichols to Cooke, April 1, 1854, NALS, M1072; Cooke to Brooks, April 2, 1854, AFUC, vol. 2, 124.

45. Messervy to Manypenny, March 31, 1854, OIA.

46. Nichols to Backus, April 4, 1854, NALS, M1072.

47. Thompson to Nichols, April 5, 1854, NALS, M1120.

48. Garland to Cooke, April 7, 1854, NALS, M1072.

49. *SFWG*, April 8, 1854.

50. Nichols to Cooke, April 10, 1854, NALS, M1072.

51. Cooke to Nichols, May 24, 1854, TSDC; James H. Quinn, "Notes of a Spy Company under Col. Cooke," AFUC, vol. 2, 126 (quotations).

52. Quinn, "Notes of a Spy Company," 126 (first and second quotations); Cooke to Nichols, May 24, 1854, TSDC (third quotation). From Quinn and Cooke's reports I place the camp in an S-shaped bend of the Rio Vallecitos below the present-day village of Ancones. Cooke called the river the Agua Caliente (Ojo Caliente), although that river begins about three miles downstream where the Rio Tusas and Rio Vallecitos converge. The subsequent passages concerning the battle are from these two sources.

53. Cooke to Nichols, May 24, 1854, TSDC (quotations); Quinn, "Notes of a Spy Company," 126–27. The soldier killed was Private John Casey of Company G, 1st Dragoons, and the wounded man was Isaac Bass, Company D, 2nd Artillery.

54. Cooke to Nichols, May 24, 1854, TSDC; Quinn, "Notes of a Spy Company," 127.

55. Carson to Messervy, April 12, 1854, AFUC, vol. 2, 138.

56. Nichols to Cooke, April 13, 1854, NALS, M1072.

57. Carson to Messervy, April 19, 1854, AFUC, vol. 2, 147–48.

58. Quinn, "Notes of a Spy Company," 128–29.

59. Nichols to Thompson, April 16, 1854, NALS, M1072; Nichols to Cooke, April 29, 1854, NALS, M1072 (quotation).

60. Davidson to Brooks, May 1, 1854, NALS, M1120.

61. James H. Quinn, "Brooks Expedition," AFUC, vol. 2, 165–66; Brooks to Cooke, May 13, 1854, NALS, M1120 (quotations).

62. *SFWG*, April 22, 1854 (first and second quotations), April 29, 1854 (third and fourth quotations).

63. Garland to Thomas, April 30, 1854, TSDC.

64. *SFWG*, June 3, 1854.

65. *SFWG*, June 3, 1854, June 17, 1854, June 24, 1854.

66. Messervy to Manypenny, May 30, 1854, OIA.

67. Meriwether to Manypenny, May 28, 1854, OIA. Governor John Evans of Colorado Territory found himself in a situation in 1863 and 1864 similar to that of Messervy and Meriwether: engulfed by exaggerated claims of raiding Indians who were about to combine against him in a general war, while constantly calling for more military protection and chastisement of the "savages."

68. Garland to Thomas, June 5, 1854, Ransom to Maxwell, June 3, 1854, TSDC.

69. For instance, Pablo Trujillo filed a claim stating that on May 15 Jicarillas stole horses from him worth $470. Trujillo's place near Guadalupita was only about twenty-five miles north of Fort Union on the road to Taos, and at this time there probably was

not a Jicarilla within 150 miles. Vincente García and Anastacio Sandoval claimed that Kaws in Santa Fe County stole mules and horses from them in June worth $800. The Kaws lived about six hundred miles away in eastern Kansas! The claims were first approved but then denied when the claimants could offer no proof that Kaws were anywhere near Santa Fe.

70. Garland to Thomas, June 5, 1854, TSDC; Cooke to Nichols, June 6, 1854, AFUC, vol. 2, 186 (quotations).

71. Cooke, Orders No. 10, May 17, 1854, NALS, M1120.

72. Carleton to Cooke, June 5, 1854, TSDC (following quotations about this incident also from this source). Morris F. Taylor, "Campaigns against the Jicarilla Apache, 1854," *New Mexico Historical Review* 44, no. 4 (October 1969): 281–84.

73. Quaife, *Kit Carson's Autobiography*, 155, 160 (quotations).

74. Carson to Messervy, June 12, 1854, AFUC, vol. 2. 193; Cooke to Nichols, June 7, 1854, AFUC, vol. 2, 189; Cooke, Orders No. 12, June 9, 1854, NALS, M1120.

75. Cordoba to Carson, June 17, 1854, Davidson to Nichols, June 20, 1854, NALS, M1120 (quotation).

76. Garland to Thomas, June 30, 1854, AFUC, vol. 2, 203.

77. Garland to Thomas, June 30, 1854, AGO, RG 94, M567, R0497.

78. Sykes to Cooke, July 2, 1854, AGO, RG 94, M567, R0498 (following quotations on this incident also from this source).

79. Cooke to Cooper, July 1, 1854 (first quotation), Cooke to Cooper, September 12, 1854 (second quotation), AGO, RG 94, M567, R0495.

80. Blake to Nichols, July 6, 1854, NALS, M1120 (quotation); Nichols to Cooke, July 9, 1854, NALS, M1072.

81. *SFWG*, July 15, 1854.

82. Garland to Thomas, July 30, 1854, AGO, RG 94, M567, R0498.

83. Meriwether, *My Life in the Mountains and on the Plains*, 188, 193–94. Meriwether's confusion may have resulted from the fact that he dictated his story in 1886 when he was eighty-six years old.

84. Graves to Manypenny, June 8, 1854, *Annual Report of the Commissioner of Indian Affairs, 1854* (Washington, A. O. Nicholson, 1855), 177–84 (following quotations also from this source).

85. Steck to Meriwether, August 22, 1854, OIA; Garland to Thomas, August 30, 1854, TSDC (quotations).

86. Averam B. Bender, "Frontier Defense in the Territory of New Mexico, 1853–1861," *New Mexico Historical Review* 9, no. 4 (October 1934): 350.

87. Meriwether to Manypenny, August 31, 1854, OIA.

88. Meriwether to Manypenny, September 1, 1854, *Commissioner of Indian Affairs, 1854,* 166–70. Depredation records indicate that Navajos were blamed more often than any other tribes, outnumbering Jicarilla accusations by about three to one.

89. Ibid., 171–72, 307. Meriwether's comment about the Indians not obeying the Ten Commandments is noteworthy, as is Manypenny's mandate that all superintendencies must keep the Sabbath—including the Indians.

90. Ibid., 173–76.

91. Meriwether to Manypenny, September 29, 1854, OIA (quotations); Meriwether, *My Life in the Mountains*, 196. Meriwether confused Chacón with Chico Velásquez in his memoir.

92. Garland to Thomas, September 30, 1854, AFUC, vol. 2, 219; Garland, October 3, 1854, Special Orders No. 63, Department of New Mexico, U. S. A. Commands, Series 4, RG 98; Thompson to Nichols, October 25, 1854, NALS, M1120 (quotation).

93. Meriwether to Manypenny, October 29, 1854, OIA (quotation); Meriwether, *My Life in the Mountains*, 198–99. Given Meriwether's confusion, he may have meant Chacón, not Chico.

94. An example is a letter from John A. Fairchild of Detroit, Michigan, who wrote to Commissioner Manypenny that Fairchild's son had been traveling through New Mexico the previous fall when Apaches killed him. Fairchild said that his son's horses, mules, wagons, and supplies were stolen and that he had heard that there was a law "by virtue of which they may be compelled to pay out of their annuities, for the loss of said property &c." Fairchild wanted Manypenny to tell him how he could get the money. Fairchild to Manypenny, December 17, 1854, OIA.

95. Carson to Meriwether, November 25, 1854, OIA; Meriwether to Manypenny, November 30, 1854, OIA; Dunlay, *Kit Carson and the Indians*, 170.

96. McNitt, *Navajo Wars*, 251–54; Dodge to Meriwether, November 13, 1854, OIA (quotation).

97. Meriwether to Manypenny, November 30, 1854, OIA; Garland to Thomas, December 31, 1854, AGO, RG 94, M567, R0498.

98. Meriwether to Manypenny, October 29, 1854, OIA; Meriwether, *My Life in the Mountains*, 199–202 (following quotations on this incident also from this source).

99. Meriwether to Manypenny, November 30, 1854, OIA (quotations); Meriwether, *My Life in the Mountains*, 201; Lecompte, *Pueblo, Hardscrabble, Greenhorn*, 244–45, 322n21.

100. Lecompte, *Pueblo, Hardscrabble, Greenhorn*, 244–45; Meriwether, *My Life in the Mountains*, 228 (quotations). DeWitt C. Peters, assistant surgeon at Fort Massachusetts, described Tierra Blanca's face as having regular, even statuesque features. Perhaps Meriwether's grotesque description was the result of a conscious or subconscious need to demonize his enemy.

101. Quaife, *Kit Carson's Autobiography*, 162.

102. Lecompte, *Pueblo, Hardscrabble, Greenhorn*, 239–43; Simmons, *Ute Indians of Utah, Colorado, and New Mexico*, 99.

103. Lecompte, *Pueblo, Hardscrabble, Greenhorn*, 244.

Chapter 6

1. Lecompte, *Pueblo, Hardscrabble, Greenhorn*, 246–51 (following quotations also from this source).

2. Baca to Meriwether, January 13, 1855, OIA.

3. Nichols to Brooks, January 12, 1855, AFUC, vol. 3, 5 (quotation); Nichols to Blake, January 12, 1855, NALS, M1072.

4. Nichols to Fauntleroy, January 19, 1855, AFUC, vol. 3, 11.

5. Meriwether to Manypenny, January 31, 1855, OIA.

6. Sturgis to Nichols, January 22, 1855, TSDC (quotations); Theophilus F. Rodenbough, *From Everglade to Canyon with the Second United States Cavalry* (Norman: University of Oklahoma Press, 2000), 201–2.

7. Ewell to Nichols, February 10, 1855, AFUC, vol. 3, 34–35.

8. Meriwether to Manypenny, January 31, 1855, OIA; Nichols to Stewart, January 29, 1855, AFUC, vol. 3, 14 (first quotation); Garland to Thomas, January 31, 1855, in TSDC (second and third quotations).

9. Lecompte, *Pueblo, Hardscrabble, Greenhorn,* 251. Wootton said seven were killed: TSDC.

10. Hammond, *Alexander Barclay,* 58–59.

11. TSDC. William Kronig and José M. Baca also filed loss claims for the January 19 attack (see appendix A).

12. Ibid. The bulk of this 200-plus page claim consists of military reports and legal briefs supporting the government contention that the Utes and Jicarillas were not in amity with the United States, thus negating any depredation claims that only could be collected from tribes at peace.

13. Watts, *Indian Depredations in New Mexico,* 2. Watts's protest was based on "Claims for Indian Depredations in New Mexico."

14. Watts, *Indian Depredations in New Mexico,* 3, 4, 64.

15. Ibid., 17, 21, 22, 23, 24.

16. We are all motivated by self-interest. Anyone testifying, telling a story, or writing a letter is subject to false memories, implanted memories, leading questions, cognitive dissonance, confirmation bias, self-affirmation, motivated reasoning, and social, cultural, and political mores—almost all of which operate on a subconscious level. Given all these obstacles, factual accuracy is a chimera. Introducing monetary compensation into the equation almost guarantees that the story will be adjusted to serve the storyteller's purpose, with truth being only incidental. This is a jaded view of human motivations, but it is well-documented. Several examples are found in Christopher Chabris and Daniel Simons, *The Invisible Gorilla: How Our Intuitions Deceive Us* (New York: Broadway Paperbacks, 2009); Richard Wiseman, *Paranormality: Why We See What Isn't There* (Lexington, Ky.: Spin Solutions, 2010); Joseph T. Hallinan, *Why We Make Mistakes* (New York: Broadway Books, 2009); Joel Cooper, *Cognitive Dissonance: Fifty Years of a Classic Theory* (London: Sage, 2007); Carol Tavris and Elliot Aronson, *Mistakes Were Made (But Not by Me): Why We Justify Foolish Beliefs, Bad Decisions, and Hurtful Acts* (Orlando, Fla.: Harcourt, 2007); Daniel Gardner, *The Science of Fear: How the Culture of Fear Manipulates Your Brain* (New York: Plume, 2009); Daniel L. Schacter, *Searching for Memory: The Brain, the Mind, and the Past* (New York: Basic Books, 1996).

17. Watts, *Indian Depredations in New Mexico,* 63.

18. The historical value of these depredation claims has been praised and damned. One author who has collected depredation claims believes that despite the exaggerations

in losses, "seldom was it determined that an attack had not been made. The facts of the attack were not challenged." He also said that "it was seldom that the claimant was dishonest in putting forth an account of an Indian attack, who was there, what happened, how it happened, etc.," but just a "human tendency" to inflate losses (Jeff Broome, *The Cheyenne War: Indian Raids on the Roads to Denver, 1864–1869* [Sheridan, Colo: Aberdeen Books, 2013], 17, 20, 23). In contrast, another researcher warned of the danger in using claims loaded with numerous lies, because of the overwhelming concern that "in every nook and cranny hides a sinister, but obvious, motive: financial remuneration." He said that the claimants "were motivated to exaggerate their material possessions and to make Native Americans a larger-than-life threat" (Larry Skogen, "The Bittersweet Reality of Depredation Cases," *Prologue Magazine of the National Archives* [Fall 1992]: 290–96).

19. Meriwether to Manypenny, February 28, 1855, OIA.
20. The 9th Military Department became the Department of New Mexico on October 31, 1853.
21. Fauntleroy to Cooper, November 30, 1853, McDowell to Fauntleroy, January 4, 1854 (quotations), AGO, RG 94, M567, R0496.
22. Garland, Special Orders No. 12, February 5, 1855, NALS; *SFWG*, March 17, 1855. James Quinn, who had provided great service with his spy company the year before, was not available this time around—he was driving fifteen thousand sheep to the market in California. *SFWG*, April 28, 1855.
23. Taylor, "Campaigns against the Jicarilla Apache," 123 (see also appendix A).
24. Ibid., 124; Morris F. Taylor, "Action at Fort Massachusetts: The Indian Campaign of 1855," *Colorado Magazine* 42, no. 4 (Fall 1965): 297.
25. Labadi to Meriwether, February 18, 1855 (quotations), Labadi to Meriwether, February 24, 1855, OIA.
26. Labadi to Meriwether, February 24, 1855, OIA.
27. Meriwether to Manypenny, February 28, 1855, OIA.
28. Nichols to Fauntleroy, February 16, 1855, AFUC, vol. 3, 36; Fauntleroy to Nichols, February 20, 1855, NALS, M1120.
29. Kiser, *Dragoons in Apacheland*, 249–50 (first quotation); Garland to Thomas, February 28, 1855, TSDC; *SWFG*, March 10, 1855 (second and third quotations).
30. Garland to Fauntleroy, February 6, 1855, AGO, RG 94, M567, R0523.
31. Fauntleroy to Sturgis, February 27, 1855, NALS, M1120.
32. Thompson to Magruder, March 10, 1855, NALS, M1120. For an excellent sketch of this affair, see Will Gorenfeld and John Gorenfeld, "Taos Mutiny of 1855," *Wild West*, 27, no. 3 (October 2014). As a result of the mutiny, four dragoons were sentenced to death, but President Pierce commuted the sentences to three years of hard labor. Captain Thompson was cashiered from the service. Major Blake found good counsel for his defense, including Judge Joab Houghton, and got most of the charges dismissed except for his failure to discipline Thompson. He was to be suspended without pay for one year, but Garland restored him to active duty after one month. Many of the Company F men were distributed to different companies.

33. Garland, Special Order No. 27, March 8, 1855, Blake to Sturgis, March 14, 1855, April 11, 1855 (quotation), NALS, M1120.
34. Taylor, "Action at Fort Massachusetts," 297; Fauntleroy to Sturgis, March 8, 1855 (quotation), March 21, 1855, March 28, 1855, NALS, M1120.
35. Fauntleroy to Sturgis, March 28, 1855, NALS, M1120 (first and second quotations); Twitchell, *The History of the Occupation*, 301–2 (third quotation); Taylor, "Action at Fort Massachusetts," 299 (fourth quotation).
36. Fauntleroy to Sturgis, March 28, 1855, NALS, M1120 (quotations); Guild and Carter, *Kit Carson*, 206; Twitchell, *The History of the Occupation*, 302. In two of Fauntleroy's reports he called the scene of the fight Cochetopa Pass. He later corrected this to Saguache Pass. Fauntleroy to Sturgis, May 5, 1855, TSDC. There is no actual Saguache Pass. I place this fight where Saguache Creek enters from a valley to the west and is constricted in a slight canyon about eight miles west of the town of Saguache, which could easily be considered a "pass." Cochetopa Pass is about eighteen miles west of this point.
37. Fauntleroy to Sturgis, March 28, 1855, NALS, M1120; Sabin, *Kit Carson Days*, 668 (first quotation); Rafael Chacon, "Campaign against the Utes and Apaches in Southern Colorado, 1855, from the Memoirs of Major Rafael Chacon," *Colorado Magazine* 11 (May 1934): 109 (second and third quotations).
38. Fauntleroy to Sturgis, March 21, 1855, March 28, 1855 (quotation), NALS, M1120; Taylor, "Action at Fort Massachusetts," 300.
39. Fauntleroy to Sturgis, March 28, 1855, NALS, M1120. Tracing their route is difficult. Modern maps show no Beaver Creek in the area that Fauntleroy described, but there is one about sixty miles to the east. It seems that they went up today's Badger Creek and the next day found themselves back in the vicinity of the Arkansas near or perhaps a little downstream from Salida. Rafael Chacón drew a map that placed their coming fight in the Salida area. DeWitt Peters also wrote about hot springs in this vicinity on the opposite side of Poncha Pass that "were sending their fumes to heaven." There is a hot spring in the vicinity of Wellsville, about four miles down from Salida.
40. Fauntleroy to Sturgis, March 28, 1855, NALS, M1120 (quotations); Taylor, "Action at Fort Massachusetts," 300.
41. Chacon, "Campaign against the Utes and Apaches," 109, 111 (quotation); Taylor, "Campaigns against the Jicarilla Apache, 1855," 125. Harvey L. Carter in *"Dear Old Kit": The Historical Kit Carson* (Norman: University of Oklahoma Press, 1968), 146–47, uses Peters's letter as quoted in Taylor's "Action at Fort Massachusetts" article to show that this fight took place at the confluence of Chalk Creek and the Arkansas because of the reference to a hot spring. But a hot spring located below Mt. Princeton is not the one that Peters was talking about. Peters described the springs in a letter written on April 5, so he had to be talking about the battle on March 23. Fauntleroy's and Chacon's descriptions place the fight in the Salida area, not near Buena Vista. Their next march of fifteen miles took them into the Wet Mountain Valley, which proves they left from the Salida area—from Chalk Creek the march would have been nearer

to forty miles. It was the coming battle on April 29 that would take place near the hot spring by Chalk Creek.

42. Fauntleroy to Sturgis, March 28, 1855, NALS, M1120 (first quotation); Chacon, "Campaign against the Utes and Apaches," 111 (second quotation); Taylor, "Action at Fort Massachusetts," 302.

43. Fauntleroy to Sturgis, March 28, 1855, NALS, M1120.

44. Ibid.

45. Garland to Thomas, March 31, 1855, TSDC (quotation); Fauntleroy, Orders No. 16, April 5, 1855, NALS.

46. Sturgis to Fauntleroy, April 6, 1855, AFUC, vol. 3, 60.

47. Fauntleroy to Sturgis, April 10, 1855, NALS, M1120; Fauntleroy to Sturgis, April 10, 1855, TSDC (quotations).

48. Taylor, "Action at Fort Massachusetts," 304; Fauntleroy to Sturgis, April 10, 1855, TSDC (quotations). From Fauntleroy's description, I trace their track as going partway up Poncha Creek, then west and north to either Little Cochetopa or Green Creek, then down to the South Arkansas River, which comes out of a canyon from Monarch Pass and would appear to come from the direction of the Grand (Colorado) River.

49. Fauntleroy to Sturgis, April 30, 1855, Fauntleroy to Sturgis, May 10, 1855, TSDC (quotation). This seems to place the camp perhaps along Chalk Creek below Mount Princeton, about seven miles south of present Buena Vista.

50. Fauntleroy to Sturgis, April 30, 1855, Fauntleroy to Sturgis, May 10, 1855, TSDC (quotations); Taylor, "Action at Fort Massachusetts," 305, 307–8.

51. Fauntleroy to Sturgis, May 10, 1855, TSDC (first, third, and fourth quotations); Taylor, "Action at Fort Massachusetts," 307 (second quotation).

52. Fauntleroy to Sturgis, April 30, 1855 (quotation), Fauntleroy to Sturgis, May 5, 1855, TSDC.

53. Fauntleroy to Sturgis, May 5, 1855, TSDC (quotations); Taylor, "Action at Fort Massachusetts," 308–9.

54. Garland to Thomas, May 31, 1855, TSDC; Carson to Meriwether, June 27, 1855, OIA (quotation). Meriwether pointed out this inconsistency to Manypenny in a letter on June 30, saying that Carson was told not to accompany the troops but did so anyway.

55. Wetherington, *Ceran St. Vrain*, 79–80.

56. Taylor, "Campaigns against the Jicarilla Apaches," 126–27; Sabin, *Kit Carson Days*, 669; Chacon, "Campaign against the Utes and Apaches," 111 (quotations). In Jacqueline Dorgan Meketa, ed., *Legacy of Honor: The Life of Rafael Chacon, a Nineteenth Century New Mexican* (Albuquerque: University of New Mexico Press, 1986), 103, Chacón elaborated on the "proof," saying that the soldier "castrated him and brought the parts to the colonel, tied to a stick."

57. Taylor, "Campaigns against the Jicarilla Apaches," 127; Chacon, "Campaign against the Utes and Apaches," 111 (quotation).

58. Fauntleroy to Sturgis, April 30, 1855, TSDC; Chacon, "Campaign against the Utes and Apaches," 111.

59. Sturgis to Fauntleroy, May 18, 1855, AFUC, vol. 3, 72.

60. St. Vrain to Craig, June 17, 1855, TSDC. Either St. Vrain's landmarks or mileages are wrong. Hole in the Rock was on Timpas Creek near present Thatcher, Colorado, beyond the Apishapa, but it is barely forty miles from where they left the Cucharas.

61. St. Vrain to Craig, June 17, 1855, TSDC (following St. Vrain quotations also from this source); Taylor, "Campaigns against the Jicarilla Apaches," 128–30.

62. Taylor, "Campaigns against the Jicarilla Apaches," 129–30.

63. Garland to Thomas, May 31, 1855, TSDC (first, second, and third quotations); Taylor, "Campaigns against the Jicarilla Apaches," 130–31; Quaife, *Kit Carson's Autobiography*, 166–67 (fourth, fifth, and sixth quotations). The casualty count shows that Fauntleroy's command killed 55, wounded 32, and captured 13; St. Vrain's command killed 19, wounded 7, and captured 61.

64. Sturgis to Miles, May 25, 1855, AFUC, vol. 3, 78; Garland to Thomas, May 31, 1855, TSDC (quotations); Kiser, *Dragoons in Apacheland*, 254–55.

65. C. L. Sonnichsen, *The Mescalero Apaches* (Norman: University of Oklahoma Press, 1958), 89 (quotation); Deloria and DeMallie, *Documents of American Indian Diplomacy*, 1309–16.

66. Eaton to Cunningham, June 17, 1855, AFUC, vol. 3, 92.

67. Blake to Magruder, July 20, 1855, NALS, M1120.

68. Carson to Meriwether, June 27, 1855, OIA.

69. Labadi to Meriwether, June 30, 1855, OIA; Meriwether to Manypenny, June 30, 1855, OIA.

70. Meriwether to Manypenny, July 1, 1855, OIA.

71. Whittlesey to Sturgis, May 26, 1855, AFUC, vol. 3, 79; Carson to Meriwether, July 26, 1855, OIA (quotations).

72. Brooks, *Captives and Cousins*, 258, 331–34.

73. Blake to Magruder, July 20, 1855, NALS, M1120 (first quotation); Carson to Meriwether, July 26, 1855, OIA (second quotation).

74. Garland to Thomas, July 31, 1855, TSDC.

75. Meriwether to Manypenny, July 31, 1855, OIA.

76. Deloria and DeMallie, *Documents of American Indian Diplomacy*, 1317–20.

77. Meriwether to Manypenny, September 1, 1855, OIA.

78. Labadi to Manypenny, August 31, 1855, *Annual Report of the Commissioner of Indian Affairs, 1855* (Washington, D.C.: A. O. P. Nicholson, 1856), 191.

79. Meriwether, *My Life in the Mountains*, 227–30 (following Meriwether quotations also from this source); Dunlay, *Kit Carson and the Indians*, 174–75.

80. Dunlay, *Kit Carson and the Indians*, 179.

81. Dunlay, *Kit Carson and the Indians*, 175 (first quotation); Quaife, *Kit Carson's Autobiography*, 168–69 (second quotation).

82. *SFWG*, September 1, 1855.

83. *SFWG*, September 15, 1855.

84. Carson to Meriwether, September 26, 1855, in *Annual Report of the Commissioner of Indian Affairs, 1855*, 192.

85. Deloria and DeMallie, *Documents of American Indian Diplomacy*, 1328–33; Garland to Thomas, September 30, 1855, AGO, RG 94, M567, R0523.

86. Meriwether to Manypenny, September, 1855, *Annual Report of the Commissioner of Indian Affairs, 1855*, 187–90 (following Meriwether quotations also from this source).

87. Manypenny to McClelland, November 26, 1855, *Annual Report of the Commissioner of Indian Affairs, 1855*, 11, 13–14, 19.

88. Miles to Steck and Nichols, cited in Kiser, *Dragoons in Apacheland*, 257–59; *SFWG*, November 24, 1855.

89. Kiser, *Dragoons in Apacheland*, 259. Although Kiser stated that Miles's "type of thorough analysis seldom occurred among military officers," it happened quite often. Recording the military reaction to the allegations was not the main focus of Kiser's study, but he did speculate: "One cannot help but wonder how much raiding and plundering was perpetrated by non-Indians."

90. Garland to Thomas, October 31, 1855, TSDC.

91. Moore to Nichols, November 6, 1855, Garland to Thomas, November 30, 1855, AGO, RG 94, M567, R0523.

92. Kiser, *Dragoons in Apacheland*, 165 (first quotation); Horn, *New Mexico's Troubled Years*, 63 (second quotation). Bender, in *The March of Empire*, 160, described the settlers as "violently opposed" to Meriwether's treaties for being "too favorable to the savages." They closed off too much good land for settlement and grazing. Dragoon James A. Bennett, whose diary is suspect for its numerous errors, nevertheless has an 1855 entry that states: "Last night the Governor of the Territory was hung in effigy from the flag staff in the main plaza. Cause: his course taken with the Indians." Bennett et al., *Forts and Forays*, 66–67.

93. Steck to Pelham, October 4, 1855, OIA.

94. Pelham to Hendricks, October 22, 8155, OIA; Hendricks to McClelland, December 6, 1855, OIA.

95. *SFWG*, January 26, 1856. Fauntleroy took command of the Department of New Mexico in October 1859. Tasked with assessing the situation, he wrote to Gen. Winfield Scott: "The greatest embarrassment arises from the fact that many of the claims set up against the Indians of New Mexico for plundering, stealing stock and the like, are either fabricated, or to a considerable degree exaggerated, and if war is to be commenced upon the simple presentation of these claims, the cause for war becomes interminable, or the Indians must be extirpated." Cited in Keleher, *Turmoil in New Mexico*, 138n94.

96. *SFWG*, September 29, 1855.

97. *SFWG*, March 8, 1856.

98. Ibid.

99. Ibid. The Legislature contended that thirty thousand Indians still roamed about at will, at one time driving off ten thousand sheep! Bender, "Frontier Defense in the Territory of New Mexico," 354.

100. *SWFG*, November 17, 1855; Baxter, *Las Carneradas*, 140–44.

101. Appendix C and D. The documents that I located focused on New Mexico from the late 1840s through the 1850s. Very likely some claimants filed decades later, after the statute of limitations was changed, purporting to have been robbed in the years 1846 to 1859. Still, the decline and near disappearance of formal claims is notable. After 1856 only ten more claims were filed through the remainder of the decade.

102. Bender, "Frontier Defense in the Territory of New Mexico," 353. Before 1857 the territorial governor was also *ex-officio* superintendent of Indian Affairs. In 1857 the jobs were separated. Collins became superintendent and Abraham R. Rencher succeeded Meriwether as governor.

103. Benjamin Franklin, *The Life and Writings of Benjamin Franklin*, vol. 2 (Philadelphia: McCarty and Davis, 1834), 460.

104. Bruce Schneier, *Beyond Fear: Thinking Sensibly about Security in an Uncertain World* (New York: Copernicus Books, 2003), 14, 31, 61–63, 74, 82, 133, 138, 176; Stanton E. Samenow, *Inside the Criminal Mind* (New York: Broadway Books, 1984), 99.

105. Schneier, *Beyond Fear*, 8, 27, 28, 244.

106. Mark Stein, *American Panic: A History of Who Scares Us and Why* (New York: Palgrave Macmillan, 2014), 2, 7, 11 (quotations), 48, 109.

107. W. A. Croffut, ed., *Fifty Years in Camp and Field: Diary of Major-General Ethan Allen Hitchcock, U.S.A.* (New York: G. P. Putnam's Sons, 1909), 396. The problems that army officers had with white frontiersmen are aptly illustrated in a number of sources, including Robert Wooster, *American Military Frontiers: The United States Army in the West, 1783–1900* (Albuquerque: University of New Mexico Press, 2009); Samuel J. Watson, *Peacekeepers and Conquerors: The Army Officer Corps on the American Frontier, 1821–1846* (Lawrence: University Press of Kansas, 2013); William B. Skelton, *An American Profession of Arms: The Army Officer Corps, 1784–1861* (Lawrence: University Press of Kansas, 1992); Bernard W. Sheehan, *Seeds of Extinction: Jeffersonian Philanthropy and the American Indian* (Chapel Hill: University of North Carolina Press, 1973); Francis Paul Prucha, *Sword of the Republic: The United States Army on the Frontier, 1783–1846* (Bloomington: Indiana University Press, 1969); Durwood Ball, *Army Regulars on the Western Frontier, 1848–1861* (Norman: University of Oklahoma Press, 2001).

Bibliography

Abel, Annie Heloise, ed. "The Journal of John Greiner." *Old Santa Fe: A Magazine of History, Archaeology, Genealogy and Biography* 3, no. 11 (July 1916): 189–243.

———, ed. *The Official Correspondence of James S. Calhoun While Indian Agent at Santa Fe and Superintendent of Indian Affairs in New Mexico*. Washington, D.C.: Government Printing Office, 1915.

American State Papers, Indian Affairs. Vol. 1. "An Act to Regulate Trade and Intercourse with the Indian Tribes and to Preserve Peace on the Frontiers." 2008. http://avalon. law.yale.edu/18th_century/na030.asp.

Andreas, A. T. *History of Cook County, Illinois, from the Earliest Period to the Present*. Chicago: A. T. Andreas, Publisher, 1884.

Annals of the Congress of the United States, 1789–1824. 4th Congress, 1st Session, vol. 5, December 7, 1795, to June 1, 1796. Washington, D.C.: Gales and Seaton, 1834–1856.

Annual Report of the Commissioner of Indian Affairs, 1846–1850. 32nd Congress, 1st Session. Washington, D.C.: Government Printing Office, 1850.

Annual Report of the Commissioner of Indian Affairs, 1851. Washington, D.C.: Gideon and Co., Printer, 1851.

Annual Report of the Commissioner of Indian Affairs, 1852. Senate Executive Documents, Exec. Doc. 1. 2nd Session, 32nd Congress. Washington, D.C.: Government Printing Office, 1852.

Annual Report of the Commissioner of Indian Affairs, 1853. Washington, D.C.: Robert Armstrong, Printer, 1853.

Annual Report of the Commissioner of Indian Affairs, 1854. Washington, D.C.: A. O. P. Nicholson, 1855.

Annual Report of the Commissioner of Indian Affairs, 1855. Washington, D.C.: A. O. P. Nicholson, 1856.

Ball, Durwood. *Army Regulars on the Western Frontier, 1848–1861*. Norman: University of Oklahoma Press, 2001.

Barry, Louise. *The Beginning of the West: Annals of the Kansas Gateway to the American West, 1540–1854.* Topeka: Kansas State Historical Society, 1972.

Bartlett, John Russell. *Personal Narrative of Exploration and Incidents in Texas, New Mexico, California, Sonora, and Chihuahua Connected with the United States and Mexican Boundary Commission during the Years 1850, '51, '52, and '53.* New York: D. Appleton and Company, 1854.

Baxter, John O. *Las Carneradas: Sheep Trade in New Mexico, 1700–1860.* Albuquerque: University of New Mexico Press, 1987.

Belich, James. *Replenishing the Earth: The Settler Revolution and the Rise of the Anglo-World, 1783–1939.* New York: Oxford University Press, 2009.

Bender, Averam B. "Frontier Defense in the Territory of New Mexico, 1853–1861." *New Mexico Historical Review* 9, no. 4 (October 1934): 345–73.

———. *The March of Empire: Frontier Defense in the Southwest, 1848–1860.* New York: Greenwood Press, 1968. Originally published by University of Kansas Press, 1952.

Bennett, James A., Clinton E. Brooks, and Frank D. Reeve, eds. *Forts and Forays: A Dragoon in New Mexico, 1850–1856.* Foreword by Jerry Thompson. Albuquerque: University of New Mexico Press, 1996.

Berwanger, Eugene H. *The Frontier against Slavery: Western Anti-Negro Prejudice and the Slavery Extension Controversy.* Urbana: University of Illinois Press, 1967.

Bieber, Ralph P., ed. "Letters of William Carr Lane." *New Mexico Historical Review* 3, no. 2 (April 1928): 179–203.

Brooks, James F. *Captives and Cousins: Slavery, Kinship, and Community in the Southwest Borderlands.* Chapel Hill: University of North Carolina Press, 2002.

Broome, Jeff. *The Cheyenne War: Indian Raids on the Roads to Denver, 1864–1869.* Sheridan, Colo.: Aberdeen Books, 2013.

Carson, William B., ed. "William Carr Lane, Diary." *New Mexico Historical Review* 39 (July 1964): 181–233.

Carter, Harvey L. *"Dear Old Kit": The Historical Kit Carson.* Norman: University of Oklahoma Press, 1968.

Chabris, Christopher, and Daniel Simons, *The Invisible Gorilla: How Our Intuitions Deceive Us.* New York: Broadway Paperbacks, 2009.

Chacon, Rafael. "Campaign against the Utes and Apaches in Southern Colorado, 1855, from the Memoirs of Major Rafael Chacon." *Colorado Magazine* 11 (May 1934): 108–12.

Chamberlain, Samuel E. *My Confession: The Recollections of a Rogue.* Introduction by Roger Butterfield. New York: Harper and Brothers, 1956.

"Claims for Indian Depredations in New Mexico." Letter from the Secretary of the Interior. In U.S. House of Representatives, Exec. Doc. No. 123, 1st Session, 35th Congress, 1857–58, 1–62. Washington, D.C.: James B. Steedman, 1858.

Cooper, Joel. *Cognitive Dissonance: Fifty Years of a Classic Theory.* London: Sage, 2007.

Croffut, W. A., ed. *Fifty Years in Camp and Field: Diary of Major-General Ethan Allen Hitchcock, U.S.A.* New York: G. P. Putnam's Sons, 1909.

Dary, David. *The Santa Fe Trail: Its History, Legends, and Lore.* New York: Alfred A. Knopf, 2000.

Davidson, Homer K. *Black Jack Davidson, a Cavalry Commander on the Western Frontier: The Life of General John W. Davidson.* Glendale, Calif.: Arthur H. Clark Company, 1974.

Davis, W. W. H. *El Gringo: New Mexico and Her People.* Lincoln: University of Nebraska Press, 1982.

Dawson, Joseph G., III. *Doniphan's Epic March: The 1st Missouri Volunteers in the Mexican War.* Lawrence: University Press of Kansas, 1999.

Decker, Peter R. *"The Utes Must Go!": American Expansion and the Removal of a People.* Golden, Colo.: Fulcrum Publishing, 2004.

DeLay, Brian. *War of a Thousand Deserts: Indian Raids and the U.S.-Mexican War.* New Haven, Conn.: Yale University Press, 2008.

Del Castillo, Richard Griswold. *The Treaty of Guadalupe Hidalgo: A Legacy of Conflict.* Norman: University of Oklahoma Press, 1990.

Deloria, Vine, Jr., and Raymond J. DeMallie. *Documents of American Indian Diplomacy: Treaties, Agreements, and Conventions, 1775–1979.* Vol. 2. Norman: University of Oklahoma Press, 1999.

Dunlay, Tom. *Kit Carson and the Indians.* Lincoln: University of Nebraska Press, 2000.

Eisenhower, John S. D. *So Far from God: The U.S. War with Mexico, 1846–1848.* New York: Anchor Books, 1989.

Emmett, Chris. *Fort Union and the Winning of the Southwest.* Norman: University of Oklahoma Press, 1965.

Favour, Alpheus H. *Old Bill Williams, Mountain Man.* Norman: University of Oklahoma Press, 1962.

Foreman, Grant. *Marcy and the Gold Seekers: The Journal of Captain R. B. Marcy, with an Account of the Gold Rush over the Southern Route.* Norman: University of Oklahoma Press, 1939.

"Fraud Statistics." *Coalition against Insurance Fraud.* September 2016. http://www.insurancefraud.org/statistics.htm.

Frazer, Robert W. *Forts and Supplies: The Role of the Army in the Economy of the Southwest, 1846–1861.* Albuquerque: University of New Mexico Press, 1983.

———. *Forts of the West: Military Forts and Presidios and Posts Commonly Called Forts West of the Mississippi River.* Norman: University of Oklahoma Press, 1965.

Gardner, Daniel. *The Science of Fear: How the Culture of Fear Manipulates Your Brain.* New York, Plume, 2009.

Gorenfeld, Will. "The Historical Record." In *Battles and Massacres on the Southwestern Frontier: Historical and Archaeological Perspectives,* edited by Ronald K. Wetherington and Frances Levine, 12–42. Norman: University of Oklahoma Press, 2014.

Gorenfeld, Will, and John Gorenfeld. "Taos Mutiny of 1855." *Wild West* 27, no. 3 (October 2014): 46–51.

Gregg, Josiah. *Commerce of the Prairies: Life on the Great Plains in the 1830's and 1840's.* Santa Barbara: Narrative Press, 2001.

Guild, Thelma S., and Harvey L. Carter. *Kit Carson: A Pattern for Heroes.* Lincoln: University of Nebraska Press, 1984.

Hallinan, Joseph T. *Why We Make Mistakes.* New York: Broadway Books, 2009.

Hämäläinen, Pekka. *The Comanche Empire*. New Haven, Conn.: Yale University Press, 2008.

Hammond, George P. *Alexander Barclay, Mountain Man*. Denver, Colo.: Fred A. Rosenstock Old West Publishing Company, 1976.

Hofstadter, Richard. *The Paranoid Style in American Politics*. New York: Vintage Books, 1967.

Horn, Calvin. *New Mexico's Troubled Years: The Story of the Early Territorial Governors*. Foreword by John F. Kennedy. Albuquerque: Horn and Wallace, 1963.

"How Many U. S. Citizens Cheat on Their Taxes?" *Answers*. 2016. http://www.answers.com/Q/How_many_US_citizens_cheat_on_their_taxes.

Hunter, J. Marvin, ed. "The Capture of Mrs. Wilson." *Frontier Times* 1, no. 9 (June 1924): 22–23.

"Insurance Fraud." *FindLaw*. 2016. http://criminal.findlaw.com/criminal-charges/insurance-fraud.html.

The Jicarilla Apache Tribe of the Jicarilla Apache Reservation, New Mexico, Petitioner, v. The United States of America, Defendant, Docket No. 22-A, November 9, 1966. http://digital.library.okstate.edu/icc/v17/iccv17p338.pdf.

Johnson, David M. "The Archaeological Record." In *Battles and Massacres on the Southwestern Frontier: Historical and Archaeological Perspectives*, edited by Ronald K. Wetherington and Frances Levine, 43–76. Norman: University of Oklahoma Press, 2014.

Johnson, David M., et al. *Final Report on the Battle of Cieneguilla: A Jicarilla Apache Victory over the U.S. Dragoons. March 30, 1854*. Albuquerque, N.Mex.: U.S. Department of Agriculture, Forest Service, Southwestern Region, 2009.

Kappler, Charles J., ed. *Indian Treaties, 1778–1883*. Mattituck, N.Y.: Amereon House, 1972.

Keleher, William A. *Turmoil in New Mexico, 1846–1868*. Santa Fe: Rydal Press, 1952.

Kenner, Charles L. *The Comanchero Frontier: A History of New Mexican–Plains Indian Relations*. Norman: University of Oklahoma Press, 1969.

Kiser, William S. *Dragoons in Apacheland: Conquest and Resistance in Southern New Mexico, 1846–1861*. Norman: University of Oklahoma Press, 2012.

Kvasnicka, Robert M., and Herman J. Viola, eds. *The Commissioners of Indian Affairs, 1824–1977*. Lincoln: University of Nebraska Press, 1979.

Larson, Robert W. *New Mexico's Quest for Statehood, 1846–1912*. Albuquerque: University of New Mexico Press, 1969.

Lecompte, Janet. "The Manco Burro Pass Massacre." *New Mexico Historical Review* 41, no. 4 (October 1966): 305–18.

———. *Pueblo, Hardscrabble, Greenhorn: Society on the High Plains, 1832–1856*. Norman: University of Oklahoma Press, 1978.

"Manuel Abrew [*sic*] et al. v. the United States and Utah and Apache Indians." In *Cases Decided in the Court of Claims of the United States at the Term of 1901–1902: With Abstracts of Decisions of the Supreme Court in Appealed Cases from October 1901 to May 1902*, 510–14. Vol. 37. Washington, D.C.: Government Printing Office, 1902.

McCall, George Archibald. *New Mexico in 1850: A Military View*. Edited by Robert Frazer. Norman: University of Oklahoma Press, 1968.

McNierney, Michael, ed. *Taos 1847: The Revolt in Contemporary Accounts.* Boulder, Colo.: Johnson Publishing Company, 1980.

McNitt, Frank. *Navajo Wars: Military Campaigns, Slave Raids, and Reprisals.* Albuquerque: University of New Mexico Press, 1972.

Meketa, Jacqueline Dorgan, ed. *Legacy of Honor: The Life of Rafael Chacon, a Nineteenth Century New Mexican.* Albuquerque: University of New Mexico Press, 1986.

Meriwether, David. *My Life in the Mountains and on the Plains.* Edited and with an introduction by Robert A. Griffen. Norman: University of Oklahoma Press, 1965.

Message from the President of the United States to the Two Houses of Congress, December 24, 1849. Exec. Doc. No. 5, 1st Session, 31st Congress. Washington, D.C.: GPO, 1849.

Message from the President of the United States to the Two Houses of Congress, January 31, 1850. Exec. Doc. No. 24, 1st Session, 31st Congress. Washington, D.C.: William M. Belt, 1850.

Message from the President of the United States to the Two Houses of Congress, December 2, 1851. Exec. Doc. No. 1, 1st Session, 32nd Congress. Washington, D.C.: A. Boyd Hamilton, 1851.

Message of the President of the United States to the Two Houses of Congress, December 7, 1847. Exec. Doc. No. 1, 1st Session, 30th Congress. Washington, D.C.: Wendell and Van Benthuysen, 1847.

Messages and Documents of the Second Session of the Forty-First Congress. Washington, D.C.: GPO, 1869.

Michno, Gregory. *The Settlers' War: The Struggle for the Texas Frontier in the 1860s.* Caldwell, Idaho: Caxton Press, 2011.

Michno, Gregory, and Susan Michno. *A Fate Worse Than Death: Indian Captivities in the West.* Caldwell, Idaho: Caxton Press, 2007.

Nevins, Allan. *Fremont: Pathmarker of the West.* New York: Longmans, Green and Co., 1955.

Oliva, Leo E. *Fort Union and the Frontier Army in the Southwest.* Southwest Cultural Resources Center Professional Papers No. 41. Santa Fe: National Park Service, 1993. https://www.nps.gov/foun/learn/management/upload/FOUNandFrontierArmyOfSW-2 .pdf.

Palacio, Francisco Gómez. *Claims of Mexican Citizens against the United States for Indian Depredations, Being the Opinion of the Mexican Commissioner in the Joint Claims Commission, under the Convention of July 4, 1868, between Mexico and the United States.* Washington, D.C.: Judd and Detweiler, 1871.

Prucha, Francis Paul. *Sword of the Republic: The United States Army on the Frontier, 1783–1846.* Bloomington: Indiana University Press, 1969.

Prucha, Francis Paul, ed. *Army Life on the Western Frontier: Selections from the Official Reports Made between 1826 and 1845 by Colonel George Croghan.* Norman: University of Oklahoma Press, 1958.

———. *Documents of United States Indian Policy.* Lincoln: University of Nebraska Press, 1990.

Quaife, Milo Milton, ed. *Kit Carson's Autobiography*. Lincoln: University of Nebraska Press, 1966.

Quinn, James H. "Brooks Expedition." Arrott Fort Union Collection, vol. 2, 164–66. New Mexico Highlands University, Las Vegas, N.Mex.

———. "Notes of a Spy Company Under Col. Cooke." Arrott Fort Union Collection, vol. 2, 125–29. New Mexico Highlands University, Las Vegas, N.Mex.

Report of the Quartermaster General. November 22, 1851. U.S. Congress, Exec. Doc. No. 2, 1st Session, 32nd Congress. Washington, D.C.: A. Boyd Hamilton, 1851.

Report of the Secretary of War. November 29, 1851. U.S. Congress, Exec. Doc. No. 1, 1st Session, 32nd Congress. Washington, D.C.: A. Boyd Hamilton, 1851.

Roberts, William H. *Mexican War Veterans: A Complete Roster*. Washington, D.C.: Bretano's, A. S. Witherbee and Co., Proprietors, 1887.

Rodenbough, Theophilus F. *From Everglade to Canyon with the Second United States Cavalry*. Norman: University of Oklahoma Press, 2000. Originally published New York: D. Van Nostrand, 1875.

Sabin, Edwin L. *Kit Carson Days, 1809–1868*. Vol. 2: *Adventures in the Path of Empire*. Lincoln: University of Nebraska Press, 1995.

Samenow, Stanton E. *Inside the Criminal Mind*. New York: Broadway Books, 1984.

Schacter, Daniel L. *Searching for Memory: The Brain, the Mind, and the Past*. New York: Basic Books, 1996.

Schneier, Bruce. *Beyond Fear: Thinking Sensibly about Security in an Uncertain World*. New York: Copernicus Books, 2003.

Sheehan, Bernard W. *Seeds of Extinction: Jeffersonian Philanthropy and the American Indian*. Chapel Hill: University of North Carolina Press, 1973.

Simmons, Virginia McConnell. *The Ute Indians of Utah, Colorado, and New Mexico*. Boulder: University Press of Colorado, 2000.

Skelton, William B. *An American Profession of Arms: The Army Officer Corps, 1784–1861*. Lawrence: University Press of Kansas, 1992.

Skogen, Larry C. "The Bittersweet Reality of Depredation Cases." *Prologue Magazine of the National Archives* (Fall 1992): 290–96.

———. *Indian Depredation Claims, 1796–1920*. Norman: University of Oklahoma Press, 1996.

Smith, Ralph Adam. *Borderlander: The Life of James Kirker, 1793–1852*. Norman: University of Oklahoma Press, 1999.

Sonnichsen, C. L. *The Mescalero Apaches*. Norman: University of Oklahoma Press, 1958.

Stein, Mark. *American Panic: A History of Who Scares Us and Why*. New York: Palgrave Macmillan, 2014.

Tavris, Carol, and Elliot Aronson. *Mistakes Were Made (But Not by Me): Why We Justify Foolish Beliefs, Bad Decisions, and Hurtful Acts*. Orlando, Fla.: Harcourt, 2007.

Taylor, Morris F. "Action at Fort Massachusetts: The Indian Campaign of 1855." *Colorado Magazine* 42, no. 4 (Fall 1965): 292–310.

———. "Campaigns against the Jicarilla Apache, 1854." *New Mexico Historical Review* 44, no. 4 (October 1969): 269–91.

———. "Campaigns against the Jicarilla Apache, 1855." *New Mexico Historical Review* 45, no. 2 (April 1970): 119–36.

Tiller, Veronica E. Velarde. *The Jicarilla Apache Tribe: A History.* Albuquerque: BowArrow Publishing Company, 2000.

Twitchell, Ralph Emerson. "Historical Sketch of Governor William Carr Lane." *Historical Society of New Mexico* 4 (November 1, 1917): 1–21.

———. *The History of the Occupation of the Territory of New Mexico from 1846 to 1851.* Denver, Colo.: Smith-Brooks Company, 1909.

U.S. House of Representatives. *Exec. Doc. No. 34,* 1st Session, 50th Congress, 1887–89. Washington, D.C.: Government Printing Office, 1889.

———. *Exec. Doc. No. 77,* 2nd Session, 49th Congress, 1886–87. Washington, D.C.: Government Printing Office, 1887.

———. *Exec. Doc. No. 125,* 1st Session, 49th Congress, 1885–86. Indian Depredation Claims. Letter from the Secretary of the Interior. Washington, D.C.: Government Printing Office, 1886.

———. *Exec. Doc. No. 182,* 2nd Session, 48th Congress, 1884–85. Washington, D.C.: Government Printing Office, 1885.

U.S. Senate. *Exec. Doc. No. 1,* 1st Session, 32nd Congress, December 2, 1851. Washington, D.C.: A. Boyd Hamilton, 1851.

———. *Exec. Doc. No. 55,* 1st Session, 35th Congress, 1857–58. Washington, D.C: William Harris, 1858.

Unrau, William E. *Indians, Alcohol, and the Roads to Taos and Santa Fe.* Lawrence: University Press of Kansas, 2013.

Utley, Robert M., ed. "Captain John Pope's Plan of 1853 for the Frontier Defense of New Mexico." *Arizona and the West: A Quarterly Journal of History* 5 no. 2 (Summer 1963): 149–63.

Ward, John. "Indian Affairs in New Mexico under the Administration of William Carr Lane from the Journal of John Ward." Edited by Annie Heloise Abel. *New Mexico Historical Review,* 16, no. 2 (April 1941): 206–32; 16, no. 3 (July 1941): 328–59.

Watson, Samuel J. *Peacekeepers and Conquerors: The Army Officer Corps on the American Frontier, 1821–1846.* Lawrence: University Press of Kansas, 2013.

Watts, John S. *Indian Depredations in New Mexico.* Washington, D.C.: Gideon, 1858.

West, Eliot. *The Contested Plains Indians, Goldseekers, and the Rush to Colorado.* Lawrence: University Press of Kansas, 1998.

Wetherington, Ronald K. *Ceran St. Vrain: American Frontier Entrepreneur.* Foreword by Marc Simmons. Santa Fe: Sunstone Press, 2012.

Winn, William W. *Triumph of the Ecunnau-Nuxulgee: Land Speculators, George M. Troup, State Rights, and the Removal of the Creek Indians from Georgia and Alabama, 1825–38.* Macon, Ga.: Mercer University Press, 2015.

Wiseman, Richard. *Paranormality: Why We See What Isn't There.* Lexington, Ky.: Spin Solutions, 2010.

Wooster, Robert. *American Military Frontiers: The United States Army in the West, 1783–1900.* Albuquerque: University of New Mexico Press, 2009.

Index